Language and Communicative Practices

CRITICAL ESSAYS IN ANTHROPOLOGY

Series Editors **John Comaroff,** *University of Chicago*
Pierre Bourdieu, *Collège de France*
Maurice Bloch, *London School of Economics*

Language and Communicative Practices, William F. Hanks

FORTHCOMING

Reconceptualizing the Peasantry, Michael Kearney

Discourse, Knowledge, and Culture, John D. Kelly

Imaginary Subjects, Illusory Sovereignties: States, Nations, Cultures, Derek Sayer

Mind in Society, Society in Mind: A Critical Anthropology of Cognition, Dorothy C. Holland and Claudia Strauss

Language & Communicative Practices

William F. Hanks

The University of Chicago

WestviewPress

A Division of HarperCollins*Publishers*

Critical Essays in Anthropology

Published in 1996 in the United States of America by Westview Press, Inc., 5500 Central Avenue, Boulder, Colorado 80301-2877, and in the United Kingdom by Westview Press, 12 Hid's Copse Road, Cumnor Hill, Oxford OX2 9JJ

Library of Congress Cataloging-in-Publication Data
Hanks, William F.
Language and communicative practices / William F. Hanks
p. cm.
Includes bibliographical references (p.) and index.
ISBN 0-8133-1216-7 — ISBN 0-8133-1217-5 (pbk.)
1. Language and languages. 2. Linguistics. 3. Language and culture. 4. Social interaction. I. Title.
P106.H295 1996
410—dc20 95-19534
CIP

Printed and bound in the United States of America

The paper used in this publication meets the requirements of the American National Standard for Permanence of Paper for Printed Library Materials Z39.48-1984.

10 9 8 7 6 5 4 3 2 1

Contents

Part 2. Language the Nexus of Context

Part 3. Communicative Practices

Tables and Figures

Tables

Figures

Preface

How do we make meaning with language? How is it that the things we say come to convey so much more than the simple words we use in saying them? A language, like English or Spanish, can be summarized in a dictionary or a grammar and discussed in the abstract as the speech native to a certain place, say, Chicago or Mexico City. But how do such abstractions stack up against the infinite utterances that can be, or have already been, spoken in the languages? It is a matter of common sense that words are spoken in context, that if we take them out of context they can be made to mean many different things. But what is a context? And how long does it last—a minute, an hour? Next to real action, speech seems as weightless as it is fleeting, and yet we have all experienced words that made a difference. Promises, threats, judgments, and plain conversations that have consequences—some intended, some not. Talk seems wrapped up in thinking, and thinking in the mind, but we talk through our bodies, and language is as much a practice of the body as it is of the mind. What happens when we look at speech as bodily gesture? And what is the proper framework in which to understand it—the species, the individual mind-body-speaker, the social community?

These and other questions arise from a series of contradictions in language: It is both an abstract system and an intimate part of our daily experience, an individual capacity for expression and a social fact, a form and an activity. These contradictions are the starting point of this book. We will approach them from several perspectives. The first is through considering a few simple examples of speech, asking how they are understood in context, how what is said ties into what is taken for granted, how the values that speakers bring to talk shape their understandings. Here the goal is to analyze the tension between language and nonlanguage. The second approach is more synthetic and focuses on major theories of language from several disciplines. As we attempt to piece together significant questions and plausible answers, we will engage with a range of works in linguistics, philosophy, and anthropology. The aim is to develop an approach to communicative practice that combines the formal properties of linguistic systems with the dynamics of speech as social activity. Clearly, the analysis of examples and the synthesis of theories are interdependent parts of a single study, and a third major goal of the book is to show how they combine in practice.

The book is divided into three parts, each marking a moment in the overall life of language. The first, entitled "Language the System," explores classic grammatical and semiotic theories, focusing on works by Saussure, Peirce, Morris, Bloomfield, and Chomsky. We want to locate the distinctive properties of linguistic systems in comparison to other kinds of semiotic systems, while clarifying the strengths and weaknesses of linguistic approaches to verbal meaning. The second part, "Language the Nexus of Context," examines the idea of context, starting from linguistic pragmatics and moving on to phenomenology, Voloshinov's Marxist theory of utterance meaning, ethnographic studies of relativity and verbal style, and sociolinguistic theories of interaction. As we work through these different, sometimes contradictory, perspectives, we will successively recast the relation between verbal meaning and social context. The third and final part of the book, "Communicative Practices," proposes a synthesis in three steps: the basic elements of communicative practice, corporeality in language, and meaning in history.

As a critical essay, this book is neutral neither in the choice of topics it addresses nor in the way it does so. There is a historical sequence in some of the works I discuss, notably in the first five chapters, and I treat many topics familiar to students of language. But my aim is to provoke reflection and to develop a framework for analyzing language as communicative practice, not to examine a history or survey a field. Chapters 1 through 5 lay the foundations of standard approaches to language. Subsequent chapters depart substantially from these, drawing on my own research and bringing together a wide range of literature beyond the scope of current frameworks. Although much of contemporary theory draws a sharp distinction between "discourse" and "practice," this book argues that *discourse is practice,* and practice depends crucially upon discourse. In other words, the two are overlapping, mutually constituting parts of social life. The problems addressed here are relevant to the interpretation of all cultural artifacts and particularly to the work of anthropologists, archaeologists, historians, and students of literature and cultural studies. Accordingly, the book is intended to open up fruitful lines of research to readers not already trained in linguistics or committed to the study of language. To that end, I have tried to observe a simple maxim: The more technical the topic, the more transparent the language and the examples I use to explain it. For the sake of clarity, I wrote the first draft in the form of lectures presented in introductory courses at the University of Chicago and elsewhere. The pacing and style of the prose reflect this, and I believe that the full import of the text is likely to be clearest on an oral reading. Each chapter ends with suggestions for further readings, and the table of contents and index are designed to make the book accessible as a tool in teaching and research. It is my conviction that language is basic to human sociality; that it can be properly understood only through a principled, interdisciplinary approach; and that theory and empirical description are inseparable.

I have benefited greatly from the questions and criticisms of my students, friends, and colleagues at the University of Chicago; the École des Hautes Études et Sciences Sociales, Paris; and the Casa de América, Madrid. I alone am responsible for the book, but it reflects the support and efforts of many. Among these, I owe a special thanks to Costas Canakis, Ben Lee, George Nielson, and Asli Özyürek, each of whom read the entire manuscript and made many helpful suggestions. As my research assistant, Costas also proofed and printed several versions of the whole and turned my cryptic notes into a coherent bibliography. Thanks also go to Aurore Becquelin Monod, Olga Beloded, Dean Birkenkamp, Aaron Cicourel, John Comaroff, Tom Cummins, Alessandro Duranti, Nancy M. Farriss, Stephane Gerson, Neil Goodman, Serge Gruzinski, Manuel Gutierrez Estevez, Anne M. Hanks, John Haviland, Stephen Hershler, Jean Lave, Stephen Levinson, Craig Luchsinger, Alicia Menanteau F., Nancy D. Munn, Elinor Ochs, Matthew Restall, Peter Thompson, Terry Turner, and the reviewers who read the manuscript for Westview Press. One of these reviewers, who turned out to be Dell Hymes, gave extensive and very helpful comments, for which I am grateful. The index was done by Lynn MacLeod Hand, whose assistance I gratefully acknowledge. During the time of the writings, I have been concurrently working on a research project entitled "History and Discourse," in collaboration with Nancy Farriss and Sebastian Castillo Moo (better known as Don Chabo), supported by the National Endowment for the Humanities (Interpretive Research Grant #RO-22303-91). My discussions with Nancy and Don Chabo and the support of David Wise, program officer of the NEH, have made a real contribution to my development. I gratefully acknowledge the help of these individuals and institutions.

William F. Hanks

Chapter 1

Introduction: Meaning and Matters of Context

START WITH A SIMPLE SCENARIO. It is 7:28 A.M. on September 19, 1993. Chicago. Jack has just walked into the kitchen. He is standing at the counter by the sink, pouring a cup of coffee. Natalia is wiping off the dining room table. Gazing vacantly at his coffee cup, still drowsy, Jack says,

"D'the paper come today, sweetheart?"

She says,

"It's right on the table."

Turning to the small table inside the kitchen, he picks up the paper and his cup of coffee. He joins her out in the dining room, where they sit in affectionate silence. She scribbles a list of the day's chores: "Review headlines in Trib, Times, Globe, Post in re: UN role in peacekeeping efforts; prepare handout for PoliSci seminar; call AMH re: Friday; gym at 2:00; renew books at lib; dentist 4:15." Unfocused, his eyes wander over the headlines: "The Moment of Truth," "Duke Learns of Pitfalls in Promise of Hiring More Black Professors," "In a Less Arid Russia, Jewish Life Flowers Again (A Faith Reviving. Jews in Russia. *A Special Report*)," "Perot, at Rally, Upsets Members of Both Parties." They kiss. He lowers his face, rests it on the nape of her neck. After a moment, he turns back to the paper, still vague with sleep. She returns to her list. He sips his coffee, thinking of the day ahead.

In itself, language is neither the cause nor the measure of the world as we live it. Much of what makes the headlines would happen without talk, and we are instinctively wary of words for their ability to deceive. The dining room would still be there, and Jack and Natalia could still take their coffee, by habit, at the table. He would undoubtedly have found the paper on the table even if he never asked, and she could have just pointed. Virtually asleep, his words express little that we would call meaningful, and his eyes glaze over the paper, barely focusing on the information it announces. They embrace in the silence of intimacy. In other words, the consequential features of the scenario don't really depend upon the words spoken

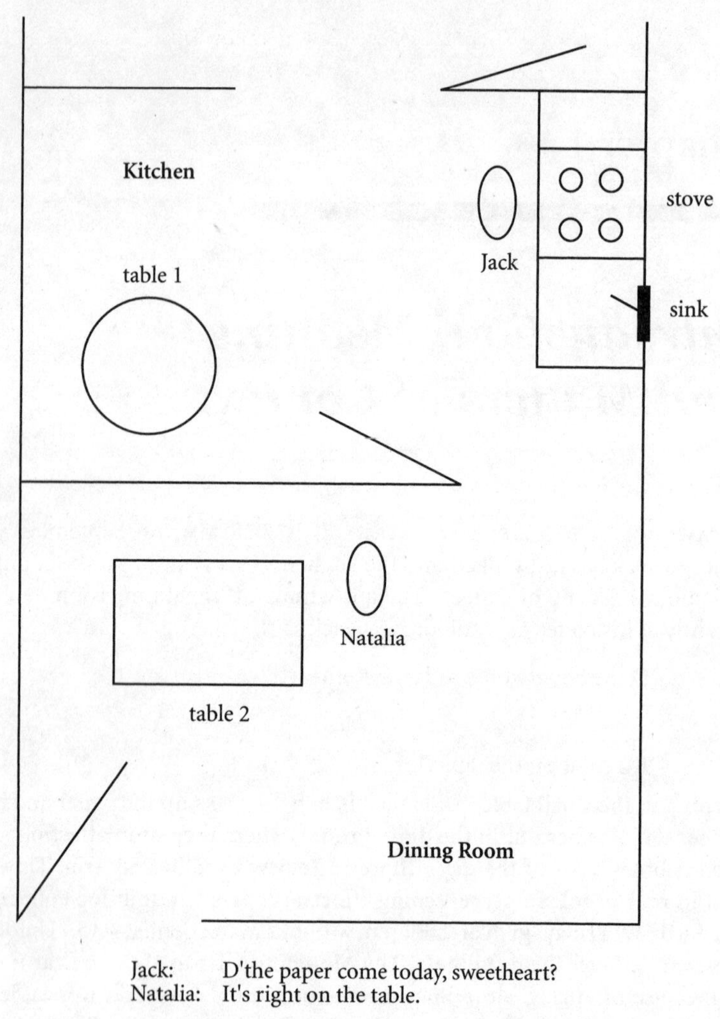

FIGURE 1.1 Floorplan for a Routine Exchange.

or even the speaking of words. The telegraphic exchanges between intimates can be virtually predictable or so idiosyncratic as to lack general interest. We need not even assume that they are wide awake. Next to disease, the environment, racism, and terror, speech seems oddly weightless. Talk is cheap.

True enough. But language permeates our daily lives, from the kitchen to the UN, and all the media in between. This sheer commonality should give us pause. The news might still happen without speech, but it would be difficult to call it news if it were never reported, and this happens only through language and other symbolic media. Jack and Natalia—or any other couple, for that matter—can do many things in silence, but this does not cut them loose from the horizon of words. There is always a history of conversation, intimate tellings. There are moments of withdrawal, when language is present by its painful absence. Common sense tells us that speech involves sound, but language inhabits silence, too (for the same reason that people are social beings even when they are alone). The truth has its moments because a pledge has been made. A university finds its present measured by a promise in the past. A third-party candidate breaks in with speech. And of course the newspaper is a printed form of language, whatever else it is. Sitting in the dining room in silence, Jack and Natalia are embedded in an unseen dialogue.

The notion that talk is trivial compared to real action is often paired with the assumption that the meanings of words and utterances are transparent. We feel confident glossing Jack's utterance as a request for information about the paper or perhaps for the paper itself. Natalia's response appears equally simple and virtually literal. A closer look at their words, however, suffices to muddle this picture. Jack's question only asks whether the paper came that day, which should merit a simple yes or no response. Knowing that he reads the paper with breakfast and that he has no independent interest in newspaper delivery, Natalia hears his question as a request to locate the paper for him at that moment. It is this unspoken utterance that she answers. Her answer in turn introduces further tacit knowledge. Notice in Figure 1.1 that there are two tables on the scene, not one. The tables are in different rooms, as are the two people. Yet Jack hears her statement as making reference to the one nearest him, the one farthest from her. She cannot even see the table in the kitchen, and he knows this without having to think of it. How does he understand her? One might reason that he would expect her to say, "It's in here," or some such, if the paper were already on the dining room table. That she does *not* say this becomes meaningful. The assertive tone of her statement further reinforces the inference that she is giving him just the information he needs to find the paper. Maybe the words "right on the table" convey that it is close to Jack, that he should be able to see it clearly.

But which inferences are actually made by such people, half asleep, in the familiar surround of their own home? Neither of them specifies that it was the newspaper of September 19 that Jack wants and not, say, the one from the day before. Yet this is implied, too. If the paper routinely came a day or a week late, then Natalia would understand him to be asking about *that* edition of the paper, and not the one of September 19. Papers can't move around by themselves anyway, so why does he ask if the paper "came" instead of asking if it was delivered? Moreover, although he never says so, Jack is obviously referring to a certain newspaper and not the wax paper, the toilet paper, or the computer paper, and his use of the word "today" suggests that there are some days on which it doesn't come (and therefore others on which it does). This gives the entire scenario an air of routine.

It should be clear that simple exchanges like this one can be tinkered with indefinitely and that much of the transparency that we sense on first hearing can be made opaque. The very telegraphic quality of the exchange, the presence of all

"All the News That's Fit to Print"

The New York Times

National Edition
Midwest: In the Great Lakes, sunshine yielding to clouds, showers arriving from the west, cool. Plains, rain, heavy at times. Ohio Valley, cloudy. Weather map is on page 19.

VOL.CXLIII . . . No. 49,459 SUNDAY, SEPTEMBER 19, 1993 Printed in Chicago $3.50

The Moment of Truth

For Clinton, a Pledge on Troops for Bosnia Will Vie With Issues Like Health and Jobs

By R. W. APPLE Jr.

News Analysis

WASHINGTON, Sept. 18 — With a settlement of the war in Bosnia apparently one step closer, President Clinton may be forced in coming weeks to confront the prospect of sending a ... American troops to the Balkans as part of an international peacekeeping force.

Question of Credibility

Doubts About Commitment

Continued on Page 6, Column 1

Connecticut Tribe Gathers Indians From Around Nation

American Indians from all over North America met in Hartford for a singing and dancing competition sponsored by the tiny Pequot tribe. The Connecticut tribe became extremely wealthy on casino gambling in the last year, but discovered that it had lost its traditions over the centuries. Page 16.

SIDE AGREEMENTS TO TRADE ACCORD VARY IN AMBITION

UNIONS ARE DISSATISFIED

Environmental Groups Receive More Than Labor, Leading to Imbalance in Support

By KEITH BRADSHER

Reasons for Broader Pact

Continued on Page 15, Column 1

Political Memo

Streetwise Politics Put to Use In Quest for Health Overhaul

By ROBIN TONER

Continued on Page 21, Column 1

Drawbacks for Couples

Perot, at Rally, Upsets Members Of Both Parties

By RICHARD L. BERKE

Presidential Embarrassment

Continued on Page 18, Column 1

Duke Learns of Pitfalls in Promise Of Hiring More Black Professors

By PETER APPLEBOME

Fault Lines Are Exposed

Continued on Page 17, Column 1

Tomorrow's Jordan: State of Uncertainty

Article, page 12.

Jewish life is blossoming in a more democratic Russia. Igor Bukharov, right, moved a sign at the first kosher restaurant in Moscow. Rabbi Berel Lazar, left, supervised the kosher approval.

In a Less Arid Russia, Jewish Life Flowers Again

By STEVEN ERLANGER

A Faith Reviving
Jews in Russia
A special report.

MOSCOW, Sept. 18 — Ilya Drutz, an agile, round-cheeked boy of 12, was calmly describing his decision to become circumcised. Last summer, he attended the first Jewish camp in Moscow.

"Before I went to the camp I knew nothing about my religion, and I felt very uncomfortable," he said. "My father is a writer and my mother a librarian, and religion wasn't talked about at home."

Continued on Page 16, Column 1

INSIDE

The Talk of Kentucky

The Tale of the Tape

Polish Leader Pushed Aside

More Asbestos Confusion

TODAY'S SECTIONS

FIGURE 1.2 Morning Headlines

that is unsaid, is part of what makes it appear routine. And we, as native actors, are curiously comfortable amidst an infinity of assumptions, beneath a horizon as familiar and unnoticed as the night sky. That is, provided we have the right kinds of background. Provided, for this example, that we come from a world in which people have dining rooms and read newspapers, in which men and women act as couples in certain common ways, in which English is spoken and coffee is drunk in cups in the morning. All of these things could be different, yet the coherence of words among silence would be similar—until something happens to break up the pieces, and the meanings shift about.

If the same exchange took place in a commercial kitchen in which large quantities of wax paper were needed, and Jack and Natalia were coworkers, he the short-order chef and she the manager, then it might be the wax paper that he was wondering about, taking for granted a history of problems with the supplier. Or Natalia might be the one who uses the paper because she works in the kitchen, and so Jack, the bartender, asks a real question whether the paper was delivered and not a request for information about its current whereabouts. What if Natalia, a native Spanish speaker, is actually practicing her English and the entire dialogue is a pedagogical exercise? Or if they are acting on the stage or running over an exchange they plan to perform at a later date in front of some third party, for reasons undisclosed? Back in the dining room, Natalia might know that Jack really wanted the newspaper, but she remembers that she happened to leave a new roll of toilet paper on the table when they returned from shopping the night before, and she playfully sends him to it, twisting his words mischievously. And so on. As we change the setting, making different assumptions, the meanings of the words shift around, become opaque, or change entirely.

The same applies to the boundary between language and gesture in much of everyday talk. Meanings understood without reflection turn out to depend in intricate ways on the cooperation of body posture and motion with speech. Jack's grasp of which table Natalia means is based on his body sense of her physical location outside the built space of the kitchen, relative to his own inside it. He is standing, about to walk to the dining room, and so can easily turn and pick up the paper as he comes to her. The two tables are in turn anchored to this relation and the habitual motion through the doorway between the two rooms. They sit close enough so that their embrace can happen as if by itself, without comment or preparation. Like the other tacit features of the scenario, most of this is so banal that a reader can digest the example easily. It takes a special effort and a certain perversity to make it strange. It takes a certain remove to unstick the words from their context, bringing their specific form into the foreground.

The goal of this book is to develop a perspective on language and speech, to ask how meaning happens through speech and silence, bodies and minds. The field is what has come to be called linguistic anthropology, although I will attempt neither a review nor a history. My method includes taking simple examples and showing the ways in which they depend on social context and some of the ways this dependency has been thought about. The purpose of questioning the obvious is not just to muddle things but to induce certain logical breaks. The first of these involves alienating our notion of language from the deceiving concreteness of common sense. In the commonsense perspective, we usually "hear through" the words people speak and "see through" their gestures, to seize directly on a larger meaning. This tendency to hear through is the first thing we must suspend in order to rediscover what gets said when people speak. In a sense, we have to unlearn some of the skills that make it possible for us to interact or read things like the newspaper.

We will inevitably continue to trade on common sense throughout such an exercise. There is no other alternative. But the point is to make this part of the problem by examining the relation between what is actually said and what is understood. It is more a matter of bracketing, or temporarily suspending, contextual inferences rather than rejecting them outright. This first break, then, is what will allow us to separate the speech form from its own commonsense horizons, which in turn allows us to hear the words within the speech—which is in turn the first step toward language as a pure form with an inner logic of its own. "D'the paper come today, sweetheart?" Yes-no question; past tense verb of motion with singular, inanimate subject; inverted word order of auxiliary verb and subject noun phrase; temporal adverb referring to the day of the utterance; utterance-final vocative, [+ familiar]; primary stress on first syllable of "pépr"; intonation peak on primary stress and final syllable of "tədéy." This is the path of formalism, and that is why formalist understanding often runs counter to common sense.

To talk of an inner logic is to say that language is irreducible, that its structure and evolution cannot be explained by appeals to nonlinguistic behavior, to emotion, desire, psychology, rationality, strategy, social structure, or indeed any other phenomenon outside the linguistic fact itself. We can pile on as many contingent facts of contexts as we wish, but language the code remains relatively autonomous. We associate this idea with such names as Ferdinand de Saussure, Leonard Bloomfield, Noam Chomsky, and Roman Jakobson, among the founders of modern linguistics, but its reach goes far beyond a single field. For ease of reference, we can call this the irreducibility thesis. It says simply that verbal systems have their own properties, and it fits well with a number of widely known facts: Languages are pervasively systematic in the sense of exhibiting patterned regularity across time and space. Sentences can be extracted from the ephemera of utterances, and languages are more than the accidents of speech. They have universal features such that regardless of the differences between any two anywhere in the world, one can predict that they share certain traits and exclude certain others. A verbal form, such as the sentence "It's right on the table," can be repeated a dozen times by speakers in as many different accents and for as many distinct purposes, and yet it is still recognizable and somehow the same. Jack could describe the table before him in great detail and you could photograph it without special effects; a comparison with the object itself would reveal that the verbal description employs things like nouns, definite articles, and verbs that have only tenuous analogues in the photo and none really in the physical thing.

Languages rest for their meaningfulness on a special sort of arbitrariness that is of a piece with irreducibility. In French one calls it *la table,* in German *der Tisch,* and in Spanish *la mesa,* yet these verbal differences appear to correlate with no differences in the thing itself, indeed no differences other than the ones we summarize in the names of the languages. Irreducibility is a grand way of saying what any working linguist or language learner already knows, namely, that languages have grammar and grammar has its own properties. The thresholds between grammar and utterance, expressions and things, may be difficult to draw, but this does not mean that they cannot be defined precisely. Moreover, the same common sense that obscures the line by making it invisible also affirms it. We know that words have relatively stable meanings fit for the dictionary, that they can be repeated, that a text can be separated from the situation in which it is read aloud, that a language can be written without being spoken, that it can be learned, to a degree, without being lived. The first break arises from the effort to make explicit this partial independence of language as a system.

There is a second break that will concern us throughout this essay. If verbal forms are patterned, abstractable, universal, repeatable, and arbitrary, in brief sui generis, all the opposites also hold with equal force. They are variable, locally adapted, saturated by context, never quite the same, and constantly adjusting to the world beyond their own limits. And there is always an ideological dimension: people have ideas about their language, its value, meanings, history, and these ideas help shape the language itself. Here we come to the inverse thesis, which I call relationality. It is actually a family of approaches that have in common a focus on the cross-linkages between language and context and a commitment to encompass language within them. Irreducibility is of course built on a logic of relations, too, as we will see in Part 1 of this book. But the critical difference is that formalisms based on the irreducible system of language always posit a boundary between relations inside the system and relations between the system and the world outside of it. The former include things like the syntax or phonology of a language, and the latter things like the psychology or sociology of talk. Knowledge of a language, under this view, is inherently distinct from knowledge of the world. It is the idea of a boundary between language and nonlanguage that makes all these other divisions possible. The system is at once more abstract, more general, and inherently longer lasting than any of the activities in which it is put to use. Proceeding from the break with particularity, formalist understanding leads to general laws of language and models of the combinatory potential of linguistic systems. This potential logically precedes any actual manifestation of speech. Relational understanding, on the contrary, proceeds from the break with formalist generality and leads back into particularity. It foregrounds the actual forms of talk under historically specific circumstances: not what could be said under all imaginable conditions but what *is* said under given ones. Here we come into contact with an endless array of particulars, with momentary circumstances and their contingencies. Language appears as a historical nexus of human relationships, a sudden patchwork that defies our ability to generalize. The line between knowing a language and knowing the world comes into question. It is unsurprising that social sciences in recent decades have seen a return to historical specificity, partly in reaction to the universalizing sweep of structuralist thought. Formalism loses in verisimilitude what it gains in internal rigor. Yet the really hard part is to achieve this second break without merely replicating the pathways of common sense, since this would mistake the problem for the solution.

Relationality has been argued for by Franz Boas, Edward Sapir, and their students in anthropology, for whom the interaction among language, culture, and individual lived worlds was, and still is, of basic import. It fits the later Ludwig Wittgenstein, for whom actions in the world were formative of and not dependent upon the regularities that we summarize as a grammar. It fits Nelson Goodman's irrealism, according to which language provides the means of formulating versions of the world that are comparable to musical scores, pictures, and other nonverbal representations. It applies to phenomenologists such as Roman Ingarden, Maurice Merleau-Ponty, and Alfred Schutz, for whom one of the primordial facts of language is its interpenetration with experience. It applies to the work of the Marxist V. N. Voloshinov, the psycholinguist Ragnar Rommetveit, and the political philosopher Charles Taylor, who have attempted to synthesize inner logics with relational dependencies in interestingly different ways. We deal with most of these works in the chapters ahead.

Relationality can combine with irreducibility in various ways. One could say simply that the irreducible uniqueness of language lies precisely in how it relates to the world around itself. This yields a view in which what is essential is not inside the linguistic system as such but in its potential for entering into further relations in the world. Alternatively, one could maintain that language is capable of entering into coherent relations because in fact it remains stable, repeatable, and sui generis. It is precisely because an expression like "the table" has the meaning it does that it can be used in reference to both a kitchen table and a dining room table. This yields an expanded version of irreducibility, for it amounts to the claim that the sui generis system is a precondition and relationality is a contingent factor. First we define form, and then we add an overlay of context. Only by combining the two do we arrive at meanings as full as the ones in our opening exchange between Natalia and Jack. We need not try to decide among such alternatives in the abstract, as though we could legislate an answer. Rather, we ought to take the general point that the two theses are just that: propositions about the foundation of language, not exhaustive descriptions or categories of things that one could sort out like so many marbles. Indeed, irreducibility and relationality are best seen as foregrounding different but interacting aspects of a single phenomenon, for it is in attempts to unify and transcend them that we arrive at the starting point for our analysis.

Contemporary linguistic anthropology draws on both these lines of thought, and its most pressing questions lie at their intersection. This is part of what distinguishes the field from related ones such as formal linguistics, in which irreducibility has a clear priority over relationality, and any of the humanities or social science disciplines, in which relationality is so dominant that the exact forms of speech and language are taken to be inconsequential or somehow matters of subjective opinion. From the vantage point of communicative practice, it is clear that linguistic systems provide resources for categorizing and classifying experience. Boas addressed this directly in his classic "Introduction to the Handbook of American Indian Languages," Sapir developed it still further, and several generations of scholars have demonstrated its accuracy through field research in scores of languages. Although this work does not cast doubt on the irreducibility of linguistic facts, it does lead one to recognize that linguistic facts have consequences, corollaries, and motivating factors across the span of social life. The linguistic genius that characterized the work of Jakobson developed out of an earlier synthesis of Russian formalism and the particular sort of functionalism that has come to be associated with Prague School linguistics. True, language has radically systematic features, and yet these appear to be almost constantly locked into the kinds of activities that speakers carry on with speech. How to draw out the lines connecting the two?

The very traditions in philosophy that produced classical correspondence theories of truth, which rest on the irreducibility thesis, also produced ordinary-language philosophy, which emphasizes the relation between words and actions. In overly simplified terms, correspondence theories hold that language is inherently distinct from the objective world it is used to describe (or at least that it should be). Moreover, the defining function of language, the very measure of meaning, is taken to consist in formulating propositions about the objective world that can be compared to it and judged true or false. Alongside Wittgenstein, John Austin was among the most influential proponents of the opposing view that ordinary language rarely works this way. Austin showed instead that many aspects of language are describable only in terms of what speaking accomplishes, and this is rarely mere description. When Jack asked about the paper and Natalia said, "It's right on the table," she did more than form a proposition that could be true or false. She engaged in a speech act (or several), which could be felicitous or not, successful or not, sincere or not, but not merely true or false. For one who wishes to hold firmly to the irreducibility thesis, the point of speech act theory is that the inner logic somehow bridges the language-world divide. The issue is the same whether one envisions a bare-bones grammar complemented by a set of pragmatic principles or a greatly expanded grammar in which aspects of speech are treated as formal rules. It depends on how one draws the line between language and nonlanguage. The rise during the 1970s and 1980s of linguistic pragmatics as a subfield, with its focus on speech acts and conversational inference, can be seen as an extended attempt to solve this basic tension. How to connect language the system with speech the activity? The literature gives ample evidence that neither relationality nor irreducibility, when taken alone, can answer this question.

Where are we left, then, on the matter of language as irreducible system or relational nexus? We need a way of integrating the insights of both approaches yet avoiding the pitfall of privileging one over the other. This is much easier said than done. It is not obvious, for instance, that one can go halfway with a formal analysis, using what is appealing and rejecting the rest, without calling the entire analysis into question. Can we say, without contradiction, that the meaningful aspects of language (what is commonly called the semantics, and perhaps pragmatics) are relational, but the organization of pure form (say, the morphology, syntax, and phonology) is subject to the systematic rules of a highly abstract grammar? This sort of division of labor has been tried in the past and inevitably engenders border skirmishes among those who argue that grammar is meaningful and meaning is grammatically structured. In any case, such a stark division between elements of a language forces the additional question of how the thing hangs together as a whole.

Is it, then, a matter of scale, such that most facts of language are both formal and relational but in differing degrees and maybe differing ways? Perhaps. Jack's utterance of "the paper" is both a grammatical form and a practical engagement. Perhaps the two ways of combining the perspectives should be used together, or some third solution will suggest itself. In a real sense, this problem is the central and most difficult one addressed in this book. My aim is to clarify and open fruitful avenues of research, not to resolve the issue. At a time when proponents of these two views have grown increasingly distant and disinterested in talking to one another, there is a critical need to reexamine their respective contributions. As surely as speech practices are both formal and relational, the two approaches must somehow fit together. Yet the solution cannot be to build bridges between them, as if we could leave the two sides intact and merely seek pathways to get from one to the other. It is more likely that combining them will change both, and the result will come out looking like an unfamiliar hybrid. The task is synthesis, and the goal is to find a third approach. This is where "communicative practice" enters the picture. The title and last part of the book are devoted to this explicitly. In effect, the entire discussion builds toward it, and my selection of topics and theories for discussion reflects this.

Drawing on the preceding chapters, we start by separating the formal system of language, the activity of speaking, and the ways that native speakers evaluate both of these: a three-way split. When Jack and Natalia talk over coffee, they speak in a language that they share, to some degree, despite differences in gender, profession, ethnic background, age, and outlook. As innocent as it might seem, to recognize this fact is to start on the path of formalism, for we recognize that part of the morning scene depends upon that system we call English. They also act in ways that are familiar to them, as would any couple or group finding themselves in space, time, and the routine contexts of their daily lives.

However we cut it, there is a difference between the linguistic forms uttered and the act of speaking—roughly equivalent in this case to the difference between a singular animate noun, "sweetheart," and a gesture of affection. Linguistically, the noun and the kiss that followed it are unrelated. Actionally, they form a pair. Both people come to the breakfast table with ideas about this English they share, ideas about the paper, the table, and words like "sweetheart." For him, the word is like a warm pulse, an affirmation of love. He sometimes thinks: Why does she not answer me with a special word? For her, well, she accepts the word as his expression, a holdover of some past they did not share. She hears the gender-loading, the tacky, vaguely kitschy patina, but knows that for him it is different. She hears the word in gross parody when catcalled to her on the street, but this, too, she takes in, at once loading the word with overtones and separating the overtones by their source. For those formed in formalism, all these ideas are external opinions about a clean form whose essence only the well-trained can define. Tacky, kitsch, gender—these are secondary reflections on something that is first a form. For those given to relational understanding, the reflections of a Jack or Natalia are as real as the wall between the kitchen and the dining room. You can't motivate a speaker's choice of words by formalist description because people follow their *own* values, not the ones enshrined in logical analysis. Natalia's values might tell her that Jack's question is really an expression of love or an ironic parody on their conversation of the night before or a tedious jab at her attitudes. Whatever it is, she both uses linguistic categories and goes beyond them. Whereas a formalist understanding makes such evaluations marginal and secondary, for a relational approach they are primary facts, different from the facts of form. However else one chooses to define "practice," it is the point at which three things converge: the law of system, the quick of activity, and the reflective gaze of value.

It is crucial to see that the three aspects of form, activity, and ideology require three different modes of analysis. The task is to integrate them without destroying them. This requires carefully considering their respective domains of relevance and validity. Many of the problems raised in the literature stem from the mistaken attempt to apply methods derived from one aspect to problems proper to another. For example, modern linguistics is based on the concept that a language is a generative system whose output is an infinite set of formal objects called "sentences." In generative grammar this was dubbed "creativity," meaning the ability of an ideal speaker-listener to produce and understand infinitely many novel sentences. This quasi-mathematical sense of creativity has no analogue in the field of social action, for actors are massively constrained by norms, their own positions, the limits of expectation, the consequences of uttering certain things at certain times, and so forth. Knowledge of language is itself a form of social capital, unevenly distributed in social groups and subject to competition and struggle. The very elements that make up what we call an action are so heterogeneous as to be incommensurate with the closed system of a grammar. To describe action using the metaphor of a grammar, in which rules predict acts and meanings, is misguided from the start. Similarly, it is wrongheaded to try to explain details of linguistic form, like word order or the morphology of the verb, without using the tools of linguistics. This despite the more exuberant claims made for free-floating signifiers, multivocality, and ad hoc production of meaning.

To describe regularities of practice, we need a different way of talking—not antistructure, which reproduces the assumptions of formal reasoning in order to contradict them, but something else. One such term is "habit," by which I mean the routine, repeated ways of acting into which speakers are inculcated through education and daily experience. Exchanges like the one between Jack and Natalia happen every day, sometimes even more often. They need not be exactly repeated, but the kinds of request, the speaking from one room to another, the affectionate epithet, the presence of things like coffee and the newspaper, the gestures that accompany talk are all part of the familiarity that makes the scenario work. By looking to habituation rather than rules to describe this, we gain flexibility but also the ability to integrate heterogeneous features of the practice. And of equal importance, we can describe regularity without reducing it to the effect of mental representation. For rules, at least in their classical form, are represented and followed by the mind, whereas habits may engage the body with or without the mediation of the mind.

Another term in describing the coherence of practices is "strategy," the idea being that under certain circumstances agents engage in action with the aim of achieving certain ends by taking certain steps along the way. This undoubtedly implies a degree of premediation and self-monitoring that is inappropriate for exchanges like that of Jack and Natalia, at least as we described it. Yet some practices, such as service transactions, professional presentations, and patient-doctor interactions, may well involve properly strategic speech. This in turn raises the question of improvisation. A major weakness in rule-bound descriptions of speech is that they imply that speakers follow conventions already established as rules, or at least that their actions are always accountable to conventions, like the ones that govern the movement of pieces in a chess game. (A brilliant chess player will use the rules to her advantage but still cannot suddenly move a knight on the diagonal or a bishop in the L shape of the knight.) In this view, if a speaker fails to follow the rules, her action is described as an exception or perhaps even a nonact (as Austin defines it in his theory of speech acts). But when we look at how actual people act under actual circumstances, the rules of play are often vague, and it is a matter of contention how they apply to situations. As a certain folk wisdom suggests, a brilliant actor bends, manipulates, or even circumvents standard rules and may go so far as to set new standards against which others will be judged. All this is fraught with risk, real and perceived, and the actor's willingness to chance an improvised utterance has much to do with the likelihood that she will "follow the rules."

Formalist descriptions of language typically build on a basic division between the linguistic system as it is at any point in time, as opposed to the ways that system or its parts change through time. In the standard terms, deriving mainly from Saussure, the former is called synchronic (i.e., in a single time) and the latter diachronic (i.e., through time). Saussure and many grammarians after him insisted that these two orders of facts are so different as to make it impossible to fit them into any unified description. As we will see in the next chapter, this division fits in with a whole series of others and is a powerful heuristic device for model building under the perspective of irreducibility. When it comes to practice, however, the synchronic/diachronic dichotomy gets in the way because it isolates the language as a system from the changing conditions of speech. As Saussure made clear, the synchronic system provides a set of ready-made forms whose structure and meaning remain constant however many times they are reproduced in practice. This very generality is what makes synchronic models so powerful. The trouble is that we need a way of describing practice as production, not merely re-production.

One of the intuitive justifications for positing the synchronic system of language is that it explains how people like Jack and Natalia understand each other: They both know the same system, and this is their common point of reference. But do we really need to explain mutual understanding by this kind of sharing? And how do you talk about sharing at the level of a community or modern public? Do you merely posit the replication of knowledge in identical form from head to head? In social terms this amounts to deriving society by the addition of individuals, all reduced to homunculi. But we know that collective facts don't work this way, and society is neither the sum of addition nor epistemologically transparent. What if, instead of sharing a grammar, speakers shared routine ways of acting, similar perspectives, a sense of space, or common ways of evaluating speech? The burden of mutual understanding could be borne by features of practice other than the formal system. This might provide a way of describing both how meanings get repeated and how they get produced for the first time. Moreover, it gives a broader basis on which to explain mutual understanding when people don't really share the same language or the same level of verbal skill. As anyone who has ever stumbled through a job interview, a meeting with a lawyer or doctor, or a written exam will recognize, knowledge of language is a valuable skill. It is a form of capital that people can acquire by training, compete for, and put to use for strategic ends. These things appear secondary from the formalist perspective, but not from the relational perspective of practice. Like verbal production, understanding in the practice perspective is an active process inflected with value. Hearers no less than speakers produce meaning, and for this they need the relevant skills.

At the same time as speaking and understanding are recast in a practice perspective, so, too, are the objects to which people make reference. For objects like the paper and the dining room table are not merely physical things whose properties can be fully understood in an objective, scientific description. Jack asked for the daily newspaper as part of a morning routine, shot full of the values and habitual ways of seeing the object. This is what distinguishes his referent from a mere sheet of folded paper with black ink printed on it. And it is what distinguishes Natalia's referent as their kitchen table from the same object as a sheet of wood with four legs. Objects are socially defined in ways both typical to the social milieu and particular to the actors. Even more, language itself and its various parts are also objectified in this way, defined by native actors as objects with certain horizons of value, meaning, and history. This is another profound point of difference between a practice approach and the formalist versions, for the latter posit a sheer division between language and the world of objects. In a practice approach, the values attached to language by native speakers are themselves social facts.

Objects of reference are socially typified, not sheer things as definable in an objective science. What we have called the ideological dimension is the social valuation of objects of reference (whether these be things like newspapers and tables or concepts or indeed language itself). Language itself is an object of value, and native speakers entertain relatively elaborate ideologies that bear on it. From the perspective of linguistic analysis, native ideologies are inherently distorting because nontrained speakers are largely unaware of the inner workings of their language, and their beliefs about it are influenced by a whole range of external factors. In the context of practice, however, these beliefs have a decisive impact on defining both utterance meaning and speech contexts. Furthermore, this reflexive effect of ideology applies to linguists and social theorists as well and requires that formal or social description are themselves inflected with value. This is a point with far-reaching consequences that will be addressed at several points in the book (most centrally in Part 3).

In accord with the foregoing, a practice approach does not assume that the central function of language is to convey objective information that can be judged cleanly as true or false. Utterances are typically multifunctional, and linguistic systems reflect this fact. An utterance like Natalia's response to Jack is at once a statement, which might be true or false; an answer, which might be appropriate or inappropriate; an affective response with a certain style; an interactive move in a chain of mutually orienting gestures; and so forth. The point is to describe how these various aspects of the utterance work together and how the specific words she chooses fit into the larger scenario. Although it may not be evident in this example, even the descriptive aspects of utterances may create a world of objects and not merely describe what is already there. For things as banal as newspapers and tables, the constitutive force of speech is veiled, but this changes when we consider phrases like "the right to life" as opposed to "choice," "terrorists" as opposed to "freedom fighters," and "battery" as opposed to "self-defense." How you describe an object may have profound consequences for its social definition. Consider also the power of the media to define the terms of public discourse, the newspaper as an instrument of power. The idea is that in a practice approach, language forms and uses take on a much more active force in defining the world than they are accorded in formalist approaches. To say that language objectifies does not therefore mean that we must hold it aside in search of a nonobjectified reality. No such pristine reserve exists in social experience, nor can it be produced by a retreat to naive subjectivism. The challenge is to enter into the process of objectification with your eyes wide open and without forgetting that we, too, are part of the world we describe—as both objects and objectifiers. This follows from the value-charged status of discourse, the power dimensions of action, and the general idea that to engage in speech is to occupy the social world, the terms of engagement perhaps having real consequences.

A proper discussion of any of the lines of inquiry I have mentioned in this chapter would require a lengthy treatment of its own. Much of this book will be devoted to spelling out and illustrating the trends I have alluded to. I do not wish to suggest that the authors I have named fit snugly into either relational or irreducible perspectives or that they would necessarily assent to the terms in which I have stated them. My point here is different. I wish to indicate simply that a variety of productive, important approaches to language can be located conceptually in terms of two basic foci, the one irreducibility and the other relationality. The work of many important thinkers has in fact combined elements of both rather than asserting the sheer determinacy of one over the other. The reason they form a sort of crux in current linguistic anthropology is that they focus on basic aspects of language in context, and this is the core of our project. Neither a history nor a survey of the field, this book is a critical synthesis aimed at laying the foundation for studies of communicative practices.

The road leading from common sense to the inner logic of pure form, and then to the relational dependencies of practice, is twisted and sometimes counterintuitive. This is why we speak of breaks and not simple transitions. In order to see the irreducibility thesis in its strong form, we shall have to adopt distinctions that will later cave in under the relational perspective. The latter in turn forces us to posit certain links that are anathema to a traditional grammarian or other proponent of irreducibility. The problem seems to be that despite incremental growth in the systematic study of language, there is still no adequate way of describing actual speech in the world. Taken alone, either perspective yields a reductive and ultimately sterile caricature of our object. Taken together, they can yield contradiction and inconsistency. It is in this brackish zone of difference that we will examine meaning and matters of context, and out of it that communicative practice will emerge.

Further Readings

The Americanist tradition of Boas, Sapir, and their students is treated primarily in Chapter 8. See also

Boas, F. "Introduction to the Handbook of American Indian Languages." In *Introduction to Handbook of American Indian Languages and Indian Linguistic Families of America North of Mexico,* edited by P. Holder. Lincoln: University of Nebraska Press, 1966 [1911]. Parts 2, 4, and 5, pp. 10–39, 55–79.

Sapir, E. "Communication." In *Selected Writings of Edward Sapir in Language, Culture, and Personality,* edited by D. G. Mandelbaum. Berkeley: University of California Press, 1949 [1931], pp. 104–109.

———. "The Grammarian and His Language." In *Selected Writings of Edward Sapir in Language, Culture, and Personality,* edited by D. G. Mandelbaum. Berkeley: University of California Press, 1949 [1924], pp. 150–159.

———. "Symbolism." In *Selected Writings of Edward Sapir in Language, Culture, and Personality,* edited by D. G. Mandelbaum. Berkeley: University of California Press, 1949 [1934], pp. 564–568.

Stocking, G., ed. *A Franz Boas Reader: The Shaping of American Anthropology, 1883–1911.* Chicago: University of Chicago Press, 1982.

The classic statement of irreducibility is Saussure's *Course in General Linguistics,* the focus of Chapter 2. See

Saussure, F. de. *Course in General Linguistics.* Translated by W. Baskin. New York: McGraw-Hill, 1966. "Object of Linguistics"; part 1: "General Principles," Chaps. 1–3; part 2: "Synchronic Linguistics," Chaps. 1–6.

For a general overview of problems relating to speech context, see

Duranti, A., and Goodwin, C., eds. *Rethinking Context: Language as an Interactive Phenomenon.* Cambridge: Cambridge University Press, 1992. "An Introduction," pp. 1–42.

Lyons, J. *Semantics,* vol. 1. Cambridge: Cambridge University Press, 1977. Chaps. 3 and 4, pp. 57–119.

The Prague School approach is most commonly associated with the works of Karl Bühler, Roman Jakobson, Bohuslav Havránek, and Jan Mukarovsky. For discussion, see Chapter 5. The best overview of linguistic pragmatics (with very helpful chapters on conversation analysis, deixis, and presupposition, as well as speech act theory and implicature) is

Levinson, S. *Pragmatics.* Cambridge: Cambridge University Press, 1983.

The references to philosophers can be fruitfully pursued in the following works:

Austin, J. L. *How to Do Things with Words.* Cambridge: Harvard University Press, 1962.

Baker, G. P., and Hacker, P. M. S. *Wittgenstein: Understanding and Meaning.* Oxford: Blackwell, 1980.

Goodman, N. *Ways of Worldmaking.* Cambridge, MA: Hackett, 1978.

Taylor, C. "Language and Human Nature." In *Human Agency and Language: Philosophical Papers,* vol. 1. Cambridge: Cambridge University Press, 1985, pp. 215–247.

———. "Theories of Meaning." In *Human Agency and Language: Philosophical Papers,* vol. 1. Cambridge: Cambridge University Press, 1985, pp. 248–292.

Wittgenstein, L. *Philosophical Investigations.* Oxford: Blackwell, 1953.

The phenomenological approach is the focus of Chapter 6. The works to be discussed there include the following:

Cassirer, E. "Le Langage et la construction du monde des objets." In *Essais sur le langage.* Paris: Editions de Minuit, 1969, pp. 36–68.

Ingarden, R. *The Cognition of the Literary Work of Art.* Translated by R. A. Crowley and K. R. Olson. Evanston, IL: Northwestern University Press, 1973.

———. *The Literary Work of Art: An Investigation on the Borderlines of Ontology, Logic and Theory of Literature.* Translated by G. G. Grabowicz. Evanston, IL: Northwestern University Press, 1973.

Merleau-Ponty, M. *Phénomenologie de la perception.* Paris: Gallimard, 1967 [1945].

Schutz, A. *The Phenomenology of the Social World.* Translated by G. Walsh and F. Lehnert. Evanston, IL: Northwestern University Press, 1967 [1932].

For the practice approach, see Chapters 10 and 11 as well as the following:

Bourdieu, P. *Outline of a Theory of Practice.* Translated by R. Nice. Cambridge: Cambridge University Press, 1977 [1972].

———. *Language and Symbolic Power.* Edited and introduced by J. B. Thompson; translated by G. Raymond and M. Adamson. Cambridge: Harvard University Press, 1991.

Hanks, W. F. *Referential Practice: Language and Lived Space Among the Maya.* Chicago: University of Chicago Press, 1990. Especially Chap. 1, where the main points of difference between practice approaches and pragmatics are sketched out.

PART ONE

Language the System

Chapter 2

The Language of Saussure

IT IS DIFFICULT AT FIRST to think of language as an arbitrary formal system. Most of our daily experience reinforces the belief that it is a tool for expressing people's intentions and objectives (and sometimes for hiding them). Far from appearing to us as a system unto itself, language ordinarily seems to be the means toward other ends. In everyday interactions this instrumental focus shows up in our unreflective grasp of things like the force of Jack's utterance "D'the paper come today" as a request. It takes some prodding to even notice the grammatical structure of this utterance. But any fluent speaker of American English with the right social background can understand the utterance as an interactive move. What Jack really wants is to get a section of today's newspaper to read with his coffee, and this fact makes it relevant for Natalia, in her response, to inform him where the thing is. His utterance may have been a simple yes-no question literally, but in context it was a request for information about the whereabouts of the paper. Notice that her response gives the locative information in a way that presupposes the answer to Jack's literal question: Yes, it had come, and it was right on the table.

Why do we automatically attend more to the motives of Jack's utterance than to its formal structure? The answer seems obvious: Jack made the utterance for certain purposes, and we adopt the same goal-oriented perspective as he. My point here is that this commonsense view of ordinary language as a means to an end helps to hide the system of grammar from view. For routine purposes, we are no more inclined to look upon language as a formal system than we are to look upon the telephone as an electronic one or our next-door neighbor as a physiological one. Context also cuts down on the visibility of verbal form by overdetermining meaning. Maybe Jack was asking if Natalia had already read the paper and whether the editorial they expected had finally appeared. Or maybe he knew that the paper is delivered at exactly 7:30 A.M. and so the real point of the question was to ask, "What time is it?" But these and other similar alternatives require special contexts to imagine, and with the proper contexts, the exchange can be made to mean *anything*. Some interpretations are highly likely or even automatic, and to the extent that they go through, we hardly attend to the specific words. This sort of inattention can be a problem under cross-examination, and televised governmental hearings have in recent years provided many examples in which witnesses respond that they cannot recall specific terms they had uttered for purposes other than the ones under examination.

Beyond the goal-directedness of speech, there is also the matter of its particularity. To imagine a formal system is to postulate a unity among all the infinite cases in which the language is used. In other words, English as a linguistic system is an infinite set of sentences and the lexical items and rules of their combination. This order of generality can be forbidding and involves kinds of abstraction that are cut off from the particulars of real talk. Faced with the morning news or the request of a friend, we don't normally dwell on the form of the expression at the expense of getting its message. For all *practical* purposes, language and the world are immediately connected. As a starting point, this connectedness is closer to relationality than to the irreducibility thesis. Just as we pointed out in Chapter 1, irreducibility as a view of language focuses more on the abstract potential of language as a code, whereas relationality focuses on the actual particulars of cases in which language is used in context. To understand irreducibility, we must shift our focus from actuality in this sense to potentiality.

Speakers have a strong sense that the terms of their language are natural, and this is another factor that hides the independence of language as a system. There may be no resemblance between the sound "table" and the piece of furniture on which Natalia put the newspaper, but the tie between them is so familiar as to seem inevitable. Because it is automatic and continually reinforced by routine usage, the tie becomes unquestionable. To imagine a formal system, though, is to question this link: The organization of a language system necessarily stands apart from the tables and coffee cups that we find in the kitchen. Under the irreducibility thesis, language will emerge as both conventional and arbitrary, the opposite of natural.

The difficulty with hearing language, then, is twofold: In the first place, routine awareness makes it hard to do; in the second, when one does, the results can cloud over the transparency we so take for granted. It is disruptive to suspend the practical import of an interlocutor's speech in order to consider its grammatical form, but this is the only way to notice how much goes on through language and how utterly detailed it is. Such disruption is part of analysis, and it is the necessary first step toward the irreducibility thesis. We want to carefully separate utterance form from the particular contexts of talk in order to bring language itself into the foreground of our attention. The challenge is to hold aside everything that cannot be firmly attached to form. Such a move can only upset the normal flow of things. And it is unlikely that people do anything like it in the course of speaking or understanding. Therefore it is not a valid model of what goes on in speech. Instead, it is a tool that we, as analysts, use to produce rigorous descriptions of languages. This is a strength, not a weakness. Suspending our practical view of speech can also yield unexpected insights into what people are up to when they talk, but this is just a by-product.

If I have emphasized the resistance of common sense to seeing language as grammar, it is to underscore the great achievement of Saussure, whose *Course in General Linguistics* stands as one of the most powerful examples of how to undertake a study of form and how to draw consequences from the irreducibility thesis. Although limited in certain ways, this work also had a profound historical effect on subsequent studies of language and symbolism in a variety of fields.

Saussure begins the *Course in General Linguistics* with a brief history of the field, an ambitious outline of the scope of linguistics as he saw it, and a discussion of the object of the field. It is with the latter that we will begin, for this is where Saussure masterfully delimits the scope and fundamental dimensions of language. At the outset of chapter 3, he asks straightaway, "What is the concrete and integral object of linguistics?"[1] (Saussure 1974:23), and he responds by saying how difficult the question is. It turns out that the difficulty is caused by a special kind of relativity that recurs again and again in the study of language and other symbolic systems: Depending upon the angle from which we view it, the object seems to be entirely distinct. Unlike all studies in which an object is given in advance and can be viewed from alternative perspectives, in the case of linguistics, it is the perspective that creates the object. If we look at the phonetic qualities of Jack's utterance, we have one sort of study. But an interactive analysis of why he chose to state his request in the terms he did, a semantic analysis of the meaning of the words he used, a morphological analysis of the structure of his question, or a historical analysis of how the syntactic form of English questions evolved from its Germanic forebears will all yield different sorts of objects posing different kinds of analytic challenges. Language appears in Saussure's description to have an almost iridescent quality, since its very identity depends upon how we look at it. He goes about isolating it through a series of dichotomies. Let us briefly recapitulate them.

Language Versus Speech

Syllables in an utterance like Jack's, for Natalia, are perceived by the auditory apparatus of the human body and thus have an acoustic perceptual layer that is in play whenever speech is heard. These speech sounds do not emanate from nowhere but have an articulatory reality as well. Corresponding to the auditory capacity to hear is the articulatory one to produce speech sounds, and thus we get Saussure's first division, between the auditory and the articulatory aspects of speech. As linguistics developed, these two came to be the focal objects of two branches of phonetics, acoustic and articulatory.

---

[1]Quotations from Saussure 1974 are my translation.

If we lump under a single heading the two phonetic aspects of linguistic signs, we can oppose them to a third element, the idea expressed by the form. So we could treat the acoustic and articulatory features of the word "table" as a unity of two parts and then join these two to the idea expressed (a piece of furniture of such and such features) as a second-order unity. This would give us something like Figure 2.1

The third division Saussure introduces cuts between the individual and the social aspects of language, neither of which, he says, can be conceived of without the other. Next we get the division between a linguistic system in the present and the past of that system, what a language is and what it has been. Whereas he introduces the individual/social dimension in an almost perfunctory manner, he notes from the outset that the line between past and present is so fine that it is often impossible to draw. We learn as the *Course* progresses that Saussure develops a whole approach to this, in what will be called synchronic (presentist) versus diachronic (historical) linguistics.

The intellectual challenge of these dualities for Saussure is to find among them a proper object for linguistics. To focus exclusively on certain ones to the exclusion of others is to miss the facts, yet to try to deal with all of them is to fall into a morass of heterogeneous issues. This concern with delimitation runs throughout the *Course.* Saussure's response is to introduce another much-cited distinction: *langue* versus *parole.* He says: "From the very outset we must put both feet on the ground of language (langue) and use language (langue) as the norm of all other manifestations of speech (langage)" (Saussure 1966:9). The difficulty with this

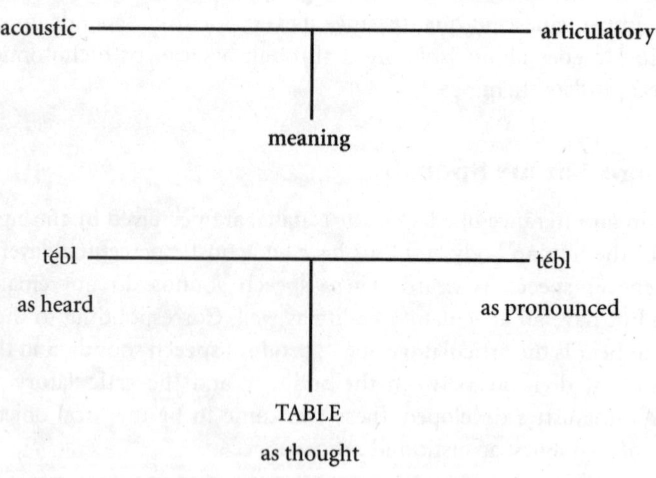

FIGURE 2.1 Three Aspects of a Sign, After Saussure.

passage is due mainly to a problem of translation. In the French Saussure distinguishes three terms, whereas in English only two are usually used:

French	*English*	*Gloss*
langue	language	the formal system of grammar
parole	speech	the realization of *langue* in actual talk
langage	language	the overall phenomenon of which *langue* and *parole* are subparts

Thus *langue* in the proper sense is only a part of the overall facts of language. It is "un tout en soi et un principe de classification. Dès que nous lui donnons la première place parmi les faits de langage, nous introduisons un ordre naturel dans un ensemble qui ne se prête à aucune autre classification" 'a whole unto itself and a principle of classification. As soon as we accord it the first place among the facts of language, we introduce a natural order into a collection which lends itself to no other classification' (Saussure 1974:25).[2] By defining this internally regular system of classification as its object, linguistics focuses on what for Saussure was the central and motivating feature of human language. Speech (*parole*), the executive or "actional" component, is nothing other than the realization of the system of *langue,* which is logically prior to it. As he says, "The faculty . . . of articulating speech can be used only with the help of the instrument [*langue*] created and provided by the collectivity" and then concludes that it is this instrument that holds language together (Saussure 1974:27).

At this point we begin to see Saussure's dualities fall into alignment, and this is key to a proper understanding of his view on language. In the preceding quote there was an identification between *langue* and the collectivity, which suggests that *parole,* as the opposite of *langue,* may be aligned with the individual, the opposite of the collective. Indeed, this is just what Saussure does. As opposed to *langue,* which is collective and systematic, *parole* is individual and accidental. It is the product of the will and intelligence of the individual subject and is never more unitary than the simple summation of all the idiosyncratic events in which it happens (Saussure 1974:30, 38). Next the synchronic/diachronic pair is brought into alignment, and we learn that *langue,* which is the system at a given phase in time, hence synchronic, is opposed to *parole,* a historically specific event of speaking that takes place over time, hence diachronic. Moreover, while *langue* is conceived of as a stable state of language, *parole* is the source of change, making it diachronic in this larger sense, too.

---

[2]Here Saussure discusses the relative naturalness of *langue* as opposed to *parole,* arguing that the American linguist William Dwight Whitney had gone too far in considering language a social institution like all others. Although we shall not pursue the discussion at this point, Saussure actually introduces a three-way division among the natural, the conventional, and the social.

Langue, then, is the social component of language. It exists beyond the reach of any individual and cannot be created or substantially modified by any single subject (Saussure 1974:32). A sort of social contract, it is learned, not instinctive, and can be understood only by abstracting away from the aleatory details of talk. The great heterogeneity of talk is offset by the relative homogeneity of *langue.* It is this which allows us to record the forms of *langue* in a fairly simple writing system, whereas *parole* is so messy that it could never be recorded adequately in a transcript.[3] At the level of the system, the only essential point is "the union of sense [sens] with the acoustic image, where the two parts of the sign are equally psychic" (Saussure 1974:32). Here Saussure reintroduces the original dualities between the acoustic/auditory aspect, which he calls the *signifier* (or sign vehicle), and the ideational aspect, which he calls the *signified* (or conceptual meaning). It is *langue* that holds together these two fundamental layers of the linguistic fact (see Figure 2.2).

Saussure's position on the relative abstractness of *langue* is subtle. He consistently reminds us that the system is only a part of the total facts of speech, that it lies somehow behind or beyond the accidents of talk, that it is collective and hence not reducible to any instance of speaking, which he takes to be individual. It is also mental in the sense of being that which fixes the relation between an acoustic image and an idea (cf."tébl" and "piece of furniture with legs and a horizontal surface"). Yet signs are not abstract, he says, because the associations of which they consist are ratified by collective consent, stored in the individual

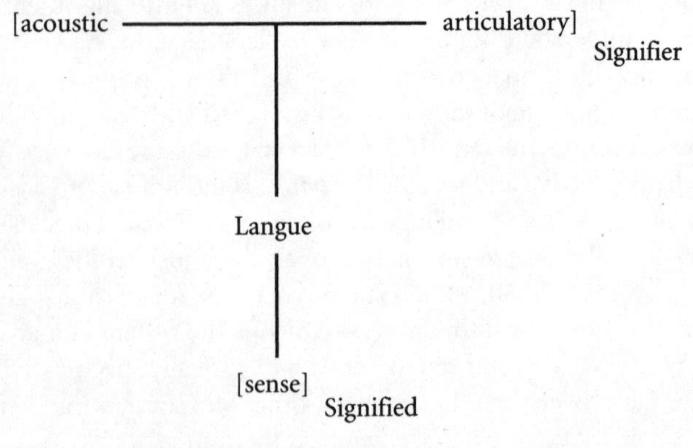

FIGURE 2.2 Signifier and Signified.

[3]Anyone who has worked with verbatim or phonetic transcriptions of talk will appreciate what Saussure is pointing to here.

brain, and sufficiently tangible to be recorded in writing. The sheer act of producing speech sounds is not properly part of *langue* because it is merely physical, whereas the "acoustic images" that are produced *are* part of *langue* because they are psychophysical units. It becomes clear that there is an intimate relation between this Saussurian system and the conceptual organization that allows us to produce meaning with language. *Langue* and *parole* are ultimately interdependent, since you cannot have the one without the other, yet they are so basically different that they could never be treated in a single framework. Whereas linguistics is the study of *langue, parole* can be studied from a variety of other fields, including physiology, sociology, history, literature. To appreciate Saussure's division of intellectual labor, one need only recall that the study of *parole* is strictly subordinate to the study of *langue.* Hence linguistics becomes the first in all those disciplines that study language, since it alone studies the core of the linguistic fact, the irreducible system.

Taken at face value, the *Course* seems to advocate that linguists turn away from *parole* and focus solely on *langue.* Being the repository of all that is conventional, *langue* alone is the basis of grammar in language. But such a gloss runs the risk of misreading Saussure, for whom the two faces of language were constantly interacting with one another. We can see this in his remarks on linguistic change, which is driven by *parole* but crystallized as structure in *langue.* It is also evident in the way he goes about locating *langue* among the facts of language (Saussure 1974:28–32). His first step is to imagine the individual acts that make up parole: "Il faut se placer devant l'acte individuel qui permet de reconstituer le circuit de la parole. Cet acte suppose au moins deux individus; c'est le minimum exigible pour que le circuit soit complet" 'One must place oneself before the individual act that makes it possible to reconstitute the circuit of speech. This act requires at least two individuals; this is the minimum necessary in order that the circuit be complete' (Saussure 1974:27).

Parole is, then, a circuit, a relational nexus, in which meanings pass between at least two interlocutors. Each party is equipped with the same conceptual and physical resources, and each performs alternately the active role of encoding meaning and the passive role of decoding it. The encoding process entails relaying concepts (signifieds) in the acoustic images of speech (signifiers). When Jack asks for the paper, he starts from a conceptual form in his brain (*cerveau*), which is associated with linguistic signs and therefore acoustic images. In phonating, he produces the physical sounds of the acoustic images. Natalia in turn can receive these sounds by auditory perception and can then decode them by relaying from audition to the brain and from sound image to signified. The one speaking is active in the sense that she produces the original concepts and also encodes them, whereas the one hearing passively decodes the other's thoughts but does not produce any new ones in doing so. The upper half of Figure 2.3 represents A speaking to B, and the lower half B speaking to A.

It is immediately evident where *langue* fits into the circuit in Figure 2.3: It is the

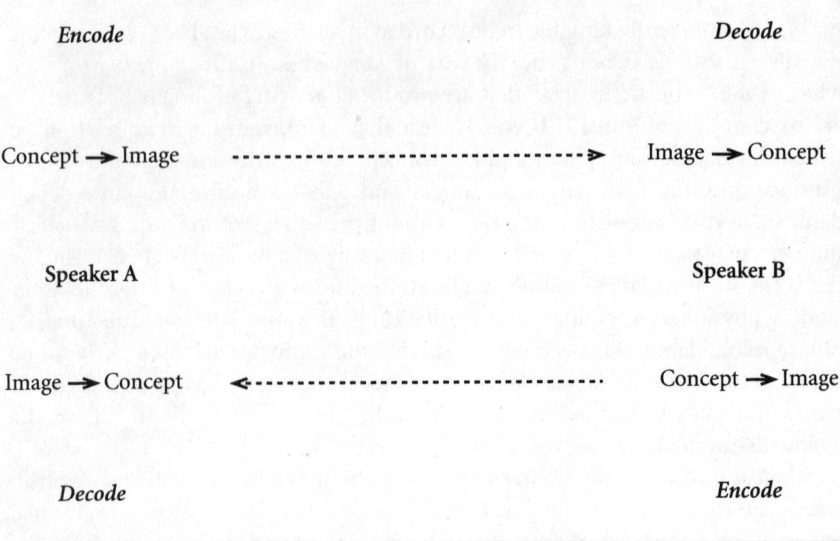

FIGURE 2.3 The Circuit of Parole.

system by which A and B encode and decode. Notice that this system is inside the brain of each speaker, and yet it is collective in the sense that all speakers have the same one. Being repeated again and again in the brains of the people, it is collective by its very distribution. Saussure holds that all speakers of a given language reproduce approximately the same associations of signifiers with signifieds. This commonality of *langue* is what makes it possible for B to understand A's meanings, even though they originate within A's head. Here Saussure resolves two key issues: how a thought, which is taken to be private, is made external and hence public; and how *langue,* which is taken to be abstract, is made concrete and hence observable. Producing and understanding speech are inverse processes (as the arrows in Figure 2.3 show), but they utilize exactly the same code. A speaker's ability to enter into the circle depends upon knowledge of *langue,* which is inherently distinct from knowledge about things like tables and newspapers. We can see in all this that whatever else it does, *parole* instantiates *langue.* Since linguists, like other people, can perceive *langue* only through its manifestation in *parole,* the two faces of language are practically interwoven, even if they are in principle distinct. This is an important point because Saussure's powerful rhetoric suggests a neat division between the two, whereas in fact the line is anything but clean. It is only through analysis that we can distinguish facts of *langue* from facts of *parole,* and how we draw the line depends ultimately upon our framework.

Arbitrariness and Linearity

Let us return to the relation between the linguistic form, or signifier, and the linguistic meaning, or signified. The two aspects of the verbal sign are not linked in any natural or "interior" way according to Saussure; the tie between them is arbitrary (1974:100). On the one hand, there is no resemblance or necessary contiguity between the phonetic form "tébl" and the concept for which it stands. Instead, it seems to be a matter of pure convention. On the other hand, there is the comparative fact that the same idea can be expressed in scores of different ways according to the language one is speaking. This cross-linguistic variation is prima facie evidence that the pairings of sounds with ideas in any one language are fixed by conventions and not by nature. To this we could add that as any language changes over time, the pairings between units at the two levels shift around, so that even in a single language viewed through time, there are variations, as there are in the dialectal variants of a language viewed across space. In each case the logic is the same: In the absence of obvious ties between sounds and ideas, variability counts as evidence of a certain sort of contingency. A bond that is both contingent and yet absolute within its own dominion is arbitrary. Saussure wants us to see that a linguistic sign functions only because there is a conventional system to hold it together and relate it to other signs, which are themselves also the products of convention.

The arbitrariness principle applies in the first instance to the relation between signifier and signified. Saussure abbreviates this by saying that the linguistic sign itself is arbitrary, but this should not obscure the specificity of the concept. One problem here is that Saussure appears to equivocate on the question of what a sign stands for. Notice that the kinds of variation that justify the arbitrariness principle actually presuppose a sameness across languages. It is only by assuming that French *soeur* and German *Schwester* or French *boeuf* and German *Ochs* really encode the same idea that their formal differences become evidence of arbitrariness. Given a commonsense understanding of kinship and cattle, the difference-relative-to-sameness seems clear. But what if the two cultures had significantly divergent kinship systems or categorized livestock in a way that overlapped with but was divergent from the way Europeans do? What if *Schwester* were used only for elder sisters or *Ochs* for horses as well as cattle? Could we adduce expressions in the language as evidence of arbitrariness? We might want to point to the sibling or the animal and use the real-world things as the pivot of sameness against which to juxtapose the different acoustic images. But this would be cheating. Under the logic of Saussure's argument, the signified is itself a concept, not a thing in the world. Therefore that two languages indicate the same physical thing with different words does *not* prove that the words have the same conceptual meanings. The signifiers differ *and so do the concepts.* To the extent that this is so, cross-linguistic variation tells us nothing whatsoever about the bond between signifier and signified.

As Emile Benveniste (1974) argued, the relation between signifier and signified is not really arbitrary; it is necessary. The concept "table," whatever its internal structure, is obligatorily tied to the acoustic image "tébl," since neither would exist without the other. An acoustic image without a signified does not count as a signifier. It is just a sound. And a concept without a signifier to encode it does not count as a signified. It is just an idea. It is only the relation between them that transforms them from noises and notions into the necessary parts of a sign. Recall from the *Course* that Saussure holds human thought to be structured by langue, which implies that verbal forms and mental representations are codependent. We can subdivide the one only in relation to the other. Here another qualification is in order: the force of arbitrariness depends upon one's perspective. For a linguist looking across languages, or for anyone adopting the objective "view from nowhere" typical of science, the phenomenon stands out clearly. Not so for a native speaker engaged in action. The commonsense perspective of a Jack or Natalia takes the link between "tébl" and the eating place as beyond question. This in no way weakens the strength of the principle for linguistics, but it should alert us to the possibility that a study of verbal practices will have to explain the appearance of naturalness as well.

Alongside arbitrariness, Saussure's second principle is the linearity of the signifier (1974:103). Although he had less to say about this than about the first principle, he considered it equally important. Being auditory (*auditive*), the signifier unfolds in time. It represents an extension that can be measured in a single dimension, a line. The grammatical system entails hierarchical structures, such as the noun phrase to which 'the' and 'paper' belong in Jack's speech. But the emergence of sound over time is linear, not hierarchical (see Figure 2.4).

Here we tread upon another fine line in the Saussurian paradigm. If the signifier is linear because its production is a physical event measurable with instruments, then does this mean that the mental event of the acoustic image is also linear? Recall that Saussure carefully specified that the signifier is more than mere sound; it is speech sound. This means that it is psychophysical, not just physical.

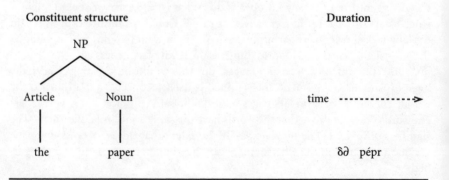

FIGURE 2.4 Structure Versus Time.

Could it be that the acoustic image, unlike the vibrations that embody it, really does have hierarchical structure? For instance, the sounds of "D'the paper come today" are divisible into syllables, which are in turn divisible into onset (first part), peak, and coda (end). If you were to show that an acoustic image is made up of syllables, this would indicate that signifiers do have at least certain hierarchical structure. This in turn suggests that linearity as temporal emergence interacts with nonlinearity in ways not apparent by Saussure's terse divisions.

Value and Opposition

If the arbitrariness principle is right, then there is a real question how words ever acquire meaning. If the table before me is not what gives sense to my utterance "It's right on the table," then what does? To answer that convention, or *langue*, confers meaning is both true and insufficient. Saussure's response is the more exacting concept of value (*valeur*). The basic idea here is that words get their meaning not by a positive tie to the things they denote but by a negative tie to the other words to which they are opposed. Two words are opposed, strictly speaking, if they are the same in all ways but one. There are of course various levels on which this difference can occur. The following illustrates minimal differences at the three levels of phonology (sound structure), morphology (word composition), and semantics (sense):

phonology:	paper	vs.	pepper
morphology:	paper	vs.	papers
semantics:	paper	vs.	magazine

The meaning (signified) of the English word "newspaper," for instance, is opposed to those terms such as "journal," "magazine," "newsletter," "publication," "broadside," that designate related ideas. It is these other concepts that delimit the sense of NEWSPAPER. The same holds for the signifier, whose identity derives in part from its oppositions to other sounds: "newsprint," "wax paper," "new sprint," "noose print" (?), "moose print," "moose sprint (quickly)." As will be clear from this list, not all oppositions are minimal or perhaps even relevant. It takes a stretch to argue that moose prints and newspapers are linguistically related. Unfortunately, Saussure does not spell out rigorous criteria according to which some differences count as true oppositions whereas others are just for fun. The important point for now is that, for Saussure, both sound and thought would be undifferentiated continua if it weren't for language (1974:155ff). It is value that fixes the subdivisions.

Value, in this technical sense, is a relation that always involves three parts. First, one must have two dissimilar things that can be exchanged for one another. The signifier and the signified fulfill this role—a sound image for an idea. Second, one must have two things that are similar and can be compared to one another: signifier 1 ≠ signifier 2, signified 1 ≠ signified 2, sign 1 ≠ sign 2. Finally, there must be a social collectivity and a system in which the exchange of dissimilars and comparison of similars are established. This third factor anchors value in the system of *langue* as it is at any point in history, making it the province of synchronic rather than diachronic study. Furthermore, although value as such could be conceived in much more abstract terms, it is specifically social value that Saussure is treating.

Examples of value are easy to come by. Compare English and Maya terms in the following, in which English happens to show more lexical distinctions.

hand k'ab'
arm k'ab'
branch k'ab'

foot ʔòok
leg ʔòok

Hence, terms in the two languages overlap extensionally; they can be properly used to refer to the same things. But they are not equivalent in meaning; the ideas are different. The value of Maya *k'ab'* is broader, less specific than the English terms because it is opposed only to *ʔòok* 'leg, foot', whereas English has five different terms for the same range of objects. We conclude that the signified of English "foot" and Maya *ʔòok* are different, even though both terms would be used to point to the extremity you put in your sneaker. Obviously, this does not mean that the Maya have no way of distinguishing their legs from their feet. It is impossible to project directly from the oppositions among words to the conceptual universe of the speakers. But it does mean that the terms most commonly used for these things have different meanings in English and Maya. Other simple examples of value are found in number systems: Language x, such as English, distinguishes singular from plural, but language y has a special form for counting things in pairs and hence makes a three-way division between singular, dual, and plural. Modern French distinguishes singular from plural in the second person pronouns (*tu* and *vous*), whereas English has only a single form (*you*). In all of these cases, it is the oppositions provided by the linguistic system that fix the meanings of its individual terms.

Paradigmatic and Syntagmatic Axes

So far we have treated value and opposition in terms of the meanings conferred on individual items due to the larger series of similar terms from which they differ. In effect our description of the value of "newspaper" could help explain why a speaker would select this word as opposed to some other to refer to the morning *Times.* Even if a nonnative speaker could get away with calling it a "bulletin" or "journal," still these terms do not fit the thing as well as "newspaper" does. The semantic potential of the expression is delimited by the others that could have been used in its place but were not. At any point in the stream of *parole,* the speaker must select the one word that best fits her idea. The field of choice may be limited or extensive depending on the case, but it is always based on the associations among the terms that make it up. Saussure dubbed this set of relations associative. Hence the value of a linguistic sign is defined by its oppositions to other terms in an associative series. Subsequent linguists called associative relations paradigmatic, because the sets they define are often organized in paradigms. Clear examples include the verb paradigms usually included in dictionaries of European languages, noun declensions in languages with case marking (Latin, German), and the pronoun paradigms made up of first, second, and third person forms, in singular and plural. Jakobson (1960) calls this the axis of selection because it is from these sets that speakers select their words. As will be familiar to anyone who has ever memorized a verb paradigm, associative relations must be remembered in order to be operative. The items they connect are not copresent in the same phrase but are relatives in absentia.

Saussure evidently thought of associative series as basically unordered and open-ended. He appears to be focused more on a mental ability than a linguistic fact when he asserts that any word might evoke any other word that is susceptible to being associated to it in one way or another (1974:175). At their most tenuous and fleeting, such associations would not even belong to the system of *langue,* and yet in other cases, such as closed paradigms, they clearly do affect language structure. This implies that in using the paradigmatic axis in linguistic description, we need to be skeptical and demand evidence that some putative relation has grammatical consequences. Otherwise we risk distorting the facts by treating a momentary association of *parole* as though it were a structural fact of *langue.* This was the point of the moose prints in the preceding section. Jack's utterance might also raise the association of the mail, since it would be delivered that day shortly after the paper, or napkins, since he uses a napkin while he reads the paper, but these associations would hardly belong in a grammar of English.

The entire discussion of arbitrariness and associative series applies to the meaning of a single word, like "table." But it tells us little about how to describe the combinations of words in sentences like "It's right on the table." How do we talk about the order and grouping of elements in verbal expressions that are longer than a single sign? The relations among sentence parts are combinations in presentia, not selections among terms related in absentia. Hence they belong to an axis that is distinct from, and indeed orthogonal to, the paradigmatic axis. Saussure called it the syntagmatic axis, and modern grammar calls it syntax.

Saussure's description of how signs combine is equivocal. On the one hand, syntagmatic combinations would appear to be the very stuff of *parole,* since they occur in speech. In particular the idiosyncratic combinations that result from freewheeling talk belong to *parole.* On the other hand, syntagmatic relations that involve fixed expressions or at least forms derived by regular grammatical rules belong to *langue.* The key difference is the degree of regularity. Such is the case with expressions like English *govern* + *ment,* which is a combination of two signs whose order is significant, according to a highly regular pattern (cf. establish + ment, embezzle + ment, settle + ment, etc.). Similarly, the word order in "The boa bit the boy" and "The boy bit the boa" is all that distinguishes the biting subject (preverbal) from the bitten object (postverbal). This highly regular fact is part of *langue* because of its rulelike status (the order subject-verb-object recurs in an infinite number of sentences with different words). Note in these examples that relative order of elements serves as a meaningful sign, distinguishing the biter from the bitten, for instance. This underscores an important feature of language, namely, that the order in which signs are combined contributes to meaning. Saussure notes this and considers the possibility that word order is itself an abstract sign (1974:190–191). He argues against this, however, asserting that the material presence of signs is primary and their order is a secondary effect. We can appreciate why he takes this position, for if he were to admit abstract signs, he would have to alter his opening dichotomies. Unlike standard lexical items, relative order has no acoustic image and therefore is not a signifier in the standard sense. So although he admits that some syntagmatic facts are part of *langue*, none are independent signs, and many fall into the patchwork of *parole*. In between is a gray zone between grammar and speech. Indeed, Saussure observes that syntagms are on the edge between the two orders of language (1974:173, section 251).

Motivation and Transparency

The final feature of Saussure's approach that must be introduced at this point is what he calls "motivation." In the relentless march of dualities that make up the *Course*, this term provides the opposite of arbitrariness. It may be easiest to start with an example: If "news" and "paper" are arbitrary signs, their combination in "newspaper" is relatively motivated. (The word is pronounced "núspepr," with primary stress on the first syllable and devoicing of the "s," as opposed to "nú:z pépr," where the two words receive equal stress and are separated by a pause.) That is, it follows a regular pattern of noun formation in which the substance term "paper" is preceded by one of a number of other nouns that qualify it, hence "fly paper," "wallpaper," "toilet paper," "tar paper," and so forth. Part of this process of compounding is the phonological change from two separate words to a single word, which I have indicated in the parenthetical note on pronunciation. For the other examples to be valid instances of compounding, they should be pronounced with similar phonological collapsing. Some motivated forms derive from an independent word plus a morpheme, as in papers (pépr + z) and government (govern + ment) and houses (haus + s, pronounced "háuziz").

Motivation in this technical sense always involves two things: (1) the syntagmatic form in which two or more signs are combined (i.e., a grammatical formation), and (2) the associative series to which the resulting compound belongs. Without the former there is no grammatical construction and therefore no possibility of motivation in Saussure's sense. Without a larger associative series, the compound could be a onetime oddity that falls outside the scope of *langue* and not a regular construction that fits into a series of related concepts. Even in cases of regular rule-governed combinations, motivation is always a matter of degree.

Even the most regular grammatical combination starts from individual signs that are themselves arbitrary. That is, examples like the ones used here illustrate what we might call first-order motivation, in which two arbitrary forms are combined. Once we consider sentences like "Did the papers come today?" the degree of motivation is much greater, since the noun is pluralized (hence motivated) but also placed in a noun phrase that is part of a sentence (hence further motivated). The sentence itself shows evidence of syntactic derivation in the inversion of the auxiliary verb with the subject noun phrase to form the question. The important point to see is that as we combine elementary linguistic forms into larger structures and alter those structures according to the rules of the language, the degree of motivation increases. We get farther and farther from the elemental arbitrariness of the simple forms.

If motivation is a relative concept, a matter of degree, it is also one whose effects may be relatively obvious or hidden. In all of the examples above, the presence of grammatical formation is immediately apparent, and anyone who understands the term "motivation" can spot these as cases of it. It doesn't always work this way, though. What about pairs like "is" versus "was," "go" versus "went," "buy" versus "bought," and the many irregular forms contained in any language? It is entirely reasonable to posit a grammatical relation between the present and past forms of such verbs, since they are organized into paradigms by person, number, and tense. This means they are related by rules, and therefore they are cases of motivation. This is true whether we argue that the past forms are derived from the present ones or the other way around. But the very irregularity of the forms in the pairs above and the inseparability of the verb stem from the past tense marker (contrast the case of I paint versus I paint + ed) obscures the grammatical derivation. In Saussurian terms, the obvious cases are highly transparent and the others relatively less transparent. Two things distinguish the two kinds of cases: whether we can isolate the constituent parts of the derived form so as to see the pieces of which it is composed, and whether the composition follows a regular pattern or is idiosyncratic. The first condition can be called segmentability, since it involves segmenting the parts, and the second generality, since it involves the scope of the process in the grammar. The greater the degree of segmentability and generality, the greater the transparency.

There is in any language a tension between motivation and arbitrariness. All of the simple elements of the language are relatively arbitrary, regardless of how natural they may appear from the perspective of a native speaker. As we combine the elements into more and more elaborate or precise constructions, the role of the grammar becomes increasingly important. It is sometimes said that the lexicon of a language, roughly the dictionary of its basic meaningful elements, is the repository of irregularity, whereas the syntax is the mechanism by which regular structures are formed. The arbitrary elements are a more or less accidental collection, but the grammar is a principle of order. In the language of Saussure, grammar is the study of rule-governed motivation, the limits of arbitrariness.

For Saussure, then, language as *langue* is a system of signs and relations among signs. This system is governed by its own internal logic, which is different from that of any other kind of social institution. Any linguistic sign can be divided into two parts, which Saussure called the signifier and the signified. From the former, language derives its fundamental linearity, the duration characteristic of the sound image that the sign defines. From the signified aspect, it derives its fundamental arbitrariness; the idea for which the sound image stands is defined by pure convention. Thus the two principles Saussure singled out intersect in the two aspects of a sign. As to the relations among signs, he distinguished another pair: Associative, or paradigmatic, relations link signs that are similar and among which a speaker must select when putting together a phrase. Syntagmatic, or syntactic, relations connect signs that are combined in a single phrase. Taken together, these two principles of sign-to-sign relations offset the original arbitrariness of every individual sign. They provide the means of deriving verbal forms by grammatical combinations and modifications. Once we see that what is arbitrary is the link of sound to idea, we can appreciate why Saussure was led to propose his concept of motivation. He needed something to oppose to the arbitrariness of individual signs, and he looked to the grammar by which signs are combined. Every arbitrary unit implies *oppositions* between itself and other comparable units, but every motivated combination implies *contrast* among the elements that make it up.

Saussure's theory is a meditation on difference—the difference between language and the rest of the world, the differences between the parts of language and the principles of their organization. The irreducible code of language is flanked and crosscut by so many boundaries based on difference that one wonders how it can ever fit in with the larger world of meaningful experience. What is one to say of the relations between such things as the words "there he goes" and the point made while uttering them; text and pictures in the newspaper; the rules of the road and the stop sign at the corner; the words "liberty," "quarter dollar," and the eagle pictured on the twenty-five-cent piece? Saussure did not attempt to answer such questions, and it should not surprise us that he offers little direction. To look out on the social world from within the system of *langue* is to see it as a world apart. This is a natural corollary of the irreducibility thesis in its Saussurian form. We could use individual concepts like value (for which he offers an economic example) and arbitrariness (which could presumably describe many nonverbal signs) in comparing language with the other ways that people make meaning. But as yet we have no terms in which to talk about the organization of these other systems except as degenerate forms of language. For this we need a broader agenda than Saussure's.

Saussure envisioned the study of signs, or semiotics, but it was the philosophers C. S. Peirce and Charles Morris who developed it in America. In the next chapter, we will briefly sketch portions of their sign theories. Each has had a profound influence on the development of modern approaches to language in context.

Further Readings

On the appearance of naturalness, see

Grice, H. P. "Meaning." In *Semantics: An Interdisciplinary Reader in Philosophy, Linguistics, and Psychology,* edited by D. Steinberg and L. Jakobovits. Cambridge: Cambridge University Press, 1971, pp. 53–60.

Ziff, P. "On Grice's Account of Meaning." *In Semantics: An Interdisciplinary Reader in Philosophy, Linguistics, and Psychology,* edited by D. Steinberg and L. Jakobovits. Cambridge: Cambridge University Press, 1971, pp. 60–66.

On the disruption of analysis, see

Polanyi, M. *On Personal Knowledge: Towards a Post-Critical Philosophy.* Chicago: University of Chicago Press, 1974.

My summary of Saussure's approach draws mainly on the following sections of his *Course:*

Saussure, F. de. *Course in General Linguistics.* Translated by W. Baskin. New York: McGraw-Hill, 1966. "Object of Linguistics"; part 1: "General Principles," chaps. 1–3; part 2: "Synchronic Linguistics," chaps. 1–6.

The French critical edition of this work has extensive and very helpful annotations; see

Saussure, F. de. *Cours de linguistique générale.* Edited by Tullio de Mauro. Paris: Payothèque, 1974.

Bloomfield, L. "Review of Saussure." In *A Leonard Bloomfield Anthology,* edited by C. Hockett. Bloomington: Indiana University Press, 1970, pp. 106–108.

Jakobson, R. *Six Lectures on Sound and Meaning.* Translated by J. Mepham. Cambridge: MIT Press, 1978. Lectures 2, 3, and 4, pp. 23–88.

For general views of language as a system, to contrast with Saussure, see

Benveniste, E. "The Semiology of Language." In *Semiotics: An Introductory Anthology,* edited by R. Innis. Bloomington: Indiana University Press, 1985, pp. 226–246.

Boas, F. "Introduction to the Handbook of American Indian Languages." In *Introduction to Handbook of American Indian Languages and Indian Linguistic Families of America North of Mexico,* edited by P. Holder. Lincoln: University of Nebraska Press, 1966 [1911]. Parts 2, 4, and 5, pp. 10–39, 55–79.

Cassirer, E. "Le Langage et la construction du monde des objets." In *Essais sur le langage.* Paris: Editions de Minuit, 1969, pp. 36–68.

Hymes, D. *Foundations in Sociolinguistics: An Ethnographic Approach.* Philadelphia: University of Pennsylvania Press, 1974, chap. 1.

Sapir, E. "The Grammarian and His Language." In *Selected Writings of Edward Sapir in Language, Culture, and Personality,* edited by D. G. Mandelbaum. Berkeley: University of California Press, 1949 [1924], pp. 150–159.

———. "Language." In *Selected Writings of Edward Sapir in Language, Culture, and Personality,* edited by D. G. Mandelbaum. Berkeley: University of California Press, 1949 [1924], pp. 7–32.

Voloshinov, V. N. *Marxism and the Philosophy of Language.* Translated by L. Matejka and I. R. Titunik. Cambridge: Harvard University Press, 1986 [1929]. Part 2, chap. 1, pp. 45–63.

On the arbitrariness principle, see

Benveniste, E. "Nature du signe linguistique." In *Problèmes de linguistique générale,* vol. 1. Paris: Gallimard, 1966 [1939], pp. 49–55.

Friedrich, P. "The Linguistic Sign and Its Relative Non-arbitrariness." *In Language, Context and the Imagination: Essays.* Selected and introduced by A. Dil. Stanford: Stanford University Press, 1979 [1970].

On opposition and the paradigmatic and syntagmatic axes, see

Jakobson, R. "Concluding Statement: Linguistics and Poetics." In *Style in Language,* edited by T. Sebeok. Cambridge: MIT Press, 1960, pp. 350–377.

———. "Signe zéro." In *Readings in Linguistics,* vol. 2, edited by E. Hamp, F. W. Householder, and R. Austerlitz. Chicago: University of Chicago Press, 1966 [1939], pp. 109–115.

Chapter 3

From Signs to Sentences

FIRST A CAVEAT and then a clarification: In this chapter we will move from the Saussurian vision of language to the more general sign theories of the American pragmatist Charles S. Peirce, the French linguist Emile Benveniste, and the American philosopher Charles Morris. Of the three, Peirce is by far the most difficult to understand. Unlike the others, his is a theory based on three-part divisions, which he calls trichotomies. The addition of a third term greatly increases the complexity of his framework, and the task of understanding is further compounded by the terseness of his explanations and the extraordinarily broad scope of the phenomena he describes. Saussure's focus on language as his object had the benefit of limiting the field of inquiry to a manageable topic. This, as we saw, was one of his goals. Peirce's intended range is well indicated by the title of the piece we will explore here, "Logic as Semiotic." Despite the difficulty of reading him, however, Peirce's work has had a profound impact on contemporary linguistic anthropology, and several of his distinctions have entered into the common language of the field. My discussion here will be partial, and, as I will indicate, some points of interpretation are open to debate.

The clarification concerns the logical status of many of the terms used in the three works. All semiotic frameworks entail classifications. These three discuss things like icons, indexes, symbols, characterizing signs, objects, interpretants, and legisigns. But none of these is a thing, and none is an object in the everyday sense of this term. All of them are *relations*—between parts of a sign, types of signs, and other elements in the semiotic process. That is, to say that a sign is an index is to say that it functions by virtue of an indexical relation between the perceivable form of the sign and whatever it stands for. The noun form "index" is a shorthand to save breath and ink. Already with Saussure, we have entered into the world of system-internal relations, in which things like the signified aspect depend for their definition upon their relation to other things, like the signifier and the associative chain. Elements in a sign theory are not like other objects in the world. We cannot say of a sign, once an index always an index, for a single sign may be simultaneously an index, a symbol, and an icon. It is crucial to bear in mind from the outset that this multiplicity is not due to inconsistency in the terms but to the logical status of the terms. We could go so far as to say that *all* signs are simultaneously of several kinds. This is only to say that they function in several relations at once. It is like saying that Natalia's response to Jack in the first chapter was a statement, a response, and an act of referring to the table all at the same time. This of course follows from the fact that the utterance enters into several relations at once, and in each one it plays a certain role. The same holds for signs, their parts, and the larger compositions made from them.

Peirce on Logic as Semiotic

So what is a sign in the first place? Peirce answers with a relational construct. "A sign, or representamen, is something which stands to somebody for something in some respect or capacity" (Peirce 1955:99). We can see both the similarity and the difference between this framework, as a first approximation, and the one proposed by Saussure: The sign form corresponds to the signifier and the object to the signified. What Peirce denotes as "in some respect or capacity" is what he terms the ground of the sign relation. It has no direct analogue in Saussure's framework, for he considered this relation to be a matter of arbitrary convention. Peirce, in other words, has recast the arbitrary link between form and meaning as a third term, which he will later subclassify into three contrasting types of ground. The initial trichotomy is shown in Figure 3.1.

We should make note of two points in this trichotomy. The first is that Peirce, like Saussure and indeed any theory based on representation, enshrines a division between meaningful forms and the things they stand for. This may seem intuitive, but it also raises a profound issue. For the inaugural rupture between form and meaning makes it impossible, ultimately, ever to join the two. An utterance cannot directly express anything; it can only stand for it. Its expressive force and meaningfulness derive entirely from its deferred relation to something other than itself. This implies that meaning can be *re-presented* but can never be directly presented. Utterances and other expressions push the mind toward things or ideas that stand apart from them, always a step removed. Try as we might in this view, we can never break through the veil of representation to the realm of meaning. The best you can do is pile on more signs, each one bringing with it another level of deferral. An alternative to this would be a theory in which meaning is taken to be immanent in human expression. We tend to think of such immanence as belonging to artistic works or performances but not to the everyday forms of expression. Asked what her painting stands for, an artist can turn the question back: "Nothing. Take it on its own terms. What does it mean to you?" Similarly for a dancer or even a poet or author of prose "fiction." But if Natalia were to ask Jack what he meant by asking her about the paper, the same response would be uncooperative, to say the least. The difference here is based on an assumption about artistic expression as something essentially unlike the everyday business of con-

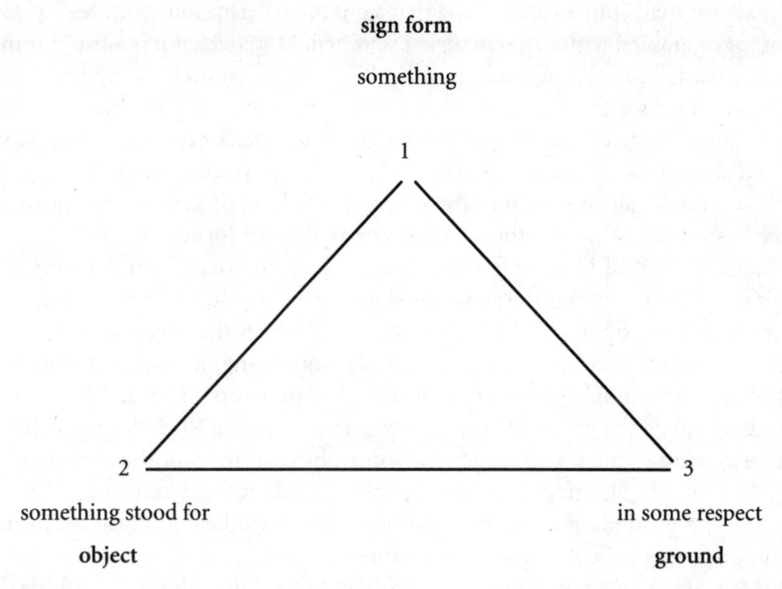

FIGURE 3.1 Parts of a Sign, After Peirce.

veying intention and information. This assumption will come into question in Part 2 of this book.

The second point concerns the status of the object stood for. There are several possible ways to understand this. By aligning Peirce with Saussure, we are assuming that the object is a concept, just as the signified was. So the object of "table" would be an idea, something like "piece of furniture made of rigid material, with flat surface raised from the ground by means of legs or some other device." In this view the sign stands for an intensional object, a conceptual entity defined within the system. The problem here is the same as with Saussure: How do we ever connect with things in the world like the newspaper and the dining room table, which are material objects and not only concepts? This level of ideal concepts creates a second-order deferral: The sign stands for an idea, and the idea stands for a thing. How many veils of correspondence separate Jack from the newspaper in his hands?

Alternatively, we could say that the object is the class of things denoted by the sign when it is used. In this view the object is what is often called the *extension* of the sign (as opposed to its intension), the collection of things to which it may properly refer. This would spare us the mediating veil of ideas, but it raises a further problem. For if the object is a real-world thing, then it cannot belong strictly to the sign system (unless we assume that signs are coterminous with reality), and it cannot be aligned with the Saussurian signified. Moreover, if it is a list of things, then the list is infinite, since any sign can be used indefinitely many times. One might wonder, as a third alternative, whether Peirce intends the object to be the actual thing denoted by an instance of a sign in use. Jack's expression "the paper" has as its object the *Times* of September 19, 1993. This reading might be accurate, but it is unlikely, since it defines the object at the level of actual utterances, and Peirce has yet to distinguish these from signs as abstract forms.

For now, the most likely definition of the object, on the one hand, seems to be that it is the class of things the sign may stand for. The ground, on the other hand, is the Saussurian signified, the idea in virtue of which the object can be represented. As Peirce puts it: "The sign stands for something, its *object.* It stands for that object, not in all respects, but in reference to a sort of idea, which I have sometimes called the *ground* of the representamen" (Peirce 1955:99). So we have a sign, or representamen, that stands for some object in the world by virtue of an idea, or ground. The linguistic sign "paper" stands for the morning *Times* in virtue of the grounding concept, something like "periodical publication printed on nonglossy paper, focusing on information, ... "

But Peirce was not content to divide the parts of a sign without also addressing the matter of understanding. Recall that for Saussure, understanding was essentially the mirror image of producing speech. That is, to understand an utterance one need only recognize its signifying forms in order to recapture the original idea of the speaker. Speech was active; understanding was passive. For Peirce, the process of understanding was more dynamic and productive. As he describes it, the sign "addresses somebody, that is, creates in the mind of that person an equivalent sign, or perhaps a more developed sign. That sign which it creates I call the *interpretant* of the first sign" (Peirce 1955:99). If we add this new term, we can say that sign form, in order to be a true sign, is associated with three parts, an interpretant, an object, and a ground (see Figure 3.2).

So understanding proceeds by way of the proliferation of signs. When Natalia hears Jack's question, there arises in her mind either an equivalent sign or a more elaborate one. She *interprets* his utterance. If her interpretation is identical to Jack's utterance, then it basically fits the Saussurian scenario, and she replicates his meaning. If it is more elaborate than his or differs in any way from his, then Natalia's understanding actually produces a *new* sign associated with its own interpretant/object/ground. And since this new sign has within it an interpretant, it in turn leads to another sign, which leads to another one, and so on indefinitely. This process is akin to Saussure's notion of the associations of signs, but it differs from it in several crucial ways. First of all, unlike the Saussurian associative series, Peirce's interpretant is not contained within the confines of a preestablished system. An interpretant might be a simple sign, or it might be an entire elaborate discourse. That is, it might be greater than a single sign. Also, an interpretant may be derived from the original sign plus other knowledge or experience that the addressee has at her dis-

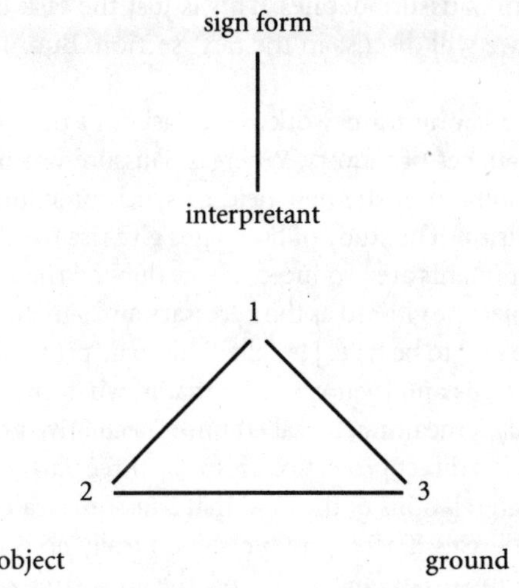

FIGURE 3.2 Peirce's Interpretant, Object, and Ground.

posal. Natalia can draw on her background knowledge of Jack's morning routines, their apartment, the newspaper, and so forth. Just as Peirce's object is a point of contact between signs and the broader world of experience, so, too, the interpretant opens out onto the world. This is a fundamental difference between Saussurian closure of the linguistic system, cut apart from the world by arbitrariness, and the more relational semiotic framework, reaching out to the world.

More than a mere sign, the interpretant is like an ideological horizon, a background of evaluative "glosses" that actors in a social group apply to any sign. Natalia understands her partner's question by virtue of her common sense, her prior experience with him, her unreflective grasp of the setting of the kitchen and dining room, her knowledge of the morning paper and the table, her ear for when a question counts as a request. All this gives her the wherewithal to fill in the blanks by grasping all that is unsaid in Jack's question. From a Saussurian perspective, this raises an acute problem, for it is unclear how Peirce would define a sign system as something with a beginning and an end. If the objects are in the world and the interpretants derive in part from the world, then how do you set limits on any sign, much less on an entire collection of them? How do you describe the difference between interpretants that are paradigmatically associated with a linguistic sign from ones that merely arise in a special context? How do you describe the syntactic relations between words (signs) in a sentence? Peirce offers no clear answers to such questions, at least in this part of his philosophy. For our purposes, he contributes a relational framework that might be useful in expanding the kind of system Saussure defines. This is just the task that Benveniste undertook in the work we will discuss in the next section. But first, there is more to be said about Peirce.

Like Saussure, Peirce saw his framework as the basis for a division of intellectual labor among several branches of inquiry. Whereas Saussure was primarily concerned to locate the proper domain of the new field of synchronic linguistics, Peirce suggested a three-way division. The study of how signs give rise to other signs, that is, the process whereby interpretants are produced, Peirce dubbed rhetoric. The relation between a sign and its object he glossed as the necessary and sufficient conditions under which the sign may be said to be true. He called this logic proper. Finally, the study of the relations between signs and their grounds, that is, what must be true of any sign in order that it embody a meaning, he called pure speculative grammar. Notice that this tripartite division is a direct projection from the three parts of a sign. There is no mention of sign-to-sign relations of the kind that Saussure treated under the syntagmatic and paradigmatic axes. There is no syntax and really no *system* of signs as such to compare with the Saussurian *langue.* Indeed, the great strength of Peirce's framework is in the ways it opens semiotics to the world, through the object, and to ideology, through the interpretant. The closure of a bounded system cut away from the world by arbitrariness, so emphasized by Saussure, is virtually missing. Peirce proposed a number of additional trichotomies, of which two will concern us here.

Modern linguistic analysis is based on a distinction that we have played upon since the outset of this book but not really stated explicitly. This is the distinction between linguistic expressions viewed as prefabricated forms, repeatable and anonymous, versus the same expressions viewed as actual utterances made under specific, idiosyncratic conditions. It is standard to designate the former, more general level as "types," and the latter, more particular, as "tokens." If you think of the word "this," for instance, it could be said that the *type* is a four-letter, singular demonstrative. There is only one type THIS, and it remains the same however many times it is repeated. There are, by contrast, more than a half dozen *tokens* of the type on this page alone, two of them in this very sentence. Whereas a type remains identical throughout all instances of its use, every token is by definition unique. A type is the class of all tokens that instantiate it. Peirce called tokens sinsigns (cf. single or singular signs) and types legisigns (cf. the sign as a general law or convention) (Peirce 1955:102). To these he opposed qualisigns, which he defined as a single property or attribute viewed as a potential. This last type has had little or no impact on the field and will not concern us here.

In relation to human language, we can speak of a division between type and token at the levels of phonology, morphology, and syntax. That is, the conceptual distinction between a general convention and an instance of its use can be applied at any level of linguistic form one wishes to consider. Let's take the word "table" as an example. The signifier or sign vehicle has a canonical phonological shape, "tébl." Now imagine that Natalia has a slight peculiarity in her English pronunciation, such that she says this word with a nasalized vowel. And since she has a slight cold on September 19, she nasalizes the vowel even more. These peculiarities are not part of English phonology but do affect the token-level variants of the phonological type. The same applies to the signified aspect. The type-level signified of table, something like "piece of furniture with horizontal surface and legs or other vertical support," is much more general than the specific meaning of "kitchen table" actualized in Natalia's utterance to Jack. Finally, considering the objects picked out by the type- and token-level forms, we can contrast the class of all tables from the specific one actually in the dining room of our domestic couple. The type level pertains to *langue*-like systems taken as abstract potential; the token level pertains to *parole*-like relations between actual instances of signs and the world around them (see Table 3.1). As long as we work within this division, the type is the domain of irreducibility, and the token the domain of relationality. Eventually we shall call this division into question, but it is a fundamental one in the various formalisms we treat in Parts 1 and 2 of this book.

I said earlier that in place of the Saussurian doctrine of arbitrariness, Peirce would offer a typology of relations. This is the focus of the next trichotomy, the last one we will address. The ground, recall, is the idea in virtue of which the sign can stand for an object. Peirce distinguishes three broad types of ground, which he calls icon, index, and symbol. An icon is a sign that stands for something by similarity, or likeness, with it. A portrait is an icon of its subject, a photo an icon of its subject, a blueprint an icon of the building design it shows. Icons may portray their object, as in the examples just mentioned. Or they may exhibit it, as a sample of cloth exhibits the pattern or color chips exhibit the hues of paint one chooses at a store. Icons may appear natural, as in the cases of exhibiting, but there is always an element of selectivity involved. No sign can resemble its object in all ways, for even the sample is partial. In most cases this selectivity implies that icons are to a degree conventional. Think of portraits from Renaissance Italy, from contemporary North America, from Japan. All demonstrate standards of posture, color choices, and ways of conveying the personal character of the subject that imply the presence of convention. Obviously, an icon as elaborate as a

TABLE 3.1 Type Versus Token

	Type	*Token*
Signifier	Canonical phonological form	Actual variants
Signified	General sense, concept	Specific sense in utterance
Referent	Class of objects designated by type	Particular object denoted by utterance

blueprint is produced according to highly specialized conventions, which one must understand in order to read it. It is sometimes suggested that onomatopoetic words, like English "bowwow," "crash," "splat," "whack" are purely iconic since they reproduce the sounds they are meant to stand for. But anyone who has learned the corresponding terms in another language will appreciate that these expressions vary a great deal across languages and so fall into the same logic of arbitrary conventionality that Saussure pointed out for other signs.

If icons are based on similarity between the sign form and its object, indexes are based on contiguity. Peirce states it like this: "An index is a sign, or representation, which refers to its object not so much because of any similarity or analogy with it, nor because it is associated with general characters which that object happens to possess, as because it is in dynamical (including spatial) connection both with the individual object, on the one hand, and with the sense or memory of the person for whom it serves as a sign, on the other hand" (Peirce 1955:107). Take, for example, a knock on the door, which indexes the presence of a visitor; the ring of the phone, which indexes the call; the voice from the other room, which indexes the presence of the speaker. Jack's question to Natalia indexed his presence in the next room, and her response indexed both her presence in the dining room and her understanding of Jack's question. It does not matter at this point whether an index gives new information or signals something that people already know. For now, it matters only that the index signals the copresence of its object in the same place and time as it occurs. Because of this dynamical relation, indexes direct the attention of their interpreters as if by blind compulsion. Given the sign, we attend directly to its object. At the token level, indexes are as direct as the doorbell is to the visitor. But it is important, if slightly more difficult, to see that indexes can also be defined at the type level. What would be an indexical type? Consider the standard difference in timbre between doorbells and phone rings or the general convention whereby a red traffic light indexes an intersection at which one must stop, but green indexes an intersection through which you can proceed apace. If Jack's voice from the kitchen indexes his presence and attention on Natalia, then the New England accent with which he pronounced "pépa" indexes the region in which he spent his childhood. Regional accents, to the degree that they are recognized and conventionally interpretable, are indexical types. If English were a language with an elaborate system of markers signaling deference or intimacy with the addressee, and Jack used an intimate form in addressing his partner, then we would say that he indexed their relation. The conventional relation between the markers and the intimacy/deferential dimension is a system of indexical types. The use of the markers in a given context is an indexical token. Thus indexes can stand for individual objects (including social relations), or they may stand for collections of objects of a certain type.

If you think about it for a moment, any sign could be said to co-occur with any object in the world. This book co-occurs with the chair in which you are sitting as you read it, and it co-occurs with the peanut butter in the pantry, the gas station at the corner, and the armed conflict in central Europe. But none of these relations is relevant to the book, at least on the face of it. Suppose you and I were standing before a large map, and I pointed to southern Mexico saying, "This is where I do my fieldwork." My pointing gesture is an index, but how do you know what its object is? Do I work in Tabasco, Campeche, Yucatán? Do I work in the Caribbean or even offshore on a boat? You need to know further information, such as the nature of the fieldwork (ethnography, not marine biology) in order to understand the index. In a general way, any indexical token could be said to be connected with any other thing in the context of its occurrence. As addressee, you need further information in order to interpret it. Even in the case of the doorbell, you need to know where the buzzer is in order to know where to go to meet the visitor. You need to know that the appropriate response to a doorbell is to answer it in person or by speaker rather than some other way. The voice indexing a person in the next room works because we assume it to be connected to a body and not a loudspeaker, and Jack's question indexes his momentary orientation toward Natalia only on the assumption that he is not practicing his pronunciation, muttering to himself, rehearsing something said to him the day before, and so forth. All these contingent facts must somehow be brought to bear on the index in order to interpret it correctly. Despite appearances, indexes require instructions, and this implies a degree of conventionality.

I emphasize the interplay between indexicality and convention precisely because Peirce's third type of sign, which he calls the symbol, is based solely on conventionality (Peirce 1955:112). A word like "table" or "paper" is symbolic in this sense, since there is no similarity nor any dynamical link between the word and its object. It is, to use a phrase combining Peirce and Saussure, a matter of arbitrary convention that these words stand for the kinds of objects they do. This is at the type level. At the token level, things look a little different. An utterance in which these two words are used *does* produce an actual relation between the sign and its object. The *Times* and kitchen table *are* in significant relations of coexistence with the words "paper" and "table" in the exchange between Jack and Natalia. But this is strictly a matter of the context of the example and not the general meaning of the two words, which could be defined adequately without ever mentioning the actual objects they refer to in the example. What this means is that at the token level many indexical relations are produced that have no place in the type-level system but that have a substantial impact on understanding. Thus while we can distinguish type from token for all three classes of sign, the token level is especially weighted toward the index because of its focus on dynamical relations of coexistence. The type level is especially weighted toward the symbol because of its focus on conventional laws. Yet just as we can define indexical types, so, too, we can define symbolic tokens. Stated in the abstract, these divisions and the connections between them can be difficult to pin down, but they will become clearer as we work through examples using them. For the moment, I want to return to a point made at the outset of this chapter.

Peirce's divisions of signs into parts, levels, and classes is in fact a classification of relations. If we try to treat terms like "object," "legisign," or "index" as denoting simple things, then the system looks hopelessly opaque. How can something be an index if it is also a symbol and the object of some other sign? The answer is that all three relations can pertain because they are just that: relations. Recall that Saussure began his meditation on language by saying that its very nature shifts depending upon one's perspective. This is a general feature of semiotic phenomena, not only language. There are no mere things in the world of signs. Just as a concept becomes a signified only by virtue of its relation to some signifier, and the sound image becomes a signifier only because it is associated with a signified, so, too, a thing becomes an object only when it is represented by a sign, which is in turn a sign only because it has an interpretant, a ground, and an object associated with it. An apparent type (legisign) can only count as a legisign if it has tokens (sinsigns) that instantiate it, and, conversely, a perceivable form is a token only if it instantiates a type. The rigorous interdependence of all these terms is one of the most basic features of a framework like Peirce's or Saussure's. Yet this interdependence is erased by the commonsense attitude that, after all, things are what they are, and an object cannot be both a this and a that at the same time. The misplaced concreteness implied in such a view is equally foreign to the symmetries of an irreducible system and to the dependencies of a relational matrix.

A Synthesis of Saussure and Peirce

There are both similarities and differences between Peirce's semiotics and Saussure's linguistics. The French linguist Benveniste (1974) was among the first to attempt a principled synthesis of the two frameworks, in the article "La Sémiologie de la langue." First published in 1969, then reprinted in his collected writings in 1974, and translated into English in 1985, this article attempts to derive an overarching framework in which language can be both related to and distinguished from other kinds of semiotic systems. Benveniste observes that Peirce's theory basically extends sign relations indefinitely by way of interpretance. Recall that the interpretant is the understanding of a sign, which may be both complex and based on knowledge outside the scope of the sign itself. The peculiarity of Peirce's system is that this understanding is at once part of the sign and yet obviously part of the broader ideological horizon. Lacking syntax and the associative relations of Saussure, Peirce gives no clue how we would draw boundaries around a sign system to define anything analogous to a *langue.* This puts his semiotics squarely in the camp of relational as opposed to irreducible perspectives. In the view of Benveniste, the domain of semiology is based on the concepts of unity and classification. The former appears to come mainly from Saussure, for whom *langue* is nothing if not unitary, and the latter from Peirce, for whom classification was a sweet obsession. What unifies *sémiologie* for Benveniste is that it deals in systems of signs that are arbitrary, that is, conventional. Taken together with his choice of the word *langue* in the title of the article, this understanding of the arbitrary nature of signs makes it clear that the Saussurian vision takes precedence in his synthesis.

Langue, according to Benveniste, is the system that produces and regulates all others. Signs like symbolic rites and codes of politeness may be quite elaborate, but they can never be at the same logical level as human language because they require language to evolve and develop. In order to fix the meaning of a pointing gesture, grasp the spatial setting of Jack and Natalia's exchange, or understand the social value of a way of dressing, we need language. But the opposite does not hold. No code of dress, politeness, or gestures could interpret the meaning of a sentence like "It's right on the table." This way of justifying the primacy of language is a classic version of what might be called linguocentricism. Benveniste's vocation as a linguist leads him to place language in the most central position among kinds of signs because it alone can interpret all others.

Elements of a Sign System

The elements of a sign system are of two kinds, internal and external. The former are divided along two dimensions, the repertoire of the signs and the functioning of the signs. The repertoire is determined according to whether the signs in the system are iconic, indexical, or symbolic and how these three are combined. The functioning of signs is what we might call the glue that binds them into a coherent system. This glue is what Saussure called "value," opposition, and the rules of combination. In this series of definitions, Benveniste reveals his debt to the dualist reasoning typical of Saussure. Human language, to take a ready example, is made up of signs that are primarily symbolic because they are arbitrary. It is held together as a system by value, paradigmatic opposition, and syntagmatic rules of combination. Road signs regulating traffic flow are also conventional, but the indexical and iconic aspects are more central given the demands of split-second decisions on the part of drivers. Table manners regulating behavior surrounding food consumption are more heavily weighted toward the conventional, for instance, the setting of a fork on the left and a knife on the right of the plate. The idea here is that by examining how the three types of sign relation combine in the elements of a given system, we can both compare and contrast it with other systems.

Whereas the internal components of a system foreground the irreducible logic of its unity, the external elements foreground its relations to other features of the social world. Interestingly, Benveniste relies heavily on dualism to describe the internal, the domain of Saussure, but proposes a three-part division of the external, the domain of Peirce. Relationality seems ill suited to binary reasoning. The first of these is the mode of signaling, sometimes called the channel, as in audible versus visible versus tactual signs. In the simple cases, gestures are visual or visual-tactual, whereas articulate speech is primarily audible. Think of the difference between the utterance "It's right on the table" and the pointing gesture that might accompany or substitute for it. The next external element is the domain of validity of the signs in question. This is the field of social life in which the signs are used and understood. Blueprints, musical scores, dance notations, flag signals, and specialized gestural codes like those of a police officer directing traffic are all relatively systematic signs with established interpretations. Yet they are restricted to certain kinds of activity, such as architecture, music or dance performance, maritime communication or traffic regulation. The last external element is the value of the sign system in relation to other systems. Here we might consider the standard relations between printed words and images in a newspaper or the notations on a typical road map in relation to the line drawings. Such examples combine highly arbitrary graphic representations of speech with conventionalized icons of spatial scenes.

Any semiotic system, then, regardless of type, must have three things. First, it must have a finite repertoire of basic signs, what in language is called a vocabulary, or lexicon. Of course the lexicon may be great or small and may contain signs of various types. Given the basic units, there must also be rules according to which the units are combined into larger ones. This corresponds to what linguists call syntax and semantics. The product of the rules is what Benveniste called a set of figures and in language we would call phrases and sentences. If the lexicon of basic units is finite, the set of figures may be infinite, as is the case with any human language. In English, Spanish, Maya, or Swahili, for instance, the set of all permissible combinations of words and morphemes into syntactic structures is infinite. The lexicon and rule-derived figures correspond to internal properties of the system. In terms of external properties, any system must have what Benveniste called a *discours*, that is, a universe of uses in which it is instantiated in actual contexts. Thus any collection of signs that meets these conditions counts as a system, regardless of other factors.

Relations Between Signs of Different Systems

Following closely in the logic of Saussure, Benveniste observes that significance is defined by opposition. The form and meaning of a sign are restricted by the other signs to which it is opposed. This has two salient consequences. First, translational equivalence between systems is in principle impossible. We can approximate the meaning of Jack's question and Natalia's response with gestures or drawings, but the gloss can never be exact. Recall the contrast between English and Maya terms for arms and legs: The words can be used to pick out the same things in a given context, but the Maya terms are more general than their English counterparts. Similarly, a verbal description of a dance routine can capture certain aspects but can never tell the whole story simply because words and dance belong to different systems. Second, it also follows from the principle of opposition that two systems could, in theory, share some of the exact same sign forms, but these would never be truly equivalent because their respective values would not be identical. Think of what the color red symbolizes in road signs, flags, and roses. Or consider the precise meaning of the word "symbol" in everyday English as opposed to its Peircean definition. Standard hand gestures like the thumbs-up sign or the forefinger-to-thumb circle (meaning OK in English) can have radically different meanings in other cultures, like Greek or Italian. As soon as we see that intrasystemic oppositions define meaning, the superficial form of a sign loses its apparent connection to meaning. All of this follows in the logic of Saussurian arbitrariness.

If signs belonging to different systems can never really be the same, they can be partially equivalent. Relying once again on the dualist reasoning typical of Saussure, Benveniste distinguishes two kinds of relation between systems. Symmetric relations are based on homology or contiguity. That is, the signs in the two systems may have corresponding shapes, values, or overall patterns. Writing, a visual system, is partly homologous with speaking, an aural one, insofar as the order of sounds and words is the same. A map showing the route through which a vehicle moves in space is partly homologous with a verbal description that follows the same order of steps (imagine the script of a tour guide moving from point to point along the route). Relations of homology are based on the Peircean notion of iconic resemblance. Contiguity, in contrast, is the basis of indexicality. Two systems that are contiguous co-occur in the same place and time. Thus, for instance, words and gestures are contiguous systems insofar as they are joined in acts of utterance. Material symbols, speech forms, and gestures are contiguous in ritual events. Any time we have different systems combined in a single event, contiguity is in play. Notice that both homology (iconicity) and contiguity (indexicality) are reversible relations. If x is similar or close to y, then y is similar or close to x. This is what Benveniste means by grouping the two relations under the rubric "symmetric." These are opposed to asymmetric relations, which are irreversible. Interpretance is an asymmetric relation because if x is the interpretant of y, it does not follow that y is the interpretant of x. Recall that the interpretant may be a more elaborate sign than the one that gives rise to it. So a lengthy driving manual may serve as the interpretant of a road sign, but the sign does not interpret the manual. The second asymmetric relation Benveniste posited is what he called "engendering" (which has nothing to do with gender). A system that engenders another gives rise to it, is the model on which the second one is constructed. Writing is clearly engendered by speech in the sense that it is based on it. Morse code, a system of long and short signals representing letters of the alphabet, numbers, and punctuation marks is doubly engendered since it is a calque on writing, which is engendered by speech. It should be emphasized here that the term "engender" implies a historical process in which one system precedes the other. But this is not necessarily the case. Two systems could in theory be devised at the same time, with one the basis for the other. It is the logical relation, not the temporal one, that concerns Benveniste. The four types are summarized in Figure 3.3.

Stated in the abstract, this typology may appear uninteresting, but in fact it provides a conceptual framework for extensive research. Notice first that these four kinds of relation can be applied to signs at any level of analysis. We can look at token events, like the exchange between Jack and Natalia, and study the relations among utterance forms, physical movement, touch, the built space of their apartment, the words and images in the newspaper, and so forth. Within a semiotic perspective, such a study would contribute significantly to understanding the event of interaction as a whole. The same set of questions can be posed at the level of types, linking things like the epithet "sweetheart" with the touching gesture, the table as a conventional place at which coffee is consumed and conversation takes place, the morning newspaper as a particular type of publication, all locking into a conventional morning routine in our society. Types are in turn organized into systems and subsystems, which provide further levels of analysis. In other words, Benveniste's typology provides a broad framework in which to connect language to other meaningful forms in social contexts. He believed language is primary because it alone interprets all other systems, many of which it also engenders.

"Double Signifiance" and the Primacy of Language

Benveniste was not content to argue that language is primary simply because of the way it relates to other systems. To do this would be to offer a purely relational justification for his linguocentric outlook. Committed to irreducibility, he had to go further, to find something intrinsic to the system that set it apart. He had to show that language is *essentially* different from all other systems, and this irreducible difference would justify putting it at the top of the hierarchy. He achieved this in two steps, in a classic example of structuralist reasoning. The internal elements of a system are by definition meaningful. Their meanings are defined by the oppositions among them, what Saussure called *valeur*, and by the rules of their combination into figures, what we might refer to as syntagmatic order of significance. All these meanings are internal to the system, just as Saussurian significance is internal to *langue*. As type-level constructs, internal meanings are invariant, regardless of the circumstances of

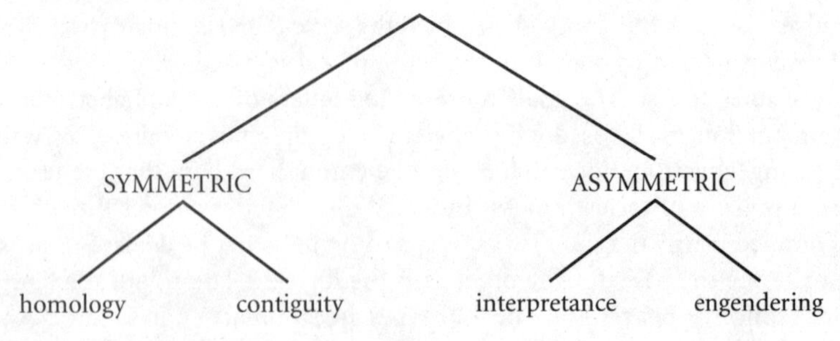

FIGURE 3.3 Relations Among Sign Systems, After Benveniste.

their use. This order of meaningfulness Benveniste called *sémiotique.* In contemporary English-language linguistics, it is called semantics. Benveniste also used the term *sémantique,* but in a different way. The *sémantique* of a system is the meaning produced in events of discourse, what English speakers would usually term the pragmatics and discourse semantics of a language. *Sémantique* is therefore a feature of *parole,* not *langue,* speech not grammar. It is the capacity of the system to generate token-level messages and to individuate objects of reference in the world. It is the domain of what we are calling relationality as opposed to irreducibility. Where Benveniste differs basically from Saussure is his claim that *sémantique,* despite its being in the domain of *parole,* is nonetheless orderly.

So what is the essential difference of language? It is the only system to have both *sémiotique* and *sémantique.* All others have one but not the other. Benveniste says:

> Language is the only system whose meaning is articulated this way in two dimensions. The other systems have a unidimensional meaning; either semiotics (gestures of politeness, mudras) without semantics; or semantics (artistic expressions) without semiotics. It is the prerogative of language to combine simultaneously the meaning of signs and the meaning of enunciation. Therein originates its major strength, that of creating a second level of enunciation, where it becomes possible to retain meaningful remarks about meaning. Through this metalinguistic faculty we discover the origin of the interpreting relationship through which language embraces all other systems. (1985:242–243)

The first part of this quote can be neatly summarized in a schema whose form, if not its content, will be familiar to any student of structuralism; see Table 3.2. The idea is quite simple. Whereas language is both conventional and capable of generating novel meanings, politeness is merely conventional and art is merely novel.

In the latter part of the quote, Benveniste returns to a central concept in the formalist tradition, metalanguage. Metalanguage is simply language about language, illustrated in statements like "'Table' is a five-letter word," "The word 'paper' designates a material derived from plants," and "The word 'today' refers to the day on which it is uttered." The capacity of language to refer to and describe itself, its inherent self-reflexivity, is what makes metalanguage possible. For Benveniste, it is precisely the fact of its double significance that accounts for this self-reflexivity. For if it had no order of *sémiotique,* there would be no invariant units to define metalinguistically, and if it had no order of *sémiotique,* it would be impossible to formulate the metalinguistic statements themselves. In Peircean terms, metalanguage is the expression of interpretance within the system. Benveniste is saying in effect that language is the only system that can be used to describe itself. This is

TABLE 3.2 A Comparison of Sign Systems

	Sémantique	Sémiotique
Language	+	+
Politeness	-	+
Art	+	-

why it is at the top of the meaning chain and why it is essentially different from all other systems. Irreducibility is thus reasserted, but on the basis of a special kind of reflexivity.

Before moving on to a rather different theory of signs, I want to underscore a question that arises out of Benveniste's proposals, a question that will remain with us throughout this book. In order to develop a semiology of *discours*, as Benveniste tries to do, one must also have a theory of the events in which *discours* happens. How else can we ever decide what counts as relations of meaningful contiguity and homology? In the exchange between Jack and Natalia, we can assume that the refrigerator, the calendar on the wall, and the cookbooks in the cupboard are all coexistent with the two people in the setting of their interaction. And these things are indisputably meaningful signs. But are they in any real way connected with the words or gestures that compose the expressive parts of the event? In order to use Benveniste's framework to describe any interaction, we need somehow to define the scope of context and the grounds of relevance. This is a daunting task for which various solutions have been proposed but none fully successful. Benveniste is trying to accomplish this while still retaining the irreducibility thesis with respect to language. The problem is that it is precisely the nonverbal factors that play a critical role in understanding and yet elude linguistic reasoning. There seem to be at least two parts to the problem: what it means to say that two objects are contiguous or copresent and whether their copresence is in any way focal as opposed to backgrounded in the event. We will return to these concepts several times in Part 2 of the book.

Charles Morris: A Behaviorist Perspective on Signs

An alternative semiotic theory was proposed by Charles Morris, a philosopher working during the interwar years in North America. Like Bloomfield and some other American linguists at the time, Morris embraced behaviorism. His semiotic framework is strongly formalist in its attempt to describe different systems and levels of structure in terms of the rules that define them. Yet his commitment to behaviorism led him to privilege what he took to be the objective tie between symbolic forms and the behavioral contexts in which they happen. The result is an interesting combination of formalism, usually associated with irreducibility, and a kind of radical relationality that smacks of reductionism from a Saussurian perspective. Despite the widespread rejection of behaviorism in modern linguistics, Morris is a pivotal figure in modern linguistic thought. He was among the first to define semiotic rules in a quasi-formal sense, and his proposals regarding the branches of semiotics as a field remain largely intact to this day. It is helpful to call attention at the outset to the behaviorist premises from which Morris proceeds. These will alert us to the profound difference between his framework and the ones of both Saussure and Peirce.

Behaviorist approaches to language are generally associated with six ideas (Lyons 1977). First, behaviorists distrust mentalist terms like "mind" and "ideas," along with the introspective methods through which they are understood. Thus the Saussurian notion of a signified and the Peircean notion of a conceptual ground and interpretant are all ruled out. They will be absent or utterly transfigured in Morris's framework. Second, language is itself observable, and thought is really inner speech. In other words, all of the more abstract features of *langue* are either erased or tied rigorously to observable features of *parole.* Third, human language is essentially the same kind of system as various forms of animal communication. This implies that they must be studied in a unified framework. And moreover, whatever is irreducible in a language system is due to its being a form of animal communication, not to its essential distinctness. Fourth, instinct and innateness play a lesser role in language than do conditioned responses. It is because we are conditioned to speak in certain ways that language has the form it does, not because we are endowed with any innate human capacities. Fifth, a behavior is no more and no less than a response to a stimulus, and the verbal interaction is therefore a chain of interconnected stimuli and responses. Finally, behaviorist approaches tend to be determinist in the sense that all events are taken to be caused in accordance with laws of causality in physical matter.

Like Peirce, Morris proposed an entire system of semiotics rather than limiting his study to one or another kind of sign or aspect of meaning production. Also like Peirce, his framework is relational in the sense that it provides terms in which to examine how speech is integrated with nonspeech in the social world. Unlike Peirce, whose theory of signs preceded the advent of behaviorist psychology, Morris was deeply influenced by behaviorism. We can see this particularly in his comments on how signs are related to the world around them, a relation that, as we will see, he considered to be quite direct. Another significant difference between the two is that Morris is closer to what we would call a formalist in that he defines a language as a formal system determined exhaustively by the rules that govern it. Formalism is intertwined with the irreducibility thesis, and the subsequent development of American linguistics through Bloomfield, Zellig Harris, and Chomsky displayed an ever more refined focus on form. Thus Morris will be a pivotal thinker in our exploration of how irreducibility and relationality have combined in contemporary thought.

We can begin with Morris's opening definition of the parts of a sign (recalling Peirce's first trichotomy).[1] He says, "S is a sign of D for I to the degree that I takes account of D in virtue of the presence of S" (Morris 1971:19). S in this formula designates the *sign vehicle*, or roughly what Saussure called the signifier and Peirce called the representamen (apart from what it stands for). D is the *designatum*, that is, the kind of object for which the sign vehicle stands. We should be careful to distinguish the kind of object from the actual object in a given case. The latter we can call the *denotatum* (verb form: denote) as opposed to the designatum (verb form: designate). To rephrase, the designatum is the Saussurian signified, a concept, whereas the denotatum is the individual thing to which the form refers in a given utterance. Hence for a sign vehicle like "newspaper," the D element is the concept "newspaper" as constituted in English language, not the *Times, Tribune,* or *El Pais,* which I may denote in uttering this word in a given context.

I is the *interpretant*, the "taking account of" that goes along with understanding; the effect of S on some agent who perceives it. Let us distinguish at this point between the interpretant and the interpreter. For Morris, "the interpretant of a sign is the habit of the organism to respond, because of the sign vehicle, to absent objects as if they were present" (1971:45). Like Peirce and his interpretant, Morris focuses here on the reception of the sign as opposed to its conventional meaning. We will designate the agent for whom the response is a habit the "interpreter." As we will see, Morris did not maintain this obvious distinction because he conflated the response with the organism for whom it is habitual.

To illustrate Morris's divisions, recall the opening example of Jack's exchange with Natalia. His question "D'the paper come today?" is a sign vehicle (a complex signifier) that designates (among other things) a kind of object (the paper), and denotes the *Times* morning edition of September 19, 1993. In this context Natalia is the interpreter, and the interpretant is her habit of responding by attending to the newspaper. It is unclear from Morris's definitions whether Natalia's utterance "It's right on the table" is part of the interpretant or itself a novel stimulus. Similarly, it is unclear whether the interpretant involves her taking account of the kind of object mentioned (the designatum) or the actual object denoted. Morris tells us only that "from the point of view of behavioristics, to take account of D by the presence of S involves responding to D in virtue of a response to S" (1971:21). Hence the interpretant arises out of the complex response:

---

[1] Page references are to the section "Writings on the General Theory of Signs," unless otherwise indicated. The original publicaiton of *Foundations of the Theory of Signs* was 1938.

S (D) > Response (S) > Response (D)
(given S associated with D, to respond to S triggers response to D).

Or simply, Natalia attends to the newspaper in responding to Jack's question. The terms of this framework are summarized in Figure 3.4.

In light of this trichotomy, Morris proposes a division of labor in terms that have become established in modern linguistics. The relation between the sign form and its designatum/denotatum is the focus of *semantics.* The relation between the sign form and the interpretant is the focus of *pragmatics.* The study of the relations among sign forms is *syntactics.* All languages have all three types of rules, and thus no language can have just one sign (fail to have syntax) or signs without designata (fail to have semantics) or signs without users (fail to have pragmatics). It is important to recognize that this program distinguishes the study of sign forms from the study of meaning in a way quite unforeseen by Saussure. For the Swiss linguist, the syntagmatic and paradigmatic dimensions applied equally to relations between signifiers and between signifieds. Since the two parts of the sign were mutually dependent, Saussure did not envision that they could become the respective objects of different subdisciplines.

By contrast, American structural and early generative linguistics were explicitly committed to the principle that form (syntax) can be studied apart from meaning (semantics). This division has been hotly disputed and is by no means universally accepted among linguists, but it remains an article of faith for many grammarians even today. For Morris, it is one of the factors that permits him to simultaneously assert that the rules of syntax form an (irreducible) system

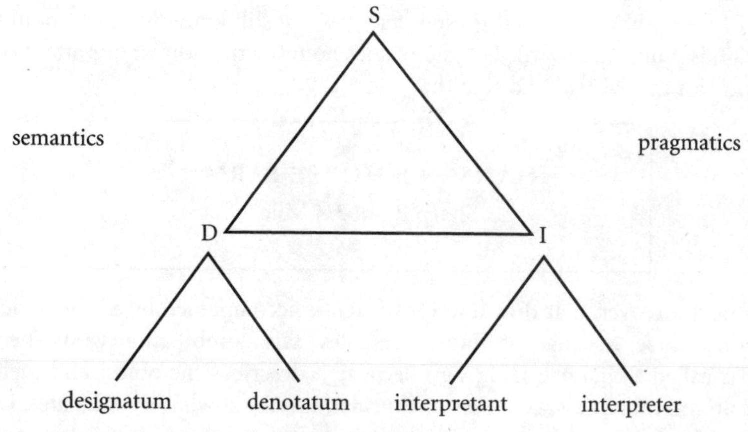

FIGURE 3.4 Morris's Branches of Semiotics.

and yet the meanings associated with the forms derive from their (relational) ties to the world of objects. By separating form from meaning and introducing the division of labor, Morris is able to maintain both theses without apparent contradiction. Bloomfield made the same move in even more trenchant terms. Given his behaviorist stance on meaning, paired with an acute sense of grammatical form, he concluded that meaning could not be defined by linguistics at all (Bloomfield 1984:145). Linguistics became the study of grammar, and grammar the repository of pure form. A similar view was to be enshrined in generative grammar.

Before we examine Morris's conception of the three kinds of rules that make up a language, it is helpful to consider his typology of signs. Recall that Peirce proposed the trichotomy icon, index, and symbol, according to the distinct relations between sign form and object that they are based on (similarity, contiguity, and convention, respectively). Morris proposed a trichotomy, too, but his terms are different from Peirce's. The three types of sign Morris distinguished are indexical, characterizing, and universal. Let us look at these one at a time.

An indexical sign is one that merely directs the attention of its interpreter, without in any way describing its object. Think of an arrow at an intersection pointing up the road on the right, without any further indication of what it is pointing toward. Coming upon such a sign, we know as drivers (interpreters) that it indicates something like a trajectory toward some kind of landmark or significant place, but we know nothing about the destination itself. Even if the road splits three ways or if the precise path of the arrow seems to transect a tree at the side of the road, we overcome these ambiguities; we assume that the sign denotes a direction-by-road, not a direction as the crow flies and, further, that the road most closely aligned with the arrow is the one it means to index. The important point here is that despite all these inferences, we still know nothing about what the sign is pointing toward. The index does no more than direct our attention.

Contrast this with a road sign that says:

HANSEN'S HORSE FARM Sharp Right 3/4 Mile

Assume, moreover, that this descriptive sign is accompanied by a schematic outline of a horse, the logo of Hansen's stables. This combination would be what Morris called a characterizing sign because it describes the object and therefore gives an interpreter a specific set of expectations about what it designates. Unlike Peirce, Morris is unconcerned with the difference between the iconic logo and the symbolic description, since both provide information about their object. They are alike in this crucial sense of providing relatively rich descriptions of their objects. We can see this even more clearly by imagining that in our example the two road signs are thirty-five years old and rusted. Hansen's Horse Farm is no longer in existence, having been sold off to a developer and replaced by a mall, say, Liberty Shopping Center. The arrow sign can still serve perfectly well to indicate the way to the mall, but the descriptive sign is no longer accurate. The reason is that the arrow, a pure index, gives no expectations about its object, and so it is compatible with any object whatsoever. The descriptive sign conveys information that severely limits the set of objects for which it can stand. At some point during the changeover from horse farm to mall, the Hansen's Horse Farm sign became inappropriate, misleading, and eventually false. An index cannot be false; the worst that can happen is that it becomes vacuous if no object is there at all (imagine the sign after a natural disaster that wiped out the mall along with the road leading to it).

Lacking the information of a characterizing sign, the index does not really have a designatum associated with it. Recall that the designatum is the kind of object for which the sign stands. But since an index, like the road arrow, can stand for anything at all, it has no fixed kind associated with it. We can say that indexes are unique among signs in that they can denote an individual object (like the horse farm) without designating it as one of any particular kind. If you assume that human language is essentially an instrument for expressing information about the world, then indexes pose a sort of conundrum. How is it that an index can denote without specifying anything about what kind of thing the denotatum is? As a further instance of the same problem, consider that you can multiply indexes without further identifying the object at all, whereas if you multiply the characterizing terms of a description, the result is increased specificity. Imagine, for example, that the road signs were replaced with even better ones: the arrow sign has been replaced by several more arrows, larger and brighter, pointing the same way, plus three more signs with the words "This way!" "Over here!" and "Up ahead!" and a set of loudspeakers blaring the theme song of the movie *Bolero*—all of the signs attached to an elaborate steel scaffolding illuminated by spotlights. None of this cartoonlike signage helps the lost motorist, though, because it conveys no more information about the destination than did the old rust-red arrow. The sound and light may well arrest our attention more effectively, but that is all it can do. From the standpoint of information, the indexes are all null, and zero plus zero is still zero. Contrast that with what happens if the old Hansen's sign is replaced by one that includes all the old information plus a line that says "Riding by the hour, all ages." This new sign tells the motorist that the horse farm also provides recreational riding, a major new piece of information.

Apart from both indexical and characterizing signs, Morris postulated a third kind, which he called universal. Universal signs can denote everything and anything; they are much more abstract than either of the other two types. Think of the English terms "somebody," "someone," "somewhere," "sometime," "anyone," "anywhere," and so on. These are distinct from characterizing signs in that they are relatively bleached of descriptive information. Yet they are distinct from indexes in that they do not require a relation of contiguity with their object, nor do they usually denote specific individuals. Instead, universal signs are related primarily to the other signs in the language itself. What they seem to represent are whole categories of signs, such as descriptions of persons (cf. "someone," "somebody"), places ("somewhere"), times ("sometime"), and so forth.

Given the three types of signs, Morris goes on to observe that they combine in languages. In fact, it is only when we have a combination of the indexical and characterizing signs that a proposition can be judged true or false (Morris 1971:32). We noted above that an index cannot, in itself, be either true or false. It can only be vacuous or unfulfilled if the object to which it points is not there. A description seems to be capable of truth and falsity because it tells us something about its object. If the description fails to fit the object, then it is false, inappropriate, or infelicitous. But even so, it is not vacuous because it is still interpretable and equally rich in information. The road sign for the horse farm still designates the farm even if it is blown away in a hurricane or taken as a souvenir by an out-of-state tourist. But notice that this power of the sign to denote the farm is not due solely to its information value. There could be two farms in the country that fit the description, so that one did not know which was intended. Or the sign could be moved to another place on the road, from which the farm was no longer a mere three-quarters of a mile but, say, 100 miles away. Or the motorist could be uncertain whether the phrase "Riding by the hour, all ages" applied to Hansen's or to some other place in the same direction. Maybe the sign was actually two signs, marking two places rather than a single one? All of these questions reflect the same fact: In understanding the road sign as we do, we are relying on both descriptive *and* indexical information. The former encodes a characterization, but it is the latter that nails down the unique object to which the description applies. Morris made the key observation that in order to make a judgment whether a sign form is true or false, it is necessary to have both kinds of sign in a combination. Neither one is sufficient by itself. This means that in order to have a language capable of formulating propositions with truth values, it is necessary that the syntactic component of the language provide rules for combining indexes with characterizing signs. In a word, semantics presupposes syntax.

Unfortunately, Morris poses these divisions in a way that invites confusion and is indeed consistent with some misinterpretations in subsequent literature. The problem turns on the grounds for distinguishing among the three types of sign. As Morris states it, it is primarily the *amount* of information that differentiates characterizing signs from the other two kinds, with indexes providing virtually no description of their object. The problem comes in when he uses natural language demonstratives to illustrate indexes. What he fails to observe is that demonstratives are not pure indexicals, by his definition, because they do contain various kinds of information foreign to sheer indexicality. A word like "this" or "there" surely does establish expectations about its object, and even more so in languages where the former might be marked for features of gender, shape, and nominal class, or the latter marked for punctual as opposed to regional spaces or spatial placement as opposed to trajectory. Morris's description suggests that they are pure indexicals, but even Peirce recognized that no natural language indexical is pure in this way. They always combine symbolic with indexical aspects. It follows that it is not just the amount of information encoded in indexicals but the *kind* of information that sets them apart. (We will return to this point in more detail in Chapters 7 and 8, where we discuss Maya demonstratives in some detail. For now, I want to alert you to the problem, which will become more pressing as we move on toward practice.)

Let's look more closely at these rules. Each of the three components of a language is made up of rules that relate the sign vehicle to another term. Native speakers of a language are usually unable to state the rules because they exist as habits, not as conscious representations. Semantic rules correlate signs with the situations they may be used to denote (Morris 1971:35). They "determine under which conditions a sign is applicable to an object or situation" (Morris 1971:36). These conditions are the designatum. So for an expression like "horse farm," the designatum would include the conditions that the object be, roughly, a farm where horses are kept or raised. This condition is abstracted away from the particulars of when and by whom the sign is used. Insofar as the designatum of a characterizing sign encodes conditions like these, we can say that it determines which things, among all the possible things in the world, can serve as its denotatum. Not so for indexes. The semantic rules of indexes are the opposite because the only determining factor is the actual object denoted. In fact, the semantic conditions of an index are null, and its designatum is no more than the sum of its denotata.

Morris distinguished two main kinds of syntactic rules, according to their function in the language. *Formation rules* define the set of permissible independent combinations. In a language like English, formation rules specify the syntax of sentences and the various phrases that can serve as independent units. Notice that the versions of English used for road signs, newspaper headlines, and other specialized forms of discourse may differ quite sharply from those of expository prose. The omission of definite articles, tense markers, and other information that can be filled in from context results in truncated phrases like "Riding by the hour, all ages." Even though chopped off, such phrases remain well formed. The other kind of syntactic rule Morris defined were *transformational rules.* These define the set of sentences that can be obtained by combining or altering the simpler units defined by formation rules. Transformational rules are at play whenever one takes an active sentence and makes it passive (as in "UN leader raises hope of hostage swap." > "Hope of hostage swap raised by UN leader.") or turns an indicative into a question ("The paper came today." > "D'the paper come today?") or condenses two sentences into a single one ("I saw a man. The man had a blue hat." > "I saw a man who had a blue hat.").

In order to decide whether some sentence is derived by formation rules or transformational rules, one may need to consider a large body of evidence and make careful judgments about how sentences are interrelated. The important point for our present purposes is that Morris recognized two levels of syntactic structure, a basic set of core or kernel sentences plus a more complex set of transformations derived from them. In subsequent years this difference became widely accepted and further refined in the linguistic notions of phrase structure rules and transformational rules (Chomsky 1957, 1965).

A pragmatic rule is the habit to use some sign under certain conditions. Whereas semantic rules define designata, pragmatic ones define the interpretants of signs. An interpretant is the habit in virtue of which the sign vehicle can designate, but it is not itself part of the designatum (Morris 1971:47). Thus the rule that a road sign be responded to as an imperative for the movement of automobile traffic and not as a mailing address or commentary on the weather is a pragmatic fact. The rules on the placement of print captions relative to images or page numbers relative to text are pragmatic habits. Morris notes that any rule, even a syntactic one, can be said to have a pragmatic dimension insofar as it is put into use. What is special about pragmatic rules as such is that they govern usage directly.

Morris arrives at a kind of irreducibility in his definition of a language as being exhaustively constituted by the syntactic, semantic, and pragmatic rules that govern its vehicles (1971:25). Although the pragmatic relations were for him ties between language and its users, hence what we are calling relational, Morris's notion of a rule effectively encompasses all language-to-context ties within the language itself. He achieves this by two steps: (1) By equating the interpretant with the social context of language use, he lumps under one heading a variety of contextual factors that are actually distinct, such as participants, time, place, and topic of discourse. (2) In the lumping of interpretant with interpreter, the former is dominant. Actual speech for Morris belongs to language only insofar as it realizes habits of behavior. The rest of what goes on in verbal behavior is pruned away and shipped over to other fields of study. Thus pragmatics is people's habits of response to verbal stimuli, embodied in rules.

This view of pragmatics is reminiscent of Saussure's view of *parole*. The scope of "language" expands to include all the rules that govern the use of linguistic forms, even in cases where the rules are determined by something nonlinguistic. Such rules could be reduced to general principles of psychology, sociology, perhaps anthropology, or some other domain of phenomena. This is similar to Saussure's position on *langage*, of which only the *langue* part, and not the *parole*, falls within the scope of linguistics. Pragmatics = *parole*; semantics and syntax = *langue*. The only difference is that Morris's pragmatic rules imply a far greater degree of regularity than Saussure's comments on the chaos of *parole*. When Jack asks, "D'the paper come today?" the properly linguistic parts of his utterance include only the designations of the words, the syntax of their combination, and the literal meaning of the whole phonological form. Facts like the routine quality of the question, the ulterior motive of getting the newspaper to read with his morning coffee, the behavioral setting of the kitchen and back porch, the interactive setting of his relation with the addressee—all this is governed by rules that fall *outside* the language proper.

Morris wrestled with the difficult question of what governs language, and in response to it he proposed a principle of "dual control," according to which conventions proper to language interact with features of the outside world to jointly produce the rules of language (1971:27). As a whole, a language is constituted by the interconnections of its signs, much like Saussurian sign-sign relations. At a deeper level, though, these interconnections derive from the linkages between actions and events in the extraverbal world. What Morris refuses at base is the principle of arbitrariness. For him, syntactic structure (which evidently includes both syntagmatic and paradigmatic axes) in *langue,* what we call grammar, is determined by how the response chains in which we make reference are connected in human behavior. He leaves little question of this: "The syntactical structure of a language is the interrelationship of signs caused by the interrelationship of the responses of which the sign vehicles are products or parts" (1971:31). Thus even the syntax is ultimately a by-product of the order of things in the world. Jack and Natalia's utterances have the syntactic form they do not because of English grammar as a system in principle apart from all others but because of where they fit in the behavioral stream of their morning interaction.

Morris introduces one further distinction that must be addressed here, if only because it will recur as a problem focus throughout this book. This is the division between metalanguage and object language. For Morris, the difference was one of principle and real consequence, although he treats it very differently from Benveniste. Any language is made up of the interrelations of its signs, by way of the three kinds of rules: semantic, syntactic, and pragmatic. In its basic uses every natural language provides the means for producing sentences that refer to and characterize the real, extralinguistic world. A sentence such as "Beneath the Mirabeau Bridge flows the Seine" refers to a real bridge and river and the spatial relation that actually holds between them in Paris. Contrast this with "'The Mirabeau Bridge' is a definite noun phrase." This sentence makes no statement about the bridge but only about the linguistic forms. It's like saying, "'Under' is a five-letter word," which contains no spatial reference at all, despite the preposition. Similarly, recall the original example we started from. Natalia's statement "It's right on the table" makes reference to real things like the *Times* and the kitchen table, whereas the statement "'Table' has five letters" does not.

Any sentence that contains terms designating language or its parts is metalinguistic in function. By contrast, all other sentences are "thing sentences," a label Morris (1971:30) adopted from Rudolph Carnap. The reason Morris appears to have attached such importance to the distinction between language and metalanguage is that only the former contains thing sentences, and only thing sentences are valid as descriptions of the physical world. A logical positivist, Carnap was in the business of debunking statements that purported to be objective but turned out on closer inspection to be little more than word games. Instead of scientific statements that can be verified by examining the world of objects, metalanguage slips into the discourse unnoticed in the form of quasi definitions, word games involving semantic distinctions, and metaphysical statements that could never be verified and hence degenerate into literal non-sense. Coming from this perspective, metalanguage is a pitfall to be avoided when one is trying to make meaningful statements about the physical world.

From the perspective of general semiotics, a metalanguage is a special kind of language, no better and no worse than other kinds. Its distinctive property is that it can be used to refer to, describe, or otherwise characterize language. This means that a metalanguage stands apart from its object language in just the way that a verbal description of the landscape stands apart from the natural environment. The remove between the two is in both cases the remove of a sign from the objects to which it refers, another instance of what we called the originary deferral of meanings from signs in semiotic theories. Thus designation, interpretance, and syntactic relations can be found in both kinds of language. In effect metalanguages are special only because they treat some other language as their object, whereas nonmetalanguages don't. The grammarian uses grammatical notation, a metalanguage of symbols, to designate the relations among signs. The lawyer uses Latin terminology, a metalanguage of legal discourse, to designate laws and conventions stated in English.

Note that since the metalanguage/object language distinction is strictly a matter of relation and not of essence, a single language could in principle function in both modes. In fact this is just what is going on when we use English to define words in English, as in "A table is a piece of furniture with a flat surface," or "'Paper' is a word commonly used to refer to the newspaper." Benveniste of course postulated this reflexivity as one of the distinctive features of human languages. Every human language can be used as its own metalanguage, and no other kind of sign system can be so used. It would follow that metalanguage about the syntax of a language would be metasyntactic; about the semantics, metasemantic; and about the pragmatics, metapragmatic. Similarly, any metalanguage, just because it *is* a language, must have its own syntax, semantics, and pragmatics corresponding to its grammar, meanings, and usage patterns. The move from signs to sentences entails a concomitant move from first-order languages to metalanguages.

Further Readings

Benveniste, E. "Les Niveaux de l'analyse linguistique." In *Problèmes de linguistique générale*, vol. 1. Paris: Gallimard, 1966 [1964], pp. 119–131.

———. "'Structure' en linguistique." In *Problèmes de linguistique générale*, vol. 1. Paris: Gallimard, 1966 [1962], pp. 91–98.

———. "The Semiology of Language." In *Semiotics: An Introductory Anthology*, edited by R. Innis. Bloomington: Indiana University Press, 1985, pp. 226–246.

Burks, A. W. "Icon, Index and Symbol." *Philosophy and Phenomenological Research* 9 (1949):673–689.

Eco, U., et al., eds. *Meaning and Mental Representations.* Bloomington: Indiana University Press, 1988.

Hanks, W. F. *Referential Practice: Language and Lived Space Among the Maya.* Chicago: University of Chicago Press, 1990.

———. "The Indexical Ground of Deictic Reference." In *Rethinking Context: Language as an Interactive Phenomenon,* edited by A. Duranti and C. Goodwin. Cambridge: Cambridge University Press, 1992, pp. 43–77.

———. "Metalanguage and Pragmatics of Deixis." In *Reflexive Language: Reported Speech and Metapragmatics,* edited by J. Lucy. Cambridge: Cambridge University Press, 1993, pp. 127–158.

Jakobson, R. "Quest for the Essence of Language." In *Selected Writings of Roman Jakobson,* vol 2. The Hague: Mouton, 1971, pp. 130–147.

———. *Six Lectures on Sound and Meaning.* Translated by J. Mepham. Cambridge: MIT Press, 1978. Lectures 2, 3, and 4 (on the Saussurian view of sound systems), pp. 23–88.

Lyons, J. *Semantics,* vol 1. Cambridge: Cambridge University Press, 1977. Chaps. 3 and 4 on language as a kind of system, pp. 57–119.

Morris, C. *Foundations of the Theory of Signs.* Chicago: University of Chicago Press, 1971 [1938]. Secs. 1–4, pp. 17–54.

Peirce, C. S. "Logic as Semiotic: A Theory of Signs." In *Philosophical Writings of Peirce,* edited by J. Buchler. New York: Dover Publications, 1955. Chap. 7, pp. 98–119.

Weinreich, U. "Semantics and Semiotics." *International Encyclopedia of Social Science* 14 (1968):164–169.

Chapter 4

North American Formalism and the Problem of Meaning

DURING THE PERIOD in which Morris was writing, a significant sector of American linguistics was becoming increasingly focused on syntax, to the exclusion of semantics and pragmatics. Under the influence of behaviorism, both the latter were taken to involve aspects of the world outside language. This gave rise to formalisms and versions of irreducibility quite distinct from Saussure's. Thus Bloomfield held in his later writings that meaning (including both designation and interpretance) was in principle undefinable by linguistics and therefore beyond the scope of the field. Just as Saussure had banished phonetics and *parole* to other disciplines, so Bloomfield banished meaning to psychology, sociology, and other external fields. The key is that because it involves things in no way specific to language, he took the study of meaning to be speculative, metaphysical, and in any case not properly linguistic. What emerges from the line connecting Morris with Bloomfield and early transformational grammar is the successive contraction of the object of linguistics. First the relation of interpretance is left behind, since it is wrapped up in habits of reaction that are surely more general than language. The search for specifically linguistic laws made this irrelevant. Then the relation of designation is reduced to minimal judgments of sameness and difference, effectively overlooking the qualitative study of meaning. The rationale is that since it is associated with habits of behavior and real things outside language, meaning is beyond the pale of linguistics. Although Chomsky's early writings marked a number of significant breaks with his intellectual forebears, he retained many of the essential features already present in Bloomfield—and even more of the ones present in the work of his teacher, Zellig Harris (although we will pass over these for the sake of maintaining our focus on meaning).

In this chapter we will trace Bloomfield's approach to grammatical meaning in order to show how irreducibility came to be linked with syntax to the exclusion of other aspects of language. Following this we will examine Chomsky's "Methodological Preliminaries," originally a section of the book *Aspects of the Theory of*

Syntax (Chomsky 1965). These two linguists stand out for their impact on the field and the force with which they argued for irreducibility. Their reflections on meaning serve as a diagnostic for the shifting boundary between grammar and the relational contexts of speech. They do not add up to a representative sample of linguistics, since there were always multiple perspectives and the history is a complex one (see, for instance, Hymes and Fought 1981). Nor will their works be treated in the depth or detail that they merit. My aim is more limited: to consider them as representatives of distinct versions of irreducibility and to trace the key problem of linguistic meaning through their writings. This will then serve as a background against which to weigh the arguments of those who have attacked formal linguistics and proposed relational alternatives to it. From a historical perspective, there is no justification for jumping from Bloomfield to Chomsky without filling in the context of their work. This would include minimally the writings of numerous other scholars, including Edward Sapir, Floyd Lounsbury, and the extensive apparatus of Americanist linguistics (Hymes and Fought 1981). Neither of the linguists discussed in the present chapter wrote in a vacuum, and both wrote on topics other than the ones we shall focus on. Chomsky's work, in particular, has continued to change and evolve, leaving little of the early framework intact. Still, the works in question have a significance of their own, and the Chomsky piece marked a critical turning point in formalist reasoning about language. It is the nature of this shift that will concern us. For further references on historical context and subsequent developments, see the suggested readings at the end of this chapter.

Bloomfield on Meaning in Language

In order to discern what version of irreducibility underlay Bloomfield's linguistics, it is helpful to focus on his treatment of meaning. We can grant that of Morris's three dimensions, syntax is the one most likely to provide examples of pure form, whereas semantics and pragmatics both tie into the behavioral context of speech, the former by way of reference to objects and the latter by habitual responses to situations. Therefore they are the most likely to provide telling examples of how any linguist draws the line between the inner system and the extraverbal world. Bloomfield is commonly associated with the sort of mechanistic view of language that Chomsky later lampooned as "simply an expression of lack of interest in theory and explanation" (1985:81). In fact Bloomfield struggled throughout his writings with the problem of meaning, and his own positions became subtle and complicated as a result. He espoused behaviorism in the 1920s and again in the 1940s. Yet he also proposed an elaborate system of linguistic meaning types based on syntax and insisted that no grammatical analysis could proceed without reference to meaning. In this section I briefly trace Bloomfield's statements on meaning in his 1926 "Postulates" article, his 1927 review of recent trends in the field, and his 1943 essay entitled "Meaning." In the course of these accounts, he adjusts and realigns the boundaries of grammar and the role of meaning in linguistics. His ultimate stance on irreducibility must be understood in relation to this evolving framework. The interest of his work for our purposes is, however, more to explore the problems posed by meaning in a formalist framework than to reveal the multistranded complexity of Bloomfield's thought.

In his 1926 essay Bloomfield decried the futility of discussions of the "fundamentals" of linguistics. He wanted to limit discussion by disposing of all the vapid debate about linguistics and psychology. The method would be to define assumptions and axioms and then work rigorously with them. This would provide a common set of agreed-upon terms, while "merely naming certain [other] concepts as belonging to the domain of other sciences" (1970:129). In particular, he ruled out the objects of psychology and acoustics from the outset. This effectively excises the material properties of speech, as well as the conceptual categorizations embodied in linguistic signs. The interactions among social groups sharing a language, in turn, belonged to sociology and anthropology, not to linguistics. By these opening excisions, Bloomfield cuts away the two dimensions of semantics and pragmatics, along with the physical features of sign vehicles. At this point he is heading toward a kind of sheer irreducibility in which syntax is the sole object of linguistics and the essential core of language.

In the next paragraph, though, he introduces a behavioral sequence: Stimulus causes a response, which is in turn a stimulus for another response. This construct justifies linguists in speaking of vocal features (phonetic material that can serve as stimulus) and stimulus-reaction features of speech, without further discussion. What follows is a set of seventy-seven definitions and assumptions organized by theme and ordered logically, in which Bloomfield sets out his vision of linguistics. The first section is "Form and Meaning" and the first assumption is that successive utterances (i.e., successive verbal moves in the stimulus-response chain) are partly alike. This seemingly innocuous and surely well grounded assumption defines the boundary between linguistics and other fields as well as the line between irreducibility and relationality.

To postulate partial similarity is to say that certain features of language recur again and again, no matter how different the speaker or circumstances of utterance. All the aspects of speech that are idiosyncratic, or peculiar to given situations, fall outside the scope of linguistics. By virtue of their repeatability, then, aspects of *parole* earn the right to belong to *langue,* and so to grammar. Shortly after this Bloomfield further specifies that linguists treat similarity as sameness and dissimilarity as difference. This sharpens the cutting edge of grammar still further by taking the relative notion of likeness and redefining it as the absolute opposition (dichotomy) between identity and nonidentity. Now when two unrelated people utter "D'the paper come today?"—the one dropping the final "r" of "pépr" and the other not, the one referring to the *Times* and the other to the Audubon newsletter—we can still say that their utterances are identical. The phonetic difference is insufficient to signal a different word, and the semantic one is insufficient to signal a different designation. Such variation in physical sound and actual denotata is simply below the threshold of the grammar. The identical sentence is repeated, even though no two utterances of it are really the same. Recall that this criterion applied to the Peircean distinction between sinsigns and legisigns, too, the former being token instances and the latter type-level forms. What Bloomfield is saying is that only those aspects of speech that can be treated as types belong in the grammar. To put it in negative terms, the only part of meaning that a linguist need pay attention to is whether two forms are the same or different. All further qualitative characterizations would derive from other disciplines. The importance of this fixing of the threshold of difference cannot be overstated, for it is one of the preconditions of grammar.

It is striking in the following entries of the "Postulates" that Bloomfield builds up a typology of meanings—constructional (postulate 23), functional (postulate 31), and class (postulate 34). Each of these depends upon syntactic relations between elements that are combined in sentences and phrases. They make up what could be called a "syntagmatic semantics." Constructional meaning attaches to the positions in syntactic constructions, as in the sequence article + noun in a noun phrase (the paper), which would mean something like "quantified object." Similarly, the word "book-s" is a construction of formative plus formative, with the constructional meaning "object in number." In postulate 31 it is further stipulated that constructions can be analyzed into positions, or slots, and that each of these positions may be said to have a meaning, called its functional meaning. So in "the paper," the first position means roughly degree of definiteness and is restricted to possessive pronouns, articles, and demonstratives. Transitive clauses (such as "Jack poured the coffee") have the positional meanings "actor acting on a goal" corresponding to what we would call agent verb object (1970:133).

All forms that can occur in the same position in constructions make up a form class, and form classes, too, have meaning. Bloomfield calls this "class meaning" (1970:134). For example, the set of all object expressions in English (roughly, all nouns denoting persons and things) makes up a form class on the basis of their distribution in clause constructions, for instance, transitive and intransitive verbs of motion, and the class meanings of these forms include actor, goal, patient, and so on. Obviously, class meaning is relatively abstract and is defined by the distribution of linguistic forms in functional positions in sentences. In postulate 35 Bloomfield then defines linguistic categories as the union of functional meanings and class meanings. This reflects the degree of centrality that he accorded meaning in the grammar. Grammatical categories, unquestionably part of the system of *langue*, are the precipitate of syntactic meanings. Thus under one reading (albeit a perverse one), the "Postulates" could be argued to make a major step *toward* a linguistics based on meaning, not away from it.

A year later, in his 1927 review of recent work, Bloomfield returned to the relation between denotata and designata. He used the example of an apple to illustrate how words are usually defined. We proceed to define a word, he says, as if the thing it designates were actually present when the word is spoken. In other words, we assume that the type APPLE can be defined on the basis of those tokens "apple" that actually make reference to a piece of fruit in the immediate perceptible context of the utterance. We assume, that is, a case of ostensive reference in which the thing fits the term so closely that a description of the thing will yield a definition of the word. So APPLE is "the well known firm fleshed smooth skinned round or long pome fruit of the trees of the genus Malus, etc." (1970:177). Under such a view, we understand Jack's request for "the paper" by imagining that a paper were actually present to us and then treating his utterance as if it connected with the real thing. How, Bloomfield then asks, can a dictionary meaning based on this fiction be adequate, given that words like "apple" are used frequently, as everyone knows, even when there is no fruit around. How can language have meaning when the things it is pegged to are missing? This problem is psychologic, he says, but could be answered with "magic ease" by assuming that there is a mental image or concept in play when the thing is not there (1970:177). He goes on to review Saussure's description of denotation, which involved four terms: the actual object (referent), the concept (signified), the acoustic image, and the speech utterance (an event of *parole*). The concept and the acoustic image are both mental for Saussure, as we saw, and it should come as no surprise that Bloomfield proposes to delete both of them from the definition of *langue. Langue* is made up instead of socially determined correspondences between things and utterances, without the mediating level of mind. Stated in terms of concepts, meaning was a metaphysical notion, giving rise to "incantations about whose value no two even of 'the psychologic shamans' will agree" (1970:177).

In his 1943 article "Meaning," Bloomfield struggled once again to get a fix on meaning. He started by rejecting popular notions in favor of direct study of how language is used in behavior. This is consistent with his earlier stance that word meanings are based on the properties of things and also consistent with Morris's caution on the difference between metalanguage and language itself, since Bloomfield is rejecting the study of commonsense metalanguage in favor of what actually happens in speech. According to Bloomfield, it is impossible to conduct a scientific study of what native speakers think the words of their language mean within the purview of linguistics. Indeed, in an article published the next year, he rejects outright the confused and fanciful notions of native speakers (Bloomfield 1944). Next he rejects the physicalist definition of meaning based on properties of things, observing that it cannot even explain the meanings of words like "but," "and," and "unicorn," nor of tokens of "apple" for which there is no real fruit around. His critique goes beyond his early statement of syntactic semantics in the "Postulates" and adds to it the problems of nonostensive reference, what he calls "displaced" reference to absent objects and description of fictive objects.

Ultimately, he appears to adopt an almost mentalist perspective, but he consigns it to psychology and other fields apart from linguistics. "In language, forms cannot be separated from their meanings," he says, and yet it is only sameness and difference that the linguist can deal with systematically (1970:401). The rest is so variable and tied to the particulars of speech that it cannot be part of linguistics. He reasserts that what he had earlier termed "function," or form class meaning, is valid, but he redefines it as a matter of form, not meaning at all. Indeed, it seems that Bloomfield's appreciation for the problem of meaning in language remained sharp, even acute, but this led him to take an increasingly exclusionary stance in relation to it. He recognized that you couldn't do grammar without it, but his premises would not permit its being fully integrated into the grammar. As linguistics consolidated itself as a science based on form, issues in meaning became increasingly lost in the morass of *parole.* The inconsistent, zigzag quality of Bloomfield's writings on the topic attests to the difficulty of describing meaning within a formalism based on behaviorist premises.

Chomsky's Early Method

Chomsky's "Methodological Preliminaries" outlines the early program of generative grammar. It represents a sharp break with the kind of structural linguistics of Bloomfield, in which behaviorist psychology was granted the role of defining meaning, and the behavioral status of linguistic structure. Chomsky had written a sweeping critique of B. F. Skinner (Chomsky 1959), and in his "Preliminaries" distinguishes the proper object of linguistics from the kinds of habits and dispositions proposed under behaviorism. Linguistics would be fundamentally mentalist. Its object would be the deep mental reality that underlies verbal performance. Furthermore, it would be universalist in the sense of incorporating an account of the properties common to all human languages. Universal features would be the foundation on which the grammars of all individual languages would be based. Although there are precedents for this universalism in earlier American and continental linguistics, Chomsky's statement of it was stark and provocative. His approach incorporated a strong form of irreducibility in which a language like English, Spanish, or Russian is governed by a mental capacity for grammar that is more basic than thought itself. This innate capacity for language makes it possible for humans to acquire their own native tongue as children and to continue using it creatively as adults. Linguistic competence is itself mental, and the study of grammar is therefore a form of psychology. The contrast with behaviorism on this first principle is decisive.

Chomsky's linguistics starts from the ideal speaker-hearer, an analytic reduction of the heterogeneous facts of speech to the purely linguistic competence of one who perfectly masters her language. This is parallel to the Saussurian description of language users as actors who share the system of *langue* perfectly and use it identically in producing and understanding language. "Linguistic theory," he says, "is concerned primarily with an ideal speaker-listener, in a completely homogeneous speech community, who knows its language perfectly and is unaffected by such grammatically irrelevant conditions as memory limitations, distractions, shifts of attention and interest, and errors (random or characteristic) in applying his knowledge of language in actual performance" (1985:80). Just as *parole* was for Saussure a residuum of irregularity, language use for Chomsky is equally degenerate. The proper object for grammatical theory is gained by idealization of the system behind the superficial facts of speech. From this it follows that actual speech is examined only insofar as it is the realization of the system. Just as Bloomfield raised the threshold of difference between forms in order to achieve the ideal of sameness over the messy facts of relative similarity, Chomsky idealizes individual language ability in order to achieve identical competence among speakers who in fact vary greatly in their ability to use language. While Chomsky starts off defining linguistic performance as "the actual use of language in concrete situations" (1985:81), we soon learn that he examines actuality only to the degree in which it realizes a potential already inscribed in the grammar. In other words, his theory of performance is not a theory of speech communication but of the use under idealized conditions of structures that are predefined by the grammar.

As a corollary of his focus on the potential of linguistic systems to generate an infinite number of structures, Chomsky underscores what he called the creative aspect of the ideal speaker's knowledge. In the first instance, this creativity is merely that any language provides the means for expressing indefinitely many thoughts and reacting appropriately to an indefinite range of situations (1985:83). Thus it is primarily a feature of generative grammar and only derivatively a feature of speakers. Moreover, creativity under this definition fits closely with the syntactic component of language, since it is the combinatory rules that create the infinite number of sentences. On this point there is a fundamental difference between Chomsky and Saussure, for whom syntax, to the degree that it belonged to *langue* at all, was secondary to the more basic facts of lexical relations. In generative grammar, syntax is the core of language, not a peripheral feature of speech.

Another major domain in which generative grammar contrasts with its historical predecessors is what we might call the cast of characters it posits. The child occupies a pivotal role because her acquisition of a native language is guided by her innate knowledge of language. To acquire a language is to construct its grammar, tacitly building up the underlying generalizations that permit the speaker to produce and understand novel utterances. The neophyte achieves this impressive result based on exposure to real talk and other performance data that are full of errors and irrelevancies. Guided by an innate capacity for language, the new speaker overcomes the insufficiency of her own actual experience and develops into a mature ideal speaker-listener. The linguist in turn seeks to derive a model of the knowledge of the ideal speaker-listener. The aim is to create a transformational grammar that will generate only and all the sentences that are grammatical in the language and accord with the intuitions of the ideal speaker-listener. Universals play a similar role for the linguist as for the child: They guide her construction of the grammar. Features common to all languages do not need to be restated every time since they are redundant. In effect, such features are definitional and follow from the fact that the particular language under study is but an instance of language. Universals therefore simplify the description of the individual language a given ideal speaker-listener knows.

Competence Versus Performance

The ideal speaker-listener's competence is an abstract knowledge of the grammar of his own language. Competence is what makes it possible to produce infinitely many different sentences. It is language as potential. Performance is language as actual utterance. Of the two the former is the deeper and more significant. This follows in the logic of types, for types possess all of the invariant features replicated by their tokens. An understanding of the former can explain much of the latter, but the inverse does not hold. That is, performance is to be studied from the perspective of competence, not the other way around (1985:86). So if we were attempting to model English language, we might start from a scenario like the exchange between Jack and Natalia, but the only relevant part of the scenario would be the linguistic forms and their literal meanings, leaving aside all other features of the scene. The forms would then provide evidence for strictly grammatical relations, like the inverted word order of Jack's question, the contracted form "it's" in Natalia's response, the structure of the locative phrase "right on the table," and so forth. We would *not* attempt to understand the various situational factors that make the exchange typical, the relation between gesture and utterance, or the familiar style of the words chosen. Such factors may impinge on the couple's morning routine, but they have no relevance to the grammar of English and no value as data for deriving that grammar. Strictly speaking, these external facts are not even part of linguistic performance, since this is defined as the realization of grammatical competence. This sheer division between the linguistic system and speech is embedded in the way we judge whether or not a form fits with the patterns of the language. The ability to make such judgments is a critical part of the knowledge of the ideal speaker-listener and it provides a basic form of evidence about the language. Sentences that are well formed are said to be *grammatical.* Utterances that are appropriate in context are said to be *acceptable.* Acceptability is affected by an undisclosed range of things, many of them having nothing to do with language. It would be impossible to characterize it in grammatical terms because unacceptability can be produced by many factors, including the repeated application of certain rules or the combination of several rules (1985:88).

In light of these facts, Chomsky proposes to study acceptability by starting from simple formal structures in grammatical sentences and examining their effects on relative acceptability (1985:89ff). The overall thrust of his argument is that grammatical features do determine acceptability in interesting ways. This asymmetry defines the direction of performance studies, from grammar to its usage. From this perspective, it is wrongheaded to tape-record what people actually say and use this as the primary data from which to infer grammatical properties. This is just the process that Chomsky attributes to the structuralists and repudiates as sterile. Rather than selecting a corpus and describing the structures in it, he defines a corpus of grammatical forms and describes what happens when they are combined and used. In Saussurian terms *parole* enters into the study only insofar as it exhibits *langue.* Nothing new here.

Part of the mentalism of Chomskyan linguistics lies in the role of introspection in working out a grammar. The ideal speaker-listener's competence is embodied in the grammar and reflected in her intuitions regarding acceptability and grammaticality of sentences. Introspection is necessary in linguistic research because no amount of elicitation from native speakers can produce an adequate corpus.

This follows from the infinite generativity of language. Hence linguistic description must match the intuitions of the ideal speaker-listener as closely as possible. By intuitions Chomsky does not mean the conscious thoughts that you or I might have about our own language, but rather the more abstract, largely unconscious ability to recognize sentences as grammatical or ungrammatical. This represents a small, highly selective portion of a speaker's metalinguistic ability. It is closer in scope to Bloomfieldian judgments of sameness versus difference than it is to the broader Peircean process of understanding by way of interpretance. Furthermore, since these judgments are often quite subtle and require the knowledge of a native speaker, linguists working in this paradigm came to rely upon their own judgments when working on the grammar of their native language. Indeed, due to the demand for native intuitions, the practice of linguistic analysis on one's own language became the rule among generative linguists, rather than the exception. With this shift in its data, generative grammar came to alter the practice of linguistics in a basic way. Linguists no longer took as their task to describe exotic languages in which they could not possibly have native competence and undertook increasingly detailed studies of their own languages. In the early years this resulted in a proliferation of studies on English and other well-known European languages spoken natively by linguists. At the same time the judgments on which their descriptions were based became ever more delicate as the theory became more fine grained. This often resulted in disagreements among linguists as to the relative acceptability of given structures. Even in a small seminar on syntax, for instance, it might be impossible to reach agreement on the judgments needed as evidence for a grammatical analysis. Since the 1970s this lack of consensus on basic facts has led many to doubt the foundations of the method, for good reasons. The malaise was indicative of a basic contradiction in the scientific practice of linguistics: The theory sought to obviate any reference to the social world by linking language exclusively to human mental capacities, defined as universal. Thus at no moment did it become necessary even to consider the social situation as anything other than an afterthought. Yet linguists are no less social beings than are the people whose language they study, and their own differences in intuitions, in many cases driven by differences of background and region of origin, got in the way. In the specifically social settings of graduate seminars, conferences, and publication networks, the very social factors the theory sought to erase or repress reasserted themselves in the judgments of the theorists.

The Organization of the Grammar

A generative grammar is made up of three components: the syntactic, semantic, and phonological. The syntactic is the core and includes both syntagmatic structures and the lexicon of minimal meaningful words and morphemes. It specifies the infinite set of formal objects corresponding to sentences, "each of which incorporates all the information relevant to a single interpretation of a single sentence" (Chomsky 1985:94). A sentence at this level is a string of formatives, not a string of words or phones. The phonological component takes as its input sentences as defined by syntax and assigns to each a phonetic structure. The semantic component also takes structures defined by syntax and assigns to each a semantic interpretation. The syntax is divided into two subcomponents, a base and a transformational component. The former is a system of rules that generate basic strings, each with an associated structural description (called a base phrase marker). These are "deep structures." In general, deep structures are distinct from surface structures. This difference is due in part to transformations, rules that change base phrase markers into surface structures. It is helpful in this regard to recall Morris's distinction between formation rules and transformational rules, where the former correspond roughly to the base component in Chomsky's model and the latter to the transformational component. One difference between the two frameworks is that Chomsky's transformations operate on abstract configurations of symbols, not on actual sentences, whereas Morris conceived transformations as operating on basic sentences. With this qualification, the basic idea of a two-tiered syntax is the same. In Saussurian terms, sentences that have been derived by transformations are that much more *motivated* than the base phrases, which are more elementary, although still rule-derived. Deep structures determine semantic interpretation, and surface ones determine phonological interpretation (Chomsky 1985:95).

At this point in the development of generative grammar, the semantic interpretation of a sentence was treated as the product of the semantic component operating on deep structure. Whereas the syntactic component is generative, the semantic is interpretive. That is, all the information necessary to its operation is available in the deep structure. This information includes (1) syntactic features of lexical items (like N, V, Adv); (2) selection restrictions, to distinguish categories such as human, animate, mass, count; (3) subcategorization in certain syntactic contexts (for instance, a V is [+ transitive] when followed by an NP, as in "read the paper"); (4) any idiosyncratic features. The overall model has the parts displayed in Figure 4.1.

I pointed out above that deep structures are in general different from surface ones. Chomsky described this as one of the central ideas of generative grammar. In order to demonstrate their distinctness, and also to justify the study of abstract form, he adduces a series of examples in which the surface structure of a sentence corresponds to more than one deep structure—or to a deep structure different from what one might expect. So given sentences like "I had a book stolen" and "Flying planes can be dangerous," he shows that each corresponds to more than one deep structure. That is, they are grammatically ambiguous. The first step is to point out the ambiguities in the original examples. For instance, the first one can be understood as "A book was stolen from me" or as "I induced someone else to steal a book from someone." The reader's ability to recognize and understand these ambiguities is due to their own native-speaker intuitions about language—in this case difference of meaning and sameness of form. It is against this intuition that the descriptive adequacy of the grammar is to be evaluated (1985:82, 100–101). Inversely, with pairs like

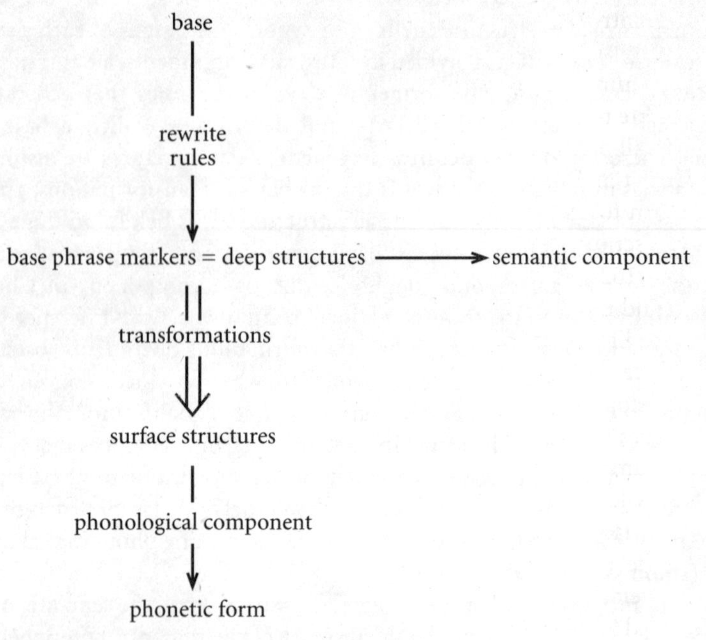

FIGURE 4.1 Outline of Generative Grammar, After Chomsky (1965).

I persuaded Kevin to shag fly balls

I expected Kevin to shag fly balls

Chomsky demonstrates that the apparent similarity in their surface form in fact hides a fundamental difference in their deep structures. Roughly, [I persuaded Kevin [Kevin shags fly balls]] but [I expected [Kevin shags fly balls]]. As evidence of the difference indicated by the brackets, consider that the two structures behave differently under transformation: [I expected fly balls to be shagged by Kevin] is grammatical, but *[I persuaded fly balls to be shagged by Kevin] is not, as indicated by the asterisk. The latter violates the selection restrictions of the verb "to persuade," which requires an animate object.

These examples indicate two points: Surface structure may not reveal the underlying deep structure; and intuitions and tacit knowledge of language, which make up the ultimate object of grammatical modeling, are elusive and must sometimes be teased out by paraphrasing, transforming, or otherwise altering the form under study. From here it is a small step to assert that the grammar of a language is really a theory of that language. Its accuracy is a function of how closely it describes the intrinsic competence of the ideal speaker-listener, whose intuitive judgments it must fit in a large number of crucial cases (1985:102). This involves providing an infinite range of structural descriptions, since the language is made up of an infinite number of sentences.

There is in all of this a deep-seated parallelism between the grammar as an analytic construct and the mental reality of the ideal speaker-listener. This corresponds in turn to the parallelism between the child, who must acquire the language from scratch, and the linguist, who must describe it from scratch (1985:81, 85, 102–103). Both characters draw on universal properties of language, the child in the form of an innate mental capacity to acquire human language and the linguist in the form of a knowledge gained by cross-linguistic research into the underlying features of languages. Every child who acquires a language develops a grammar—more precisely, an internal mental representation of the rules that determine how sentences are to be formed and understood. The term "grammar" is used to designate both the linguist's product and the speaker's knowledge. Chomsky says, "Using the term 'grammar' with a systematic ambiguity (to refer, first to the native speaker's internally represented 'theory of his language' and, second, to a linguist's account of this), we can say that the child has developed and internally represented a generative grammar, in the sense described" (1985:103). It is important to keep in mind that generative linguistics does not impute to speakers conscious thoughts about their grammar. On the contrary, it is axiomatic that most of the interesting features of grammar are far too abstract to be accessible to the consciousness of speakers. Nor is it asserted that speakers follow a grammatical derivation stepwise in the course of actually producing an utterance in talk. The system schematized in Figure 4.1 is not a model of performance but of competence. Therefore, hypotheses, rules, and theories have to do not with the things people think about but with the process of arriving at a generative system (1985:121). Presumably, the ideal speaker-listener has acquired a full range of intuitions and is beyond the stage of hypotheses.

The Semantic Component of Generative Grammar

As a model of the ideal speaker-listener's knowledge of language, a generative grammar must accurately reflect semantic intuitions. But what is the content of such intuitions, and what is semantic competence? Chomsky's answer was that competent speakers can perform at least the following operations:

1. They can recognize nonsyntactic ambiguities and assign readings to each pole (e.g., "the entire construction will be supported by the bank" [as financial backing vs. as the ground on which something like a dock would be built], where the ambiguity turns on the words "support" and "bank").

2. They can paraphrase sentences to create other ones whose meanings are roughly the same. For instance, "The bank will underwrite the building of the dock" and "The dock will rest on top of and be attached to the riverbank" (a dubious architectural decision but a fine sentence).

3. They can recognize anomaly and in some cases make sense of it. For example, consider "Sorrow floats," "Jack scattered on his way to the dining room," and "The paper is seated comfortably on the table." Anomaly in semantics corresponds roughly to ungrammaticality in syntax. Given a theory in which sentences are first generated by a syntactic component, and only then interpreted in the semantics, the ability to recognize anomaly is crucial. Without it, there would be no way to limit the class of semantically well formed sentences and, without that, no way to make significant generalizations.

4. They can exploit syntactic structure to reduce potential ambiguities. For instance, although "bank" may be ambiguous between the river and the lending institution, "The bank was closed" is not ambiguous. "Flying planes can be dangerous" is several ways ambiguous, but "It can be dangerous to fly planes" is not.

5. They can recognize equivalence and difference of meaning, even when the surface form provides no clue. (This overlaps with 1 above). So "Visiting relatives are quite nice" means something very different from "Visiting relatives is quite nice," whereas "It is quite nice to visit relatives" is roughly equivalent to the second reading.

These five abilities that make up the semantic competence of the ideal speaker-listener correspond to the features of grammatical forms. A constituent that is ambiguous in n ways is one to which n readings are assigned. An anomalous sentence is one whose semantic readings are null, and so forth (Katz 1971:305). Recall from Figure 4.1 that the semantic component takes as its "input" the deep structures that are produced by the syntactic base. To each deep structure, it assigns a set of interpretations called readings (potentially Ø or >1). It does this by the cooperation of two subcomponents, a dictionary and a set of projection rules. The dictionary entry for a word contains various kinds of information:

- syntactic features (N, V, Adv, etc.);
- markers, or major class features that crosscut whole sets of words (such as color vs. evaluative for the item "colorful");
- distinguishing features that differentiate at a lower level (such as [having distinctive character, picturesque] vs. [abounding in contrast or bright colors]);
- *strict subcategorization* features (such as [———NP] for transitive verbs);
- and selection restrictions (such as <aesthetic object>, <physical object> under the two poles of "colorful").

In other words, the dictionary entries give you basic representations of words and other lexical items in the form of bundles of features. The correspondence between features in the syntactic and semantic component is what allows you to map the one into the other. This is not unlike the use of features in phonology, and there has been a considerable amount of discussion about the relation between these two.

The meaning of any syntactically compound constituent of a sentence is a function of the meanings of its parts. Projection rules combine the meanings of individual words into meanings of whole sentences. They get us from a lexical, paradigmatic semantics to a syntagmatic one. The rules are sensitive to the different syntactic structures that relate words and reflect them in the readings they project. These rules operate from the bottom of a syntactic tree up to the top, progressively amalgamating features. In "The paper is on the table," for instance, the first level of amalgamation combines the definiteness of the article "the" with the nouns "paper," "table." The next steps would combine the preposition with the NP in [on [the table]], the verb with its subject, and the adverbial constituent made up of the preposition plus NP, yielding the constituent structure

$[_S\ [_{NP}$ the paper$]\ [_{VP}$ is $[_{PP}$ on $[_{NP}$ the table$]]]]$.

The selection restrictions play a key role in this process, since they constrain the way constituents combine. For instance, in the sentence "Jack scattered from the kitchen," there is a violated selection restriction: The intransitive verb "scatter" requires a plural subject. Hence it can be corrected by saying "Jack left the kitchen" or "The group of which Jack was a part scattered from the kitchen."

It is evident that the treatment of meaning in generative grammar is both related to and far more complex than that of earlier formalist models. The emphasis on judgments of sameness and difference is continued but refined considerably into judgments of ambiguity, the ability to resolve ambiguity using the syntactic resources of the grammar, and the ability to recognize and rectify semantic anomaly. The view of understanding implicit in generative grammar is considerably more active and surely more powerful than the Saussurian view of passive recognition of fixed correspondences between lexical forms and meanings. Much of the difference here is due to the centrality of syntax in generative grammar, the push for a semantic description that engaged fully with the combinatorial capacity of language. The need to prove that deep and surface structures were in principle distinct foregrounded the phenomenon of structural ambiguity in a way virtually absent from pregenerative theory.

Still, it is only the propositional, referential-descriptive aspects of linguistic meaning that are considered worthy of treatment in grammar. It does not deal with questions of style, indexicality, discourse structure, verbal interaction, relations between utterance and gesture, affective expressivity, or how speakers actually work out understandings. On this point semantics in a generative framework maintains the narrow focus typical of traditional irreducibility theories. Much of what constitutes the relational matrix of speech is swept away and left for other disciplines. The idea that language is acquired through an innate, specifically linguistic, specifically human capacity pushes irreducibility to its logical extreme. Jack and Natalia come out looking like identical stick figures or transposable minds in a vat. And yet by making it a strictly mental phenomenon, Chomsky is able to assert without contradiction that linguistics is a branch of psychology. There is in all this a fundamental shift in linguistics away from social sciences and problems of historical context toward individual psychology and computer modeling. Although the models have evolved a great deal between the 1960s and the present, and there are today a number of competing grammatical frameworks, it is fair to say that much of formal linguistics has continued in the direction marked by Chomsky's early pieces.

Dissenting Voices: Voloshinov and Rommetveit

Although generative linguistics caused major changes in linguistic analysis, there were dissenting voices all along. Some of these came from scholars engaged in heated debate with generative grammarians. Others come from more distant times and places and offer alternative views that challenge the formalist paradigm without ever making reference to things like transformations and semantic components. For our purposes, the key point is to understand the strengths and weaknesses of the paradigm, in order to better determine its potential contribution to a practice approach. We begin by making explicit the idealizations and priorities embedded in the early generative perspective. They include at least the following, which I number for ease of reference:

1. *Language use is regular both within and across speakers.* This must hold at least to the extent that utterances can be treated as performance, and performance is always the realization of competence, the nature and content of which is constant among speakers of the same language.

2. *Native speakers' intuitions about their language are also regular within and across individuals.* This is the product and clearest indicator of competence.

3. *The ideal speaker-listener is a single complex mental system, and innate language ability is a distinct system, virtually an organ.* These related assumptions undergird the essential distinctness of linguistic competence from all other kinds of knowledge, innate or acquired. They also assure that language production and understanding derive from a unified mental capacity.

4. *A language is a set of sentences, whose properties can be studied apart from the discourse and other contexts in which they occur.* That is, a language is no more and no less than a collection of formal objects. These objects are sentences, and not words, phrases, or other units. The sentence is the privileged level of structure around which grammatical processes are organized. It is

therefore the highest unit of grammatical description, as opposed to, say, connected discourse at a higher level of complexity or other units like the interactive move.

5. *The sentences of which the language is a set are a synchronic unity.* That is, they coexist in the linguistic present of the grammar, rendering irrelevant historical, geographical, or social considerations leading to variation.

6. *The meanings of a word are constant from use to use.* This assumption justifies the linguist in positing a lexicon of semantic feature bundles that are all in play whenever the word figures in a sentence.

7. *The child and the linguist face equivalent tasks.* This is the basis of the systematic ambiguity of the term "grammar" for both a child's emerging command of her language and the linguist's model of the language. Both must construct a generative model on the basis of defective and partial evidence.

8. *The linguist can play the role of ideal speaker-listener to the extent of using her own intuitions about grammaticalness and meaning in constructing the grammar.* Introspective data are as valid as or more valid than observations of actual speech. The proper training allows a linguist to overcome the otherwise obvious temptation to engage in circular reasoning by adjusting her intuitions to fit a theory.

9. *Syntax takes priority over both sound and meaning.* The grammar models the irreducibly linguistic aspects of language the total phenomenon, and it is the combinatorial capacity of the system, the syntax, that is the heart of irreducibility.

10. *The best grammar is the simplest one.* Because the grammar is a mental model, it is a point of method that a grammar that imputes excessively complex, cumbersome, or redundant structures to the mind is to be rejected in favor of one that describes the same facts more simply. Hence the search for universals of language is in part a search for ways to simplify the statement of individual grammars.

Many of these assumptions have analogues in earlier grammatical frameworks, but one of the great strengths of the generative one was to make them explicit. We can see them at work in the notion of selectional restrictions, which are designed to block out otherwise possible sentences, such as "The wind backed in through the window and scattered Ziggy's new plaid shirt" or "Colorless blue thoughts fell onto the floor, splattering the furniture." That is, we know as a matter of linguistic competence that "wind" cannot be the subject of the verb "back in" (enter posterior first), nor "Ziggy's new plaid shirt" the subject of "scatter," nor can "thought" amalgamate with "colorless blue" nor serve as the subject of "splatter," and so forth. But are these things really linguistic facts with the solidity of rules?

Obviously people say many things that are semantically anomalous, judging from the literal meanings of their words. There are two obvious factors here. A lot of apparently anomalous speech is actually resolved into nonanomalous meanings by way of metaphor and other tropes. The semantic component is not intended to be a theory of tropes, and yet it could contribute substantially to an understanding of them. Second, people's assumptions about things may be somewhat opaque on occasion, such that what looks semantically anomalous may actually be quite straightforward. Or it may be anomalous on some very strict reading but well formed on a looser one. The cumulative effect of the generativist assumptions is to treat sense as the relatively rigid content of form. But in human speech meaning production is obviously more elastic, and it is virtually always possible to imagine a context in which an otherwise outlandish statement can be semantically well formed. This merely makes explicit the well-known idealization of the object.

The main problem with the semantic component overall is that its shape and object are determined precisely by factors other than meaning. Voloshinov (1986:66) was right when he said that, objectively, the synchronic system of *langue* does not correspond to any real moment in the historical process of becoming. What a grammar represents is rather a fiction, "a conventional scale on which to register the deviations occurring at every real instant in time." Language use in any community of speaker-listeners is constantly changing, being nudged this way and that, being used in unforeseen ways. Of course any serious linguist recognizes this fact, and Saussure and Chomsky even discuss it. But Voloshinov wants to suggest that a grammar, like any system of social norms, actually exists "only with respect to the subjective consciousness of individuals" (1986:66). The problem is that too many proponents of abstract formalism assume that what a grammar represents is an objective system of normatively identical forms. Voloshinov argues that it would be more accurate to say that language appears as a synchronic given only to those for whom it is the native tongue. In an ironic twist of what we might otherwise expect, he accuses grammarians of falling prey to native-speaker common sense in assuming that something as mutable as language has a synchronic reality in the first place.

Next Voloshinov calls into question the actual correspondence between a grammar and how speaker-listeners experience language (1986:67). Here his argument takes a wrong turn because he slips from "the speaker's subjective consciousness" to "the speaker's focus of attention." The two are obviously distinct. One's typical focus of attention in talk is not on language forms at all, but on understanding. The grammatical tradition from Saussure to Chomsky reduces the reception of sentences in context to the recognition of their type-level meanings. So when we hear a question like "D'the paper come today?" we proceed by recognizing that this phonetic image corresponds to certain recurrent pairings of form and meaning, that is, certain words, in a syntactically defined structure. Given all that we already know and simply actualize in recognizing the sentence, the meaning falls out quite automatically. The designations are captured in the dictionary, the syntagmatic meanings in the syntax and reflected in the projection rules, and plop! the ideal speaker-listener yields its reading. And yet this strong form of irreducibility does not really purport to represent the conscious, focused thoughts of a speaker. Chomsky in particular proposed the mentalism of competence at a far deeper level of abstraction than that of conscious thought. Voloshinov may be right when he asserts that norms exist in respect to individuals, but he is wrong in claiming that this implies that they contemplate or even have any awareness of the norm. That speakers do not usually contemplate the forms or rules of their grammar is quite simply irrelevant to the grammar. This point has been recognized in linguistics at least since Boas and Saussure, and it applies *mutatis mutandis* to any social norms. In fact, it is a basic part of the early Americanist reflections on linguistic relativity as well (see Chapter 8).

Instead of starting from the assumption that word meaning is constant, Voloshinov begins with the opposite claim. "The meaning of a word is determined entirely by its context. In fact, there are as many meanings of a word as there are contexts of its usage" (1986:79). This fundamental fact of "polysemanticity" then provokes what he took to be the cardinal question of semantics, namely, How does a word ever cohere as a unit? What holds it together in the face of such variability? The objectivist linguist starts from a stiff unity and treats variation as mere overtones and shadings around a constant core. His concern is to define the unity as an invariant bundle of features, identified by comparing instances of the word across a variety of contexts. This is precisely the inverse of the practical attitude of the speaker who wants to understand the present utterance of an interlocutor. Natalia does not draw together and compare all the instances of "paper" that she has heard before with Jack's utterance as she hears it now, just to make sure that it is all consistent. She hears and immediately understands the request of her partner. Voloshinov also attacks what he takes to be the associated fiction that words have real things with objective properties as their designata. This idea further encourages the reification of meaning. Here he seems to imply that even though the meanings of utterances are token-specific, and hence variable, still they are a step removed from the material realities to which they may refer. Whatever accounts for the variation, it is not the sheer thingness of the speech situation. It is, instead, the socially constituted ideological screen through which speakers apprehend their world and produce meanings. The final error of objectivist semantics is in treating the various contexts in which a sentence occurs as though they were all of equal status, a series of contexts all of which instantiate the same constant meaning. According to Voloshinov, this entire knot of erroneous assumptions reflects that linguistics as a field grew out of the philological study of dead languages and is by nature incapable of shedding light on living languages. This somewhat radical critique should be understood in relation to Saussure and his neogrammarian forebears, not Chomsky and modern studies of living languages.

Closer to the truth for Voloshinov is the notion that contexts themselves are crosscut by conflicting subcontexts for the same words, so that not all example usages can be explained by the same semantic representation. Consider the fate of words like "life," "right," "choice," and "human being" in the abortion debate. This better approximates the sort of discourse that Voloshinov took to be the proper object of theorizing. Recall the Saussurian model of meaning being passed between identical heads, encoding and decoding being merely inverse versions of the same process linking signifier and signified. Chomsky's semantic component is vastly more precise than that and takes a more productive position on the importance of syntax, but it still portrays a homunculus. We can say that, of course, the facts of *parole* look daunting and underexplained when we gaze out onto them from within the capsule of grammar. No one has denied this, and none of Voloshinov's arguments can really call into question the existence of grammar in its modern forms. They can only make pointedly clear what the limitations are.

As we begin to explore the relational critiques of formal grammar, it is important to keep in mind that relationality and irreducibility combine precisely because they do not always correspond to the same sets of facts. A grammarian with strong ties to the irreducibility of form can easily allow the relationality of speech. She simply focuses on where the system is and backgrounds the rest. Conversely, a student of speech can maintain a full commitment to relationality of meaning production in dialogue while still assuming certain forms of irreducibility with respect to verbal form and semantic potential. But Voloshinov's challenge runs deeper and cannot be dealt with by this familiar move. He is prodding us to consider that even the apparently stable meanings we describe in a dictionary are really the crystallizations of speech processes. These processes take place at the token level, and a focus on them naturally throws into question the status of abstract types. His real challenge is to explore the ways in which this system, however it hangs together, provides *a logic for the interpenetration of social context with dictionary meaning.* Note that this is quite different from saying that the grammatical system is a logic unto itself whose features are in principle apart from those of contexts. Part of the challenge for us is to develop a metalanguage in which to describe what goes on in language at the token level. As will become increasingly clear, the status of tokens and the very notion that speech instantiates prefabricated types will come into question.

Rommetveit's *On Message Structure* (1974) makes an interesting companion piece to Voloshinov because Rommetveit criticizes Chomsky in much the same way Chomsky criticizes Saussure. By 1974 it had become obvious that many aspects of the generative paradigm were far from intuitive. Judgments of synonymy in particular turn out to be subtle and occasionally technical. This calls into question just how clear a native speaker's intuitions are. The generativist equation of native speakers with practicing linguists also gives rise to questionable uses of introspective data by linguists themselves. Judgments about the underlying conceptual reality of semantic representations, which appear to Western academics to be merely commonsensical, turn out on inspection to trade on esoteric definitions of the objects words denote. Thus "buy" and "sell" are described in a semantic framework owing much to economic theory and little to investigation of what speakers actually take the words to mean. Rommetveit had already conducted extensive research on the experimental reality of intuitive judgments and even questioned the stability of such judgments (in light of the well-known fact that judgments are always made relative to assumptions about the nature of the task). To the extent that this critique is well founded, it suggests that the body of linguistic intuitions that Chomsky placed in the center of grammar is in fact not systematic at all but the epiphenomenon of a false vision of how people judge language. This is one of Rommetveit's strong critiques.

He goes on to criticize Charles Fillmore's analysis of verbs like "buy" and "sell," which appear to be semantic converses of one another (Rommetveit 1974:16). Fillmore claims that

John sells roses to schoolgirls

is equivalent in terms of truth conditions to

Schoolgirls buy roses from John.

Rommetveit's line of attack is to shift the question in a way typical of his work. He asks, "What can be made known by uttering these two sentences?" This way of asking places the burden of meaning on the utterance of the sentence and not on the sentence itself. He then shows that indeed the *sells* sentence can be uttered truthfully when John works as a flower vendor but has not in fact sold any flowers yet. Hence the first can be true and the second false. The two are therefore not equivalent. Later he severely critiques Chomsky for defining the term "uncle," in other examples, strictly in relation to biological kinship. This "bourgeois reification" betrays no knowledge of contemporary studies of kinship by anthropologists.

It could be claimed on these matters that Rommetveit, like Voloshinov before him, has confused facts of *langue* with facts of *parole* and hits below the belt, as it were, in his talk of bourgeois reification and formalist escapism (1974:17–18). These responses fail to take into account the discourse to which Rommetveit addressed his work. The severity of linguistic rhetoric in the mid-1970s is adequately foreshadowed by Chomsky's 1965 monograph, in which he cites the social sciences as having produced objective knowledge without insight or explanation. It is not untoward to point out that he assumes simplistic notions of kinship that have been undone by the very fields he scorns. Furthermore, Rommetveit is not confusing the study of tokens for the study of types. He is questioning the very status of the distinction.

Rommetveit's alternative is to start from semantic potential rather than semantic content and to ask what can be made known by uttering a sentence, not what the sentence means in a vacuum. This way of posing the question leads him directly to the relation between the interlocutors and specifically to the "contract" that they share in the act of communication. This move will be familiar from Wittgenstein's discussion of language games. We can see in the case of the exchange

Jack: D'the paper come today, sweetheart?

Natalia: It's right on the table.

that the "contract" between Jack and Natalia orients them to locating the morning newspaper and thus rules out all sorts of potential ambiguities and other meanings that could be made known with the exact same sentences in another context (e.g., the litmus paper on a conference table in a lab). Notice, that it is the metacontract, and not the grammar, that rules out alternative meanings. The key shift here is to see lexical and sentential meaning as something that remains *indeterminate* until one places it in the framework of a context, where "context" entails intersubjective contracts, ongoing discourse, and a horizon of background experience. This is consonant with Voloshinov's arguments on the variability of meaning as well. One of its important consequences is that the meaning of a word cannot be treated as a self-same unity, even for the purposes of idealization. For Rommetveit, the facts that all actors know the world under numerous perspectives and that they assign multiple meanings to the same words jointly call into question the assumption that speaker and listener have the same understandings. In short, understanding becomes a constructive process in a social world in which knowledge and experience are differential, not an interpretive one in an epistemologically unitary and transparent thought world, in which ideal speaker-listeners trade messages whose meanings are determined once and for all by their common grammar.

Further Readings

Bloomfield, L. "On Recent Work in General Linguistics." *Modern Philology* 25 (1927): 211–230.

———. "Meaning." *Monatshefte für deutschen Unterricht* 35 (1943):101–116.

———. "Secondary and Tertiary Responses to Language." *Language* 20 (1944):45–55.

———. "A Set of Postulates for the Science of Language." In *A Leonard Bloomfield Anthology,* edited by C. Hockett. Bloomington: Indiana University Press, 1970, pp. 128–138.

———. *Language.* Chicago: University of Chicago Press, 1984 [1933]. Chap. 10: "Grammatical Forms," pp. 158–170.

For a view of linguistic structure and meaning just prior to the emergence of Chomsky's oeuvre, see

Harris, Z. "Distributional Structure." *Word* 10(2-3) (1954):775–793.

And for further discussion of American linguistics between the 1930s and the 1950s, see

Hymes, D., and Fought, J. *American Structuralism.* The Hague: Mouton, 1981.

On the break between Chomsky and earlier models, see

Chomsky, N. Review of *Verbal Behavior,* by B. F. Skinner. *Language* 35 (1959):26–58.

Chomsky, N. *Syntactic Structures.* The Hague: Mouton, 1957.
———. "Methodological Preliminaries." In *The Philosophy of Linguistics,* edited by J. Katz. Oxford: Oxford University Press, 1985, pp. 80–125.
Devitt, M., and Sterelny, K. *Language and Reality: An Introduction to the Philosophy of Language.* Cambridge: MIT Press, 1987. Chaps. 3–9; chap. 8, pp. 130–160.
Fillmore, C. "Types of Lexical Information." In *Semantics: An Interdisciplinary Reader in Philosophy, Linguistics, and Psychology,* edited by D. Steinberg and L. Jakobovits. Cambridge: Cambridge University Press, 1971, pp. 370–393.
Katz, J. "Semantic Theory." In *Semantics: An Interdisciplinary Reader in Philosophy, Linguistics, and Psychology,* edited by D. Steinberg and L. Jakobovits. Cambridge: Cambridge University Press, 1971, pp. 297–307.
Lees, R. Review of *Syntactic Structures,* by N. Chomsky. *Language* 33 (1957):375–407.
Maclay, H. "Overview." In *Semantics: An Interdisciplinary Reader in Philosophy, Linguistics, and Psychology,* edited by D. Steinberg and L. Jakobovits. Cambridge: Cambridge University Press, 1971, pp. 157–182.
Newmeyer, F. *Grammatical Theory: Its Limits and Its Possibilities.* Chicago: University of Chicago Press, 1983. Chap. 1, pp. 1–47.
Putnam, H. "Some Issues in the Theory of Grammar." In *On Noam Chomsky: Critical Essays,* edited by G. Harman. New York: Doubleday, 1974, pp. 80–163.
———. "Is Semantics Possible?" In *Mind, Language and Reality: Philosophical Papers,* vol. 1. Cambridge: Cambridge University Press, 1975, pp. 139–152.
Quine, W. "Methodological Reflections on Current Linguistic Theory." In *On Noam Chomsky: Critical Essays,* edited by G. Harman. New York: Doubleday, 1974, pp. 104–117.
Weinreich, U. "Explorations in Semantic Theory." In *Semantics: An Interdisciplinary Reader in Philosophy, Linguistics, and Psychology,* edited by D. Steinberg and L. Jakobovits. Cambridge: Cambridge University Press, 1971, pp. 308–328.

For dissenting voices, see

Harman, G. "Against Universal Semantic Representation." In *Proceedings of the Texas Conference on Performatives, Presuppositions and Implicatures,* edited by A. Rogers et al. Washington, DC: Center for Applied Linguistics, 1977, pp. 1–12.
Hymes, D. "Linguistics: The Field." *International Encyclopedia of Social Sciences* 9 (1968):351–371.
———. Review of *Noam Chomsky,* by J. Lyons. *Language* 48 (1972):416–427.
Rommetveit, R. *On Message Structure: A Framework for the Study of Language and Communication.* New York: Wiley, 1974.
Voloshinov, V. N. *Marxism and the Philosophy of Language.* Translated by L. Matejka and I. R. Titunik. Cambridge: Harvard University Press, 1986 [1929].
Weinreich, U. "On the Semantic Structure of Language." In *Universals of Language,* edited by J. Greenberg. Cambridge: MIT Press, 1966, pp. 142–216.

PART TWO

Language the Nexus of Context

Chapter 5

Sentences, Speech Acts, and Utterances

DURING THE SAME PERIOD that Chomsky and his collaborators were developing the early transformational model of syntax and syntactically based semantics, a number of important developments were taking place in the related field of pragmatics. It should be said in the first instance that Rommetveit's critique, published in the early 1970s, had little or no impact on mainstream linguistics and was not, to my knowledge, widely read or taught in graduate linguistics seminars of the time. Nor was Voloshinov's *Marxism and the Philosophy of Language* used as the basis of any reorientation. Although it was somewhat more widely read than Rommetveit, it was rarely cited or addressed in detail. More influential, and in keeping with the self-image of the burgeoning field of formal linguistics, was Thomas Kuhn's framework for describing scientific revolutions. For linguistics was presenting itself as a science in a state of revolution, a shifting of the paradigm from American descriptive to a universalizing generative framework. Among the key events in this shift were the publication of Chomsky's first major piece, *Syntactic Structures* (1957), and Robert Lees's influential review of the book (Lees 1957); the appearance of *Aspects,* which we discussed in the previous chapter; the appearance of Chomsky and Morris Halle's *Sound Pattern of English* (1968), which applied the generative paradigm to the phonological component of English; and the appearance of such classics as John Ross's MIT dissertation "Constraints on Variables in Syntax" (1967), which was taught in basic syntax courses for many years thereafter. In addition MIT was producing a whole new generation of linguists whose primary training was in this paradigm and who went on to form a productive and highly influential core of the field. Among them were some of the leading figures to argue against the kind of model put forth in *Aspects,* and in favor of what came to be known as generative semantics and, more recently, cognitive linguistics. With some noteworthy exceptions, most of these scholars maintained the central premises of generative syntax with respect to the irreducibility of language form and the idealized view of speakers and understanding that it entailed.

Alongside the generative paradigm there developed specifically linguistic approaches to language use that broke away from the reductionism of formal notions of performance while still attempting to retain its focus on competence. These approaches will be the first theme of the present chapter. Chief among them are two that derived from philosophy and that proved congenial with the linguistic view of structure. The first was speech act theory, whose prime movers in philosophy were John Austin and John Searle. Austin, an ordinary-language philosopher whose 1955 William James Lectures were published in 1962 as *How to Do Things with Words*, advanced the views that (1) the proper object of philosophical description was ordinary language use, not the rarified speech that would result from using language in accordance with formalist doctrines of logical truth, or "performance," in the linguistic sense;[1] and that (2) ordinary language was not organized around the functions of reference and description but rather a wide range of speech acts whose analysis required a basically different kind of framework.

Five years after the appearance of Austin's influential little book, the William James Lectures were presented by another philosopher, H. P. Grice, whose proposals grammarians adopted as they progressively extended the scope of linguistic description into language use. Grice's theory of "conversational implicatures" is based on the observation that utterances typically convey more information in context than is encoded in their semantic structure. Like Austin, Grice provided a language in which to describe a range of speech phenomena beyond the grammar, yet without calling into question the existence of grammar or its semantic component. This is part of what distinguishes the two from writers like Voloshinov and Rommetveit, who did call into question the entire formalist enterprise. And it is doubtless one of the reasons that their writings were congenial to the emerging generative paradigm. Unlike Austin, Grice proposed no typology of the speech acts that utterances routinely achieve. Nor did he define a specific class of expressions akin to Austin's explicit performative verbs. Rather, he focused on the relatively diffuse and widespread phenomenon of conversational inference, arguing that literal semantic meaning interacts with utterance context according to what he called the cooperative principle and its associated maxims.

Although they were pursued as universal frameworks applicable to all languages, the foregoing developments emanated almost exclusively from the English-speaking scholarly world, forming a kind of arc, ironically, between England and New England. But equally important lines of thought had developed

---

[1] In the 1950s, when he first advanced his theory, Austin was arguing against the view of language derived from the logical positivist doctrine of meaning as verification, although in the 1960s, when his writings were widely read, they were used to argue against the view of "performance" enshrined in generative grammar.

in Europe and took a different tack on a similar range of problems. The first of them, Prague School functional linguistics, took shape largely in the interwar years, its intellectual roots reaching back to Saussure, earlier Russian and Czech formalism, literary criticism, and phenomenology. Among the central figures in this "school" were Karl Bühler, Yuri Tynianov, Roman Jakobson, Jan Mukarovsky, and Bohuslav Havránek. By the early 1960s Jakobson was already collaborating with the Chomsky-Halle group at MIT and was doubtless the most prolific and influential of the Prague group. A number of key concepts were associated with the Prague School:

1. Grammatical form is oriented toward, and costructured with, utterance context.
2. Utterances, and by extension sentences, are multifunctional, and their organization is determined by the relative salience or hierarchy of functions.
3. The encoding of information in lexical items is asymmetric such that paradigmatic oppositions (cf. Saussure) commonly consist in one member whose meaning is more specific than the other; this insight became the basis for marking theory.
4. No human language is a single system, nor can it be described properly as if it were; a language is a system of systems, and its relation to the social world is defined by functional differentiation, not functional homogeneity.

Drawing on developments on both sides of the Atlantic (and the Channel), French-speaking linguists have also played a central role in creating functionally based frameworks. These include, among others, Saussure, Benveniste, André Martinet, and a more recent generation of scholars whose work relates language form to context in ways unthinkable to the North American formalists. Of these, the work of Oswald Ducrot has a special interest for our purposes. In the mid-1980s Ducrot proposed a framework for semantic description that incorporated the idea that the meaning content of sentences derives from the interaction of relatively underdetermined linguistic sense with context. Unlike the work of Grice and even Austin, Ducrot's approach implies that literal meaning is itself the product of context. Hence it becomes impossible to study pragmatics as the contextual overlay upon a core meaning, a move characteristic of formalist-derived approaches. Rather than discussing Ducrot's proposals in the abstract, we will do so using an extended example from Maya, the language of my field research.

This chapter is unlike the previous ones in that it traces a somewhat larger trajectory of ideas and integrates the work of a more diverse set of thinkers. In relation to language and communicative practices, it makes a break from the formalist core of Part 1, and prepares the ground for subsequent chapters in which we explore phenomenology (Chapter 6), the full saturation of language by context (Chapter 7), ethnographically based studies of language in culture (Chapter 8), and recent work on participant roles and the embedding of speakers in social relations of broader scope (Chapter 9). The first section of this chapter, "The Use of Form, the Overlay of Context," treats both speech act theory and Gricean implicatures. The unifying concept here is the idea that utterances correspond to sentences and sentences encode full propositional meanings. Propositional content, literal meaning, is analytically separable from the penumbra of situational factors engaged in its use. This is, as it were, the last stand of irreducibility, for it amounts to the claim that grammar is a prerequisite of speech. Still, it goes beyond pure grammar in trying to classify and describe a much wider range of phenomena. And this makes it ambiguous between the irreducible and relational perspectives, an uneasy ambiguity reflected in much of linguistic pragmatics. The second section addresses the Praguean framework, which retains a properly linguistic commitment to form but attempts to motivate form in terms of speaking, not abstract competence in the generative sense. The third and final section draws out the consequences of the preceding ones and advances the idea that even literal meaning is the product of context, not its invariant precondition. Hence the chapter effects a basic shift, or turns a corner, moving away from irreducibility toward a more deeply relational approach. The pivotal issue is how to define literal meaning relative to the diverse interactive meanings that arise in speech. Subsequent chapters amplify on this and follow the path of relationality to some of its logical conclusions.

The Use of Form, the Overlay of Context

If utterances have literal meanings that are "contextualized," what kind of information is it, and how is it integrated into context? Austin's answer to these questions marks a basic departure from previous approaches within analytic philosophy and linguistics. He started from the observation that much of ordinary language, even when it consists of apparently simple declarative sentences, does not involve statements that can be said to be true or false. It involves rather the doing of things with words. So if Jack says to Natalia,

1. I promise to be home by 6:00.
2. I request that you leave me a section of the paper to read with my coffee.

then he has done more than merely make statements. To the first sentence Natalia could hardly respond by saying, "That's not true," even if she knew he wouldn't get home until 7:00, and she might wonder at the stilted style of the second utterance, but she couldn't directly question its truth. The former makes a promise and the latter a request. The key insight here is that the saying of certain words *is* the doing of certain kinds of acts. The term Austin proposed to describe this effect was "performative," and both examples illustrate performative utterances. Imagine now that Jack were talking in his sleep, or a bit tipsy, and instead of sentences 1 or 2 he uttered 3 or 4:

3. I promise you will be home by 6:00.
4. I request an audience with the president.

Clearly, example 3 could not count as a promise unless Jack had some special right to make a commitment that Natalia had to fulfill or was responsible for her getting home. Similarly, example 4 could not count as a real request unless Natalia has the right to book appointments for the president. So although performative utterances cannot be true or false in the standard sense, they can still be appropriate or inappropriate. They can work or fail. At this point three questions arise: How can we specify the conditions under which performatives are and are not appropriate? Can we distinguish among types of inappropriateness, so as to specify exactly what aspect of the utterance failed? What is the class of utterances to which the term "performative" properly applies? We take these up in order.

The term that Austin used for appropriate performatives was "felicitous," and the requisite conditions are "felicity conditions." He distinguished among three classes of conditions, which jointly define a set of contextual dimensions. The alpha conditions stipulate that the context must be properly "prepared" for the act, the beta conditions that it must be appropriately executed, and the gamma conditions that it must be followed up on in the appropriate manner. They are, in summary:

A (i) There must exist a conventional procedure with a certain effect, and (ii) the situation of utterance must fit the procedure.
B The procedure must be done (i) correctly and (ii) completely.
G (i) The procedure must be done with the requisite intentions, feelings, and (ii) if it is such as to require subsequent action to follow through, then this must be fulfilled.

Note in this formulation that the "procedure" is the central element. It is the saying of the specified words. For example 3, there does exist a procedure whereby a speaker can promise, and the dyad of Jack and Natalia appears to fit the requisite conditions. However, Jack has violated the B(i) condition by incorrectly invoking the promise since he does so in the name of his interlocutor instead of in his own name. Similarly, in example 4 he makes his otherwise appropriate request to an inappropriate party. These are what Austin called "misfires." If Jack were to have uttered sentences 1 or 2 but without the intention to come home at 6:00 or without the desire to read the paper, then his utterances would be infelicitous and what Austin called "abuses." In the case of misfires, no act is performed since the rules that define it have been misapplied. This is akin to moving a chess piece in a way it cannot move: the knight on the diagonal, the rook or bishop on the L shape of the knight, and so forth. With abuses, a verbal act still takes place, but it is done in bad faith, like someone who enters into a contract with his fingers crossed beneath the table, intending all along to violate its terms later.

With regard to the class of utterances to which this kind of analysis applies, Austin's position evolves during the lectures. After having presented the basic framework in disarmingly simple terms, he introduces the distinction between "explicit" and "primary" performatives. The former are verbs of speaking, such as "promise," "declare," "christen," "warn," "bet," "admit," "apologize," "approve," "pronounce." These have in common two properties definable in linguistic terms. First, they may all be used to describe an utterance after the fact, and in such case they define the type of act the utterance is taken to have performed. So if Jack says, "I give you my word that I'll be home at 6:00," Natalia can later say of him that "he promised." Her report of his utterance labels it as being of the type PROMISE. Similar examples can be constructed for the other explicit performatives. The second feature is that when used in the first person present, these same verbs execute the relevant act in mentioning its name. So Jack could say, "I promise," "I apologize," "I bet 10 dollars the paper wasn't delivered today," and so forth, and in so saying, he would have executed the act, providing the felicity conditions are all met. The class of primary performatives is broader and formally more diverse. It consists of the various routine expressions whereby speakers accomplish acts that are later reportable using the same verbs that are explicit performatives when used in the first person present tense. So promises can often be accomplished by assuring the addressee of the intention to do some later action or by otherwise committing to it. Similarly, apologies are typically done with expressions of regret and so forth. The implication is that the list of explicit performative verbs provides a sort of lexical repertoire of speech acts, most of which can actually be accomplished either by using the verb itself or by uttering some other expression commonly understood to express the act. Notice that this repertoire is made up of metalinguistic expressions, and it is the play between metalanguage and direct speech that is the defining moment of explicit performativity.

In a sense the typology of performatives opens up a larger question regarding the kinds of acts accomplished with speaking. When Jack asked Natalia whether the paper had come that morning, he might be said to have accomplished a request for information, using the primary performative form of a yes-no question. But what about the implicit request for information about the location of the paper at that moment, or the more humble acts of having made an utterance in English and addressed his partner? If by asking about the paper he had managed to convey to Natalia that he was concerned about the fate of a piece of legislation that he expected to be reported in the morning edition, is this a performative also? Not really. For this range of acts, we need a more robust set of terms. In his seventh lecture, Austin turns to this broader question and generalizes the notion of performatives to a more general doctrine of "forces." The force of an utterance is its effectiveness in enacting an act, whatever the kind. The relatively precise kinds we have discussed so far all fit under the rubric of what he called "illocutionary forces." These have in common that they center on the performative value of the utterance, that is, its core conventional effect as distinct from both its propositional meaning and its side effects. By promising to be home at 6:00, Jack might have managed to confuse, insult, frighten, amuse, bewitch, bore, or distract Natalia, but none of these effects is part of the illocutionary force of promising.

He also managed to make reference to home and to the time when the little hand is on the six and the big hand on the twelve, but these things do not belong to the class of promises as such either. They are part of the propositional content of his promise on this occasion.

In contrast to illocutionary forces, then, Austin distinguished locutionary acts and perlocutionary effects. Locutionary acts basically inhere in the making of the utterance as a viable instance of English language. The "phonetic" act is the pronunciation of the forms. The "phatic" act is the uttering of a grammatically well formed expression of English, and the "rhetic" act is the saying of something semantically well formed. Notice that direct quotation, assuming it is accurate, reproduces all three locutionary acts of the original utterance, whereas indirect reported speech captures the rhetic aspects but not the phonetic or phatic. So if Natalia says, "It's on the table," and Jack reports her to have said, "The paper was on the dining room table," he has accurately reported the thematic content of her utterance but changed the words. In general, locutionary acts correspond to the producing of linguistic objects properly definable by the grammar of the language. Perlocutions are of a quite different order and are much more far-flung. As suggested by the label, they are the side effects and consequences of making the utterance. Whereas illocutions are conventional, tied to the saying of specific words, and involve requisite intentions and follow-through, perlocutions need not be conventional. They can often be accomplished without any words: Gestures can be frightening, amusing, distracting, and so forth, whereas it takes words to "promise." Similarly, perlocutionary effects can be triggered by accident, irrespective of the actor's intentions or subsequent follow-through. In making an utterance, speakers usually accomplish all three kinds of act simultaneously.

Perhaps the most interesting aspect of Austin's framework, for our purposes, is the way he walks the line between parts of speech acts that belong strictly to language and parts that do not. On a plausible reading, speech act theory is basically formalist and provides further evidence for the irreducibility of the linguistic system. The set of locutionary acts that must be part of any speech act basically consists of the appropriate token realization of the phonetic, syntactic, and semantic rules of the language. The locutionary acts in no way put those rules into question. Moreover, the difference between illocutionary and perlocutionary acts has to do, at base, with the difference between, on the one hand, what is encoded in the language and conventionalized as the automatic effect of using it under the right conditions and, on the other hand, the nonlinguistic by-products that might ensue from actions, whether verbal or not. It is no accident that explicit performatives are *words,* whose semantic values are such that they can be used to describe utterances after the fact or, when produced in the first person singular present tense, to accomplish the act itself. That is, the definition of the class relies upon the properties of the linguistic forms. Context, defined radially as the parameters required by the forms, serves as the setting in which the utterance is a catalyst whose causal effect is the speech act.

As Austin's work was taken up by linguists during the 1970s, the ties between the doctrine of forces and linguistic structure were examined all the more intently. The William James Lectures were taught in pragmatics seminars around the country, linguistics conferences focused on speech act theory, and the typology of illocutionary forces was brought into ever closer alignment with the linguistic evidence of distinct act types. In a real sense, the subfield of pragmatics, foreseen and labeled by Morris, was born as a fact of the sociology of academic knowledge. Various attempts were made to assimilate the notion of illocutionary force to the propositional content of utterances, such attempts motivated in part by the fact that explicit performative verbs, like "promise," achieve their effect precisely because of their conventional meaning. This trend (discussed in Levinson 1983:243–260) led to reduction of speech acts to matters of truth and falsity (an ironic development, given Austin's objectives). In a related development an increasing number of linguists worked toward assimilating speech acts to grammatical structure, even positing higher performative clauses in the grammatical deep structure of sentences to account for their contextual effects. So Jack's question to Natalia might be derived from an underlying structure roughly of the form: [*I ask you* [did the paper come today]], with the italicized portion deleted in the course of the derivation. Such an approach obviously stretches the grammar to its limit—or, some would argue, beyond it. Probably the most far-reaching and revealing attempt to argue for this approach was by Jerrold Sadock (1974), who proposes a typology of speech acts on the basis of a wide range of linguistic evidence. Sadock's basic thrust is to demonstrate that linguistic form, that is, facts of co-occurrence, syntactic transformations, and their constraints, systematically respond to speech act phenomena. To the extent that this is so, those phenomena, be they bits of context or classes of acts, must be represented somehow in the grammar. Thus progressively more of pragmatics, or *parole,* is assimilated to the grammar, or *langue.*

Like Austin's, Grice's work is a response to the tradition of formal philosophy in which natural languages, like English and Spanish, are described on the model of formal logic. Whereas Austin argues from the perspective of ordinary language that human speech is basically different from and irreducible to logic, Grice argues the opposite. He takes the two to be similar, despite the appearance of difference. His task is to explain this appearance in such a way as to retain a logical model of the semantic structure of language, while adding to it principles sufficient to explain the nonlogical effects of speech in context. Although he never says so in so many words, Grice is trading on the distinction between *langue* and *parole,* with the former logical and the latter something else. The first step in this direction is his observation that utterances in context convey a good deal more information than is encoded in their semantic structure. In general the relation between logical content and situationally conveyed meaning is one of a lean, literal core expanded into a thicker, more concrete situated meaning. To use Grice's terms, the literal meaning is what is *said,* and the situated meaning is what is *conveyed.*

The observation that conveyed meaning is generally greater than literal meaning is not new. What was new was the way Grice went about getting from the one to the other, by what he called a "cooperative principle" and an associated set of maxims. The principle is as powerful as it is vague: Conversation being a cooperative effort with a shared set of purposes, conversants are held to make their respective contributions such as is required. The guidelines that define this sense of the required are divided into four kinds, adopting the Kantian categories of quality, quantity, relation, and manner.

1. Quality
   a. Do not say what you believe to be false
   b. Do not say that for which you lack sufficient evidence
2. Quantity
   a. Make your contribution as informative as is required
   b. Do not give more information than is required
3. Relation
   a. Be relevant
4. Manner
   a. Avoid obscurity
   b. Avoid ambiguity
   c. Be brief
   d. Be orderly

The cooperative principle and maxims obviously rest on an idealized, and particularly Anglo-Saxon, view of conversation as a rational exchange of information. Grice makes this explicit in his general observations on cooperative transactions, including talk, but other things as well. All such transactions, he says, involve a shared set of aims among the participants, however vague these may be. Furthermore, the respective contributions of interactants interlock or dovetail and are mutually dependent. The terminating of talk, like its initiation, is something that comes about jointly, not by the abrupt action of a single party. On the face of it, this view of Grice's is at odds with much of our daily experience, and it is surely a culturally specific vision to which an endless list of ethnographic counterexamples could be adduced. With disarming candor, it reflects what Rommetveit called the idealization of a fully shared, epistemologically transparent world. In simpler terms, it looks like a British philosopher's vision of what the world should be like, if only everyone had the sense to be like him. Before we get carried away with criticism, however, Grice is more subtle than appears. He is aware that people don't really talk this way, and this discrepancy between principle and fact is precisely how the framework operates.

It works like this: People almost never behave exactly as prescribed by the maxims. But they do interpret each other as if their behavior fit the cooperative principle. So when Jack asks "D'the paper come today?" Natalia figures he has no interest in kinds of paper other than the newspaper, even though he doesn't say so; that he has no burning interest in paper delivery, despite the question; that he's getting his coffee and is probably interested in reading a section, even though he never says so. Therefore his question probably has some aim other than merely eliciting information. Hence because he is probably being perspicuous, not too wordy, relevant, and not excessively informative, he must mean to convey something slightly different than the logical content of his words. In order to correct the apparent discrepancy between the words and what would be appropriate in the setting, she expands on the words, using the maxims as guide, and derives the inference that he is asking her where the paper is so he can read it. She in turn says, "It's right on the table," answering the inferred question, not the literal one. He reasons that she is telling the truth, and enough of it to answer what she takes to be his question, and that, despite appearances, she is being cooperative. So he derives the inferences that the newspaper was delivered that day (even though she might in fact have lifted the neighbor's copy if theirs never came), it's OK with her if he picks it up and reads it (even though he might be wrong), it's on the table where he can do so (even though, perversely, she might have glued it to the table as a practical joke). All these situated inferences that allow the couple to get from words to deeds are what Grice called "implicatures." They are all generated by the apparent failure of the speaker to be cooperative at the level of literal meaning, and the resolution of that failure by adding inferences to what was said.

What exactly is an implicature? A speaker, in saying that p, implicates that q if and only if the following three conditions apply: (1) The speaker is presumed by his interlocutor to be following the maxims, or at least the overarching cooperative principle. So obvious violations are treated as only apparent, and the work of going beyond appearances is needed to get from p, what is *said,* to q, what is implicated. (2) In addition, the addressee assumes that the speaker is aware that q (the implicatum) is, or thinks that it is, consistent with the assumption that she is being cooperative. In other words, the implicatum is intended and resolves the apparent violation of the ground rules. (3) And finally, the speaker thinks that the addressee can work out the implicatum. That is, the connection is not so tenuous or convoluted as to be obviously inaccessible to the addressee. In order to meet these three criteria, both parties to the conversation must have at their disposal the conventional or literal meaning of the utterance, the cooperative principle and its maxims, the context of utterance, and certain relevant background knowledge. Given these factors, implicatures are clearly multiple, in that a single utterance can give rise to more than one inference. And any individual implicature can be blocked or canceled, either by context or by accompanying words, without resulting in contradiction. So Natalia could respond, "It's right on the table—the neighbor's table of course. They forgot ours again" or "It's right on the table—but don't bury your nose in it like you always do. Talk to me, for Christ's sake!" or "It's right on the table—the toilet paper, that is. The newspaper never came, ha ha." What Grice calls the cancelability of implicatures is what others call defeasibility. It indicates that the implicated meaning is not part of the words but part of the context, and so it changes as the context changes. Notice that if the meaning were part of the literal sense, to cancel it would result in contradiction: "It's right on the table—well, it's not on the table really."

Grice's framework offers an interesting twist on Austin's felicity conditions. It assumes that speakers routinely make utterances that are infelicitous, at the level of what they literally *say.* And in this sense it appears decidedly antirationalist. At the very least it implies that speech, or performance, to use the grammatical term, follows a logic quite distinct from that of literal meaning and that the interpretation of utterances is always more than mere recognition. Yet it supports the formalist position in arguing that natural languages really *are* like formal logic in their semantics. Conversational practices, in contrast, seem to be nonlogical. So, to be provocative, we could say that logic reigns both at the deep level of literal sense and at the most superficial level of conveyed meaning. It is in the middle, in the fit between literal content and context, that problems arise. Like the sociological notion of latent functions, implicature intervenes to save the system from the appearance of nonlogicality. There is a grain of truth in this provocation. Grice's framework was rapidly adopted by linguists looking for ways to describe pragmatics, precisely because it answered the need to save semantics from the flood of pragmatic nuances. As Stephen Levinson (1983) observed, implicatures allow linguists to greatly simplify and contract the scope of semantics while still taking into account a broad range of nonsemantic meaning. Whereas Austinian performatives had led to an ever expanding semantics, as linguists assimilated more and more speech acts to the grammar, Grice responded to the desire for a simpler, more minimal semantics. If the description of conversational implicature could be made rigorous, it was hoped, the semantic component of the grammar could be kept simple. Grammar based on irreducibility could coexist with pragmatics based on relationality.

This is the point at which the vagueness and ethnocentric overtones of Gricean pragmatics come home to haunt it. Grice's promissory notes about relevance, context of utterance, and background knowledge left many students of talk dissatisfied. What is relevance, and how can we describe utterance context beyond assuming our own commonsense categories? What would a Gricean description of a non-Western culture look like? When a Mayan shaman is purposely vague with a patient, is it a violation of the maxim of manner, or are there as many readings of the maxim as there are cultures? If the framework was intended to be universal, it would need an enormous ethnographic foundation in order to be applicable—and that foundation would probably render the framework itself redundant. Yet if relevance, perspicacity, and cooperation were all defined relative to cultural and historical contexts, then what generality is there in the Gricean framework? What do we gain from it? It looked alternately like ethnocentric prescriptivism or common-sensism too vague and turned in on itself to explain anything. This queasy duality may explain why the implicature framework had little impact on ethnographers of speaking, whereas Austin's notion of performativity elicited an enormous range of responses in other fields (see Levinson 1983 for remarks on this point). In the end Grice answered his own questions about the proper place of logic in describing natural languages, but he did not really open up new vistas for language study beyond the purview of formalism. I think the reason for the limitations of Grice's work is that he retained the view of language as essentially an instrument of thought, with the dynamics of communication serving as little more than a foil for the more basic conceptual structure.

Prague School Functionalism

Austin and Grice both extended the focus of formalism from language structure to the dynamics of language use. And both, as we saw, maintained that speech is the use of predefined forms and that context figures as a sort of overlay on the formal core. With Prague School functionalist linguistics, we return to the basic question of relating sentences to utterances in context, but the solutions the Prague thinkers offer are different. The main source of difference lies in that the Prague School theories assume that grammatical structure and utterance are two faces of the same thing. That is, they deny the original division between language and the social world, on which formalism rests.

What was to become the Prague Linguistic Circle came into existence in October 1926 and first took shape over a series of lectures and discussions during the following months. By 1929 the group had more than doubled in size and adopted the explicit goal of developing a unified approach to language in its formal, social, and historical dimensions. This vision was expressed in the theses presented in 1929 at the First Congress of Slavic Philologists. A key aspect of this unified view was the premise that language is a tool of communication or, as they put it, a system of goal-oriented means of expression. Where Saussure (and formalist approaches after him) had posited an essential difference between synchrony and diachrony, the Prague Circle posited a "dynamic synchrony," characterized by innovation, retention, and variation. The linguistic present would not be defined by a monolithic system in equilibrium but instead by a constant tension among pasts, presents, and futures, played out on the stage of a diverse social landscape. Finally, where the formalist tradition has been based on the function of encoding information of the sort modeled in logic, the Pragueans started from the idea of multiple functions defined by the multiple goals that speakers pursue through speech. Language would not be a system with a single inner logic but a system of systems whose subparts had their own distinct logics.

This last idea is what was called "functional differentiation." When speakers make utterances, they do so with certain purposes, goals, in mind. Different social situations make different communicative goals appropriate. For instance, everyday face-to-face interaction, like the one between Jack and Natalia, involves speech aimed at ends different from the ones typical of technical exchanges in the workplace, scientific argumentation, poetic expression, or the sheerly instrumental speech between a surgeon and her assistants. The idea is that the correspondences between contexts and motives of speaking serve as a kind of selection device and call forth different kinds of language. Intellectual language is focused on the goal of communicating specific information; emotional language on the goal of discharging and evoking affect; poetic language on the aestheticizing of verbal expression itself; communicative language on the goal of individuating and describing objects. Each functional kind corresponds to a set of conventions, or a specialized *langue.* So from this perspective, Grice's framework appears as the privileging of a certain kind of information exchange and the mistaken attempt to use this as the measure of all speech. Despite the more or less obvious problems inherent in functionalist schemes, such as the endless multiplication of functions, still we can see that this one opens up an entire array of approaches to verbal practice missing from formalist reasoning.

A special instance of functional differentiation was what Havránek called "intellectualized" speech. In situations calling for the exchange of precise information, the linguistic resources of the standard language tend to be adapted to the demand for unambiguous, propositional, highly rational speech. This often involves the creation of new vocabularies and jargons, as is evident, say, in the talk of doctors, lawyers, mechanics, and academics. In the clearest cases intellectualization leads to speech with the following features: (1) unambiguous, self-contained statements whose meaning remains constant regardless of utterance context; (2) specialized, narrowly defined distinctions between concepts; (3) the use of abstract summarizing terms to facilitate abstract reasoning; and (4) a preference in syntax for the maximal parallelism between linguistic form and the logical relations among concepts discussed. In general, intellectualized speech is aimed at maximally definite, semantically transparent messages. It is important to note in this regard that this overall process results in a wide range of speech forms, from the minimally to the maximally intellectual. On the lower end, everyday speech is relatively context-bound and marked by ellipsis and repetition. Task-oriented speech in the workplace tends to be relatively more definite and therefore less dependent upon idiosyncratic features of context. Fully intellectualized speech, such as the language of contracts or logical argument, aims at minimal context dependency and maximal transparency within a specialized code. That highly intellectualized speech is usually opaque to those not familiar with its conventions is a straightforward result of this hyperspecialization.

In view of the differentiated goals of talk and the kinds of language adapted to them, Prague theorists proposed another useful dimension, what they called foregrounded as opposed to automatized speech. Automatized utterances are those closely matched to their setting, so that the chain linking communicative intent, speaker-addressee expectations, and outcomes is unbroken. This connection presupposes the existence of routine, habitual ways of speaking, to which the automatized utterance fits. Foregrounded utterances, by contrast, are unexpected, uncommon in their context, and for this reason attract special attention. Their atypicality may be due to a mismatch between functional style and setting, to the use of common expressions for uncommon meanings, or indeed the use of grammatically peculiar forms that would be unexpected under any circumstances. It should be clear that judgments of relative foregrounding can be made only against the horizon of what is typical for a given kind of context and that automaticity is a matter of degree. It is therefore wrongheaded, in the Praguean view, to elevate any one functional style to the level of the standard against which others are judged, just as it is impossible to evaluate appropriateness out of context. The problem with the Gricean framework of the cooperative principle and associated maxims is precisely that it is a decontextualized theory of context.

What about context in the sense of the immediate conditions of utterances? On this point the Pragueans proposed a set of dimensions and principles designed to relate linguistic forms to the speech events in which they occur. Although the basic elements of this framework were in place as early as Bühler's writings in the 1930s, it is Jakobson's (1960) article on verbal style that is usually considered the standard source. Jakobson proposed that utterance contexts always entail six minimal dimensions: speaker, addressee, message (form and semantic content of the utterance), context (the objects talked about), code (the linguistic system that makes it possible to form the message), and contact between the participants. In any utterance event one or more of these factors will take prominence over the others, although all are to a degree present. For example, when Jack asks "D'the paper come today?" the interrogative force of his utterance centers on the newspaper (context) and elicits from the addressee a response of a certain kind. If he had simply called out Natalia's name to see if she were in the dining room, his utterance would have been focused on the contact between the two. If he were explaining the meaning of some specialized expression to her, the focus would be the message or perhaps the code. The idea here is that utterances tend to focus on one or another component of the event, leaving the remaining ones in the background. This focusing is what Jakobson called the *Einstellung*, or "set," of the utterance. Each selective focus is a "function."

Utterances, or utterance portions, focusing on the speaker (whom Jakobson called the addresser) are expressive in function. Their main object is the speaker's subjective attitude toward the message, as can be seen, for instance, in many interjections and expressive intonation, like "Tch! The damn paper is late AGAIN?!" Speech set mainly on the addressee is conative in function. This is illustrated by special vocatives, like Jack's "sweetheart," the use of imperative verb forms, commands, reverential and deferential speech. Focus on the contact between participants is phatic in function, illustrated by back-channel cues like "yeah," "OK," "right," that speakers utter to let their interlocutors know they are paying attention and understanding them. Similarly, expressions like "See what I mean?" "Follow me?" and "Catch my drift?" are phatic in that they are aimed primarily at securing the understanding of the addressee. A focus on the code yields the metalinguistic function, in evidence any time speakers comment on, define, call into question the forms of an utterance. For instance, "What do you mean, 'right on the table'? Someone threw it in the rubbish and it's covered with coffee grounds." The referential function is defined as a focus on the objects described (which Jakobson unfortunately called context). This is the main concern of traditional formalist theories. Finally, the poetic function is defined as the set or focus on the message itself, bringing into the foreground its own form. We will return to this in Chapter 8 in discussing discourse style and textuality.

Overall, the differences between Prague School approaches and the ones typical of modern formalism are decisive. From the functional perspective, formalism privileges the referential function and evaluates all language from the viewpoint of highly intellectualized styles typical of academic or formal settings. The commitment to sheer synchrony flattens out the interplay between past and future in the linguistic present, and the isolation of language from its social context misses completely the phenomenon of functional differentiation. Yet formalists have traditionally derided functionalism as reductionist, since it rejects formal irreducibility in favor of a more deeply relational approach. Similarly, the commitment to a means-ends view has been widely criticized as circular, and the central place of communication in functionalist theory is rejected by formalists who see the essence of language to be its role in thinking.

There is one further aspect of Prague theories that is relevant to our discussion at this point: their approach to paradigmatic oppositions among linguistic forms. Recall from Saussure that the paradigmatic dimension concerns the differences between closely related forms, be they lexical items, phrases, or, in an extended sense, sentences. Building on the work of N. S. Trubetzkoy in phonology, Jakobson in 1939 proposed a general theory of "markedness," whose key insight is that linguistic expressions differ systematically in terms of how much information they encode (Jakobson 1966). Expressions with relatively more specific information content are more "marked" than those with less specific meaning. To use a standard example, the term "man" is generally considered to be less marked than "woman" because it encodes features for [+ human, + adult] but no feature for gender. "Woman," by contrast, encodes both [+ human, + adult] but is also specified [+ female]. The evidence for this is the use of "man" in reference to the entire human race (cf. "Man is the only animal that laughs"). This illustrates a "privative" opposition in which the marked term is specified [+ female], and the unmarked term is [Ø female]. Privative oppositions are actually widespread in human languages, occurring at three distinct levels: (1) superficial phonological, morphological, or syntactic form; (2) the encoded meaning or semantics of the forms; and (3) the stylistic organization of discourse. At the semantic level, which is our primary concern here, unmarked forms tend to have a wider grammatical distribution and a wider range of contextually derived meanings. Both of these correlates come about because of the unmarked terms' relative vagueness compared to the more marked counterparts. Privative oppositions are logically part-whole relations, with the marked term being included in the broader field of the unmarked. Or to put the same point in terms of hierarchy, the unmarked term is superordinate to the marked, as shown in Figure 5.1.

If privative relations are asymmetric in this special sense, "equipollent" oppositions are symmetric. They involve pairs of expressions both of which are positively specified for some feature. For instance, "boy" and "girl" form such a pair because each carries a specific gender feature and there is no evidence that either is more specific. Here the opposition would be [+ human, – adult, + male] versus

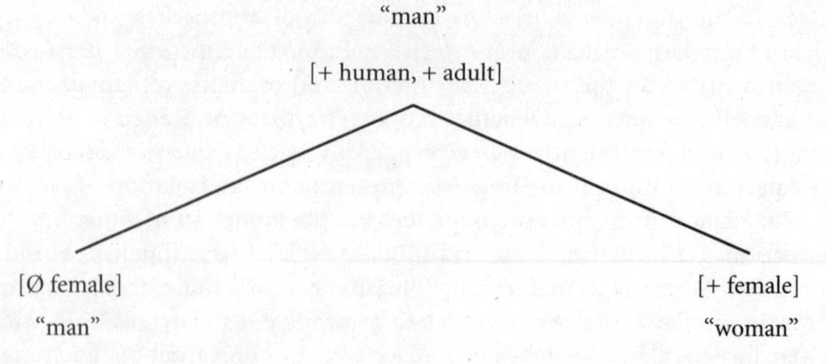

FIGURE 5.1 A Privative Opposition.

[+ human, – adult, + female] (or, for the final feature in the second set, [- male]; a negative specification counts as a marked feature). In order to better understand how these kinds of oppositions work in actual cases, we turn in the last section of this chapter to an extended example. Before doing so, note that although marking theory could be formalized in logic, it is nonetheless different from logic in positing unmarked terms, whose sense is underspecified. This is consistent with the Praguean focus on human language as a communicative system with its own peculiar properties.

The Context Dependency of Literal Meaning

Speech act theory, conversational implicature, and functionalism have in common the attempt to relate aspects of linguistic form to utterance context. The three obviously pursue this objective in different ways and with different starting points. Key among these starting points is the basic conception of literal meaning, for, as we saw, this is the first element in the inferential chains of implicatures, just as it includes both the propositional content and conventional illocutionary force of speech acts. The status of literal meaning has become one of the central problems in modern linguistic semantics. Since the early 1980s, there have been increasingly many attempts to formulate semantic content in such a way as to recognize its intimate relation with the situation in which it is produced. In other words, the idea of a fixed literal sense inhering in grammatical form has come under scrutiny, and many of the meaning components traditionally assumed to be properly linguistic have been shown to be the product of context. To the extent that this is so, the traditional division between semantics and pragmatics is itself brought into question. This general trend characterizes cognitive semantic approaches, as illustrated in George Lakoff (1988), Ronald Langacker (1987, 1991), and Gilles Fauconnier (1988). It is also prefigured in Hilary Putnam's (1975) article "The Meaning of Meaning," in which he argues against the traditional conception of encoded intensional meaning as the precondition of extension. Instead, Putnam proposed that the meaning potential of linguistic expressions is fixed by local standards of use (see Chapter 9). This implies that as those standards change, the meanings of the terms change with them. Hence semantics is not encapsulated in the grammar but depends on the relation between that system and what Putnam called the "division of linguistic labor."

Another influential framework that goes in the same direction is situation semantics, associated centrally with the writings of Jon Barwise and John Perry. Barwise (1988:25) observed that the circumstantial relation between meaning and semantic content is "perhaps the most basic fact about meaning." "Meaning," he points out, is an ambiguous concept, standing for three quite different things: (1) the encoded sense of a grammatical form, such as the English sentence "It's right on the table"; (2) the use of the sentence by a certain speaker to say something to an interlocutor, which he called "content"; and (3) whatever larger meaning the speaker intended to convey on that occasion, which he called "user's meaning." Content, in this set of meanings, arises only under the circumstances of an utterance. It does not inhere in the forms themselves.

Barwise (1988:29) goes on to distinguish four constituents of content: (1) the part that contributes articulated constituents; (2) the part that contributes unarticulated constituents; (3) the part that contributes articulated nonconstituents; and (4) the part that contributes unarticulated nonconstituents. An *articulated constituent* is a part of content individuated by a specific linguistic form, such as the objects of pronouns and deictics "I," "here," "now," "today," and deictic uses of tense, demonstratives, and pronouns. *Unarticulated constituents* are aspects of content not denoted by specific forms but nonetheless presupposed or directly inferable from it. For example, in the sentence "It's raining," the location of utterance would be an unarticulated constituent. Similarly, in "It's right on the table," the kitchen in which the table is located is an unarticulated constituent. The overall class of *nonconstituents* is made up of factors that aid in deriving the content but are not themselves part of it. Barwise illustrates *articulated nonconstituents* with the sentence "She is a philosopher," in which the gender of the individual is articulated in the pronoun but is not part of the content. Evidently, only those factors that contribute to the truth functional value of the utterance are part of content, and hence a word like "right" in "It's right on the table" would fit this category as well. Notice that this word, however we describe its meaning, does not alter the truth conditions of Natalia's utterance, but it does aid Jack in recognizing which table the newspaper is on. *Unarticulated nonconstituents*, as one might expect from the label, are the negative instance on both dimensions of articulation and constituenthood. They include a grab bag of background assumptions that speakers make and that help them to derive specific content, even though they are not part of the content. Jack, for instance, assumes that "on the table" means above the table and not stuck to the underside, that the table sits on the floor rather than being suspended from the ceiling, and so forth. But we don't want to say that these and similar assumptions actually belong to the content of Natalia's utterance. A fifth factor contributing to the derivation of content is of course the conventions of the language being spoken and the awareness of both interactants that they share the same grammar.

Another attempt to contextualize semantics is the framework proposed by Ducrot (1984). Like Barwise and indeed subsequent cognitive theorists, Ducrot starts from the premise that only part of what appears as the content of an utterance is encoded in its formal structure; the rest derives from the combination of language with context. Ducrot's framework has the following parts. An uttered form, or *énoncé,* is defined as a linguistic structure with an inherent signification. The latter corresponds to encoded meaning in Barwise's sense. It is schematic and less determinate than fully propositional meaning measured by truth conditions. If we assume the signification of the *énoncé,* the situation of utterance then comes into play, the combination of the two yielding the literal sense of the utterance. This is the level at which propositional meanings are sufficiently well defined and complete to be judged true or false. Given this, there is, as it were, a second-order infusion of context, resulting in many of the inferential and perlocutionary effects Austin and Grice discussed. So Ducrot's framework assumes a relatively lean inherent content in verbal form, which combines with the utterance situation in two steps, the first yielding the literal meaning and the second yielding more fully pragmatic effects. Notice that this shares with Barwise's approach, and indeed with the others mentioned at the outset of this section, the notion that literal meaning is defeasible: If you alter the situation of utterance, the literal meaning of the form will change. To use the terms of Peirce, we can summarize these approaches by saying that literality is itself the product of indexical relations between utterance tokens and contexts.

Let's look at these proposals with the help of an example. The following exchange took place in the evening in a Maya household in Oxkutzcab, Yucatán. The first speaker, a young man named Yuum, had come to visit the senior man of the household, Don Chabo. Margot, his interlocutor, was the wife of Don Chabo's oldest son, making her the senior resident woman (since Don Chabo was divorced and living alone). This exchange will be discussed in much greater detail in Chapter 7. At this point I want to focus on the expression *uy uk' ul.*

Yuum: *kul áˀ an wá dón čàabo*
'Is Don Chabo seated?'

Margot: *šén toloˀ taán uy uk' ul. šeén to ič nah oˀ*
'Go over there. He's drinking. Go over there inside.'

At the time of this utterance, Don Chabo was not actually ingesting a liquid. He was sitting in Margot's kitchen, relaxing after supper. The question is how we describe the meaning of *uy uk' ul.* It cannot be simply that the subject (Don Chabo) was actually drinking, since this was false and would be inappropriate to the context. Yet this is at least one of the literal meanings of the phrase. Another, more appropriate reading was that Don Chabo is engaged in his evening meal, which happens to be called "drinking" in local usage. That he was relaxing after the meal can be understood by saying that mealtime includes both the lead-up and relaxation after consuming.

So *uy uk' ul* could mean either "drinking" or "having supper." The solution toward which the frameworks of Barwise and Ducrot lead is to say that the properly linguistic "signification" of the form is relatively vague. It is only once we take into account the situation that a particular literal sense, or "content," arises. The question for Yuum was to grasp the relevant situation assumed by Margot in making the utterance: the ingestion of nonsolids through the mouth or participation in the diurnal eating cycle. In fact, it is highly unlikely that Yuum had to wonder what Margot was claiming when she made this assertion, since the force of the thing was transparent in context. Everything suggested that the diurnal cycle was her frame of reference: the time of day, her location in the kitchen area as she spoke, her refusal to interrupt Don Chabo. Part of what specifies this interpretation is strictly linguistic.

Margot uses the intransitive verb form *ˀuk'ul* 'drink,' not the corresponding transitive form *ˀuk'ik* 'drink it'. This is an important aspect of her knowledge of Maya, shared by Yuum, since the transitive form, which requires a direct object (what is being drunk), unambiguously has the content "ingest liquid through the mouth." So this is the form required if the speaker specifies what is being ingested.

taán uyuk'ik k'eyem 'he's drinking *pozole*'
taán uyuk'ik cafe 'he's drinking coffee'
taán uyk'ik le b'aˀ al oˀ 'he's drinking that stuff (booze)'

Whereas the intransitive form *ˀuk'ul* can be used to describe acts of ingestion involving both liquids and solids, as is the case with "supper," the transitive one requires a liquid object. So you cannot say in Maya

****taán uyuk'ik coka yetel tacos*** 'he's drinking Coke and tacos'
****taán uyuk'ik cafe yete frances*** 'he's drinking coffee and bread'

In order to read such assertions, it is necessary to imagine the subject drinking a thick substance derived by pulverizing the bread and tortilla products and mixing them into the liquids. Even so, it is unlikely by local standards that the result would be said to be "drunk."

These facts suggest that the transitive forms marked by [*-ik*] are positively specified for some feature such as [+ liquid] that must amalgamate with the object, but the intransitive form *ˀuk'ul,* with the suffix [*-ul*] instead of [*-ik*], has no such marking. The expression *taán kuy uk'ul* 'he's drinking' could be used to describe a simple act of drinking, without regard to the substance being drunk, but as a matter of fact it usually is not used this way. It usually indicates routine acts of consumption within the daily eating cycle, involving both liquids and solids. This suggests that the opposition between the two words is a privative one, with the transitive form being positively specified for the liquid object and the intransitive one being unmarked (see Figure 5.2).

In favor of this interpretation, note that there is a parallel distinction in the verb *han* 'to eat.' The transitive form, ending in [*-ik*], requires a solid object, and the intransitive form, ending in [*-al*], designates the routine event of eating the main meal at midday. Just as supper involves liquids and solids, so does the main midday meal. So if the transitive is used, the direct object has to be solid, although with the intransitive the implied object can be either solid or liquid:

taán uhanal 'he's having dinner' or 'he's eating'
taán uhàantik waàh 'he's eating tortillas'
taán uhàantik tacos 'he's eating tacos'

but not

****taán uhàantik coka yetel tacos*** 'he's eating Coke and tacos'
****taán uhàantik cafe*** 'he's eating coffee'
****taán uhàantik k'eyem*** 'he's eating *pozole*'

The upshot of these observations is that *hanal,* like *ˀuk'ul,* is the unmarked member of a privative opposition, in which the transitive form is the marked member. In order therefore to derive a specific content from the use of the intransitive verbs, a speaker must know whether the relevant situation is one of the bodily activity of ingestion or the daily activity of consumption according to local standards.

Even the bodily actions of ingestion are defined by local standards, implying a hidden indexical component in their meaning. Acts of consumption described as

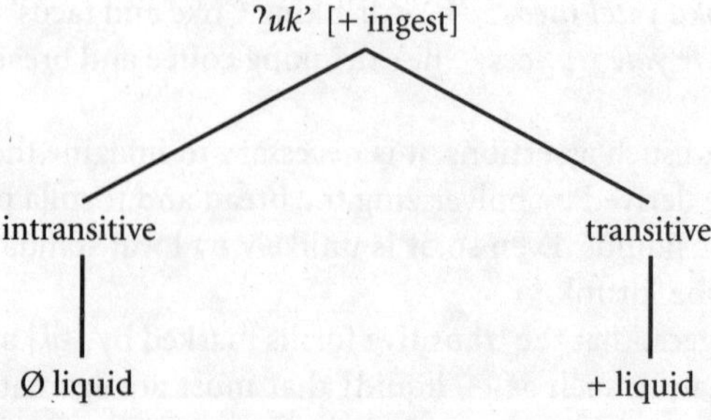

FIGURE 5.2 Semantic Structure of ˀuk' *'to drink'.*

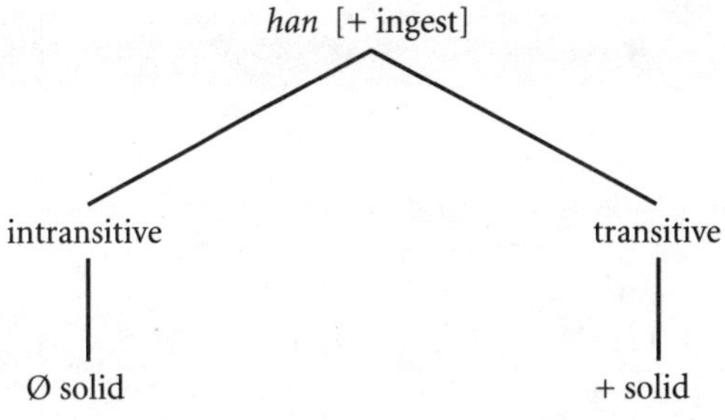

FIGURE 5.3 Semantic Structure of han *'to eat'.*

"eating" canonically involve chewing and swallowing a nutritive substance. In some cases the substance may itself be what we would call liquid and yet the action is described in Maya as eating a solid. For example, a style of black bean "soup" called *k'abaš bú'ul* is objectively the liquid broth from boiling black beans, and yet in standard Maya one "eats" it rather than "drinking" it. By contrast, "drink" canonically designates the swallowing of nonsolid substances. Yet the *pozole* that Maya farmers drink during their midmorning break from work is a thick, chunky corn gruel that requires chewing to ingest. For such cases, one would have to probe further into the classifications of food types among Maya people than we can in this context. It is likely that the roots of the division would ultimately be found in cultural understandings of the growth cycle, the symbolic values of food, hot-cold values, preparation, and place in which different foods are canonically consumed. All such elements would be unarticulated nonconstituents in Barwise's terms. They are part of the commonsense background against which exchanges like the one between Yuum and Margot was automatic and hence unreflectively intelligible.

With respect to the diurnal cycle, there are relatively clear phases to which the two intransitive verb forms correspond, as shown in Figure 5.4. These phases may figure as unarticulated nonconstituents or as articulated constituents in utterances like Margot's, depending upon how close we claim them to be to the invariant meanings of the corresponding verbs (in bold across the top). At the bottom the rough time of day is noted; in the middle, remarks indicate what activities tend to be ongoing. Notice that these periods of food consumption are separated by different kinds of engagement and that both the engagements and the foods consumed are describable in terms of being hot or cool. This dimension is of central importance for Maya people.

It is clear even in the gross schematization above that eating and drinking are complementary activities, focused on different portions of the overall round of the day. Periods associated with drinking in fact involve consumption of light

ˀuk'ul		ˀuk'ik k'eyem		hanal		ˀuk'ul	
Between rest and work: consume hot liquid, light food. Dip food in drink.		Rest during work: mix and drink cool *pozole* at worksite.		Rest after work: cool off, sit at table in home. Food, prepared by female, with hot dish and cool drink. Relax after eating.		Rest after work. Light meal with warm beverage, bread dipped in beverage.	
	HEAVY LABOR (hot)		HEAVY LABOR (hot)		LIGHT LABOR (cool)		SLEEP
Early Morning		Midmorning		Afternoon		Evening	

FIGURE 5.4 Mayan Daily Work and Food Consumption Schedule.

solid foods, but their nutritional value is less than that of the foods consumed at midday. Interestingly, "drinking" in this sense is associated with warm beverages, in which the solid foods (bread or tortillas) are dipped. Although the midmorning break and consumption of *k'eyem* (*pozole*) is an act of drinking, it is a specific one, with a particular object. It is inappropriate in contemporary Maya to describe this as simply *ˀuk'ul*, even though *pozole* is drunk. The implication is that *ˀuk'ul* 'drinking' in the intransitive describes consumption on the periphery in the food cycle.

Notice that both the midday meal and the two peripheral meals typically involve consuming both liquids and solids, though the relation between them is inverted. So in the *ˀuk'ul* 'drinking' cases, the liquid is typically hot, not cold (i.e., coffee, hot chocolate, hot milk, or, rarely, *atole*, a kind of thin, cooked corn beverage), and the bread (tortillas or French-style white) is dipped in it. The resulting meal is a balance of hot and cold in which the alignment is

hot : liquid :: cool : solid

At this phase the human body is itself in a state of relative coolness. (It is common sense for Maya people that one is in a cool state upon first awakening in the morning and after relaxing, before bed.) By midday, in contrast, the body is understood to be in a relatively hotter state due to the action of intense labor and the shining of the sun. The rough time of the midday meal is from 2:00 to 3:00 in the afternoon, the period of peak heat. Men return to their homes and relax before eating. Women rarely eat with the men, although they may follow immediately after. At this time women are usually considered to be in a state of intense heat because of their proximity to the cooking fire and the heating of the tortillas. At this meal the beverage, if there is one, is always cool, and the main meal is considered warm (even if it is in fact tepid, it will have been cooked food, served from the pan in which it is cooked). Thus the alignment is roughly

hot : solid :: cool : liquid

Thus we could say that the two verbs *ˀuk'ul* 'drinking' and *hanal* 'eating' get their specific meanings from their relation to the daily round of work, relaxation, and social food consumption. However, they focus on different portions of the daily routine. This background is immediately relevant to Yuum's understanding of Margot's utterance, which is highly automatized in the Praguean sense. Also, as the Praguean concept of functional differentiation suggests, this everyday exchange displays considerable context-dependency. To summarize, then, the aspects of the diurnal frame that were made understood when Margot told Yuum that Don Chabo was "drinking" included the following: Don Chabo was sitting in a customary place; relaxing and conversing with other coresidents; being attended to by a woman (Margot) currently occupying the female sphere of the kitchen; and consuming a meal that was warm and relatively light, its centerpiece a bever-

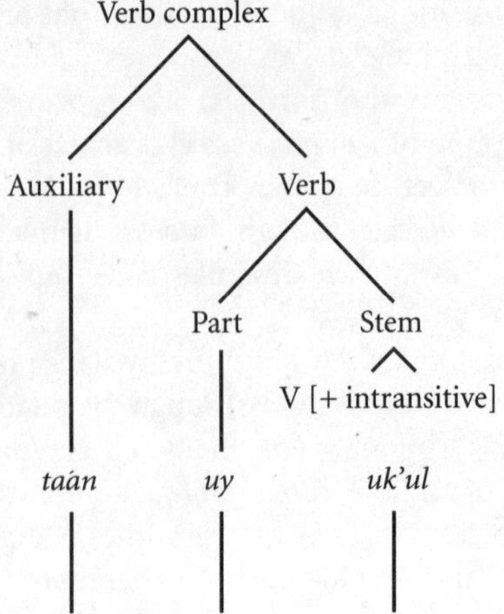

Level 1: Signification [progressive [other (x,i) [+ ingest Ø liquid]]]

Level 2: Literal content [drinking/margins of day [he (i) now (i)]]

Level 3: Conveyed sense Don Chabo is having supper. He will not be interrupted. Go wait.

FIGURE 5.5 Three Levels of Analysis of taán uy uk'ul *'he is drinking'.*

age, on the margins of the workday (i.e., after the main labor of the day), in transition to rest.

Given this relatively rich background knowledge, we can describe the semantic content of Margot's utterance *taán uy uk'ul* 'he's drinking' roughly in terms of three levels of analysis, diagrammed in Figure 5.5. At the simplest and most sparse level of semantic representation is the "signification" of the linguistic forms uttered. This much inheres in the forms and their syntactic structure. Note that it is too underspecified to make a proposition. In particular, the unmarked term *ˀuk'ul* 'drink' can be read as either ingesting a liquid (irrespective of time of day) or as the social activity of eating on the margins of the workday. The third person pronoun indicates reference to some other relative to the indexical frame of utterance, but as yet it has no specific referent, as indicated by the (x). At the second level, this sparse linguistic signification is fleshed out with the circumstantial information that the relevant activity frame is the margins of the day, the time of the utterance, and that the subject of the activity is a specific individual in the discourse context, namely, the same person mentioned in Yuum's immediately preceding question. That is, the Ø features from level 1 are specified in light of the temporal and activity setting, and the indexical ground, marked by (i) at level 1, is filled in with the particular personal and temporal reference (Don Chabo, at this time of day).

At level 3 the pragmatic force of the utterance is filled in by inferences and the side effects of making this utterance under these circumstances. These include its value as a negative response to Yuum's implicit request for an audience with the man. Moreover, the myriad background facts that form part of the diurnal cycle are available, including the understanding that supper lasts beyond the time in which food and drink are actually consumed, the justification for Margot's refusing Yuum the chance to see her father-in-law at this time, and the relation between her home and her father-in-law's.

Conclusion

If this brief analysis goes in the right direction, then the literal meaning of Margot's utterance has everything to do with the time of day at which she uttered it, as defined by the routine activities of people like herself. It also depends to a degree on the other simultaneous acts she accomplished in the saying. This has the effect of making literal meaning dependent upon the context of utterance. Furthermore, the process of meaning construction at the utterance level involves a whole range of factors that have a different status from formal features, that have to do with how Maya speakers engage with and experience their social world. Austin's framework led to a progressive expansion of the scope of grammar, as speech acts were assimilated to the conventional meanings of form. Grice's implicatures provided a way of simplifying the semantics by linking it to logic and treating conversational inferences as the pragmatic side effects of using forms with literal meanings in context. The Prague School theorists in turn introduced the concepts of functional differentiation and the differential focus of utterances of aspects of speech setting. Their approach linked linguistic meaning still more closely to utterance context. Finally, contextualized approaches to semantics take the next logical step of arguing that literal meaning itself is derived from the intersection of linguistic form with context. In the next chapter we explore three phenomenological frameworks for describing language. Among the features they share is a fundamental rejection of the separation between language the system and the field of human activities. Although the vocabulary and philosophical backdrop is thoroughly nonformalist (if not antiformalist), the focus on meaning in context builds conceptually on the developments explored in this chapter.

Further Readings

The Use of Form, the Overlay of Context

Austin, J. L. *How to Do Things with Words.* Cambridge: Harvard University Press, 1962.

DuBois, J. "Meaning Without Intention: Lessons from Divination." In *Responsibility and Evidence in Oral Discourse,* edited by J. H. Hill and J. T. Irvine. Cambridge: Cambridge University Press, 1993, pp. 48–71.

Garver, N. "Varieties of Use and Mention." *Philosophy and Phenomenological Research* 26 (1965):230–238.

Grice, H. P. "Meaning." In *Semantics: An Interdisciplinary Reader in Philosophy, Linguistics, and Psychology,* edited by D. Steinberg and L. Jakobovits. Cambridge: Cambridge University Press, 1971, pp. 53–60.

Harman, G. "Three Levels of Meaning." In *Semantics: An Interdisciplinary Reader in Philosophy, Linguistics, and Psychology,* edited by D. Steinberg and L. Jakobovits. Cambridge: Cambridge University Press, 1971, pp. 66–76.

Levinson, S. *Pragmatics.* Cambridge: Cambridge University Press, 1983. Chap. 1, pp. 1–53; chap. 3, pp. 97–166; chap. 5, pp. 226–284.

Lyons, J. *Semantics,* vol. 1. Cambridge: Cambridge University Press, 1977. Chaps. 1.2–1.4, 1.6, 2, 3.1–3.4.

Newmeyer, F. *Grammatical Theory: Its Limits and Its Possibilities.* Chicago: University of Chicago Press, 1983, pp. 48–73.

Searle, J. "What Is a Speech Act?" In *Language and Social Context,* edited by P. P. Giglioli. Harmondsworth, England: Penguin, 1972, pp. 136–154.

———. *Speech Acts: An Essay in the Philosophy of Language.* Cambridge: Cambridge University Press, 1976, chap. 2, "Expressions, Meaning and Speech Acts," pp. 22–53.

Prague School Functionalism

Bühler, K. *Sprachtheorie: Die Darstellungsfunktion der Sprache.* Stuttgart: Gustav Fischer Verlag, 1982.

Havránek, B. "The Functional Differentiation of the Standard Language." In *A Prague School Reader on Esthetics, Literary Structure, and Style,* edited and translated by P. L. Garvin. Washington, DC: Georgetown University Press, 1964, pp. 3–16.

Jakobson, R. "Linguistics in Relation to Other Sciences." In *Selected Writings of Roman Jakobson, vol 2.* The Hague: Mouton, 1971, pp. 655–696.

———. "Parts and Wholes in Language." In *Selected Writings of Roman Jakobson, vol 2.* The Hague: Mouton, 1971, pp. 280–284.

Mukarovsky, J. "Standard Language and Poetic Language." In *A Prague School Reader on Esthetics, Literary Structure, and Style,* edited and translated by P. L. Garvin. Washington, DC: Georgetown University Press, 1964, pp. 17–30.

———. "Structuralism in Esthetics and Literary Studies." In *The Prague School: Selected Writings,* edited by P. Steiner. Austin: University of Texas Press, 1982 [1941], pp. 65–82.

Trubetzkoy, N. *Principles of Phonology.* Translated by C.A.M. Baltaxe. Berkeley: University of California Press, 1969.

Context Dependency of Literal Meaning

Barwise, J. "On the Circumstantial Relation Between Meaning and Content." In *Meaning and Mental Representations,* edited by U. Eco et al. Bloomington: Indiana University Press, 1988, pp. 23–40.

Coleman, L., and Kay, P. "Prototype Semantics: The English Verb *Lie.*" *Language* 57(1) (1981):26–44.

Ducrot, O. "La Description sémantique en linguistique." In *Le Dire et le dit.* Paris: Editions de Minuit, 1984, pp. 47–66.

———. "Structuralism, énnonciation et sémantique." In *Le Dire et le dit.* Paris: Editions de Minuit, 1984, pp. 67–94.

Fillmore, C. "Frames and the Semantics of Understanding." *Quaderni di semantica* 6(2) (1985):222–254.

Goffman, E. "The Neglected Situation." In *Language and Social Context,* edited by P. P. Giglioli. Harmondsworth, England: Penguin, 1972, pp. 61–66.

Gumperz, J. "Contextualization and Understanding." In *Rethinking Context: Language as an Interactive Phenomenon,* edited by A. Duranti and C. Goodwin. Cambridge: Cambridge University Press, 1992. Chap 8, pp. 229–252.

Lakoff, G. "Cognitive Semantics." In *Meaning and Mental Representations,* edited by U. Eco et al. Bloomington: Indiana University Press, 1988, pp. 119–154.

Rommetveit, R. *On Message Structure: A Framework for the Study of Language and Communication.* New York: Wiley, 1974. Chaps. 1–3, pp. 1–28; chap. 5, "On Message Structure," pp. 87–123.

Voloshinov, V. N. *Marxism and the Philosophy of Language.* Translated by L. Matejka and I. R. Titunik. Cambridge: Harvard University Press, 1986 [1929]. Chap. 2, "Language, Speech and Utterance," pp. 65–82.

Chapter 6

Three Phenomenologies of Language

MOST FORMALIST APPROACHES TO LANGUAGE, from Saussure through Chomsky, posit a dichotomy between language and the extralinguistic world to which language refers. In the case of Saussure, we confront a series of dichotomies whose joint effect is to so isolate the system of language from the real-world objects of reference as to make reference itself somewhat mysterious. In fact, if we take seriously the arbitrariness thesis, the steadfastly mental ground of *valeur,* and the divide between *langue* and *parole,* there is a real question how reference in context ever takes place. Recall in the same vein the clarity with which this division is stated in Chomsky's early writings and maintained in subsequent transformational approaches to semantics: Knowledge of language was taken to be inherently distinct from knowledge of the world. Although Bloomfield's commitment to behaviorism clouded the issue, his description of grammatical form makes clear that he held linguistic structure to be part of a system of language whose properties could be (indeed had to be) studied apart from the stimulus-response chains in which utterances came to be subjectively meaningful for individual speakers. Thus there is a tradition in linguistics of theorizing language as something intrinsically different from every other aspect of human experience.

One semantic corollary of this inherent difference is the opposition between designation and denotation. The former is a linguistic category defining the class of object to which an expression refers as a semantic type. For instance, the designation of "table" is the class of all horizontal surfaces, suspended or supported, produced or used by humans for placing objects, such as the kitchen table, the dining room table, and the coffee table. Similarly, "paper" designates the flat, dry pulp product used for wrapping, writing, and printing, such as the daily paper, wax paper, and the dollar bill. Opposed to this level of generality are the myriad objects speakers use these terms to denote on given occasions: the *Tribune* of March 28, the sheet in which I wrapped my sandwich yesterday, and the slightly shredded dollar bill in my wallet right now. In a sense, denotation is a matter of indexical specificity and designation of symbolic generality. This basic division ramifics throughout pragmatics as well, as we saw in Chapter 5. The notion that utterances can be decomposed into the components of sense and illocutionary and perlocutionary force is another way of projecting it, for sense and encoded illocutionary force, like designation, belong to language, whereas the situationally specific perlocutions that an utterance may engender belong to the world in which speech acts transpire. The Gricean approach to inference further enshrines the division by distinguishing the literal meaning of an utterance from its implicatures. The former belongs to language as a code and the latter to conversation as an activity informed by nonlinguistic maxims of rational behavior.

But this way of distinguishing language and knowledge of language from the world and our ways of knowing it is itself a historical product. It is equally plausible to assert that language and the world are everywhere interconnected, that any sheer dichotomy between the two is condemned to distort both, whether it is advanced with the aim of securing a distinct place for language among the facts of human existence or to preserve the possibility of a scientific understanding of objective reality. Knowledge of language can be seen also as thoroughly interpenetrated with knowledge of the world. This is a new starting point, foreign to the formalist tradition. Yet it is, in effect, what Voloshinov and Rommetveit argued. It is also one of the common elements in the work of phenomenologists.

When we call into question the ontological distinction between language and the world and the epistemological one between knowledge of language and knowledge of the world, we are by implication questioning the division between types and tokens. This may explain why phenomenology has been virtually ignored by modern formalists and why Prague School functionalism, which integrated phenomenology from the beginning, was for many years marginalized by formal linguistics. For tokens have always been recognized to pose problems of connectedness to nonlinguistic context. *Parole* and performance have always been viewed as belonging to the world, a sort of patchwork of heterogeneous, accidental facts, ever since they were named. The oppositions between *langue* and *parole* as between competence and performance are asymmetric, since it is the first term in each pair that is taken to motivate the second. It was because of the units of *langue* that *parole* could be meaningful and because of speakers' competence in the grammar of their language that their performance could make sense despite its eclectic, degenerate character. In other words, tokens are meaningful just insofar as they instantiate types. Or so it looked.

Language as speech is part of the world, a social activity on a par with others. In this respect, words don't stand for something apart any more than my fingers stand for my arms or the print stands for the paper on which it is impressed. Utterances are of a piece with the "outer world," and so are the formal features of which they are made up. If we accept the division between the two orders as a privileged starting point, then we are led inevitably to search for an underlying signification lodged within language, by which it corresponds to an external reality. This, roughly, is the project of traditional linguistic semantics. By contrast, if we start from the codependence between the two, then we are led to search for the common elements and pathways by which they communicate. We can see this search already in recent cognitive and indexical versions of semantics, in which the circumstances of utterances play a key role in determining even the literal meaning of expressions.

Hence situation semantics takes as its point of departure the combination of speech circumstances with linguistic content in producing literal meaning, and cognitive theories posit a conceptual level at which active minds produce literal meaning based on the "instructions" of linguistic form. For our purposes, both of these frameworks are excessively limited, the former by an oversimplified theory of "circumstance" and the latter by an overemphasis on individual speakers and cognitive representations. These are holdovers from formalism. Still, they take the crucial step of opening up the domain of literal meaning to include factors beyond the strictly linguistic. In this way they break from the formalist traditions of strict division between sense and reference, intension and extension, sense and force, designation and denotation. They say, in effect, that the capacity of verbal expressions to refer to and describe the world is *a function of the combination* of abstract senselike components with human contexts. Taken out of context, sense is too vague to be literal. Meaning then emerges as the product of utterances combining with contexts, not the mere instantiation of types in a series of identical tokens.

This relational perspective struggling to emerge indicates that there are many factors that come between language forms and reality. These include the immediate social setting of speech, the cultural and ideological values that participants bring to interaction, their cognitive activities, and particular projects. To posit a dichotomy between language and the world is erroneous because it ignores these mediating factors. The more productive challenge from our perspective is to find a way of systematically describing the social embeddedness of language. We already have some clues.

The Peircean concepts of iconicity and indexicality both presuppose a sociocultural framework in order to be applicable to actual language phenomena. The reason is that resemblance and contiguity, the underlying relations that define the terms, are always relative to local criteria. What counts as resemblance can be defined only relative to a standard of difference and similarity. We saw this in Chapter 3. The same applies to contiguity. From a sufficiently detached perspective, we might say that all things that coexist are contiguous, but natural language indexicals never work this way: They always link up with contexts whose dimensions are defined simultaneously by language and other modes of engagement. In order to fix the objects of indexes we must rely upon definitions of the speech event, the interactive situation, and the framework beyond the indexical token itself. Similarly, we can accept with modern linguistics the premise that syntax is the repository of pure form, belonging to the system of grammar. But semantics and pragmatics require a more relational approach, as Voloshinov and Rommetveit argued. Recall from Chapter 5 the trajectory from pragmatics based on abstract intensional meaning through the cognitive and situational approaches to sense as the product of language-context relations. Moreover, language is an expressive medium far richer than the functions of description and reference. Through speech, actors continually reach beyond themselves and the preestablished forms of language to create meanings that were not there before. Functional linguists, starting with the Prague School, have proposed various theories to describe this, distinguishing, for instance, how utterances express the subjective attitudes of a speaker (the so-called expressive function), how they create a relation of mutual attentiveness between interlocutors (phatic function), how they serve to orient attention (directive function), and so forth. The point is that in the overall range of linguistic usage, only certain kinds of utterances involve correspondences between words and things that exist apart from them.

Even in the case of referring, language does more than just point to things outside itself. As surely as it corresponds to the world, speech helps to create it through objectification. This is so for everyday conversation, where people reproduce objects like newspapers and tables through the terms of their references, or the way that social theory objectifies its subjects. In contemporary theory the concept of objectification tends to have a negative loading, standing for a way of treating people and processes as if they were things. But in the more properly analytic sense, every time language stands for something, it stands for it *as its object.* To put it strongly, we *always* objectify, without which we could not make reference. One corollary of this observation is that although speech as sound may be ephemeral, its objective products are not. The world as we live it is populated by innumerable objects produced by the action of innumerable utterances. Even if we could sort through all these sedimented objects and decide which ones are real things and which ones merely the spin-offs of talk, little would be gained by way of understanding language. The fact would remain that language is part of what makes the world.

The phenomenologists have a special place in our emerging discussion because they start from the interconnection of language and human experience. That is, they provide a contradictory response to the challenge of formal dichotomies between inner form and the language-external world. For our purposes, they shift the focus from conventional systems to speech as something primary in itself. In order to illustrate phenomenological approaches and their potential contribution to the study of linguistic practice, we will briefly review three thinkers, Roman Ingarden, Alfred Schutz, and Maurice Merleau-Ponty. Although they differ in emphasis and on certain points of analysis, they share a set of premises that jointly define them as representatives of phenomenology. The premises are the following:

1. The study of speech tokens is something distinct from and irreducible to the study of linguistic or symbolic types.
2. Linguistic meaning is inherently indeterminate or underspecified with respect to the experienced meanings of utterances.

3. In the production of meaning, silence and the tacit dimension play as great a role as—if not an even greater role than—does articulate speech.
4. The proper unit of description is not the sentence but rather the utterance. This may involve formal units of greater or lesser scope than the sentence.
5. Understanding is not a matter of recognizing the forms used in an utterance but of producing meaning based on linguistic and nonlinguistic dimensions of experience.
6. Meaning is historically specific, not subsumable under universals of grammar.

Expanding from these common concerns, Ingarden, Schutz, and Merleau-Ponty focus on three different aspects of experience, with three corresponding sets of implications for our approach to language. Ingarden constructed a theory of artistic works, essentially a theory of discourse semantics, along with a model of how discourse is interpreted by its readers. His framework was to become the basis for reader reception theory in literary criticism and resonates with recent semantic frameworks based on cognitive and situational dimensions. Schutz proposed an encompassing theory of human interaction, an interactive pragmatics in which speech activities mediate among the actor's consciousness, the world as known, and other people. Although Schutz wrote about a variety of social relationships, his work has been most influential in terms of face-to-face interaction and the articulation of utterances with gestures. His framework was to provide the basis for interpretive sociology and especially ethnomethodology (see Chapter 9). Merleau-Ponty built his approach to language upon his analyses of meaning production in the phenomenal field of experience. His work has had relatively little impact on studies of language but is fundamental to theorizing the sphere of contiguity for indexical relations, what he calls the phenomenal field, and especially the body (a theme treated at length in Chapter 11).

In general, both Ingarden and Schutz accord language a central place in their overall projects, whereas Schutz and Merleau-Ponty accord the body a more central place than does Ingarden. One salient limitation of all three frameworks, from an anthropological perspective, is that they focus on individual experience, paying relatively little attention to the social world apart from the ways that individuals experience it. In Part 3 of this book we return to this theme and attempt to adapt several key phenomenological concepts to a more thoroughly social description of communicative practice.

Ingarden: Incompleteness and Concretization

Ingarden was a student of Edmund Husserl between 1912 and 1918 in Göttingen and later at Freiburg, Germany, and the two corresponded throughout Husserl's lifetime. He was also the first nonpositivist to write a critical piece about the Vienna Circle's principle of verification, that is, the idea that the meaning of a concept is equivalent to the method by which its truth could be verified (Spiegelberg 1960:229). His writing in general is marked by analytic precision and clarity, reflecting his training in Polish analytic philosophy, and by a deep commitment to understanding things in the world as a logical prerequisite to understanding how these things are constituted in experience. Thus his early work *The Literary Work of Art* was followed by *The Cognition of the Literary Work of Art,* in which he reanalyzed the literary text from the perspective of its interpretation by a reader (or, more generally, from the perspective of its reception by a cognizing public). In the first book he was concerned to locate the distinctive properties of literary works, as opposed to other kinds of works (scientific, everyday, confessional, etc.). For our purposes, we read him for an approach to verbal discourse more generally, without limiting ourselves to any category or genre such as "literature." This is not to deny that such a category may be definable nor to obliterate all distinctions among genres but rather to leave open the possibility that Ingarden has put his finger on phenomena of much broader scope than Western literature as he knew it.

Literary works are part of the real world, but what kind of thing are they? Ingarden starts his book by rejecting two obvious responses. A work is not entirely physical: A novel obviously transcends the paper and ink in which it is embodied. Nor is it psychological: It cannot be equated with the individual psychological processes of the people who read it. Both alternatives are reductionist in the strong sense of denying that the work has an inherent structure and organization of its own. Where would the physicalist look for meaning, and how would the psychologist explain the constant identity of the work across greatly varied readerships? The third alternative that Ingarden proposes is to treat works as purely intentional structures, as if they were endowed with a meaning content toward which they are directed—irrespective of whether they correspond to real physical things, to unicornlike fictions, or to sheer conceptual relations like the inferences of the detective in a mystery novel.[1] We can think of the intentional object as a sort of target toward which the meaningful expression projects, like an arc or vector: "expression" ⟶ object. Like Peirce's "standing for" relation, this one is asymmetric in that the sign stands for (intentionally projects) its object, not the other way around. Unlike the Peircean concept, which could apply to natural relations like smoke standing for fire and movement of leaves standing for wind, an intentional structure is the work of human cognition. Hence "intentionality" is linked to human thought and intention as well as to the sign-object relation.

The target or intentional object of a verbal expression transcends the utterance in two senses: Objects are repeatable and can be targeted by various expressions, and any object can be presented under indefinitely many aspects. So when Jack

---

[1]Ingarden's use of the term "intentional" appears to follow Husserl's usage, which was derived in turn from Franz Brentano's theory of intentionality.

asks "D'the paper come today?" he uses the expression "the paper" to refer to the *New York Times.* The "object" of his utterance is the newspaper of that day—not the actual thing on the kitchen table, but anything that fits the description in this context, that is, any copy of the morning *Times* from that day. Imagine that Jack continued to talk and think about the paper that morning, using the same expression in utterances like "The paper was all wet this morning," "The paper had a gruesome picture on page one," or "You take the paper, I'll read the Cheerios box," and so forth. This amounts to repeating the identical intentional object in a series of different individual acts. Or instead imagine that he had referred to the *Times* that morning as "the *Times,* "the daily rag," or "New York's largest daily." This would then show that the same intentional object can be referred to and described under various aspects. Notice that the constancy of the intentional object does not depend upon the material thing to which Jack is referring. It would still remain constant in these examples even if it turned out that there was no paper that day, or the *Tribune* was delivered mistakenly instead of the *Times.* Just as the object can be repeated an infinite number of times, so, too, there are indefinitely many aspects under which it could be individuated.

This notion of an "intentional object" has direct consequences for how Ingarden describes verbal discourse. As much as any other single factor, it is the basis of his semantics. Notice that the "object" is neither the designation nor the denotation of the phrase, if we take these terms in their original meanings. We would not want to say that the constant designation of "the paper" in English is the "*New York Times* of September 19, 1993." This content arises only in the context of Jack's utterance, which happened to take place on that day at that time. It is too particular to be a designation. And yet it is not the denotation either, if by this we mean the actual object to which Jack referred—the one copy of the *Times* that was destined to be delivered to their home. Somewhere in between the two is a level of meaning that is contextual and yet also inherent in the intentional structure of the utterance. This level stands apart from the supposed duality of words with dictionary meanings and things with objective properties. Moreover, because intentional objects are repeatable and describable under multiple aspects, they always somehow exceed the terms by which they are projected. No single expression can totally fix the object because it exists as a system of relations to indefinitely many potential contexts. Think of all the ways you could make unique reference to the daily newspaper. This open-endedness is the root of what will become Ingarden's provocative notion of "blank spots of indeterminacy."

A single work, like a novel or short story, naturally corresponds to many intentional objects, not to a single one. Works are internally complex in the sense of being built up of several "strata" or levels (sound structure and meaningful units), and Ingarden treats each individual element at each level as inherently intentional. This results in a multitude of intentional objects, all interrelated according to the unfolding structure of the discourse. Coming from a linguistic perspective, this is like saying that any discourse that is built up out of sentences is, quite naturally, structured at several levels (phonology, morphology, syntax, semantics, pragmatics). But it is unlike linguistics in making the claim that every unit at each level is intentionally meaningful. Ingarden's levels therefore differ from the standard linguistic ones, and yet they provide a powerful metalanguage in which to describe discourse. Before we explore what he calls the "basic structure" common to all literary works, we should ask one more initial question: What does *not* belong to the work? The author as an individual, the attributes and psychic and emotional states of the reader, and the entire world of objects and states of affairs that may serve as the model for the work—these three spheres of facts are excluded and taken to exist apart from the work (Ingarden 1973:22). The city of Rome, as he says, is not part of a novel that happens to be set there, nor am I part of the novel I read. Thus Ingarden starts from a strong insistence on the irreducibility of the literary fact. This is not unlike Chomsky's grammar or Saussure's claim of the irreducibility of *langue.* They differ on where they peg the irreducible core, but not on irreducibility as such. Ingarden is saying that literary forms are deeply systematic. This runs counter to Saussure's *parole* as chaos, and it posits structure at a level far beyond the sentence, the highest unit of traditional grammar.

Ingarden (1973:30) distinguishes four basic strata in literary works: (1) word sounds and phonetic formations of higher order; (2) meaning units at various orders from minimal to maximal units of form; (3) schematized aspects; (4) objects represented (i.e., intentional objects; see Ingarden 1973:117ff). Of these, we will be most concerned here with the first two. These strata differ from one another in their characteristic material (phonic, conceptual, etc.) and in the role each plays in relation to the whole (Ingarden 1973:29). In addition to its strata, any work also has a beginning and an end, which jointly define a longitudinal or sequential structure apart from the strata. The overall work is then a "polyphonous construction" (1973:58) to which every separate element contributes its own voice. Ingarden insists that the dynamics of literary and discourse form be studied from the perspective of the interactions among elements, not from any single component.

The treatment of the sound stratum shows important differences from grammatical approaches to phonology. In a Saussurian framework, sounds contribute to meaning only by providing the vehicles for expressing difference. A phoneme, say, "t," can distinguish among lexical items but has no positive meaning of its own. It can have no intentional object apart from that of the word to which it belongs, say, "tébl" 'table'. For Ingarden, the sound stratum of a work *does* have intentional objects, however. He speaks of rhythm, pacing, prosodic contour, and sound formations of long stretches of discourse. Each of these contributes "irreducibly" to the whole (1973:56). And yet the superabundance of meaning that Ingarden derives from sound is not a matter of casting about in the wilds of *parole.* It is more systematic and abstract, much like Saussure's acoustic image was. For both, the word (signifier) corresponds to a stable phonological type that is realized by actual acoustic material in speech production. The key difference is the range of meaning to which this unit corresponds. Whereas Saussure's signified element, like the semantic units in modern theories, is restricted to referential-descriptive meaning, Ingarden is concerned with a much broader range of signification.

In a living language, as opposed to a dead one, word sounds hold in a state of readiness aspects of the objects that the word intends. Thus in understanding the word sound "tébl," we draw both on the history of our use of the word and our experience with the kind of object for which it stands. Here Ingarden is pointing out that the objects picked out by words in a literary work are usually ones with which we have prior experience. In the little vignette in which Jack asks Natalia "D'the paper come today?" and she responds "It's right on the table," the word "table" holds in ready aspects such as "locus of eating," certain likely dimensions, certain probable range of materials, and so forth. Drawing on this horizon, we can grasp the object +table+ in a sort of intuitive fullness upon hearing the sound (I adopt the notation+——+ for intentional objects, as opposed to semantic features and things). Thus what Ingarden puts in the place of the Saussurian signified is the network of aspects that define the intentional object, not only a single distinctive "idea." This is related to his rejection of the arbitrariness thesis as well (1973:59).

Ingarden distinguishes five components in the meaning of words (1973:63), but for our purposes it is his discussion of actual versus potential meaning that is most important (1973:84ff). The actual meaning of an expression is the aspect of the intentional object that it actualizes. For instance, the expression "the table" in our scenario corresponds to an intentional object that could be alternatively described in terms of its material, color, size, location, use, and so forth. But of all this, the noun phrase focuses particularly on the geometry of the thing—roughly flat, at a height suitable for human use, made of a material sufficiently rigid to support everyday objects. These are the aspects that make up the qualitative meaning of "table"; they are its actual meaning. It also has a potential stock of meaning. This is obviously broader than the actual, and indeed can never be fully realized because description is finite, but meaning potential is not. For "table," the potential stock would include all those other features that we can reconstruct about +tables+, and especially ones likely to be in a kitchen. The potential stock serves as a horizon of alternative aspects that are apart from the specific meaning of a word yet held in ready by it.

Ingarden distinguishes two kinds of potential meaning according to how close they are to actual meaning. Merely potential meanings associated with "table" would include things like the assumptions that a table is manmade, designed to stand upright, supported by its legs, subject to gravity, planar in shape rather than a solid mass. The list would go on as long as we could think of aspects of the conceptual object that provide alternative portrayals and draw on further background meanings. But this open-ended list is a space of unweighted possibilities and at some point drifts off into irrelevance. Potential meanings that are "almost actualized" are different because they are much closer to the meanings of the words and correspondingly closer to probable meanings rather than merely possible ones. In the example of Jack and Natalia, these include things like the aspects clustered around the location of the table in question in the dining room, its probable use for eating, and its likely size for use by a single household. None of these things were stated in so many words, but they are readily available. They are what Ingarden considered the zone of potential most closely surrounding actual meaning. Using linguistic terms, we would be likely to describe these as the readily inferable features of the referent of "table" in this discourse context, as opposed to merely imaginable ones. In all cases Ingarden insists that potential meaning cannot be actualized without reference to the discourse context. That is, it remains indeterminate if cut away from the context of other words.[2]

The discrepancy between actual and potential meaning becomes the basis of what Ingarden calls "blank spots in description" (1973:205). Given only the description of Jack and Natalia's exchange about the morning newspaper, we fill in various unstated aspects, relying on our grasp of potential meaning and the objects represented. Blank spots are simply the result of the inherent partiality of description. It is strictly impossible to recount every object in an event such that no leaps would be required in order to fill in the connections. On the contrary, through description a literary work builds up an encompassing frame of reference in which these blank spots can be filled in according to a coherent whole. It is important to recall that for Ingarden the presence of blank spots was unavoidable and related to the fact that discourse represents objects only as schematic constructs. Ultimately, he defines the schematic aspects of meaning, both at the level of words and larger discourse, as "a structure of infinitely many spots of indeterminacy" (1973:250).

His definition, then, raises questions regarding which blank spots can be filled in and which not (1973:252), how far one goes in filling them in, and how different types of work require different levels of engagement in realizing meaning potential. It is obvious, for instance, that we read newspaper headlines and recipe instructions differently from the sentences in a poem or novel. Among the salient differences in our approaches would be (1) the degree to which one expands on the schematic structure to derive an expanded interpretation; (2) the range of contexts to which one refers in deriving the expanded understanding; (3) the degree to which one attempts to ascertain authorial intent; (4) the degree to which the interpretive process reflects the relatively unconscious, habituated patterns of interpretation characteristic of the historical era in which the reading takes place; and (5) the kind and level of self-consciousness with which one checks one's reading against textual form and standards of interpretation. Compare the three sentences

1. Shake well before using. (on the back of a can of spray paint)
2. D'the paper come today? (in our opening scenario)

---

[2]He goes on to distinguish a gradience between actual meaning and potential meaning, with co-given meanings and ones held in readiness coming between the two extremes (1973:265ff).

3. Among twenty snowy mountains, the only moving thing was the eye of a blackbird. (the opening line in Wallace Stevens's poem "Thirteen Ways of Looking at a Blackbird")

Each of these is incomplete in Ingarden's sense, and each requires of the reader/addressee the effort of interpretation. Yet the interpretations proceed quite differently and to a different level of understanding, according to the purposes and relevant context of reception. The instructions can be read and followed in an instant, taking account of the unmentioned spray paint can itself and the assumed use of the paint. The question fits into its own morning scenario, in which a specific range of the potential meanings of the words is actualized. The poem, itself a meditation on the blackbird as an intentional object, provokes a more reflective reading in which we extend potential, entering into the world of the blackbird and the cadence of the verse. Ingarden helps us to understand these different ways of reading as a function of different kinds of text and distinct modes of reception. Thus the kind and organization of indeterminacy becomes a crucial feature in the identity of the work. As Ingarden puts it:

> This schematic structure of represented objects cannot be removed in any finite literary work, even though in the course of the work, new spots of indeterminacy may continually be filled out and hence removed through the completion of newer, positively projected properties. We can say that, with regard to the determination of the objectivities represented within it, every literary work is in principle incomplete and always in need of further supplementation. In terms of the text, however, this supplementation can never be completed. (1973:251)

The interplay between indeterminacy and intentional projection leads Ingarden to distinguish the literary work as a relatively abstract structure from the concretization of the work in some actual understanding of it. Concretization is the process whereby the work as a meaning potential is actualized in human understanding and the blank spots are at least partly filled in. By "understanding," Ingarden does not mean the psychology of interpretation but the social reception of the work. The key difference is that a work in the abstract is a potential, with many more blank spots and indeterminacies than the same work in the context of its actual concretization. When actualized, potential meanings interact with one another, and the order of phrases in the work is transformed into real temporal asymmetries (i.e., it takes time to read a book or process an utterance). The meaningfulness of a concretized work is therefore distinct from that of the same work in the abstract (1973:337–353). For one thing, the work as potential usually goes far beyond what is actualized in any specific reception of it.

Schutz: Typification and the Meaning of Interaction

Schutz in a sense picks up where Ingarden leaves off. He also paid a great deal of attention to the stock of background knowledge, as this defines a range of potential meanings that interactants draw on in understanding one another. But unlike Ingarden, whose focus was the structure of discourse works, Schutz investigated the dynamics of human interaction and the organization of background knowledge in the total context of what he called the "life world" (*Lebenswelt*). He studied spoken language in the context of common sense, not written text in the context of literary reception. He combined Husserl's phenomenology with Max Weber's theory of social action to produce a phenomenology of the social world, centered on modes of interaction and meaning production among members of various kinds of social relationships. As part of this, Schutz explored how actors orient themselves toward prospective ends (which he called "in-order-to motives"), on the basis of past and present experiences (which he called "because motives"). He tried to explain how interactants come to understand one another and orient themselves to each other by dovetailing their respective motives. Schutz is much more concerned with "intention" in the sense of actors' projected goals, whereas Ingarden treated intentionality in the more abstract sense of how signs stand for objects. In this section we concentrate on three features of Schutz's approach, what he calls the stock of knowledge, typification, and relevance. These three link his writings to those of Ingarden and add several more features to our understanding of the meaning of utterance tokens.

The Stock of Knowledge

The stock of knowledge is a background of ready-made meanings that are socially distributed among members of a language community. It is the stuff of common sense, which is never truly common, but instead differs according to one's social identity and experience. In our opening scenario, our unreflective grasp of the meaning of "the paper," "the table," and the notion that the paper can "come today" all depend upon our background knowledge. If we lived in a society in which papers were neither read nor delivered and coffee were not drunk at tables, then the same simple sentences of the example would be opaque. Without the routine knowledge of newspapers, the printed page of the *Times* would appear as a unique object whose kind remained a mystery. Without a sense of the kinds, or *types*, of objects, it becomes in turn difficult, or even impossible, to recognize two things as being instances of the same thing. If the page is printed in color, or the sheet of paper cut smaller or rounded, or the texture made stiff and glossy, do we still have a "paper"? The answer lies not in a scientific analysis of the physical object but in a sociological analysis of the category "paper." Such questions lie behind Schutz's writings on the stock of knowledge. What he wants to explain is how we, as actors with common sense, can recognize different things as instances of the same—how we can understand two actions that are never really identical as repetitions of the same action, and how, upon perceiving a small fragment of an object, we can anticipate and mentally fill in the parts we do not perceive. As Schutz observed, the vast majority of our knowledge of the social world comes not from direct experience with objects and other people but from the system of social typifications, through which we understand direct experience in terms of typical categories. Once we apply this line of questions to utterances, it becomes clear that Schutz's project is very close to Ingarden's. He is exploring the knowledge background required to fill in the indeterminacies that Ingarden defined.

For Schutz, the stock of knowledge was *practical* or instrumental in nature, that is, tied to practical activities and their routine goals. This means that it is encyclopedic in scope but without any fixed order. Rather than being structured rigidly, background knowledge is subject to a situation-by-situation ordering according to priorities at hand. It is also incomplete, or selective, and contains numerous contradictions. Consider, for instance, how we know an appliance like the telephone. Unless we have some special interest in the matter, we are unlikely to consider the telephone as an electronic system locked into a larger electronic system with specific technical design features. In commonsense understanding, the phone is what you use to call someone. Our knowledge of it is "recipe-like" in that it is embodied in the routines according to which we use the thing. You pick up the phone's receiver, listen for a dial tone, mark out the number of someone you want to talk to, wait for the ring and the response, identify yourself, and so on. In other words, the stock of knowledge pertaining to things like telephones and tables is organized according to the actional patterns in which people interact with them, not according to a scientific, detached understanding. This is Schutz's way of saying that what Ingarden called meaning potential is preeminently practical in its organization. To use a spatial metaphor, potential meanings do not "radiate in all directions" from intentional objects, but rather they are directed, weighted, skewed according to some actional project. It could be said in this sense that Schutz does not conceive of potential meanings apart from practical engagements. Ingarden, as we saw, has a less instrumental and more open-ended view of the matter. Finally, Schutz, more than Ingarden, underscores the status of the stock of knowledge as *taken for granted.* In everyday interaction we rarely attend explicitly to background assumptions, unless there is some sort of a hitch. On the contrary, we tend to assume until further notice that our own commonsense know-how and expectations are also available to our interlocutors (Schutz 1970:74–80). I say "tend to" because in social settings as differentiated as the ones in the world today, where people of radically different backgrounds interact routinely, it is also a matter of common sense that much of common sense is not in fact common to all. This surely qualifies Schutz's observations, but it does not alter the essential point that most of what we know as social beings appears in our activities under the cover of the taken-for-granted.

Typification and Frames of Reference

To understand objects as being of certain kinds, as is characteristic of commonsense knowledge, is to typify them. The stock of knowledge is organized into types. Typification was for Schutz a fundamental process that to a large degree forms our relation to the world. Without it, there would be no prefabricated structures with which to derive socially viable understandings. We perceive things as instances of types—such as the table before you that you perceive as a "table," not usually as a swatch of color, mass, or pure form. Each time we reexperience the type in a token instance of it, it is rectified and corroborated by supervening experience, and therefore types are always subject to changes wrought by their tokens (Schutz 1970:116–117). Our ability to recollect prior instances and anticipate unstated features of typical objects make up an "inner horizon" of the type. This means that every instance of a type points back to the history of its instantiations and anticipates the future of its potential but as yet unrealized uses. We can see here that what Schutz calls the inner horizon is another way of defining what Ingarden called the potential meanings of an expression. Ingarden's blank spots of indeterminacy show up in Schutz's terms in the incompleteness of any token with respect to the larger history of which it is a part. Just as potential meaning provides the horizon for actuality, so, too, the history of a type through its tokens provides the ground on which it is understood.

Language is the typifying medium par excellence and comprises a vast repository of preconstituted types, each of which has further meaning horizons that are usually left unexplored. Here we can see that Schutz echoes Ingarden's point that intentional objects in a literary work are multiply describable and repeatable. Hence the actual use of an expression in a given context defines an *occasional meaning* that carries with it a sort of haze of other potential meanings that are not directly in play. Occasional meanings, in the clearest examples, are projected by indexicals, emotive expressions, incomplete phrases, and other verbal forms whose understanding crucially depends upon the discourse context in which they occur. Dictionary meanings, by contrast, are relatively stable and do not depend so much on the circumstances of their use (Schutz 1970:108). Schutz makes the interesting observation that even terms like "paper" and "table," which appear to have stable dictionary meanings, nonetheless take on occasional meanings in use. The example exchange between Jack and Natalia gives ample evidence of this, and indeed it was introduced in order to illustrate the division between occasional and dictionary meanings. Of course the great analytic challenge becomes how we distinguish between the two.

Schutz anticipates subsequent developments in linguistics when he observes that the study of occasional meaning can proceed in two directions: (1) We could investigate how meaning is built up in discourse as it unfolds. In this case we would be dealing with asymmetric progression from earlier to later and the "life cycle" of meaning in discourse over time. One could readily imagine plotting the specific meanings a term takes on as it recurs in a series of local contexts, in a conversation or over several conversations. (2) We could also investigate the kinds of "situational baggage" (my term) that an expression picks up by virtue of the various contexts in which it is situated. This recalls Ingarden's notes on how an actual meaning is built upon a potential that is in turn the cumulative result of the myriad ways that people interact with the intentional object. Like the first approach, this one has to do with a history of familiarity with the type and the contexts of its usage. And like the first, this dimension has to do with the dynamic by which aspects of meaning that originate in the contexts of speech become attached to the type-level units of language. Thus the expression "the paper" summarizes a prefabricated typification having to do with regularly appearing journalistic texts on a certain sort of paper with certain highly typical features of format and layout. Yet on the occasions of its use in the city of Chicago, it tends to become associated with a certain range of publications (*Tribune, Craine's, Reader,* or, for some, the *New York Times*). And when used over morning coffee, its associations become increasingly more specific. The general expression and its dictionary meaning are augmented by occasional meanings, and the linguistic type attracts situational features the way a magnet attracts steel filings.

Relevance

This elaborate system of background knowledge is unevenly distributed among members of a community, and it naturally contains many contradictory elements. The sum total of typifications makes up what Schutz called the "frame of reference" (1970:119–120). The frame of reference establishes connections among features, objects, events, and so forth and in this way constitutes an anonymous structure of relevancies. It is the overall frame of reference that transforms the utter uniqueness of any act of speech into a repeatable type of utterance. That is, it fixes the threshold of difference and identity against which we decide when a new experience is another case of a familiar one and when it is truly novel. It is a scheme of both interpretation and orientation, serving all interactants in both response and production modes of their action. Part of the taken-for-granted status of the frame of relevance is the actor's further assumption that their own frame is commensurate with that of others. Until further notice, I assume that you, my interlocutor, share more or less my understanding of how things hang together and "what is going on here." This Schutz calls the "congruence of perspectives." We can state it alternatively as the assumption that although you and I have different experiences of the world, if I were to occupy your shoes, as it were, the world would look to me the way it does to you, and vice versa. Thus a common relation to the world, mediated by types, becomes a basis for intersubjectivity.

Schutz was continuously aware of the practical basis of knowledge and the ways in which it is organized by the goals and purposes of actors. He described this as the "interests-at-hand" and the "motivations" of actors. It is important to realize that he posited no single interest for any actor but a plurality of them. Furthermore, one's interests change continuously as the "now" to which they pertain emerges over time. Finally, even at a given moment, one's interests may include inconsistent elements because every actor figures in plural social roles (Schutz 1970:112–113). Speaking with you now, I am simultaneously an author, an academic anthropologist, a man, a linguist, a proponent of a certain way of doing theory, and so forth. And each aspect of my identity is activated relationally, relative to you, my projected interlocutor. Of course I am also a son, a brother, a father, an English speaker, a former bartender, an apartment dweller, and any number of other types whose relevance is determined by the situation at hand.

The frame of reference is vast if taken as a whole, but it is split up into what Schutz called "zones of relevance," according to the network of interests in which I live. The most immediate zone is the world within my reach, the observable social landscape co-occupied by my *consociates,* with whom I have direct, often face-to-face interactions. At this first level, knowledge and practical skill are relatively precise. At a step removed is the world of *contemporaries,* the other actors who coinhabit the contemporary world of objects that are familiar but not known in intimate detail. The zone of relevance anchored to contemporaries includes things like the institutions that define the objects we manipulate, such as the phone company, the manufacturer of my kitchen table, the publishing company who produces my newspaper, and the editors who decide its content. Knowledge pertaining to this zone is relatively more vague and anonymous than that of consociates. A third zone of relevance, that much more removed from the fine point of engagement, is the world of *predecessors* and relatively irrelevant features of the past lives of my contemporaries. The idea here is that there is a gradience of specificity and determinacy: We all have zones of relatively vague knowledge that is insufficiently precise to give a basis for decisive action but still retrievable and recruitable for purposes of understanding. At the farthest remove, Schutz posits a *zone of irrelevance* for which vague suppositions or beliefs are adequate. At this level interlocutors need not even share the knowledge, although they may be able to draw it into play if motivated to do so. So in our example both Jack and Natalia may be assumed to know that the people who deliver the morning *Times* are union members whose jobs may be threatened by electronic production of the paper, and yet this knowledge may be strictly irrelevant to their interaction.

Schutz's zones of relevance summarize the typification of knowledge in terms of decreasingly direct experience with its objects. To posit four rough zones is not to attempt to draw a solid line around them but to imagine a scale of relative remove from direct experience. This is an important addition to our discussion of knowledge of language, since it allows us to get beyond the Saussurian and Chomskyan idealizations that all speaker-listeners know their language identically. For social description, this idealization is otiose and simply untenable. It must be broken down into ways of describing partial and presumptive overlap of knowledge, even when speakers do not in fact have the same. These zones, then, are not meaningfully centered on certain topics but are defined as levels of differentiation, so that knowledge at a given level is highly diverse and bears on many themes. Schutz likens relevance to a topographical map on which lines connect points of similar salience that may be nonadjacent. That is, it is not thematic foci that organize a relevancy structure but instead the socially constituted experience that people have and the shifting centers of their practical interests. For one thing, relevancy structures are automatically altered when background elements are drawn into the foreground—this follows from the linkage to interests. But notice that this has profound implications for the methods by which we can study social knowledge. It means that it is impossible to investigate zones of relevance by asking people to discuss them, because to do so would be to make them thematic, and this would alter their status, leading to a totally different picture of the overall frame of reference (Schutz 1970:116). The figure-ground structuring of commonsense knowledge is a critical part of such knowledge, and it is vulnerable to the methods of direct interrogation. I won't dwell on their impact here, but this has far-reaching consequences for the methodology of empirical fieldwork. By asking about a topic, the fieldworker thematizes it and therefore changes its meaning.

There are some problems with Schutz's framework from an ethnographic perspective. For one, he assumes that consociates are the most familiar and relevant to actors, whereas predecessors are the least. However, it is relatively easy to imagine a cultural context in which certain actors, such as shamans, priests, or historians, cultivate an extensive body of knowledge of predecessors or even expected successors. This knowledge may actually be greater than their familiarity with the consociates around them in their everyday lives. In such a case, Schutz could respond in one of two ways. He could redefine the spheres of social actors in such a way that whatever class of actor is most routinely encountered and most intimately known counts as consociates, even if they happen to be dead, spiritual beings, or potential successors. This would allow him to retain the notion of zones of relevance yet detach the concept of consociates from actual copresence in a physical sense. Alternatively, he could recast the notion of relevancy, saying in effect that certain classes of actor have different relevancy structures from others precisely because nonconsociates are among those they know most intimately. This would retain the divisions among consociates, contemporaries, and predecessors but implies that relevancy structures, like common sense, are not really common. The problem seems to be with Schutz's basic assumption that common sense maintains a single relation between spheres of actors and spheres of interests, so relevancy structures can be defined in terms of the historical situation of the actor. A more realistic assumption is that the interrelations Schutz perceived among these factors are themselves relevant to all kinds of actors but that the specific correspondences are likely to change depending on the agents and cultural contexts one examines.

In order to resolve this uncertainty in Schutz's framework, it is necessary to turn from the total life world to interaction relationships, in which the acting subject is actually engaged in conversation with other subjects. In such contexts the actor knows his or her interlocutors not merely through anonymous types but through the body. The gestures, gaze, and corporeal engagements of the other provide, according to Schutz, a direct form of knowledge distinct from background knowing. Schutz went so far as to assert that through perception we can grasp our interlocutor in the vivid present of bodily gestures, whereas we grasp ourselves only through our reflection in others. In understanding an utterance, we integrate the following orders of information: (1) recognition of the sound and linguistic form of the utterance; (2) grasping of the anonymous, dictionary meaning of the linguistic forms uttered; (3) grasping the utterance as an indication (*Anzeichen*) of the speaker's subjective expression, that is, the expression of an in-order-to motive and the indication of what the utterance means to the interlocutor. Whether invested with conscious intention or not, the utterance act serves as the direct expression of the inner states of consciousness of its speaker. Part of this process is the relation among gestures, facial expression, and words. Although Schutz did little by way of analyzing different kinds of gestures, the expressive effectiveness of perceptible movement and expression is a critical part of what he termed the vivid present. Thus, returning to the question of the preceding paragraph, it is unlikely that Schutz would countenance an actor for whom predecessors are more vividly present in the "now" than are actors to whom he or she has perceptible access over the course of their emerging expression. It follows that an actor for whom predecessors are more intimately accessible and defining of interest is one with a nontypical relevancy structure. This in turn implies a plurality of relevancy structures in any social world.

In comparison to Ingarden, Schutz may be said to focus on the ways in which meaning potential is organized by the actual focus of an interaction. Schutz thematizes interaction relations rather than discourse works, and he therefore disengages aspects of background knowledge that are sensitive to social experiences that may have nothing to do with language as such. Both tacitly treat language as a typifying medium, although it is Schutz in particular who explains how this works. From our perspective, we can integrate (a qualified version of) Schutz's theory of typification and relevance as another major step toward understanding how speakers access and can share background knowledge in relation to their shifting actional foci. Some such understanding is a necessary prerequisite to the study of tokens, lest we fall back into the reductionism of treating speech as a state of chaos whose sole ordering principle is grammar.

Merleau-Ponty: The Phenomenal Present and the Body as Ground

Of the three phenomenologists, Merleau-Ponty is in many ways the most difficult, for he treats language at a still deeper level of relationality to other forms of knowing and experiencing. And yet we can see clearly the family of themes that unite his thought to that of the others: the irreducible role of a background horizon of cultural understandings (Merleau-Ponty 1964:39–83); the role of silence and blank spots in defining sound and the meaning of what is actually said (1964:87–89); the nontrivial relation between verbal art and other kinds of art (1964: chapter 1); the surplus of meaning created in expression but not predefined in the language as a system (1964:91); the nondetachability of meaning from the occasions of its production (1964:77ff); the role of history in shaping language at any "synchronic" phase of its development, by way of sedimented meanings. More than the other two, however, Merleau-Ponty was concerned to relate perception, language, and meaning production. This led him in turn to accord a greater role to the human body in expression and understanding and to more firmly reject any form of linguocentric theory. Thus, for instance, he takes a position quite opposed to that of Benveniste regarding the comparability of literature and painting (see Chapter 3).

Merleau-Ponty was the first French philosopher to use the term *phénoménologie* in the title of a work, and he went farther than any other in identifying *phénoménologie* with philosophy as a whole. In 1952 he took the chair in philosophy at the Collège de France, once held by Henri Bergson. He had a long friendship with Jean-Paul Sartre, but by the mid-1950s he was very critical of what he called Sartre's "ultra-Bolshevism." One point of difference between the two was the contradiction between self and other, which Sartre considered irresolvable but Merleau-Ponty treated as a stage of antithesis that led to a higher synthesis. He had come into contact with Aron Gurwitsch, who interpreted Gestalt psychology, and he also knew Schutz and read his works (Spiegelberg 1960:547). Thus it should come as little surprise that we find the recurrent features of figure-ground structuring, indeterminacy, and intersubjectivity in his work.

Merleau-Ponty's research from the outset concerned perception. He saw this at base as the relation between consciousness and nature. And he refused to choose between the solipsism of Cartesian subjectivity, which he abhorred, and the opacity of a world conceived as a meaningless objectivity. We have seen a parallel rejection on the part of Ingarden in respect to the literary work. Merleau-Ponty rejected the Cartesian cogito in its subjectivistic interpretation and argued instead that the relations between self and other "dovetail into one another [of] two experiences which, without ever coinciding, stem from one and the same world" (Spiegelberg 1960:541; cited from Merleau-Ponty). In other words, he treated the world as the context in which initial antitheses were resolved through the mutual interpretation of the terms. I, as experiencer, am in the world with you, and we are both occupied by it even as we inhabit it. As he stated, "There is no such thing as an inner man: man is within the world [*au monde*]; it is in the world that he recognizes himself. What I find in myself is 'a subject vowed to the world'" (Spiegelberg 1960:551).

Where Ingarden proposed the ontological category of purely intentional constructs, Merleau-Ponty proposed a new form of reason, a reason that was only partly rational. For him, "what is real is only part rational, and what is rational is only part real" (Spiegelberg 1960:543). This means that expression cannot be reduced to a set of correspondences between symbolic forms and the world of objects, effected according to a consistent logic of realist description. He argues repeatedly that the intentional objects of expression are not definable apart from expression itself but must be seen as literally created by it. Obviously, the kind of creativity that concerned him differs sharply from the generative creativity of a transformational grammar. It has more to do with the agent's ability to project a world of new objects in every act of speech than with the combinatorial capacities of the linguistic system through which such projection occurs.

As a corollary of this stance, Merleau-Ponty considered that the "true philosopher" is equally interested in clarity (*évidence*) and ambiguity. By the latter he underscored the incomplete character of much meaning production (once again a feature common to phenomenologists) and the imperative that philosophers return to the world as it is in actuality rather than viewing it through the lens of analytically purified systems. The contrast is stark when we consider Merleau-Ponty's discussion of meaning alongside the models produced by transformational linguistics. As we emphasized, the latter classically start from an analytic construct and study its use only insofar as it elucidates the preexisting system. Meaning is merely a diacritic of grammatical form, and our ability to engage in meaningful speech is a function of our competence in using the system as predefined. For Merleau-Ponty, the starting and ending point was the world as experienced in all its ambiguity.

Merleau-Ponty's "return to the phenomena" of perception was based on three factors. The first two are the body as vantage point of perception, that is, corporeal involvement in the world through the senses and motion, and the world as perceived, that is, the objects that we construct in meaningful encounters with the world, taking as point of departure our bodily mediated access to it. Some of these may correspond rather closely to physical things, but some, as we have seen, may not. These two elements make up the "phenomenal field" as lived. But the phenomenal field is itself not a sufficient basis for description. There are phenomena of Gestalt structuring (figure-ground aggregation of parts into wholes) and meaning that belong neither to the world of objects as perceived nor to the body as a vantage point. These require a third term—our consciousness *of* the phenomenal field. Thus Merleau-Ponty ends up positing the three-leveled context shown in Figure 6.1. We will return to this construct, and indeed to the ideas of Ingarden and Schutz, in Part 3 of this book, particularly when we explore corporeality in language (Chapter 11). At this stage it is interesting to note that the phenomenal field is a construct shared by Schutz and Merleau-Ponty. But whereas the former augmented it with his theory of the life world and background knowledge, the latter embedded it within the self-consciousness of the agent. That is, in acting, I not only perceive the world through the modalities of my body, but I perceive that I perceive. Consciousness has among its objects both the world as perceived and the perception itself. Recall the similar reflexivity of metalanguage: In speaking, I

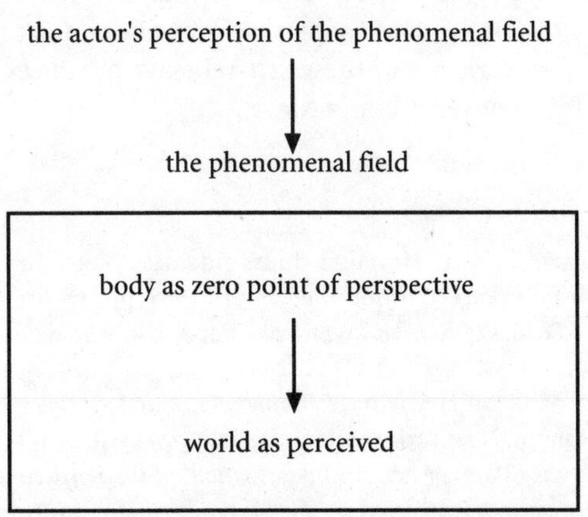

FIGURE 6.1 Three Moments of Perception, After Merleau-Ponty.

not only objectify the world through the modalities of linguistic representation, but through metalanguage I also objectify the objectification.

In his fascinating exploration of corporeality, which will be one of the main themes of Chapter 11, Merleau-Ponty applies this three-part theory of the field of experience to an understanding of the human body. Breaking sharply with what he calls intellectualist understandings of the body, he defines the "corporeal schema" of an actor—the posture and ongoing gestures that are part of speech—in terms of three elements: (1) the actual current state of posture and motion (cf. the body as part of the world), (2) the actor's awareness of his or her current posture and of the whole bodily field as a synthetic unity (cf. the body as an origin point of perspective), and (3) the actor's unreflective grasp of the infinity of other potential postures and motions that could be engaged but are not. So recall Jack standing in the kitchen, pouring coffee, and asking his partner, in the next room, if the paper had arrived. We posit that in making his utterance, he was aware of the kitchen and the range of objects within his perceptual field; that he unreflectively grasped his own bodily disposition in this context, separated by a wall and doorway from Natalia, but sharing her auditory field and emerging present; and that he was conscious of his current disposition as one of indefinitely many potential ones. Thus he could pour his coffee, anticipating his ability to pour the liquid accurately and stop pouring when the cup approached fullness, turn and walk into the next room to approach his interlocutor, find the paper when it was located for him, sit at the table, and so forth. This entails defining his actuality as he perceived it in relation to potentiality, which in turn requires his self-reflexive grasp of his current bodily field (cf. perception of the phenomenal field). The implication of all of this is that the here-now of utterances is irreducibly reflexive and can be defined only in relation to other, nonactual states of affairs. The two key additions of phenomenology with respect to utterance context are thus the relevance of a horizon of non-actual but potential factors and the reflexivity of human consciousness. In the next chapter we examine context from this perspective and illustrate the workings of these self-reflexive processes with an extended example from routine conversation in Maya.

Further Readings

Cassirer, E. "Le Langage et la construction du monde des objets." In *Essais sur le langage,* edited by J.-C. Pariente. Paris: Editions de Minuit, 1969, pp. 36–68.

Falk, Eugene H. *The Poetics of Roman Ingarden.* Chapel Hill: University of North Carolina Press, 1981.

Husserl, E. "Origin of Geometry." In *Phenomenology and Sociology: Selected Readings,* edited by T. Luckmann. New York: Penguin, 1978, pp. 42–70.

Ingarden, R. *The Literary Work of Art: An Investigation on the Borderlines of Ontology, Logic and Theory of Literature.* Translated by G. G. Grabowicz. Evanston, IL: Northwestern University Press, 1973, pp. 3–17, 19–37, 62–185, 246–254, 331–355.

Kellner, H. "On the Cognitive Significance of the System of Language in Communication." In *Phenomenology and Sociology: Selected Readings,* edited by T. Luckmann. New York: Penguin, 1978, pp. 324–342.

Merleau-Ponty, M. "Indirect Language and the Voices of Silence." In *Signs.* Translated and introduced by R. C. McCleary. Evanston, IL: Northwestern University Press, 1964, pp. 39–83.

———. "On the Phenomenology of Language." In *Signs.* Translated and introduced by R. C. McCleary. Evanston, IL: Northwestern University Press, 1964, pp. 84–97.

———. *Phénoménologie de la perception.* Paris: Gallimard, 1967 [1945], pp. 81–86, 114–172, 204–234.

Ricoeur, P. "Phenomenology and Hermeneutics." In *From Text to Action.* Translated by K. Blamey and J. B. Thompson. Evanston, IL: Northwestern University Press, 1991. Chap. 1, pp. 25–52.

Rommetveit, R. *On Message Structure: A Framework for the Study of Language and Communication.* New York: Wiley, 1974. Chap. 4, pp. 29–86.

Schutz, A. *The Phenomenology of the Social World.* Translated by G. Walsh and F. Lehnert. Evanston, IL: Northwestern University Press, 1967 [1932]. Chaps. 21–27, pp. 107–135.

———. *On Phenomenology and Social Relations.* Edited by H. R. Wagner. Chicago: University of Chicago Press, 1970. "The Life World," pp. 72–78; "The Cognitive Setting of the Life World," pp. 79–124; "The World of Social Relationships," pp. 163–244.

Silverman, D., and Torode, B. "Husserl's Two Phenomenologies." In *The Material Word: Some Theories of Language and Its Limits.* London: Routledge & Kegan Paul, 1980. Chap. 5, pp. 97–115.

Spiegelberg, H. *The Phenomenological Movement, a Historical Introduction.* The Hague: Nijhoff, 1960. On Roman Ingarden, pp. 223–232; on Merleau-Ponty, pp. 537–584.

Chapter 7

Saturation by Context

WHAT IS CONTEXT? Everything and nothing. Like a shadow, it flees from those who pursue it, evading the levels and categories of theory, and pursues those who try to flee from it, insinuating itself as the unnoticed ground upon which even the most explicit statements depend. If you are persuaded by the phenomenological concept of incompleteness, then context is inexhaustible. The more you try to specify it, the more blank spots you project, all in need of filling in. Ultimately, context is nothing less than the human world in which language use takes place and in relation to which language structure is organized. How we describe it and what properties of organization and duration we ascribe to it depend upon what we focus on. In other words, because context is so pervasive, "context" is necessarily a theoretical construct. From the formalist and phenomenological traditions, we are told to proceed into context, working outward from utterance form. You start with the "vivid present," as Schutz put it, or the speech form itself, and seek to determine what aspects of the larger setting are immediately relevant to it. This gives the construct a radial structure, with the verbal utterance in the middle, and the elements of its situation arrayed in a scale: from the immediately relevant, to the somewhat relevant, to the tenuously implicated, to the irrelevant. Like Schutz's domains of typification and Ingarden's aspects held in ready versus merely potential, context starts out dense and detailed in the center, and becomes thin and spotty at the fringes. This image does help to conceive of relevancy relations, but it also causes problems. It invites the false assumption that in the middle, as it were, everything is well defined. Unfortunately, even in the focal points of explicit expression, the value of context can be opaque. The opacity might involve the meaning of an utterance, the nature of the setting, the current identity of an interlocutor, or any number of other factors. We cannot mechanically equate close with clear and far with fuzzy.

This is, in a sense, what formalism does by positing a literal meaning with an overlay of context (see Chapter 5). In its strong versions formalism presumes that the encoded meaning of a sentence is transparent, however vague its implications when used on a given occasion. The Chomskyan sentence is either anomalous, unequivocal, or ambiguous, in which case it is associable with a limited number of possible semantic readings. And the tacit assumption is that fully competent speakers intend just one reading for their utterance. Thus, we add to the form features of context that serve to disambiguate it and nail down its core meaning. This view is akin to the Chomskyan program for studying performance: Start from forms that in no way depend upon the situations of their production, define them, and then observe what happens when they are realized in actual situations. The situations are never explored beyond their providing frames for the occurrence of the forms. If Saussure had discussed the study of *parole*, it is likely he would have said something similar.

This approach leads to an impossible task, however, because you never know when you have added enough context to fix the meaning. And moreover, for every meaning that arises in a context, there is always another context in which the meaning would be different. This dependency between the two is what is sometimes called defeasibility. A meaning component that is defeasible is one that changes under a change in discourse context. For instance, the force of Jack's question, "D'the paper come today?" as a request for information regarding its current location in the house, is defeasible: The same utterance issued by an employee of the publisher to verify delivery would not normally convey the request for a specific location. This follows from the indeterminacy phenomenon Ingarden discussed, but this time posed at the level of indexical relations to context instead of semantic relations to text. As long as we start from the analytic division between linguistic form and use, the problem remains insurmountable. It is both necessary and impossible to specify the point at which a description of context is adequate. Part of the challenge of doing linguistics of *parole* must therefore be to reformulate semantics. Traditional semantics as part of formal grammar rests on the idea that language consists of self-same types that are reinstantiated again and again in utterances, which are in turn always unique (cf. Chapter 4). In this view "creativity" has a double sense: It is both the generative capacity of the syntax in defining infinitely many semantic units and the referential capacity of the language, when used, to denote infinitely many objects.

A different sense of creativity comes from defining semantic units as themselves contextual products. To a degree this is in the spirit of the versions of contextual semantics described in Chapter 5. From a cognitive point of view, the semantic content of an expression is produced by the cognizing speaker, on the basis of the "instructions" encoded in linguistic forms. This requires integration of situational factors with linguistic ones. Similarly, in situation semantics it is the relation between the underspecified meaning of forms and the circumstances of speech that produces literal content. This is as much as to say that literal meaning is itself defeasible, a position quite different from the traditional one in speech act theory and Gricean pragmatics (see the first sections of Chapter 5). It also means that deriving literal content is itself a matter of producing meaning and not merely recognizing it. The importance of considering these proposals for a study of linguistic practice is precisely that referential, inferential, and descriptive aspects of language are central in speech. Therefore to recast them is to provide a different ground for explaining how context saturates linguistic form, right down to the semantic bones.

The phenomenologists achieved this break in a distinctive way, rather different from that of modern semantics. Recall from Chapter 6 that context for all three phenomenologists would necessarily be bilevel, including both the immediate sphere of relevance that pertains to the vivid present of an utterance and the broader horizon against which the immediate sphere takes shape. Furthermore, particularly in the work of Merleau-Ponty, we see that context is critically reflexive: The phenomenal field of utterance is itself an object of experience in the consciousness of the speaker. This does not imply that people always consciously think about the relations between themselves and their actual setting but that their unreflective awareness of actuality and potentiality is part of what defines the field. In linguistic terms this suggests a basically different starting point for semantics. For it is impossible to treat meaning as the correspondence between linguistically encoded sense and the world of objects. By contrast, what makes meaning possible is the anchoring of utterance forms *both* in language form and in the phenomenal field. It is *the relation between these two* that is the starting point from which literal meaning arises. As in the case of contextualized semantic theories, what is crucial in this view is not how context is represented when it is, itself, an object of commentary or symbolic representation. What is crucial is how utterances *index* their immediate contexts even when they do not symbolize them, to borrow the terms of Peirce and Morris. The point on which both cognitive-situational and phenomenological theories break down is their inadequate analysis of the social structure of the situation. They help us to get beyond the type-token division, yet they retain the assumption of a monologic speaker. In an anthropological theory of utterance, we must move beyond this notion of subjectivity, a task that will occupy us throughout Chapters 9 to 12. One way to do this is to redefine the unit of speech production, replacing speakers by the participation framework in which they are engaged (Chapter 9). Another way is to attend more closely to the cultural structuring of language and to the role of participants' metalinguistic values in defining utterances (Chapter 8). In the present chapter, we return to the approaches of Voloshinov and Rommetveit, each of whom addressed the specifically social nature of contextual meaning. In the final section of the chapter, we explore this through an extended example from Yucatec Maya.

Voloshinov on Verbal Interaction

Voloshinov (1986) treats verbal interaction from a perspective that has much in common with Rommetveit's, although the two differ with respect to the philosophical frameworks they assume, Marxism for Voloshinov and a combination of phenomenology and the later Wittgenstein for Rommetveit. In this section we briefly review Voloshinov's approach to verbal expression and his treatment of utterance theme and meaning. According to standard theories, he says, there are two sides to expression: that inner something that is expressible and the outward objectification of it for others (or for oneself). The entire event of an utterance is played out between these two poles, with experience defined prior to its exteriorization. Voloshinov's first step is to reject this view on the grounds that expression *organizes* experience rather than merely externalizing it or, worse, being caused by it (Voloshinov 1986:84–85). In a sense, his position on this can be seen as a rejection of any attempt to reduce the utterance to a mere spin-off of some more basic level of human experience or engagement in the world. Utterance is a form of engagement, and it produces experience as much as it reports about it. Notice that this is a kind of irreducibility, in the terms of Chapter 1, posed at the level of speech, not linguistic systems.

His second proposition is that utterances, which organize experience, are always oriented toward an addressee. This means that speakers' experiences, in part formed by their expressions, derive from their orientation to other people. Thus, in two short steps, Voloshinov has rejected the long-standing equation of experience with subjectivity and replaced it with strictly social experience. At the same time, he is rejecting the inner-outer division, since the source of "inner" experiences is now the "outer" social world. As he puts it, "The word is a two-sided act. It is determined equally by whose word it is and for whom it is meant. As word, it is precisely the product of the reciprocal relationship between speaker and listener, addresser and addressee" (1986:86). On this point Voloshinov foreshadows what Rommetveit later called "anticipatory decoding" and more recent sociolinguistic works have called "audience design" (see the readings listed at the end of this chapter). This is the phenomenon whereby speakers form their utterances anticipating how an intended audience will interpret them. Linking what he calls "we experience" to socially defined ideology, he pushes this line of reasoning to an extreme, pretty much denying the existence of individual subjectivity. He discusses the experience of hunger, for instance, which might seem to be so basic and universal as to transcend social interpretation. But Voloshinov argues that hunger, in the absence of any sociocultural definition, is vague and formless, hence not really *hunger* in a strict sense. In order to experience hunger per se, a subject must *evaluate* his or her sensations, and this evaluation requires the horizon of social values. By this logic even consciousness is a social fact. In order to be true consciousness, and not just a formless, objectless waking state, it must be objectified in some material. Since the material—whether thought, speech, or some other mode—is socially defined, so is the objectification, and so, in turn, is the consciousness (1986:90). It follows that language and consciousness are social phenomena governed by sociological laws (1986:96). Curiously, Voloshinov shares with Saussure the premise that thought is formless until structured by language (and other forms of objectification). Yet he applies the premise to *parole* rather than *langue* and concludes from it that *parole* is social, not individual. This reversal is explained by Voloshinov's rejection of the externalization theory of utterances and his insistence on the social orientation of all speech.

Having set out the ligaments that tie language into a social world, Voloshinov set about distinguishing aspects of utterance significance into what he called the "theme" and the "meaning." The former is the unrepeatable, unique, inherently situated meaning of an utterance in context. The *theme* of an utterance like "Oh, gee, I really like those cookies" includes a request to pass the plate, an evaluation of the cookies, a phatic contact with the addressee, a compliment to the chef, and all the other defeasible aspects that it conveys on the occasion of speech. Moreover, this emergent meaning is inflected with the history of relations that justify the speaker's request to her addressee to perform the service of passing the cookies. If we imagine a wealthy aristocrat speaking to her poor pastry chef, the same utterance might convey approval of his work and an order to make the cookies the same way in the future. All of these factors would belong to the theme. The meaning, by contrast, is necessarily leaner and more schematic, closer to what we would recognize as linguistic sense. It is what is reproducible and relatively invariant across contexts (1986:100). However, this reproducibility does not indicate that meaning can be defined in isolation from themes, an abstraction that Voloshinov rejects flatly. Instead, invariant meaning is evident only when we compare a series of utterances and figure out what remains constant across them. In every individual utterance, theme and meaning are intertwined. Thus it could be said that for Voloshinov, this level of meaning is a sort of fiction, produced by the detached perspective of a linguist, since actors do not normally undertake comparison and analysis on the spot. Up until this point, Voloshinov runs parallel to the distinction between literal meaning and conveyed utterance force in linguistic pragmatics (Chapter 5), although he is more circumspect about the ontological status of meaning. But Voloshinov also suggests that the line between theme and meaning is fuzzy, more a matter of degree than of kind. It is difficult to imagine a formal theory in which the difference between literal content and utterance force is a matter of degree, since this would imply that the borders between language and nonlanguage are gradual. Ultimately, theme is the upper limit of actual linguistic significance, and meaning is the lower threshold, a potentiality that arises only in the context of a theme.

Understanding in this view is active and productive, not merely passive reception. Moreover, it is *dialogic.* To genuinely understand an interlocutor, you don't match his or her words with the same ones in your own mental representation, the way the process appears from a Saussurian perspective. Instead, you produce your own understanding, in such a way as to anticipate the response it will in turn elicit (1986:102). On this point Voloshinov goes even farther than contextualized semantic theories and arrives at a notion of understanding similar to Peircean interpretance. Recall that Peirce defined the interpretant of a sign as another sign, which could be more elaborate than the first (i.e., not just a replica of it). So the interpretant understanding of Jack's utterance "D'the paper come today?" would include: (1) Natalia's grasp of Jack's theme in its intentional and historical fullness, (2) her assessment of the appropriate answer to the conveyed request, (3) her orientation to his likely response to her response, and (4) her spoken answer to him. It is clear that to understand at this level is to construct a maximally rich interpretation that itself counts as a move in an ongoing dialogue.

The final point in this section of Voloshinov's discussion is that linguistic meanings and themes interact constantly with *evaluation* (1986:103). He considers this linkage to be the most significant problem in semantics. The most superficial example of this is expressive intonation, such as "Wow, those cookies are reeeeallly goood!" But Voloshinov is of course aiming at a much deeper level of language, as is evident when he asserts that "referential meaning is molded by evaluation." The scale of this claim may appear difficult to justify if by evaluation we think in terms of expressing subjective opinions. But this is not the sense that Voloshinov attaches to the concept. Evaluation is the tie between a given language form or object and the ideological horizon of categories, values, and orientations that speakers bring to their interaction. Thus in placing evaluation in such a central position, he is extending just the same line of reasoning that we discussed in relation to experience at the outset of this section. Placed in that context, "every utterance is above all an evaluative orientation" (Voloshinov 1986:105). And, we might add, this evaluation comes to define the very consciousness of the speaking agent.

Rommetveit on Message Structure and Perspective

Rommetveit's description of what he called "message structure" must be understood in relation to generative grammar as it was done in the early 1970s. This was his main target of criticism and the reference point against which he argued for his own position. Whereas generative models took as their object the linguistic competence of ideal speaker-listeners (see Chapter 4), Rommetveit's object was the production of meaning in speech. Messages, for him, were not abstract, formal objects but the thematic and meaning components of situated utterances. His central question was not, "What is the abstract linguistic knowledge underlying a speaker's ability to recognize and generate forms?" but instead, "What can be made known with a sentence?" This question recurs throughout Rommetveit's monograph and implies a fundamentally different conception of semantics than that of generative grammar. For one thing, it presupposes that sentences are generated for the purpose of making things known to an interlocutor and not for the purpose of formulating thoughts. Thus, expectably, Rommetveit is centrally concerned with the way speech mediates between parties to a social relationship. Similarly, because much more can be made known by uttering a sentence than its own encoded content, Rommetveit conceives of understanding as an active process of interpretance, not a matter of recognition. From the outset, then, his framework leads away from the idea of invariant semantic structures and toward something closer to variable concretization.

On several key points his approach is consistent with that of Voloshinov. Probably the most basic commonality is their rejection of subjectivist views of speech in favor of a socially grounded framework of interaction. In addition, the two treat understanding as a dynamic production that takes place against the horizon of a preestablished stock of social knowledge. Rommetveit calls this the "perfectly understood" (1974:29), whereas Voloshinov subsumes it to ideology, the stock of evaluations, and the prior utterance-response chains.

Rejecting the search for abstract competence, Rommetveit argues that ellipsis, or incompleteness, is the natural state of language. Recall that in formal models based on type-level units, incomplete "surface" forms are derived from completely specified underlying forms. For instance, one derives contractions such as "áyd'v" and "íts" from full forms like "I would have" and "it is" by way of deletion. You don't derive the full forms from the partial ones by way of expansion. The result is often a simpler, more powerful generalization in formal terms, since the contracted forms can be predicted from the full ones but the opposite does not hold. Contractions in the auxiliary verbs {would, will, have, be} follow a simple rule: Delete all phonological material up to but not including the final consonant. This gives the contracted forms {'d, 'll, 've, 's, 'm, 're, 's} according to the person/number values of the subjects. The contraction analysis requires only four underlying auxiliaries plus a simple rule of deletion. The alternative would require about eleven underlying forms corresponding to the total list of full and contracted variants, plus a set of rules to expand the contracted forms into full ones. Clearly, this would be a more cumbersome solution, and it would probably obscure the generalization that the reductions are all part of a single phenomenon. Given the criteria of simplicity and generality, the first solution is the better one.

The use of elliptical and fragmentary forms in speech is not quite so simple as contraction, but the hope at one time was that much of it could be accounted for by grammatical rules. The idea was to start from the canonical sentence forms, the way they might be produced in a generative grammar of the sort Chomsky proposed. These forms represent the whole statement as it is understood. Then from there the fragment is derived by a regular rule of deletion, or reduction. The directionality of the logic is identical to the case of contraction, although the units are larger. For example, in an exchange like

A: Where are Peter and Dave?
B: Swimming at the Forty-ninth Street beach.
B': Right over there (pointing).

B's utterance can plausibly be derived from "Peter and Dave are swimming at the 49th Street beach," or something like that. After all, this is what it conveys, more or less, and all we need to assume is that B leaves out just those parts of his utterance that can be filled in automatically from A's question. Parts of a sentence that were missing but automatically interpretable were said to be "recoverable," a phrasing that makes explicit the logical priority accorded to the full form and the directionality of interpretation: from surface fragments to underlying wholes. Stated from the perspective of the full forms, the process was described as "deletion under identity," meaning that just those parts of B's response that were identical to A's question could be deleted. So long as linguists worked with examples in which an elliptical form was immediately preceded by its full counterpart, the identity criterion worked well and provided a way of capturing what appeared to be the understanding of otherwise incomplete sentences. Moreover, it was evident that in any case something like deletion rules would be needed to explain the interpretation of many structure types involving subordinate clauses. So consider

"I hoped to swim across the bay that morning, but Peter didn't want to."

We understand automatically that what Peter didn't want to do was "swim across the bay that morning," because this is recoverable under identity with the preceding clause. As powerful as this logic was in explaining certain types of ellipsis, the problem cases involved incompleteness with no prior overt form. Jack walks into the room carrying two bags of groceries, and Natalia says simply, "On the counter by the sink," meaning that he should put the bundles there. Do we really want to say that Natalia's utterance linguistically encodes the full imperative "Put them on the counter by the sink"? How do you know exactly what words she did not utter? Around the time that Rommetveit wrote *Message Structure,* a debate was beginning to take shape among formal linguists regarding the status of ellipsis.

Given his focus on interactive speech, it is unsurprising that Rommetveit considers ellipsis to be the prototype of speech under the idealized conditions of shared knowledge. He calls this "complete complementarity in an intersubjectively established, temporarily shared social world" (Rommetveit 1974:29). In other words it is just what we would expect of speakers: The more they share, the less they have to say. The more similar their knowledge, the more likely they are to speak in snippets whose meaning goes without saying. Such complementarity is perfect under the idealized conditions of Saussurian exchange, where the message encoded by A is identical to the one decoded by B. It is also perfect in a world inhabited by Chomskyan ideal speaker-listeners, where their flawless knowledge of the same grammar assures that they will amalgamate just the same features into the same semantic readings. How ironic, then, that this idealized view of common knowledge undergirds a theory of grammar based on full sentences, not fragments. For if people really did correspond to the identical homunculi of formalism, their language would surely be organized around incompleteness, not fully specified forms. Where does the formalist concern with full specification come from, if not from the objective conditions of language in the world? It comes from the detached perspective of scientific objectivity, in which nothing goes without saying unless it follows from the formalism. Rommetveit wants us to see the inner contradiction of this perspective when applied to human language.

This irony might be resolved by assuming that ellipsis belongs to performance, whereas a sentence-based grammar corresponds to competence. Telegraphic speech has no more to do with grammar than do other features of *parole,* such as sarcasm or singsong pronunciation. Rommetveit rejects such a view and takes the opposite position that ellipsis and other kinds of context dependency are fundamental to the system of language and to message structure. Like deictic expressions, as in B' above, ellipsis serves as a "bridge" between an utterance and the already shared world of the interlocutors. Thinking back to Ingarden and Schutz, we can say that the linguistic form of the utterance is partial in respect to what it makes understood. The blank spots point into the intersubjective context, linking verbal form to the extralinguistic horizon of social knowledge. When this knowledge is available in the perceptual field of the two parties, then reference proceeds on the basis of *recognition.* When it is accessible only through recall of prior experience or only from secondhand report, then reference relies on what he calls *identification* (Rommetveit 1974:32). The interlocutor identifies a current object with one experienced in the past. Both modes of reference are spontaneous, although the first is relatively more immediate and involves the body and perception more directly.

Rommetveit's bridges tie utterance forms into social worlds by indexical relations: The demonstrative pronoun stands in a relation of contiguity to its object in the context of speech, just as the formal blank spots of ellipsis stand in relations of contiguity with previous talk. Like other indexical relations, these all involve *copresence* of different elements in the framework of speech. Whether we can see the same things or remember them or just consider them together in the hypothetical, they are available to us both. Moreover, we are mutually available to one another in the vivid copresent of the moment—our gazes turn toward one another, if only for an instant, and we are each part of the perceptual field of the other. This reciprocal field of copresence is what provides the background information needed to fill in the unstated in speech. It takes the place for Rommetveit of the formalist notion of identity in providing the means to "recover" what is unspecified in the utterance. What are the dimensions of copresence, then, and how do they show up in language?

At this point we shift from grammatical facts to sheerly interactive ones. Rommetveit maintains a long tradition in European thought regarding the field of copresence; it is made up of three basic dimensions: space, time, and person. From the first we get contiguity as proximity, the space between here and there. From the second we get it as diachronic immediacy, the interval between now and then. In the final one we have participant roles, speaker = I, addressee = you; the two are contiguous in their engagement with one another. Thus each dimension establishes a subfield of indexical relations that jointly make up the we-here-now of speech. It is relative to this actional manifold that reference is achieved and within it that intersubjectively shared knowledge is accessed. When Rommetveit speaks to his question, "What can be made known in uttering 'X'?" he does so in terms of relations along one or more of these axes.

The partiality of what is said is complemented by a more pervasive kind of partiality, this one having to do with what is shared among social actors. This is another point on which Rommetveit takes exception to standard idealizations. Intersubjective copresence, whether conceptual, perceptual, imaginary, or other, can only be partial, never total. Hence the blank spots in expression are filled in on the basis of a context with gaping blank spots of its own (Rommetveit 1974:39). Here his framework rejoins Schutz's concern with the limitations of intersubjective understanding. Whereas identically shared knowledge of language is assumed in formalist approaches, and Rommetveit uses it to point out the internal contradiction of that approach, his own position is that the *unshared* is an unavoidable feature of social life. Perfect complementarity of knowledge is a social fiction that bolsters the more elaborate conceptual fiction of a formal grammar. With this critique in place, his next step is to argue that any object can be described in a variety of ways according to the perspective one adopts. Recall that Ingarden made the same observation regarding intentional objects. Reference is accomplished routinely under conditions of partial knowledge, according to Rommetveit, and objects cannot be equated with monadic things that remain transparently the same across descriptions (1974:48). So when I say of my friend Neil, who is a sculptor, "I like the artist and the person," I have made two references, not just one. Furthermore, I have done so by decentering my perspective, from vocation-profession to character. Imagine fifty other possible descriptions of the person, all referring to the same individual but each imparting a different bit of information about him. Any one of these descriptions is selective, the degree of sharedness between interlocutors is both limited and variable, and the proper perspective on a given object varies from situation to situation. In order to achieve understanding, therefore, speakers must to a degree anticipate the perspectives and decentering abilities of interlocutors. In other words, as Voloshinov stated it, they must anticipate the interpretive response of their addressee.

Rommetveit goes on to argue that the meaning of utterances, and even the message structure that they convey, differs significantly according to the context in which they are nested. This is the basis for recasting semantic description from a system of invariant features and rules on their combination to a contextually variable one. His strategy is to start from linguistic forms, place them in successive contexts, and show how their conveyed meanings covary with context. From this it follows that the ability of speakers to share understanding derives not from their common possession of a fixed code but from their ability to work out meanings in contexts. This in turn requires shared contracts regarding how things are to be understood, a concept Rommetveit gets from Wittgenstein's writings on language games. As he says, encoding involves anticipatory decoding, and decoding is aimed at reconstruction of the speaker's intention. That the match is always imperfect does not contradict the common commitment to reciprocity as a social contract.

The logical extension of this approach is to say that contexts are made up in part of metalinguistic contracts, which govern how speakers concretize the indeterminate meanings of the words they use with one another (Rommetveit 1974:57). What is described as semantic competence under the generative view becomes a repertoire of perspectives and modes of adopting them. Rather than a code combining literal meanings, language eventually reemerges in Rommetveit's framework as a code of potential contracts for the sharing of perspectives. Notice that under such a description, silence may be as meaningful as speech, so long as it is nested upon the proper contracts.

Saturation by Context: An Example from the Field

In the remainder of this chapter, we will examine an example of speech in context. It is a simple exchange, around the house, between two people who know each other relatively well, one a resident and the other a familiar visitor. The purpose of the example is to illustrate the interplay among linguistic meaning, the situated themes of the utterances, the "temporarily shared intersubjective world" of the interlocutors, and the broader sociocultural horizon. We will draw directly on the analysis of verbs of eating and drinking in Maya presented in Chapter 5. Also, the example anticipates another extended example of speech around the household, which appears in Chapter 11. Since these examples are from my own fieldwork in Yucatán, Mexico, and the one here depends upon this context for its intelligibility, I begin with brief remarks on the setting and my place in it before moving on to the interaction.

The Setting

Oxkutzcab, where I have conducted most of my ethnographic research, is a *municipio* (county) of approximately 20,000 inhabitants, about 100 kilometers southwest of Mérida, the capital of Yucatán (see Figure 7.1). The older map in Figure 7.2 is from the family papers of the Xiu lineage, one of the leading families in preconquest Yucatán and the rulers of Mani Province. The round shape of the map, the writing in both Spanish and Maya, the radial representation of a central church with roads leading outward toward the periphery, and the graphic and scribal style all date the map as a colonial production. In the middle of the page at the bottom, the Spanish inscription labels it "Mapa de Mani." At the time indicated on this map, 1557, the town of Mani, which is shown in the center, was the capital of the entire region of the same name, enclosed by the circular perimeter. Because of the deteriorated state of the map, it is uncertain where to place

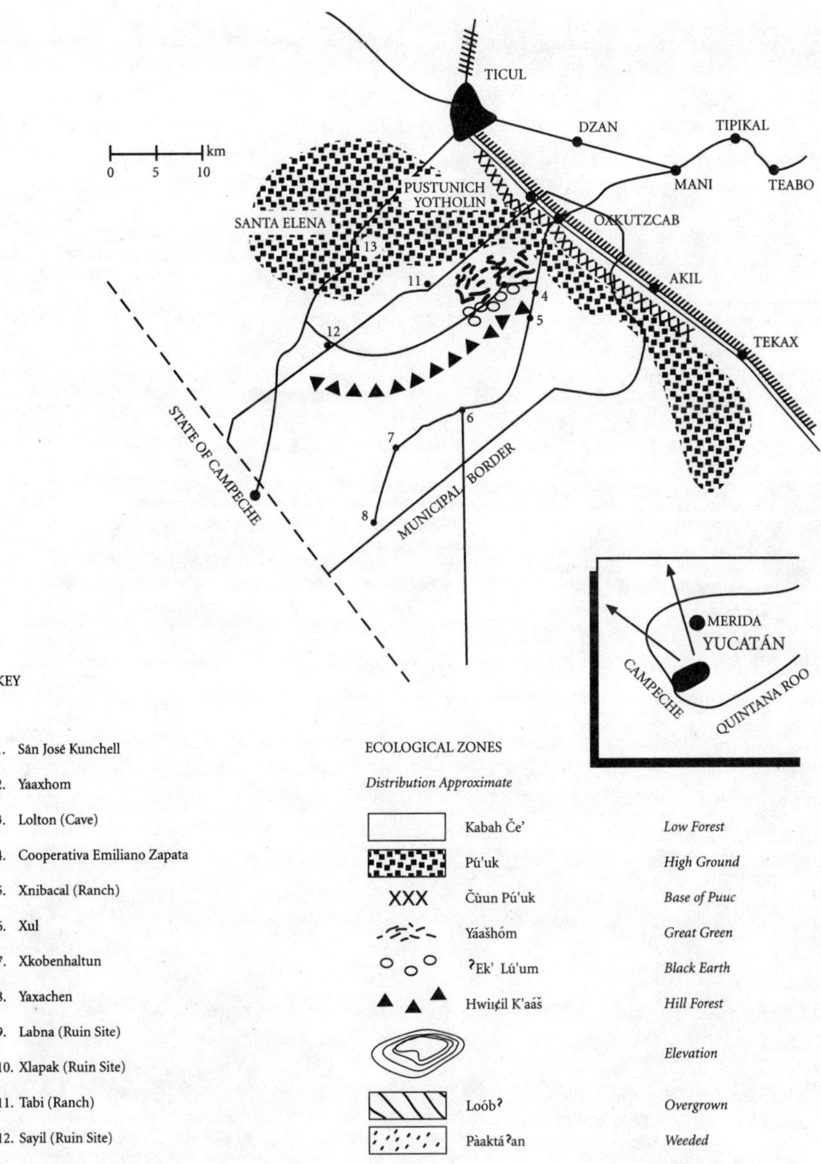

FIGURE 7.1 Map of Oxkutzcab (1990). Source: William F. Hanks, Referential Practice: Language and Lived Space Among the Maya *(Chicago and London: The University of Chicago Press, 1990), p. 309. Reprinted with permission.*

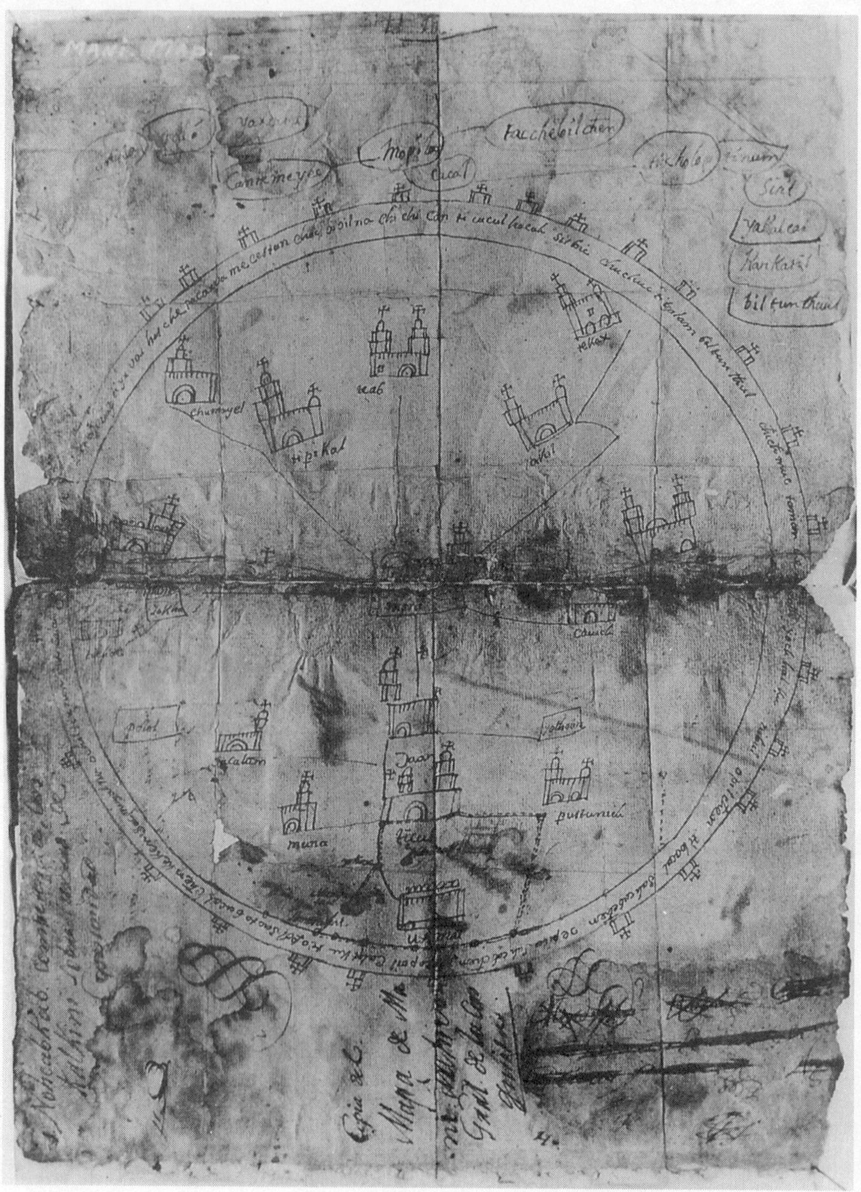

Figure 7.2 Map of the Mani Region (Sixteenth Century). Reproduced courtesy of Tulane University Library.

Oxkutzcab on it, but the best candidate is the church with twin towers shown rightmost on the map, just above the darkened area where it has been folded. Indeed, there is in the town a church, still in use today, that dates from this period and fits the twin-tower description.

Before discussing the region represented by Figure 7.1, let's have a quick look at the maps themselves. No less than verbal descriptions, maps display the tension between indeterminacy and expression, representation and tacit assumptions, that the phenomenologists focused on. If spoken language is tied into gestures and nonverbal modes of expression, maps combine verbal with graphic information. Both of these examples are highly selective, the first one skewed toward commonly used roads, contemporary municipal boundaries, and ecological zones. The first two of these features are among the most significant from an external, relatively anonymous perspective. The labels for the ecological zones are the ones used in local discourse in Maya, and their distributions reflect the state of the landscape in the late 1980s, when the map was drawn. Knowledge of the best examples and distributions of the soil types contains hidden indexical components, in that it is local standards that fix the referents. So, for instance, the areas labeled "high ground" and "hills" follow local usage even in cases where the distinction is not obvious to the eye. The hilly area to the south of Cooperativa actually lacks the steep inclines usually associated with *hwiíç*, and Maya speakers visiting the area from other parts of the peninsula often mistakenly assume it to be part of the Puuc. They know the dictionary meanings of the terms but lack the indexical ties to local standards. Terms like *yáašhóm* are defined by clusters of properties, including how the soil retains water after heavy rains, features not obvious to outside observers. The upshot is that ecological classification is based on what Rommetveit called "bridges" to local standards of description. A similar point applies to colonial maps, in which the sign of the church may either indicate the actual presence of a church in the town or serve as a symbol that the town had been evangelized, whether or not an actual church was erected. The gross contours of the roads indicated in Figure 7.2 and the fact that all roads emanate from Mani are similarly selective and reflect both the purpose of the mapmakers and local standards of interpretation. It is virtually certain that there were roads between outlying places such as Oxkutzcab, Yotholin, and Akil, although these are omitted. As part of the family papers of the Xiu lineage, centered in Mani, the map portrays the space as entirely centered on this town.

The overall orientation of the map in Figure 7.1 is common to that of contemporary maps, in which longitude and altitude coordinates define relative location. Although we can infer from the density of factors around Oxkutzcab that it is the focal point of the map, there is no center to the map, as there is to the colonial one. Notice that north is to the top, whereas in the colonial map east is at the top, with Teabo directly above Mani. Along with the centered, or radial, orientation of the colonial map and the use of churches as the primary landmarks, this east-up orientation is typical of its genre. The lesser places inscribed around the double-lined border must be read by rotating the map around the fixed point of Mani. At the same time, the written inscription to the bottom left of the sheet, outside the area of the map itself, is inscribed in Spanish, with the sheet rotated 90 degrees, so that north is at the top. It says "Copia del Mapa de Mani" (Copy of the Map of Mani), indicating that this document is a reproduction of another one. In other words, there are two simultaneous orientations in the text, one radial, centered on Mani, with east at the top, and the other with north at the top, as it would be in Spanish practice. The Spanish inscription is superordinate in that it categorizes the entire graphic as being of the genre *mapa,* while indicating its status as a secondhand report, or copy. Such features identify it as a colonial hybrid style and index the multiple perspectives to which it was addressed. We will return to these matters in more detail in Chapter 12.

Something of a backwater in the colonial period and a second-order place until the early 1970s, Oxkutzcab has become a boomtown since the paved roads connecting it to neighboring towns were finished and a state-sponsored development program installed a mechanical irrigation system, making the soil productive in a way hitherto unimagined. During the latter 1970s and into the 1980s, increasingly many orchards were developed in the area, taking advantage of the extraordinarily rich soils and the presence of irrigation. The populations of neighboring towns, including the once predominant Mani, have shifted massively into Oxkutzcab, which is now the commercial and agricultural center of the region. The map in Figure 7.1 shows rough distributions of ecological zones, which correlate but are not coextensive with soil types. Today Oxkutzcab is widely referred to as the *huerta del estado* 'garden of the state', in honor of the immense citrus and orchard produce that comes out of the area. There are virtually all shadings of bilingualism and biculturalism in this area that one is likely to find in the entire peninsula of Yucatán. Although my research and the example I adduce are focused on the far Maya end of the cultural spectrum, variation is a basic fact of life here. That I have worked almost entirely in Maya language and that the exchange presented below is entirely in Maya are already indexes of the linguistic practices of people who enter into these kinds of exchanges under these circumstances. The stock of knowledge available to all of the participants spans the rural world of outlying homesteads without water or electricity, to the semiurban setting of Oxkutzcab, and into the urban, cosmopolitan setting of Mérida. My own presence on the scene is indicative of the larger presence of foreigners in the area as well and serves to extend the sphere of contemporaries internationally.

In the light of the classic ethnographies of Yucatán produced by Robert Redfield and his collaborators, Oxkutzcab would be considered far out on the urbanized end of the continuum. A county capital, it has two paved highways through the center of town (two lanes each), several *preparatoria*-level schools, numerous clinics and private doctors, a hospital, and one of the largest regional markets in all of Yucatán, including the capital. A remarkable number of Oxkutzcabeños work abroad, and it is not uncommon to see trucks bearing California and Oregon license plates. Contrary to Redfield's predictions about urbanization, however, it is a deeply *campesino* town in which people can live virtually their entire domestic lives in Maya language, all the while interacting with non-Maya social phenomena in public and private life. It is a place where one can bring complaints against wrongdoers by accusing them in Maya before the *presidente municipal.* Local politicians campaign in Maya. Some dozen shamans perform rain ceremonies and "traditional" rituals for people with color televisions, cousins in San Francisco, and international experience themselves. Indian women cross-dress as *ladina* because the clothing is less expensive, and *ladina* women cross-dress as Indian because the clothing is more beautiful. A horde of evangelical sects peddle modern secularism in their *templos,* yet their leaders discreetly visit shamans for advice on dealing with congregation members. The study of change and gradience between Maya and Spanish is one of the classic topics in the ethnography, and the challenge posed by a place like Oxkutzcab is to theorize change that is both multilineal and multidirectional.

My fieldwork has focused on other issues. A linguist whose first contact with the Maya was through studying the language, I work entirely in Maya. This linguistic focus has undoubtedly limited the range of the community to which I have direct access, but it has provided a wealth of data on how the relatively indigenous sectors of the population live. Figure 7.3 illustrates the floor plan of a single extended household in the town, about 1 kilometer from the central plaza by paved road. By 1987, the time of the exchange we will explore, I had worked with the senior head of this household for nearly ten years, resided in it for about six months over the preceding five years, and was *compadre* to one of the children of the household. (I am still compadre, but the household has changed shape several times in the past six years. Hence my description is in the ethnographic past tense.) It will be the setting for much of the remainder of this chapter.

Note first off the rectangular perimeter that surrounds the entire area, setting it off from the neighboring homesteads. Maya households are never round, and indeed the cultural definition of inhabited space is canonically rectangular. The domestic boundary is embodied in a stone wall that outsiders are not entitled to traverse without explicit sanction from residents. Within the homestead there were three primary households, corresponding to the conjugal units of the senior male (rooms 9 and 10) and his two eldest sons (rooms 1–4 and 5–8, respectively). These are separated by boundaries of privacy that are not self-evident in the floor plan but are observed meticulously by all adult members of the households. For example, one does not merely enter the area of a sibling without first addressing the head of household. According to norms of propriety, a man never addresses the spouse of his brother, and the dogs belonging to one household typically keep out people of the adjoining household, particularly at night. Although they may help each other, the individual residence units are also economically independent.

The Opacity of Form

It was early evening, February 11, 1987, and we were sitting in the eating area having supper (in the room labeled 1 on the floor plan). We were in the house of Manuel, the oldest son of Don Chabo (whose home was rooms 9–10). Long sepa-

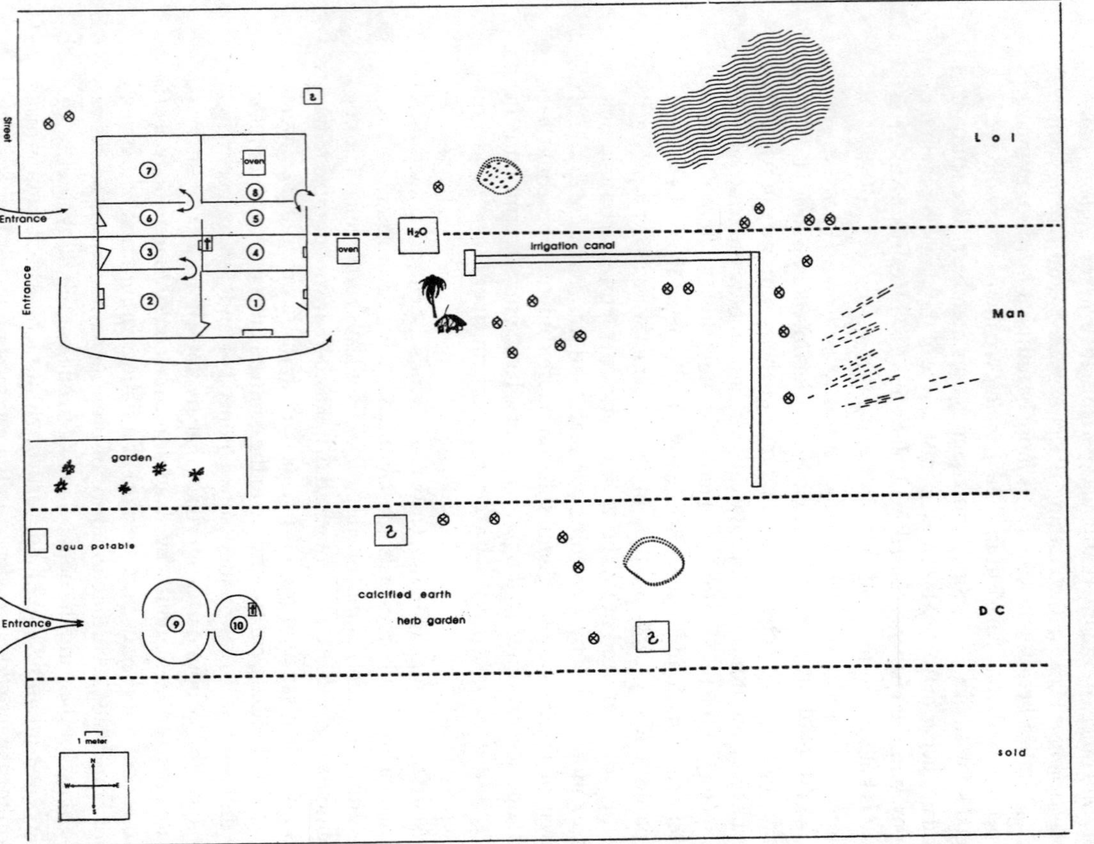

Figure 7.3. Diagram of Don Chabo's house. Source: William F. Hanks, Referential Practice: Language and Lived Space Among the Maya *(Chicago and London: The University of Chicago Press, 1990), p. 323. Reprinted with permission.*

rated from his estranged wife, who lives in Mérida, Don Chabo took his meals in Manuel's home in those days, served by Manuel's wife, Margot. *Compadre* to Manuel and Margot, I slept in room 4 during this field stay.

We were having crusty rolls and hot chocolate for supper, a typically light evening snack after the day. It was cool and dry, as it often is on February evenings, although a substantial dew would fall before morning. The family would sleep in room 2, as it usually did during the cold season, because the windows were closed with sheet metal shutters and they would be more comfortable than in the gaping space of room 1, where the windows were shutterless. Six people in two hammocks over a packed earth floor. The darkness receded before the cast of light from the bare bulb hanging above the table. Evening sounds of dogs barking, the neighbor's stereo playing *cumbias,* and our own soft conversation. The smell of wood fires. Stories of the past, plans for tomorrow, my tedious questions about the language all overlain on the comfortable silence born of familiarity. Puto Corrito, the pet parrot, was dozing on the window sill. We were midway through supper when I was startled by a voice just outside the window, in the dark. It was Yuum, a young man I had seen talking with Don Chabo in his home on numerous occasions. He had come for a blessing.

Yuum: *kul áʔan wá dón čàabo*
'Is Don Chabo seated?'
Margot: *šén tol oʔ, taán uy uk' ul. šeén to ič nah oʔ*
'Go over there. He's drinking. Go over there inside.'

Why did Yuum ask if Don Chabo was seated? What did he seek to make known by his question, and what relevance could it have? What relation could he possibly bear to this family that would permit him simply to enter the yard in the evening and greet them from just outside the window, like some intimate or some intruder? And why did Don Chabo never even react, lost in his relaxation, leaving the role of respondent to someone else? Why, with all the men present, in a society permeated by male dominance, did Margot feel at ease to respond without hesitation? Don Chabo was gazing off into space with a roll in his hand, and yet no one contradicted her claim that he was "drinking." What odd relation did she bear to Yuum that allowed her to answer his question with an imperative, telling him in effect to beat it, yet reacting to his intrusive speech as though she expected him all along? Or better, by what right did she tell him to go install himself in her father-in-law's home? If the phenomenal field of the exchange is as I have described it, in terms of placement and perceptual access, what shared consciousness of this field permitted them to have an exchange so compact as this one and still understand it with little apparent effort?

I have chosen this exchange as an example for its transparency, its almost insipid banality from a Mayan perspective. A friend visits in the evening and a woman tells him to wait until supper is finished. Don Chabo is one of the dozen or so shamans in Oxkutzcab, and he receives visitors at all hours. His daily rhythm and time sense are different from that of any other person I have met in Oxkutzcab—or elsewhere for that matter. He is a *hk'ìinil wiínik* 'sun person' in his mid-seventies, with patients from as far away as Belice and the Valley of Mexico. The neighbors consider him a harmless herbalist because he doesn't transform himself into a jaguar, nor does he cause death with the waxen hummingbird commonly associated with true shamanic power. His is a vocation of synthesis based on pre-Columbian practices saturated by local Catholicism and sedimented over the nearly 500 years of cultural hybridization. Like other shamans in contemporary Yucatán, he competes for clients with scores of "magicians," "curers," charismatics, doctors, ministers, priests, and others who offer physical and spiritual therapies. Over the years that we had worked together, I had noticed that Don Chabo usually had a few young men who sought him out regularly for advice and an occasional blessing. Often, as was the case with Yuum, their relationship was ambiguous, part shaman-patient, and part elder adviser–youth. Yuum would pay the standard fees for shamanic services when he could and visit for free when he couldn't. On this night he would pay.

Common sense in rural Yucatán has it that Maya shamans can perform evil with the same degree of effectiveness as they can cure. Ability to inflict harm is the measure of ability to effect good. Don Chabo has distilled this duality into a steadfast commitment to good, and though he can defend from the evil of jaguars and hummingbirds, he can cause none himself. Yuum is one of several regulars who seek advice, a blessing, and the occasional boost of a brush with the divine. But these are other matters. Our question is simply, What went on in this exchange? What was made known? What responses were anticipated? What can we learn about language or context from the arcane particulars of a Maya night? Let's begin with what was literally said.

Most adherents to the irreducibility thesis, and here I count myself, would recognize that speech regularly takes place in contexts that display the sort of massive relationality of this example. The question seems to be whether linguistic systems are the precondition of relationality or vice versa. The formalist answer to this question is to say that utterances have literal meanings of the sort predicted by grammar based on logic, but they acquire all manner of contextual overlays once placed in social situations. As we saw in Chapter 5, this was basically the approach of Grice in his theory of implicatures as well as the tack of speech act theorists who maintained that utterances have propositional content that is detachable from their illocutionary force and perlocutionary effects. Hence it is perfectly clear what Yuum said and what Margot said in response, even if the whys and wherefores require some explanation. He uttered a yes-no question referring to a particular individual, and she uttered an imperative referring to a particular place. She went on to inform him that the individual in question was currently drinking, and repeated her imperative. It would take scarcely a month studying Maya to parse the utterances, reduce them to their constitutive elements, and derive a literal sense.

What would take a bit longer would be to see why the exchange is senseful or, better, why it seems *natural* from the perspective of the participants. On this point the approaches of Voloshinov and Rommetveit are helpful. Margot asserted that Don Chabo was "drinking," and I can attest that her utterance is true by relevant standards. But he was not *really* drinking; he was gazing off, chomping on a roll. She told Yuum to "go over there inside" but nothing in her utterance itself told Yuum where to go. Surely, in a crowded, semiurban neighborhood like this one, there were indefinitely many places that fit the description "over there inside." In fact, if by chance she were a neighbor and not a coresident, her utterance would have been understood literally to tell Yuum to go to *her* house, not Don Chabo's. In other words, both the meaning and the theme of her sentence would be crucially different. This recalls our discussion in Chapter 1 of the reference of "the paper" to the *New York Times* on a certain day. The unspecified parts of the utterance make a bridge into the commonly known space of the homestead. Yuum's knowledge of her, her identity in the house, and his history with Don Chabo all overdetermine his understanding of where she meant. The referent is not merely a thing but a thematized intentional object in a social matrix.

Yuum for his part asked whether Don Chabo was seated. Since he was in fact sitting in a chair, Margot could have answered simply yes to affirm the positive response, just as Natalia in Chapter 1 could have said yes in response to Jack's question about the paper. That this reply would have been less than cooperative is another matter. It seems self-evident that what Margot did say subsumes the claim that Don Chabo *was* seated. And after all, he was. Things get a bit more opaque when we consider that this proposition would have been equally true if he had been off in his own home bathing at the time, out back relieving himself against a tree, standing instead of sitting, asleep in his hammock, or indeed anywhere within the perimeter of Figure 7.3. By local standards he would still have been "seated." Just as we saw in relation to verbs of eating and drinking in Chapter 5, there are hidden indexical components in the verb that make its meaning dependent upon local standards.

If Yuum was really coming for a blessing, as I have asserted, why should he care whether Don Chabo was sitting or standing when he arrived? The simple truth is that he didn't care, because Don Chabo's physical posture at the time was utterly irrelevant to the theme of his utterance. Yuum asked whether he was sitting in order to request that he be granted an audience with him. Therefore a "literal" response on this point would have been uncooperative. This holds even on the local version of literality, in which his question asks whether Don Chabo was around the house. Had Margot given a straight yes-no response, it is reasonable to expect that Don Chabo would have piped in and overridden her and probably told her to stop messing with his patients. But the manner in which Margot did respond gives a clear indication that she did not understand the greeting as a simple request for information. For if she had, then her response as stated would have been grossly irrelevant and doubtless rude. She responded, rather, to what she took to be the interactive move that Yuum sought to make known and thereby accomplish: a request to come in and talk with Don Chabo.

If we were to reject the notion of language as a system entirely, as many have done, we could start from the other end. Yuum has a certain relation to the household, and so does Margot. He is a familiar visitor, and she is the senior resident woman. They are consociates. His role and Don Chabo's particular lifestyle as a shaman sanction passage and inquiry, and hers sanctions her sending him away while the men of her household eat supper at her table. Don Chabo is a shaman and Yuum a patient. Therefore, she sends Yuum to Don Chabo's private home, where he will be treated once the old man finishes supper and is ready to go to work. The basic explanatory elements in the scene are residence, profession, gender, and rationality. This is of course just one version of relationality. One could claim alternatively that the words never make reference to an external reality, that it is all a play of self-reflexive expressions that dissolve as soon as we try to fix them into some reified order of things outside themselves. In this view it makes no difference whether Don Chabo was sitting or standing, because such facts are trivial constructions cooked up in retrospect. The so-called issue of where Margot told Yuum to go is an exercise in scholasticism; she told him to beat it. Like us, they surf along on a sea of reflexivity; literality is no more than a last wave that never arrives.

In the perspective of this book, these versions of relationality can only beg the basic questions. They can never generate explanations of why precisely these utterances were produced under these circumstances, any more than unmitigated formalism could do so. If an unbalanced commitment to irreducibility leads to sterile formalism, a commitment to sheer relationality always ends up in reductionism. By dint of generalizations, one abstracts upwards to a level at which the specifics of social interaction become irrelevant. What people actually say on a given occasion gets lost in structural factors posing as root causes or emergent ones posing as immaculate experiences. Although I tried to show in Chapter 6 that the phenomenologists have a good deal more structure to offer than is commonly assumed, this reductionism is one of the criticisms often leveled at them. Extreme relationalists who deny structure entirely fit into what Charles Taylor (1985: chapter 4) has lucidly criticized as the "false ally" of radical relativism. The inadequacy of radical relativism lies in the incorrigibility thesis, whereby our description of another culture must be in its own terms, which effectively guarantees that it will be circular. It would also be naive to think that a culture provides a single set of terms or that even if it did, there would be a single correct way to concretize them. Located at the crux of irreducible and relational explanations, the approach to language-in-context proposed here rejects both extremes. Any theory of language use that renders explanation of Margot's actual words either otiose or circular is wrong by definition.

Let's look back at our example to see whether we can recover some of the transparency we have by now lost. Yuum asked if Don Chabo was seated, but it is misleading to suggest that this exhausts the literal meaning of his question. There is a conventional pattern of usage in Maya whereby the stative participle *kul áʔan* is used to refer to the state of being in one's home, irrespective of what one is doing or where one is within the inclusive perimeter. The idea is evidently that the home is the prototypical place in which one is seated. It's a little like the English "go to the bathroom" which can describe acts of elimination quite irrespective of where they take place. Although there are about a dozen other commonly used derivational forms based on the positional root *kul* 'be seated (human)', none of them is used in this way, and *kul á'an* virtually always is. This all suggests that there is a convention in Maya and that a really accurate rendering of the literal meaning of Yuum's sentence would have to reflect it. In other words, literal meaning is fixed by local standards, and what Yuum said was, "Is Don Chabo home?"

As for the question of drinking and eating, there is another standard, as we discussed in Chapter 5. Recall that when making reference to food consumption within the diurnal cycle, morning and evening meals are described as *ˀuk'ul* 'drink' and the main meal in midafternoon is described as *hanal* 'eat'. As a matter of fact, Maya people almost never eat without accompanying beverages, nor do they usually "drink" without accompanying food, if only a bit of starch. This accounts for Don Chabo's eating bread while he was said to be drinking. But there is one more element to consider. If the eating and drinking had already been completed and Don Chabo were leaning back smoking a cigarette, as is typical, Margot's assertion would be judged equally true. This is because once we understand the activity designated by *ˀuk'ul* 'drink' within the frame of daily meals, which is the relevant one for it, then its temporal extent changes. It is not coextensive with the actual ingestion of liquids or solids but rather with the social engagement of sitting together, relaxing between periods of work, conversing with one's consociates, and sharing food. To borrow terms used by George Herbert Mead in his brilliant essay on the philosophy of the present (1980:23), we can say that the "temporal diameter" of Margot's reference is fixed not by any physical criterion of simultaneity but rather by the character of the event to which it corresponds. That is, contiguity in time, as in space, is socially defined. This is another way of saying that literality, in this case the literal present, is fixed by local standards. And the use of words like these constitutes a bridge between the vivid present of the utterance and the horizon of typical usage.

What we have done, then, is to reassert the existence of a literal meaning, but in a revised version. It is no longer the purely irreducible content of words taken in isolation from their relational contexts—no longer the kind of logical propositionality that one can compare to a world of things outside itself, in order to judge correspondence or noncorrespondence in a strictly objective way. Instead, it is a literality that is already relational in character, both irreducible and relational at the same time. Without taking into account the irreducible system of Maya language, one cannot even pose the important questions, since there is no noncircular way of identifying what speakers actually say. Without taking into account the relational matrix in which the language exists, it is equally impossible to explain verbal action, since there is no noncircular way of identifying the objects of reference and description.

The Fine Art of Reference

One of the most powerful examples of the interaction between grammatical form and context are the terms grammarians usually call demonstratives, indexicals, or sometimes deictics. Recall from Chapter 3 that both Peirce and Morris define indexicals as signs whose interpretation depends upon the coexistence of the sign form and the object. Rommetveit, among others, accords indexicals a central place in message structure. He uses the example of words like "here," "now," "I," "you," "this," and "that" which appear to point at things in the world (hence the term "deictic," from Greek "to point"). The reason they are interesting is because of the peculiar way they become meaningful. If you think about it for a moment, what does "here" mean? It seems to denote wherever I am when I utter it, or at least always some place close to me at that moment. What about "there"? On the face of it, it appears to be the opposite; "there" denotes wherever I'm not at the moment I utter it, or at least somewhere a little farther off than wherever "here" is. You can imagine that the form "I" has attracted a great deal of attention from philosophers, linguists, and others who work on discourse, since it so obviously raises issues of subjectivity, self-awareness, and the social role of speaker. Some have even claimed that this little word is actually the nexus of subjectivity, since it is the central resource we have to make reference to ourselves. Although I do not hold this position, I can see where they are coming from (see the Benveniste and Lyons references at the end of this chapter). The line of research represented by Goodwin (1990) in turn shows that whatever "I" is taken to mean, it must be understood relative to participation frameworks in which the repertoire of roles is much greater than the traditional dyad of speaker-addressee (cf. Chapter 9). Moreover, the dynamics of role occupancy go far beyond received notions of what it is to be a speaker. These issues have been central in much of my own research, and we will return to them in the next chapters. For now, we will concentrate on the special status of demonstratives and pronouns in relation to the language-context nexus. This will allow us to zero in on Margot's choice of words in responding to Yuum.

What makes indexicals interesting, for our purposes, is that they are so obviously and thoroughly relational. As indexicals, their meaning is always a matter of the relation between the utterance, the situation in which it is produced, and the object being talked about. This point is easier to get a handle on with examples, and in a moment we will look again at Margot's response to Yuum. First, though, it is important to see that demonstratives give equally forceful testimony for irreducibility as they do for relationality. Every known human language has deictics, and this fact suggests that they are part of language sui generis. Hence it is unsurprising to encounter a model of copresence based on the relations summarized as we-here-now, as we do in Schutz and Rommetveit. Even though the meaning of a word like I changes from case to case, depending upon who says it, it is also *constant* in the sense of pointing to whoever utters it.[1] Hence, the form has inherent

---

[1] I hold aside transposed uses, including quotation, until Chapter 9. For example, imagine that Natalia told a friend about her morning coffee with Jack, saying, "Jack said, 'I'll take mine black with sugar.'" In this type of utterance, the actual speaker of the quote (Natalia) is not the referent of the pronoun, but the original speaker (Jack) is. This is a case in which what Voloshinov called the meaning of the pronoun remains constant, whereas its theme changes decisively. The sense relations encoded in the pronoun form can be shown to be exactly the same as in nontransposed cases (cf. Hanks 1990: Chapter 5).

meaning alongside its relational meaning. Grammarians have long recognized that these words are intimately tied into the categorical structure of language, which is another way of saying that they have a purely formal side, and this, too, argues for irreducibility. Indeed, a recent synthesis of the literature on language use states that "the single most obvious way in which the relationship between language and context is reflected in the structures of languages themselves is through the phenomenon of deixis" (Levinson 1983:54). We have a natural locus, then, in which to examine language in context without falling into the old trap of claiming that either one is derivative of the other.

When Margot told Yuum to "go over there," she conveyed quite clearly that Don Chabo was not to be interrupted, but she did more than just this. She acknowledged Yuum's presence in the yard and her own face-to-face relation with him. This is less trivial than it might seem, since entering another person's yard at night and addressing the wife of the man of the house from just outside the window would under many circumstances be a grave violation of propriety and might even be grounds for arrest. Now it is tempting to say that this little bit of acknowledgment is a purely relational fact with no special relevance to language. After all, she could have acknowledged him with a smile or a wave, and she could have told him to go away with a gesture. What she would have had much more difficulty accomplishing without speech would be to acknowledge him, direct him to go elsewhere, and precisely signal her own relation to Don Chabo's house *all at once.* For in the very act of making this utterance, Margot set herself apart from Don Chabo's house. In order to see why I say this, we have to understand the linguistic meaning of *toloˀ* 'over there' more precisely. It is one of five basic spatial deictics in Maya, shown below.

way eˀ *'here (the region that includes me now)'*
toloˀ *'over there (outside the region that includes me)'*

téˀel aˀ *'right here (the spot I hereby point to)'*
téˀel oˀ *'there (a spot of intermediate distance from us)'*

tiˀ iˀ *'there (where we said)'*

Where English has two basic words to choose from, Maya has five. (I omit from this count the dozens of combined forms based on modifying and collocating the basic ones.) The spacing between the sets of deictics listed above is meant to reflect the minimal oppositions by which they are organized: The first two are dichotomous opposites. The second two form an opposition in which the proximal form is the more marked or informationally rich. The last form is really different from all the others, since it encodes no particular spatial value apart from denoting a place known to both interlocutors, irrespective of distance or perceptibility. The form Margot chose was the second one, which is used for places that are maximally distant from the speaker, typically on the other side of a social, perceptual, or physical boundary. So, for instance, relatives who live outside Yucatán, in other states of the Mexican republic, would be said to be *toloˀ*, just as a hunting ground seven hours away from Oxkutzcab in the southern forests, where one hunts scarcely a couple of times a year, is *toloˀ*. The key factor is not just physical distance, although this helps. Rather, it is distance in the sense of being beyond whatever one's perceived zone of immediacy is. As I pointed out above, Maya households are typically surrounded by physical barriers (like stone walls) and internally subdivided by social barriers that have powerful effects on people's behavior. Don Chabo would never enter Margot's kitchen, for instance, without an explicit invitation, and this would not happen without the consent, tacit or expressed, of her husband, Manuel. Similarly, she enters his living quarters only when she has a reason to be there. Hence, the referent of her deictic, her father-in-law's home, is in a space that excludes her in the relevant sense—even though it is no more than 10 meters away, within the same walled household.

If you put together these brief remarks about Maya households and Maya language, you will see that Margot faced a significant choice in making a response to Yuum. She could just as easily have said to him, *way yaneˀ*, *kulenˀ ič nah* 'Yeah, he's here; have a seat inside', using as her frame of reference the entire homestead whose boundary is marked by the wall. This would be equally proper Maya, and I have attested many cases like it. It would display perfect semantic competence in an idealized world. Indeed, as we saw earlier, it is precisely this total expanse of the household that defines where one is when one is *kuláˀan* 'seated'. Therefore this response would have been even more directly tied into Yuum's question than the one she actually gave, since it would have indexed precisely the same spatial frame of reference. But her position in the house is not the same as Yuum's. As an outsider, he appropriately presupposes the entire homestead as his frame of reference; to do otherwise would have been truly presumptuous. She, in contrast, is a resident member of the household, and she cannot just adopt an outsider's perspective without running a serious risk of misinterpretation. If she had said, "Yeah, he's here; have a seat inside," Margot would not merely have described Don Chabo as being in a particular place. Rather, she would have conveyed something potentially intimate about herself at the very same time. In saying "He's here; have a seat by the altar," she would have been saying as much as "He is where I am," "He is with me," "My here includes his home," "His altar is part of my here, the place in which I have the right to tell you what to do." Indeed, if she were Don Chabo's wife and not his daughter-in-law, and he were having supper in a kitchen that belonged to him and not to his son, then this is exactly what we would expect her to say. This is true even if the physical distances were much greater. And to have told Yuum to go *toloˀ* 'over there' would have been automatically interpreted as ordering him to get out of the yard.

My point in these remarks is that the intelligibility of Margot's response turns crucially on her relation to the homestead, *even though this is the one thing that never gets mentioned.* Indeed, as a resident woman, her position is usually invisible because taken for granted until further notice. As Voloshinov would have put it, the very referential content of her expression is molded by her social evaluation of the situation in which she uttered it. Just as Merleau-Ponty predicted in his philosophy of the phenomenal field, she displays a dauntingly precise consciousness of her own physical setting, her position in the setting, and the horizon of acceptable positions that she can potentially occupy. But beyond what Merleau-Ponty foresaw, it is the minute details of linguistic structure that coordinate this awareness and make it known with a delicacy unparalleled by any other mode of expression. On first appearances, Margot could be an anonymous third person observer stating an objective fact about a man and directing a visitor to his house. But when one looks more closely and takes into account the stock of knowledge on which native speakers draw, the fallacy of such a view becomes obvious. Margot has made reference to her father-in-law's house in terms that automatically situate it in a relation of exteriority to her. There are no stone walls between the two, but the social, economic, and gender divisions between her kitchen and her father-in-law's house all come into play. Furthermore, the indexical components encoded in the words of this exchange force her to situate herself in relation to her father-in-law, in the very act of answering Yuum's question. Because of the bridges between the words and the spatial setting, there is no neutral way of telling Yuum to wait for Don Chabo in his house without simultaneously taking up her own position in relation to the house. Routine examples like this one indicate that social relations between participants and the speech setting have a central place in the context through which thematic meaning emerges. They also suggest the inverse: An analysis of social relations that is deaf to linguistic practice will be blind to some of the most revealing displays of its own object.

This example and other ones like it can help us to better understand the interactions between formal and contextual poles of language. Just as being "seated" and engaged in the activity called "drinking" are social facts defined locally, to speak of things as "here" or "there," or oneself as "I" and one's other as "you," is to engage oneself in a network of social relations. In the act of making reference to the world, one takes up a position in it. It follows that we as researchers must work through social contexts in order to determine the reference of speech. There is nothing new in this observation, but it is worth emphasizing the considerable burden it places on students of human language. For as a simple matter of data collection, it is impossible to recognize meanings without situating them relationally. And this has as one of its consequences that the entire apparatus of formalism is suspended at a remove from language and meaning, so long as one fails to ground it in local understandings. Here we are merely reiterating the relational thesis, which is likely to be obvious to social scientists without much argument. The sword cuts both ways, though, and it has become equally clear that analyses of verbal meaning based solely on context never quite attain their object, so long as they fail to define it sui generis. There may be no reference without a social context, as Voloshinov and Rommetveit argued, but there would be no social context as we know it without reference either.

Conclusion

From the phenomenologists Voloshinov and Rommetveit, we learn that meaning production takes place upon a horizon of already constituted knowledge and practice. However we treat utterance context, it must include some account of this horizon. According to Ingarden, the horizon was present in discourse as a field of potential meanings, not actualized in the focal structure of text but still there as viable alternatives to it—other meanings that have been conveyed in the past and so could be conveyed with the expression in the present. For Schutz, the horizon was the background of commonsense knowledge, a sliding scale of typifications ranging from the fully saturated knowledge of the world of consociates to the relatively schematic and vague knowledge of an anonymous world of contemporaries and predecessors. For Ingarden, it is in the context of an actual concretization of the literary work that the whole field of its potential signification is subdefined into actual, potential-held-in-ready, and merely potential meanings. The implication is that "context" has several different levels whose properties may differ. The horizon is a sort of background defined in relation to the foreground of actualized meaning. "Context" includes both levels. Schutz held that the stock of knowledge at any moment was configured according to the practical interests of the actor. Hence for both philosophers, the context as horizon is continuously restructured according to the present activity. It is not that people are making knowledge de novo at every moment but that the background of what is already known is revisable according to the purposes at hand.

As we saw, the horizon(s) on which Margot's exchange with Yuum took place have elements of past verbal interactions, shared knowledge of domestic architecture, the overall organization of the household, and a commensurate knowledge of Maya language. Margot's utterance and Yuum's understanding also presuppose the paradigms of alternative spatial descriptions that she could have used but did not. All this means that the exchange has value against a social background that preexists it and will last longer than it. Context may be organized out of the vivid present of utterances, but it is equally preformed by histories and social facts that linger in the blank spots and silences of speech. Not everything is revisable.

How shall we talk about the histories and social values of actualized contexts and their horizons? Must we know and rehearse the entire history of Yuum's relations with Don Chabo, Margot, and the household in order to adequately describe the exchange at the window? Relevance is helpful in this regard, since it cuts a swath through the total background to pull out and order a selective portion of it. The notion of deictic coordinates to which Rommetveit makes appeal is another relational schema, the familiar space-time-person coordinates. It is as though these three were always relevant or somehow above the fray of shifting relevance. Rommetveit follows a long tradition when he treats space as relative contiguity, time as sequence (before and after), and person as speaker/addressee. The modern study of interaction has led to refined definitions of these dimensions, however, which effectively render Rommetveit's three axes obsolete as terms of theory. In this chapter we have seen some of the evidence of this in relation to space and participant role. The next two chapters will push the question further, exploring the cultural embeddedness of "context" and the dynamics of participation.

Further Readings

Related to utterance meaning and the unavoidability of context

Basso, E. "Contextualization in Kalapalo Narratives." In *Rethinking Context: Language as an Interactive Phenomenon,* edited by A. Duranti and C. Goodwin. Cambridge: Cambridge University Press, 1992. Chap. 9, pp. 253–269.

Basso, K. H. "Speaking with Names: Language and Landscape Among the Western Apache." *Cultural Anthropology* 3(2) (1988):99–130.

Benveniste, E. "Le Langage et l'expérience humaine." In *Problèmes de linguistique générale,* vol. 2. Paris: Gallimard, 1974 [1965], pp. 67–78.

Clark, H. "Common Ground and the Understanding of Demonstrative Reference." In *Arenas of Language Use.* Chicago: University of Chicago Press, 1992, Chap. 3, pp. 78–100.

Hanks, W. F. *Referential Practice: Language and Lived Space Among the Maya.* Chicago: University of Chicago Press, 1990. Chap. 2.4, pp. 74–80; chap. 3, pp. 81–134.

Levinson, S. *Pragmatics.* Cambridge: Cambridge University Press, 1983. Chap. 2, pp. 54–94.

Voloshinov, V. N. *Marxism and the Philosophy of Language.* Translated by L. Matejka and I. R. Titunik. Cambridge: Harvard University Press, 1986 [1929]. Part 3, chap. 3, "Verbal Interaction," pp. 83–98; chap. 4, "Theme and Meaning in Language," pp. 98–106.

Related to message structure

Goffman, E. "The Neglected Situation." In *Language and Social Context,* edited by P. P. Giglioli. Harmondsworth, England: Penguin, 1972, pp. 61–66.

Hanks, W. F. *Referential Practice: Language and Lived Space Among the Maya.* Chicago: University of Chicago Press, 1990. Chap. 2.1, pp. 33–49; chap. 2.4, pp. 74–80; chap. 3.1, pp. 81–86; chap. 4.1, pp. 137–154; chap. 5.1–5.2, pp. 192–205; chap. 5.4, pp. 252–254.

———. "The Indexical Ground of Deictic Reference." In *Rethinking Context: Language as an Interactive Phenomenon,* edited by A. Duranti and C. Goodwin. Cambridge: Cambridge University Press, 1992. Chap. 2, pp. 43–76.

Rommetveit, R. *On Message Structure: A Framework for the Study of Language and Communication.* New York: Wiley, 1974, chap. 4, "On the Architecture of Intersubjectivity," pp. 29–86.

Silverstein, M. "Shifters, Verbal Categories and Cultural Description." In *Meaning in Anthropology,* edited by K. Basso and H. Selby. Albuquerque: School of American Research, 1976, pp. 11–55.

On the linguistic treatment of ellipsis, see

Morgan, J. "Sentence Fragments and the Notion 'Sentence.'" In *Issues in Linguistics: Papers in Honor of Henry and Renée Kahane,* edited by B. B. Kachru et al. Urbana: University of Illinois Press, 1973, pp. 719–751.

Sag, I. A., and Hankamer, J. "Deep and Surface Anaphora." *Linguistic Inquiry* 7(3) (1976):391–426.

Further perspectives on context

Bourdieu, P. *Outline of a Theory of Practice.* Translated by R. Nice. Cambridge: Cambridge University Press, 1977 [1972]. Chap. 2, "Structures and the Habitus," pp. 72–95.

———. "Le Marché linguistique." In *Questions de sociologie.* Paris: Editions de Minuit, 1984, pp. 121–137.

Cicourel, A. "The Interpenetration of Communicative Contexts: Examples from Medical Encounters." In *Rethinking Context: Language as an Interactive Phenomenon,* edited by A. Duranti and C. Goodwin. Cambridge: Cambridge University Press, 1992. Chap. 11, pp. 291–310.

Clark, H. "Context for Comprehension." In *Arenas of Language Use.* Chicago: University of Chicago Press, 1992. Chap. 2, pp. 60–77.

Duranti, A. "Language in Context and Languages as Context: The Samoan Respect Vocabulary." In *Rethinking Context: Language as an Interactive Phenomenon,* edited by A. Duranti and C. Goodwin. Cambridge: Cambridge University Press, 1992. Chap. 3, pp. 77–100.

Gal, S. "Language and Political Economy." *Annual Review of Anthropology* 18 (1989):347–367.

Gumperz, J. *Discourse Strategies.* Cambridge: Cambridge University Press, 1982.

Lindstrom, L. "Context Contests: Debatable Truth Statements on Tanna (Vanuatu)." In *Rethinking Context: Language as an Interactive Phenomenon,* edited by A. Duranti and C. Goodwin. Cambridge: Cambridge University Press, 1992. Chap. 4, pp. 101–124.

An example from the field: on contemporary Yucatán and its colonial legacy, see

Bricker, V. R. *The Indian Christ, the Indian King, the Historical Substrate of Maya Myth and Ritual.* Austin: University of Texas Press, 1981.

Farriss, N. *Maya Society Under Colonial Rule: The Collective Enterprise of Survival.* Princeton: Princeton University Press, 1984.

Hanks, W. F. "Authenticity and Ambivalence in the Text: A Colonial Maya Case." *American Ethnologist* 13(4) (1986):721–744.

———. *Referential Practice: Language and Lived Space Among the Maya.* Chicago: University of Chicago Press, 1990. Chaps. 4–5 on pronouns; chaps. 6–7 on domestic space; chap. 8 on shamanic practice; chap. 9 on spatial deictics.

Redfield, R., and Villa Rojas, A. *Chan Kom: A Maya Village.* Chicago: University of Chicago Press, 1962 [1934].

Chapter 8

Relativity, Reflexivity, and Difference

WE ENDED THE LAST CHAPTER with the suggestion that "context," however we define it, is a cultural phenomenon. The engagements sustained by participants in talk are of a piece with the larger social world to which they belong; context, no less than lexical meaning or the "pragmatic" effect of utterances, must be defined in relation to the values, beliefs, and routine practices of speakers. And further, context has several levels whose properties are not all the same. This way of viewing context is at odds with any universal framework like the ones proposed by Grice (Chapter 5), Schutz (Chapter 6), and Rommetveit (Chapter 7). Or at least it forces us to ask what a properly universal basis for context would be. We cannot give a decisive answer to this question but will continue to work away at it in the present chapter.

The first topic we will address is the so-called relativity hypothesis, the idea that there is a significant relation between the language people speak and the way they understand their experience. The special relevance of this hypothesis for our purposes is that it implies a reflexive relation between ways of speaking and ways of constituting context. Although the classic formulations of relativity were based on analysis of semantic categories, we will revisit them on the basis of indexical ones. For indexicals provide the most obvious and perhaps the most central nexus between linguistic form and the situations of utterance production. From here we move on to the descriptive paradigm called ethnography of communication, a broad approach to speech analysis developed by anthropologists and sociolinguists during the 1970s. We will focus on two aspects of this paradigm, the treatment of "ways of speaking" and the description of ethnopoetics and performance. These will provide a further vantage point from which to consider the question of indexical relativity. The third major theme is discourse style and textuality, topics that ethnographers of communication have already opened up but that have become increasingly central in the field, particularly since the 1980s. It has two consequences for the language-context interface: first, that the units of language must be expanded to include discourse genres and intertextual series; second, that these same intertextual complexes are part of the context for any given discourse production. In other words, in a basic way language *is* context.

The final section of the chapter treats what I will call the ideological dimension. "Ideology" has a range of meanings in social theory, from the general values and beliefs that people hold to the self-justifying and distorted rationalizations that undergird their social positions. Although we will draw on these concepts, my use of the term here is slightly different. From our perspective the metalinguistic capacity inherent in human languages (Chapter 3) and the prevalence of metalingual discourse in everyday speech imply that native *speakers typify their own language and speech.* This means in turn that the semantics and context of speaking are partly defined by the ideas of native speakers, however distorted these may appear from an analytic perspective. The chapter moves, then, from the reflexive interplay between language and experience, through functionally differentiated modes and styles of discourse, to the second-order reflexivity of ideologies of language. Rather than conceiving of a purely formal language placed in an inert context, we end with a picture of contextualization as a set of dynamic tensions among sociocultural elements whose definitions depend critically upon one another.

Linguistic Relativity and Mediation

We begin with the early development of North American linguistic anthropology and first formulations of the relativity hypothesis in the writings of Franz Boas, Edward Sapir, and Benjamin Whorf. Despite their being in certain ways outdated, these writings make a significant contribution to contemporary issues by clearly setting forth the relations among language form, routine patterns of speaking, and the ways that people experience. From here we move on to reconsider aspects of the relativity hypothesis from the vantage point of indexical categories. What does it mean to suggest, as we did in the last chapter, that Margot's perceptions of her domestic context are "coordinated" or "channeled" by the deictic categories of her language? The question here is not so much whether Maya language is essentially different from, say, English, and hence whether Margot and Yuum inhabit a different world from Jack and Natalia. Their worlds are obviously different in some ways and alike in others. Rather, the key question is how to analyze indexical reference in such a way as to reveal the dynamics through which verbally mediated meaning is produced.

Boas's classic "Introduction to the Handbook of American Indian Languages" (1911) was a wide-ranging and influential essay that was to set the stage for the early development of anthropological linguistics. In it he focused on cross-linguistic variation and the relative boundedness of any given language. There is a strong parallel between his starting points and those of Saussure (Chapter 2), although, as we will see, his conclusions were quite different. Languages differ in two major ways, namely, the groups of sounds that they define as meaningful and the groups of ideas that they associate with fixed phonetic groups (i.e., words and morphemes). Whereas a language like English defines as meaningful the distinction between "p" and "b" (cf. pin ≠ bin) and "t" and "th" (cf. tin ≠ thin), Maya distinguishes "p" versus "p'" (glottalized; cf. *pik* 'appear' ≠ *p'ik* 'break up into pieces') and "t" from "t'" (cf. *taán* 'front' ≠ *t'àan* 'speak'). Hence the two languages have different phonemic inventories. Similarly, whereas the Maya expression *kìik* designates specifically "elder sister," the same concept requires two words in English.

The languages also have different "semantic inventories." This point is reminiscent of Saussure's evidence for arbitrariness. For Boas, it was the point of departure in relating language to thought. He reasoned that if each word is associated with a limited number of ideas and the total number of words in any language is also limited, then the total inventory of ideas expressed by words in any language must itself be limited. Like thought, language is inherently classificatory. "So the infinitely large number of ideas have been reduced by classification to a lesser number, which by constant use have established firm associations, and which can be used automatically" (Boas 1966:21). The last part of this quote underscores the repeated use of words to routinize certain associations. From a logical perspective, this routine factor is significant, because if it were not present, the expression of an infinite number of thoughts would require an equally infinite number of words, and the linguistic system would be forever unstable. Boas goes on to give a series of interesting examples to demonstrate the cross-linguistic variations in verbal classification, which help define a perspective on the relation between linguistic form, the grouping of ideas, and routine speech.

If Boas's reasoning about grammatical categories is sound, then we can see why languages have syntax. For in noting the limited number of words in any language, Boas was not suggesting that verbal expression, much less thought, was similarly limited. It was only through the combinations and modifications of stable lexical units into larger structures that the infinity of human thought could be expressed through the finite repertoire of stable units in language. Although he proposed no principle of infinite generativity such as Chomsky's, Boas did recognize the expressive power of syntax. On this point he went beyond Saussure, distinguishing what Sapir was later to label word order (order of units in phrases and sentences), composition (formation of words via compounding, subordination, and incorporation), affixation (use of prefixes, suffixes, infixes), internal modification (as in the shift from high to low tone, which marks possession in certain nouns in Maya), reduplication (which in many languages marks plurality of reference or distributive as opposed to collective plural), and accentual alteration (shifts of stress and pitch). The key point here is that a language is not a collection of words but instead a system organized around structural patterns. Indeed, as Boas pointed out with examples from Eskimo, Pawnee, and Kwakuitl, words are identifiable only through analysis. Rather than being the natural building blocks of language, as common sense might have it, they are what remains after the linguist has factored out all formal elements. Note that although Boas's concern with the relation of language to thought and culture is classically "relationalist" in the sense of our opening theses (Chapter 1), his attention to the combinatorial capacity of grammar is consistent with formal irreducibility. No less than the formalists in Part 1 of this book, Boas provided convincing evidence that languages have determinate structures that must be taken into account in any explanation of verbal practice.

The Boasian attention to grammatical pattern was further developed in the work of Sapir. In his articles "Psychological Reality of Phonemes," and "Sound Patterns in Language," Sapir showed that phonological systems (i.e., the sound systems of languages) are essentially intricate patterns in which the elements are defined by their mutual oppositions and contrasts. He called this pattern the "inner configuration" of the sounds in the language. Recall the Saussurian concept of *valeur,* by which the meaning of an expression is defined by its opposition to other, comparable ones. In the two Sapir articles cited, the focus is on sound patterns and not semantic patterns. Sapir demonstrated that two languages could actually employ just the same inventory of sounds, yet their patterned relations could be distinct. This would result in two quite different systems. So for instance, English speakers routinely pronounce the sounds ["b"], as in "boy," ["p"] as in "hip," and ["p+"] ("p" followed by a burst of air, called aspiration), as in "pin." As it happens, the difference between the two versions of "p" makes no difference in meaning, since there is no word "p+in" with a sense distinct from plain "pin," no word "hip+" with a sense different from "hip," and so forth. In another language, however, the aspirated sound might well indicate distinct words with unrelated meanings. The central idea here is that the material reality of the sounds is not really what matters in language. It is instead their value in the linguistic pattern and whether they distinguish meanings or not. There is a significant parallel between Sapir and Saussure's arbitrariness principle on this point, although Sapir never makes reference to objects in the world (compare Chapter 2).

Where Sapir's reasoning begins to break away from the Saussurian analogue and follow the path of Boas is when he observes the effect of these patterns on people's perception. In an early article entitled "Alternating Sounds," Boas had noticed that speakers of one language tend to hear the sounds in another language through the pattern of their own. So English speakers hear French through the sound system of their native language and tend to have a hard time distinguishing *tout* 'all' (pronounced roughly like English "too") from *tu* 'you' (pronounced with a fronted rounded vowel nonexistent in English). Similarly, English-speaking students of Maya tend to confuse glottalized (explosive) consonants with plain ones because this distinction makes no difference in their native language, although it makes all the difference in Maya. Boas illustrated this phenomenon with languages like Eskimo, Pawnee, and Chinook, showing that native speakers' perceptions of a foreign language shifted according to the context. Think of Japanese speakers' mistaking English "r" for "l" because the distinction is not maintained in Japanese. In a way this is a special case of the well-known phenomenon whereby we perceive the novel through the lens of the familiar. Where Boas, and later Sapir, pushed this observation to a new level was in proposing that the inner configurations of a language—any language—act as a sort of perceptual screen through which speakers experience the world. Once we move this basic concept to the level of meanings or syntactic features, it suggests that our native language predisposes us to recognize certain meanings in a foreign language while misrecognizing others. Even more, it predisposes us to perceive the world around us in terms of a specific set of categories. This predisposition is the root of what would come to be known as the "relativity hypothesis." The idea is that our ways of perceiving, and perhaps even thinking, depend nontrivially on the structure of our language. Few ideas in linguistics have provoked more widespread interest or been subject to more grotesque misunderstanding.

The name most often associated with relativity in this sense is Benjamin Lee Whorf. During the 1950s Whorf produced a series of studies of Native American languages and general issues in the conceptual consequences of language structure. Contrary to popular misconceptions, Whorf advocated the idea that all human languages share certain properties. Like Sapir before him (see Sapir 1921:107), he was a proponent of universals. In subsequent literature the notion of relativity has been frequently opposed to universality. Under this view if each language structures experience in a unique way, then it should be impossible in principle to define properties common to all languages (see Berlin and Kay 1969:2 for this position). This led to claims that if Whorf were right, and "everything were relative," it would be impossible to learn a foreign language, to translate from one to another, or even to distinguish good from bad. The fact is that the notion of relativity as it developed in Americanist linguistics was never advanced in this way, and the extreme version is more a parody of Whorf than an accurate statement of his position. To hold that language predisposes speakers to certain ways of experiencing is not to deny the existence of features common to all languages. The two ideas are logically independent. It is to posit a particular kind of mediation: to say that the pathways of habitual linguistic practice intervene between the individual and the world.

The notion of relativity as developed in the Americanist tradition was always linked to *certain aspects* of thought and experience and, correlatively, to *certain features* of language and habitual speech. The idea is not that language determines what people *can* think but that it tends to influence what they routinely *do* think. In much of the debate over relativity, this notion of *a linguistically motivated predisposition* has been misconstrued as the idea that language determines people's capacity to think and experience. This misconstrual is another by-product of formalism. For to say that a linguistic system drives the experiences of its speakers is to say that the limits of grammatical structure define the limits of thought. The systemic potential of the one constrains the systemic potential of the other. A more interesting and historically accurate interpretation, by contrast, locates the dynamic not at the level of pure potentials but of actualities. Habitual ways of speaking, the patterns of reference and description that people engage in from day to day, may influence the way they implicitly categorize experience.

In early Americanist writings this influence was taken to be rooted first in the obligatory categories of language. That is, the grammar of any human language makes the indication of certain relations obligatory in order for a phrase or sentence to be well formed. For example, an English speaker who wishes to convey that Jack chopped a log can say, "Jack chopped the log" or "Jack chopped a log" but does not have the option of saying merely "Jack chopped log." The English speaker must select among the definite or indefinite articles, which implies an obligatory decision regarding the relative definiteness of the reference to "log." Moreover, the number must also be marked—if a single log, it is singular; if more than one, it is plural. Contrast this with Maya, in which a speaker could express roughly the same idea in any of the following ways:

1. ***Juaneˀ, tu č'akah le čeˀ oˀ.*** 'Juan chopped the wood (for fire).'
2. ***Juaneˀ, tu č'akah un ꝗ'iít čeˀ.*** 'Juan chopped one elongate piece of wood.'
3. ***Juaneˀ, č'akčeˀ nahih.*** 'Juan wood-chopped.'
4. ***Juaneˀ, síˀ nahih.*** 'Juan fire-wood-chopped.'

Given the grammar of Maya, the obligatory choices are different from those in English, first, because the Maya speaker can readily express relative definiteness (1, 2) or avoid the issue entirely (3), and, second, because plural marking in Maya is not obligatory, so that example 1 could be either singular or plural in reference. Yet if the Maya speaker does count the object, as in 2, then he must include in the number a grammatical form called a numeral classifier (*un ꝗ'iít* 'one elongate piece' in example 2). The function of classifiers is to indicate something about the shape or type of the object being counted. Similarly, whereas Jack asks Natalia, "D'the paper come today?" the corresponding Maya expression would contain reference to "paper," not "the paper." The use of the definite article in the Maya translation would unambiguously imply a specific copy or edition of the newspaper. So Maya speakers are led to signal explicitly certain features of the scene that English speakers need not address, and vice versa. This signaling implies, for Whorf, a conceptual attention to the corresponding feature of the scene.

According to Sapir and Whorf, the classifications implicit in obligatory and optional categories function as templates that are extended by analogy. In Whorf's famous discussion of Hopi and English plurals, he pointed out that English speakers pluralize nonconcrete entities such as time and cyclic occurrence (cf. five times, ten steps, four visits) as though they were physical entities that could be grouped together and counted. That is, the pattern of obligatory pluralization that is established in relation to concrete count nouns (denoting things that can be collected in a single place and time) is extended by analogy to nouns designating nonconcrete entities. The latter he called "imaginary plurals."

Whorf adopted Sapir's view of linguistic categories as interrelated, and hence he looked to large-scale patterns. Yet he also treated differently distinct subsystems of a language, such as tense and time reference, pluralization, and verb semantics. As John Lucy (1985, 1991) pointed out, Whorf never sought to connect human thought directly to grammatical categories. Hence he never suggested that a mere inventory of words (such as the much-cited Eskimo words for snow) or even a set of categories could be said to cause certain ways of thinking on the part of thc nativc speakers of the language. The relation between language and thought was mediated, he said, by "fashions of speaking," generalized styles and patterns of verbal expression that belong not to grammar but to people's routine linguistic practice. The process of analogical projection from a concrete category to a nonconcrete domain of experience Whorf called "objectification." Although he used the contrast between Hopi and English to argue that English speakers "objectify" in ways that Hopi speakers do not, the implication of his argument is that all languages involve objectification, albeit of various kinds.

There has been a considerable growth of interest in the issue of relativity in recent years. In the 1970s Paul Friedrich reexamined relativity in the light of poetic analysis (see the next section), arguing that the poetic resources of language were actually the most powerful elements in establishing routine patterns that speakers project into new experiences, including the products of their imagination. Working more on the border between psychology and linguistics and focusing on referential-denotational language, Lucy has sought to reformulate the ideas of Boas, Sapir, and Whorf in a way sufficiently precise to be experimentally studied. Similarly, linguists, psycholinguists, and anthropologists at the Max Planck Institute for Psycholinguistics in Nijmegen, the Netherlands, have been working for several years on the universal and language-specific structures of spatial orientation, trying to bring the notion of relativity to the specialized but fundamental domain of spatial representation and reckoning (see the references at the end of this chapter). Any current application of this concept must take into account the kinds of semantic indeterminacy discussed in Chapters 5 to 7. For one thing, the meanings of linguistic forms are now recognized to be much less specific than was believed when Whorf and Sapir were writing. We saw this with the phenomenologists, particularly Ingarden, but it has come to be appreciated in modern semantic theories as well (as we saw in Chapters 5 and 7). There is also a wider appreciation of speakers' capacity to get around obligatory categories by rephrasing and circumlocution. This means that no set of obligatory categories can be assumed to mechanically determine people's choice of words. Similarly, the pervasive role of indexicality in language and speech has the result of recasting semantic categories once analyzed as pure forms to semantic categories whose content in any utterance is a function of their relation to speech context.

The cumulative effect of these developments is that there is a new relativity principle emerging. It says that literal meaning itself (which Whorf and many of his proponents and detractors alike took for granted) is a product of the relation between language form and utterance context. Hence the meaning of linguistic categories in use is context-relative, and this is logically prior to any relativity between habitual thought and language structure. In a sense, these developments imply that a good bit less comes along with the knowing of a language than was implied by the early relativity writings. Furthermore, it bears repeating that the issue is not whether grammar somehow constrains what people *can* think or perceive. To pose the question in this way is to buy into the formalist thesis of a direct relation between language, viewed as systemic potential, and thought, also viewed as pure potential. So stated, the relativity thesis is self-defeating. What we need instead is to examine the actuality of practice in its relational contexts. Knowing what we now know about indeterminacy, habituation, and indexicality, we can restate the issue in more productive terms. Communicative practice and the verbal categories it engages do help sediment routine ways of perceiving and acting. This in no way implies that people are *incapable* of nonroutine thought but only that socially established habits of language both guide and facilitate the ways they *typically* think, perceive, and act.

Indexicality, Relativity, and Universals of Context

During the 1950s, as Whorf was advancing the relativity hypothesis and Chomsky's early writings on transformational grammar began to appear, there emerged another important trend in anthropological linguistics: the comparative study of semantic systems and their component parts. Based mainly on analyses of paradigmatic sets of lexical items and morphemes in non-Western languages, componential analysis, as it came to be known, built upon Morris's divisions among syntax, semantics, and pragmatics. The leading question in this field was the degree to which the vocabulary, or "lexicon," of a language can be analyzed as a system organized around a limited number of underlying principles. The more traditional alternative was to view vocabularies as essentially unordered lists of words, much like the lists that make up a standard dictionary. Floyd Lounsbury proposed in his 1956 article "A Semantic Analysis of the Pawnee Kinship Usage" that kinship terms are indeed organized according to a highly systematic componential structure. This insight and the force of Lounsbury's demonstration opened up a new avenue of research that was to extend from kinship studies to color terminologies, ethnobotanical classification, and a variety of other semantic domains. The hope was that such analysis would reveal deep-seated principles according to which large portions of the vocabularies of languages would be shown to follow from a small number of primitive dimensions and distinctive features. The possibility was all the more exciting since the relations between semantic units tended to be covert. An overt distinction, such as the gender difference between Spanish *tio* 'uncle' and *tia* 'aunt', is one that is overtly signaled by a morphological difference between the forms (in this case the coding of gender in *-o* masculine vs. *-a* feminine endings). In Lounsbury's usage a covert distinction (like the one between uncle vs. aunt, nephew vs. niece, or brother vs. sister) is one in which the semantic dimension is not morphologically signaled. In order to reveal covert components of meaning, he proposed to use distinctive features, thus breaking down lexical meaning into features like [+ agnatic] (i.e., through the male line), [+ uterine] (through the female line), [+ masculine], and [+ feminine]. This breakdown of word meanings into features was based on the analogy between semantics and phonology. He further urged the necessity of examining entire semantic subsystems, not small lists of words. Thus as transformational grammar was focusing increasingly on syntax to the exclusion of semantics, the componential analysts began a series of intensive semantic studies. Unlike subsequent generative approaches to semantics, the focus was paradigmatic and not syntagmatic. Indeed, Lounsbury asserted explicitly that he viewed the semantics and syntax of a language as essentially independent, so that either could be studied without reference to the other (Lounsbury 1956:190).

One of the basic premises of componential analysis is that the terms it analyzes do indeed form a bounded domain, or "field." In the case of kinship, the field was taken to be determined by affiliation and biological descent. All terms that designated such relations were assigned what Lounsbury called the "root" feature of the paradigm, in this case K for "kinsmen." This way of defining the root of the paradigm had broad consequences for the analysis and led to fractious debate among anthropologists. On the one hand, it takes the biological facts of sexual union and descent to be universally basic in the meaning of such terms. This is parallel to Brent Berlin and Paul Kay's (1969) argument that the perceptual facts of color discrimination are basic in all "color terminologies." Both run counter to the commitment of most ethnographers to understand how members of the society define their own worlds, imposing instead an objectivist criterion. On the other hand, there is the problem of how to explain kinship terms used for people or other referents that fail to meet the biological criteria. Or in the case of color terms, how to explain the various noncolorimetric values that accrue to colors in given cultures. The standard solution was to say that all the nonobjective uses involved metaphor or other kinds of extension from literal meaning. As we saw in the preceding chapters, this commitment to an a priori literal meaning fails to explain most of what goes on in speech. But the question remains how one defines a root feature for the purpose of paradigmatic analysis. Let's look at this question in relation to indexicals.

The first problem that arises in determining a common feature for indexicals is that they vary so widely in terms of what they signal. The range includes everything from the background knowledge of Jack and Natalia—some of it spatial, some interpersonal, some dealing with the newspaper delivery service—to the time of day of Margot's exchange with Yuum, the history of their relations with Don Chabo, and so forth. In fact this heterogeneity is one of the most difficult problems in undertaking a general analysis of indexicality, for it means that any specification of indexical context must end with "etc." It is unlikely that any single feature would be common to the kind of context embeddedness of terms like Maya verbs of eating and drinking or sitting and being "home" or even the ecological terms that contain hidden indexical ties to local geography. We could of course posit a general feature like [I] to stand for "indexical," but this would tell us nothing about the semantic features of the terms that shared this would-be "root" feature. The problem is that componential analysis is basically a formalist project, whereas indexicality in the broad sense is a sheerly relational phenomenon.

More promising would be to start not from indexicality but from indexical-referential terms, such as pronouns or demonstratives. Unlike context embeddedness in general, deictics in particular are formally and functionally unified by their relational structure. They also share specific morphosyntactic features in any language and are found in all known human languages. The relational structure that sets them apart as a class is the way they define a referential figure on an indexical ground. Recall Margot's choice of the term *toloʔ* 'over there', as discussed in the previous chapter. Her utterance indexed her current location in her own kitchen as a ground from which to make reference to the home of her father-in-law, across the courtyard of the homestead. We can represent this relation graphically as in Figure 8.1.

In the case of the word *toloʔ*, the relational feature (R) would be EXCLUSIVE, since all uses of this expression make reference to a place (X) outside of (i.e., that excludes) the location of the utterance (see Hanks 1990: chapter 8). Note that by positing this structure as the root feature of deictics, we achieve the kind of formal unity required for paradigmatic analysis, without the debilitating assumptions as to what the specific relational features in a given language must be.

Perhaps the most promising aspect of indexical-referential terms for the cross-cultural study of context is that they systematically categorize utterance situations. Maya, for instance, has locative deictics formally distinguishing relations of inclusion from exclusion and regional spaces from punctate ones (according to the relative extent of the reference space). There are also other series of forms distinguishing the perceptual access that a speaker has to the referent (tactual, visual, auditory) as well as distinguishing routine reference from presentation (roughly like French *voilà,* said while handing over or showing the referent to the addressee). The pronouns (or, more accurately, "participant deictics") in turn distinguish first (I), second (you), and third (he, she, it) persons, singular and plural, as well as inclusion versus noninclusion of a plural addressee. There is a large series of temporal deictic adverbs that distinguish "now" from "then," along with an

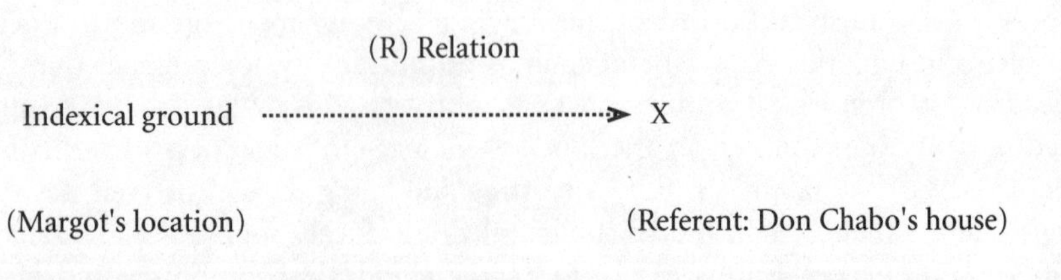

FIGURE 8.1 Indexical Ground, Relation, and Referent.

elaborate set of more subtle divisions between temporal frames such as "at this time of day in the past," "back then (which we both experienced)," "still" (or "already," depending on context), and so forth. So well developed is the deictic system in this language that the roughly twenty-eight base forms combine and can be modified to form a total inventory of over fifty forms. What is interesting for our purposes is that these forms and the ways they are routinely used in Maya speech provide a privileged window on how Maya actors categorize the experiential and interpersonal contexts of speaking.

The logic is much like Whorf's: Languages may differ in terms of which aspects of utterance contexts are explicitly encoded in the deictics. If a feature of context, such as relative distance or perceptual channel, is encoded, then speakers using the language are habituated to take notice of the corresponding aspect of context. This routinization is all the more powerful because deictic reference is a ubiquitous feature of talk. The sheer frequency with which people use indexical referential expressions serves to embed them in their routine practice. We need not assume that the Maya system or the perceptual habits implied by its use are unique or incommensurate with other languages. Rather, what is significant is the three-way relation among the linguistic system in its irreducible properties, the communicative practices of its users, and the ways that they occupy interactive settings.

This way of framing the question differs fundamentally from the way it has been framed by many opponents of the relativity hypothesis. In 1969, for example, Berlin and Kay published their path-breaking study of color categorization, in which they proposed a series of universal generalizations regarding the ways that human languages encode color distinctions and evolve over time. Their starting point was the goal, associated with Boasian anthropology, of approaching each language on its own terms, that is, without a priori assumptions as to which categories would be distinguished or how they would be combined. Applied to color terminologies, such an objective would lead, as Harold Conklin (1955) showed, to recognition that color divisions tend to be bundled in languages with a great deal of information of a noncolorimetric sort, for instance, texture, the particular objects associated with given colors, use of those objects, and other values attaching to colors and the things that bear them.

Now because Berlin and Kay were arguing explicitly against the kind of relativism they associated with the Whorfian project, they stated their own position in stark terms: "Briefly, the doctrine of extreme linguistic relativity holds that each language performs the coding of experience into sound in a unique manner. Hence each language is semantically arbitrary relative to every other language. According to this view, the search for semantic universals is fruitless in principle. . . . We suspect that this allegation of total arbitrariness in the way languages segment the color space is a gross overstatement" (Berlin and Kay 1969:1–2). Set against this background, Berlin and Kay's demonstration of similarities in color categorization among unrelated languages was taken as a disconfirmation of the strict relativity hypothesis (Berlin and Kay 1969:10). That different languages combine color information with other kinds of information was taken as merely a point of method and not a serious challenge to their universal generalizations. That is, the noncolorimetric information needed to be held apart from the color divisions in order to discern the real basis of these terminologies.

Without questioning the magnitude of Berlin and Kay's achievement, we can see that their study fails to address the concept of relativity. Instead, it disproves an unrealistically extreme version of it. There is no contradiction between observing that some feature of semantics is universal and at the same time observing that the feature tends to guide the perceptual habits of speakers. It simply means that for that feature human speakers tend to perceive the world in similar ways. Moreover, the Boasian goal of "taking each language on its own terms" is, stated in its strong form, a straw man. It is clearly impossible to achieve such an aim, as if the linguist could miraculously forget everything that she knew of human languages in order to study a language like Maya with *no assumptions.* Even if such a Herculean feat of forgetting were possible, it would be fruitless. A linguist studying a foreign language must use all that she knows of language in order to properly see the patterns. But as in the supposed contradiction between relativity and universality, the conflict here is more smoke than fire. For the real objective is to discern the interactions between linguistic form and human context, not to prove that one can submit to apparent difference or subdue difference with the brute force of "objectivity." But there is a still more basic assumption that needs to be questioned in order to study indexical universals.

As we pointed out above, the relativity hypothesis as it is usually understood is based on formalist premises. It takes as given the structure of a language and asks whether this structure in some way influences the perceptions of its speakers. Linguistic form is, as it were, the independent variable, and perception is the dependent one. This view of the thing looks all the more plausible when we consider "obligatory categories," and it seems to correspond to the plight of an individual speaker who needs to use the tool of language to express a thought. Like a rigid mold into which amorphous thought is poured, the categories of language exist independently and must be reckoned with in order to speak. If this sounds like the irreducibility thesis writ large, it is no accident. As long as you assume that language has an inner logic, hermetically sealed from the incursions of human action, you are led to ask how it influences perception. This is so whether or not you search for a universal language of which individual languages are the exemplars. But what if we rotate the axis by considering the degree to which language derives *its* properties from modes of action? What if the causality goes in the other direction, or, better, what if it cuts both ways? In some of its features, language is relatively arbitrary with respect to its actional settings. In others, it is formed by those settings. Or alternatively, the form of language is the product of an ongoing tension between an inner logic and a relational context.

What would this mean for linguistic analysis and the issue of relativity? It would imply, in the first instance, that the structural forms displayed by languages are the product of history, itself made by human agents acting in socially defined contexts. To embed language in context is to historicize it. At any point in its history, a language is the sedimented product of myriad acts in relation to the value horizons of speakers, addressees, and other receivers. Here we come back to the view put forth by Ingarden in relation to literary works. Just as the history of the work is a series of concretizations, the history of a language is a series of concretizations. The particular meaning categories configured in the language at any point depend critically upon the social world with which it articulates. And whereas Ingarden's framework accords the literary work a schematic structure irreducible to any given concretization, this view of language accords it a schematic structure irreducible to any of its specific realizations. The issue of relativity is therefore at base a matter of mediation: how the interplay between the formal system and the social world of which it is a part serves to organize and prefigure certain kinds of experience.

The first point to underscore in relation to indexicals is that they are multidimensional. As I pointed out above, indexicals in Maya encode a broad range of relational features that define types of referents (see Hanks 1990 for details). In addition to these, the forms are associated with typical communicative functions, including phatic, expressive, referential, predicative, directive, and presentative. These terms derive mainly from the functional typology of utterances worked out by Prague School linguists (see Chapter 5 for background).

The phatic dimension has to do with establishing and maintaining contact between interlocutors. It is in play in things like posture, eye contact, and backchannel responses that indicate that the addressee has understood and is attending to the speaker's utterance. In Maya deictic forms are among the preferred verbal responses that manage this relation. Expressive utterances focus on the speaker's current evaluation or attitude toward the interactive situation. Familiar examples in English include interjections, use of affectively charged expressions, tone of voice, speed of articulation, and other prosodic features. In Maya certain deictics are conventionally associated with expressive features such as the speaker's certainty about the truth of what is asserted and the speaker's judgment that a referent is obvious to a point of exaggeration. The referential function is that dimension of deixis that serves to individuate objects of reference and description. It is the most finely categorized dimension in the system as a whole, being subdivided according to the relational values. Directives have the force, roughly, of imperatives, telling an addressee to direct his or her attention to the referent, to listen to it, look at it, or take it in hand. Whereas there are no special words for this function in English, we do use syntactic expressions in this way, as when we point and say, "There he goes!" In Maya there are three lexical forms whose usage is always directive, as well as a wide range of foregrounded structures that also direct the addressee's attention (Hanks 1990: chapters 6, 9). Finally, the presentative function is in play when a speaker presents a referent to an addressee, demonstrating it ("Here's how you do it"), showing it ("Voilà!"), or literally handing it over ("Here [take this]"). As we said, there are specialized forms for these functions in Maya, whereas in English the normally locative referentials "here" and "there" tend to be used. Thus part of the multidimensionality of Maya has to do with the way that functions other than reference are combined with the relational values. The result is a set of communicatively rich forms whose conventional meanings coordinate elements of practice in a precise way.

Another set of dimensions is the indexical grounds to which the different deictics articulate. As we have treated it so far, the indexical ground of reference is an unordered bundle, a grab bag, of different aspects of context. Its very diversity seems to defy systematic description, and its tie to actual speech puts it beyond the scope of formalist reasoning. But if we study the dynamics of indexicals *in practice*, it becomes clear that they are in fact very systematic. The indexical ground of deictic reference breaks down into two main dimensions: the relation between the interacting parties and the relation between them and the object of reference. With respect to the first, the key question is the degree to which the participants have access to one another, whether by mutual perceptibility or prior knowledge. Although it may seem a truism that people talking must be able to perceive one another, in fact there are many gradations in mutual access. They may be within arm's length or separated by significant distance. They may be able to see each other or only hear each other. They may share a relatively full set of referents based on prior experience together or common knowledge of the setting, or they may be strangers. All these factors affect the usage of deictics. Similarly, the referent, whether a thing, a person, a time, or a place, may be a matter of common knowledge or something with which one party is significantly more familiar than the other. In the case of Yuum and Margot, both knew where Don Chabo's house was, as well as Margot's relation to it as his daughter-in-law. It was evening, and the semidarkness put the place out of visual contact for Margot (inside her own home) and on the periphery of Yuum's visual field. Sharing this knowledge and being close together, the two had what I will call relatively symmetric access to the reference place. If Yuum had been a stranger, lacking all the relevant knowledge, Margot's reference would have been opaque.

These aspects of the situation are similar to ones that constrain all deictic reference in Maya (and probably other languages, although I have investigated only Maya in the level of detail required by such a generalization). That is, they are part of the system design of the language and not only the particular conditions of this one exchange. We can see this in the structure of individual deictics and also in the way the total set of forms maps interactive space. Each individual form has a typical range of indexical contexts in which it is used, such that it is associated with highly symmetric contexts, in which the parties have access both to one another and to the referent, or relatively asymmetric contexts, in which their respective access is different. Hence forms like *té*ˀ *ela*ˀ 'right here', *lela*ˀ 'this (one)', and *hé*ˀ *ela* 'here it is (presentative)' are used when the speaker is making reference to an object to which she has fuller access than the addressee. These uses are commonly described in the literature as "new information," such as when a speaker initiates a new topic or draws the addressee's attention to something to which she is not already attending. What is critical, however, is not that the information is "new" but that it is salient and asymmetrically available to the interactants. By contrast, the corresponding forms *té ʔeloʔ* 'there', *toloʔ* 'over there', *leloʔ* 'that' and *héʔ eloʔ* 'there it is (pointing)' are less salient and typically lock into symmetric contexts in which both interactants are aware of the object. So each deictic form, taken individually, is based on the combination of a functional potential, a range of relational values, and an indexical value.

Looking at the total inventory of deictic forms in the language, we find another interaction between these three dimensions. For the relatively symmetric forms outnumber the relatively asymmetric ones by a wide margin. It is as if the system were especially adapted to acts of reference between people who share a common vantage point, both conceptually and perceptually. Or to put it another way, the more information you already share with your addressee, the more choices you have among alternative deictics for the purpose of making reference. Inversely, the less you share, the fewer forms can be used appropriately. In light of this, we can see that context is based on the intersection of the perspectives of the participants. This is one of the reasons that classical formalism, which incorporates the idealization of the solitary speaker, has never produced a credible analysis of an actual deictic system. Whereas such systems have irreducible formal dimensions, they have equally fundamental relational ones. A proper analysis of their structure and use requires that we integrate the two kinds of fact as complementary poles in a dynamic interplay. Having got to this point, we see that deictic systems provide an exceptionally fine-grained mapping of the interactive field of verbal practice. Through continual use of such forms, speakers are habituated to certain ways of occupying context, attending to things like perceptual access, spatial inclusion and exclusion, and the relative sharedness of these factors among participants. There is no evidence that such habits limit what people like Margot and Yuum *are capable of* experiencing or expressing. But myriad examples of actual utterances produced in real situations give powerful testimony of what they *typically do* experience and express.

One of the things that makes deixis such a fruitful focus for studying mediation is that these forms are so common in everyday talk. My field research in Maya indicates that pronouns, demonstratives, and other deictics occur in virtually every kind of talk under all circumstances. The only genre of discourse in which they appear to be rare is shamanic prayer, and even here certain forms abound. It is more a matter of restricting usage in accordance with the particular contexts of prayer rather than an outright absence of deictic practices. This raises an important question, however. For we have discussed indexicality so far as though the language were a single system and contexts were all somehow equal. But there are good reasons to believe the opposite; the language is really the sum of various subsystems, and contexts differ significantly in terms of their features. If the systematic quality of deixis tends to unify practices and contexts around a consistent set of dimensions, these other factors tend to differentiate them.

The tension between unity and differentiation is the next step that we must explore as we work toward a better understanding of language in speech. It has several parts, of which two will concern us here. The first is the differentiation of speech according to its style, that is, the formal, semantic, and rhetorical properties of the spoken language itself. Our goal is to develop a framework in which to distinguish varieties of language use that mediate experience in different ways. For this is another weakness in classical discussions of linguistic relativity: By focusing solely on referential and descriptive dimensions of language, they portray talk and its producers in overly simple terms. The flip side of stylistic variation is the notion that the speech varieties that make up a language, considered in aggregate, can be classified into recurrent types, or "ways of speaking." Here the point is not so much the formal properties of utterances themselves but rather the ways that members of the society distinguish and group kinds of language into repertoires. This grouping, which is found in all human speech communities, implies a metalinguistic evaluation on the part of native speakers. The most obvious sign of such evaluation is the words used to label kinds of language, for instance, "conversation," "prayer," "oratory," "promise," "warning," "declaration," "debate," "interview," "interrogation," and their respective verb forms. A proper description of the meaning of such terms goes a long way toward revealing the overall "ecology" of verbal practices in the community.

But such explicit terminologies are only the tip of an iceberg, and many socioculturally meaningful distinctions have no one-word labels. What is important is that native speakers recognize a putative metalinguistic type and invest it with value. For this is what binds speech to the ideological horizons against which it is meaningful. This is another major piece in the puzzle of mediation, and it implies another order of reflexivity between language forms and cultural values. If linguistic practices serve to habituate certain ways of experiencing, these practices are themselves objects of experience informed by ideology.

Style, Textuality, and Verbal Repertoires

The study of linguistic style has taken various forms in this century. Among North American linguistic anthropologists, Edward Sapir, Dell Hymes, Richard Bauman, and Paul Friedrich were some of the pioneers whose studies of poetics and discourse structure opened the way for scores of analyses of Native American literary traditions. Drawing on a combination of Prague School aesthetics, folklore studies of oral performance, and a variety of linguistic and literary approaches to discourse, they showed that speech of all kinds has stylistic dimensions. This contradicted two commonly held assumptions. The first one identifies elements of style, such as verse parallelism, meter, metaphor, and other tropes, with special kinds of language, particularly what we call literature and poetry. Within a Western context, these are usually associated with writing, and thus stylistic analysis seemed to be pretty much irrelevant to the business of speech. By demonstrating that oral traditions such as storytelling and myths are organized by intricate principles of style (many of them specifically oral), these studies broke away from the dominance of writing. Moreover, some of these same principles operate in routine conversation, as could be discovered only through careful observation of speech in day-to-day life. Thus the reified categories of literature and poetry were replaced by the recognition that all language has style. One important corollary of this broadened scope was a more finely graded, differential sense of style itself. Another was a heightened appreciation for the historical specificity of what we call literature. For to say that all language has style is not to say that it is all the same nor that poetry is a fiction, but that we need a better theory of speech forms and a better approach to literature as a sociohistorical phenomenon.

The second assumption is equally limiting and, in a way, even more disabling. It is the idea that whatever the stylistic features at play in a discourse, they are really just the outer packaging for a message whose literal meaning lies within. We can see this already in the writings of Saussure and Chomsky, for whom the referential-denotational functions make up the essence of language. Even within the generative paradigm, there were studies of metrics and verse. But what they analyzed was the sound structure of special kinds of language, rarely venturing into the woods in which style and *meaning* interact. And the commonsense appeal here is strong. After all, thought is propositional and language exists for thinking, right? Saussure might have been right in saying that linguistic forms correspond to acoustic images, but the real action is in the signified concepts. And since the relation of these to sounds is arbitrary, why involve grammar and semantics if you're studying things like alliteration and end-rhyme? Ethnographically grounded studies of style have shown these views to be as flawed as they are familiar. For one thing, stylistic features often index specific genres of discourse, which imply different ways of interpreting. A speaker who engages in obvious hyperbole or irony is doing more than merely adorning the literal meaning of his or her words. The bluntness of an order or the bite of sarcasm with a stranger can trigger a confrontation, while the radically elliptical style of a written recipe can cause confusion if spoken in a context that calls for explanation. In other words styles are associated with certain kinds of verbal practice, and a noteworthy mismatch between speech style and the current setting alters the meaning. In general the surrounding discourse in which any expression is embedded is its first tie to context.

Furthermore, the kinds of phonological, structural, and semantic parallelisms typical of verse create equivalences at the level of form, and these juxtapose meanings in such a way as to generate new understandings. We could illustrate this process with examples from the considerable literature on ethnopoetics, but a more familiar piece will do the trick. Here are the opening two stanzas of Robert Frost's poem "To Earthward."

Love at the lips was touch
As sweet as I could bear;
And once that seemed too much;
I lived on air
That crossed me from sweet things,

The flow of—was it musk
From hidden grapevine springs
Downhill at dusk?

The simplicity of Frost's language runs through a perfectly balanced verse pattern based on four-line stanzas, in which the first three lines have six syllables and the final line has four syllables. The rhyme scheme in each stanza is *abab,* setting up a positional equivalence between "lips was touch / seemed too much"; "I could bear / lived on air"; "from sweet things / grapevine springs"; "was it musk" / "downhill at dusk." Without dwelling further on the details of the language, we see how this kind of parallelism and lightness of description engages the imagination and draws the reader into a world where the touch of lips makes you light-headed, where the air bears you, the sweet thing is the grapevine spring, and the evening is musky. Of course, Frost never *says* these things; he says that the touch was sweet and too much for him, the air was sweet and musky from a grapevine down the hill—an almost trite "message." But the exact form of the lines creates a tension between what is said and what is intimated through parallelism, and this tension is what gives rise to a reading of the second degree. If we hope to describe the uniquely human capacity for verbal expression, we must also explain this ability to enter into the play of multiple readings. In varying proportions similar principles are at play in much of speech, especially in persuasive discourse such as advertising and political oratory. Indeed, one of the important results of recent research in poetics has been to show that what is distinctive about "poetry" is the degree to which it foregrounds and combines linguistic devices present in all language. Not a thing apart but the high end of a continuum.

This view of style derives in large measure from the Praguean approach to linguistic diversity, which we encountered in Chapter 5. Among Pragueans, Tynianov, Havránek, Jakobson, and Mukarovsky stand out for their brilliant contributions to the study of verbal art (see the Further Readings at the end of this chapter). The observation that verse patterns create semantic relations, which we illustrated in the preceding paragraph, was first made in Russian by Tynianov in 1924. Tynianov developed an entire theory of verse dynamics that prefigured the central elements of the Praguean approach and remains today one of the most provocative statements on the topic. But it was Jakobson who brought this to English-speaking readers many years later, particularly in his often-cited 1960 article on linguistics and poetics. Using Saussurian terminology, Jakobson restated the principle of poetic projection: Verse parallelism projects equivalence from the axis of selection (paradigmatic) to the axis of combination (syntagmatic). That is, the repeating patterns of verse are syntagmatic because they depend upon the combination of words into lines and other syntactic units, yet they serve to create equivalences similar to the partial equivalence among members of a single paradigm. In this way verse dynamics create a new kind of grammatical structure in which the Saussurian dimensions are turned in on one another. This kind of analysis is basically formalist in that it is the purely formal equivalences of meter, rhythm, rhyme, and position in the line that drive the verse and produce new meanings. In fact Tynianov was a member of the linguistic group known as Russian formalists. But we can see that unlike the North American tradition, the Russian and Prague School linguists never divorced form from meaning, and this makes all the difference.

Mukarovsky's writings are marked by a broader vision of the place of verbal art in society and the underlying aesthetic philosophy upon which analysis depends. In his 1941 article "Structuralism in Esthetics and Literary Studies," he outlined an approach that will help us conceptualize the dynamics of verbal artworks as a whole. His approach starts from the artwork (not a pair of lines or a stanza or a chapter, but the entire work), conceived as "an external manifestation of an immaterial structure, i.e., a dynamic balance of forces represented by its individual components" (1982:71). Any work so conceived is part of a broader "artistic structure," which is the historically derived social definition of verbal art in all its forms. In this larger structure, some elements are relatively foregrounded and others automatized (cf. Chapter 5). Like Ingarden, Mukarovsky situates the individual work (e.g., a poem, novel, letter) between an artist and a perceiver, and it is in the reading, or concretization, that the work is completed. Neither the producer nor the receiver enters into the work as a concrete individual, an actual "I," but as a position mediated by the artistic structure. This position may be occupied by an individual, a group, or even an entire generation. Hence the work of verbal art exists as a form of mediation between the socially defined producer(s) and receiver(s), between the individualized qualities that it has as a unique work and the broader historical structure of which it is a part.

To say that the work mediates between these different poles is to say that it is not a mechanical reflection of any of them. Rather than mirroring the society, artistic structure is a locus of interplay between two inverse tendencies, the domination of artistic production by social forces and the engagement of art in changing society (Mukarovsky 1982:74–75). The former can be seen in the classification of art into high and low forms (e.g., highbrow literature vs. gang graffiti, the opera house vs. the urban boom box, *Masterpiece Theater* vs. the soap opera) and in the social formation of taste. The engagement of art in social change is particularly evident in political art and in the myriad art forms exploring current social issues, such as sexuality, discrimination, and drug-related crime. But, again, these tendencies toward domination and engagement, which are most apparent in certain kinds of art, are taken to be at play in varying degrees in other kinds of language use as well.

Alongside this interplay with the social world, art forms in any medium interact with ones in other media, just as different elements of semiosis interact in everyday behavior (recall the relations among gesture, speech, spatial setting in our examples). The "artistic structure" approach to verbal art relates different kinds of art to one another and to other forms of human activity. Far from isolating artistic language or works as things independent of their sociocultural milieu, therefore, this approach seeks to contextualize them to the fullest extent possible. We find in the study of style and aesthetically wrought language a way to better understand the intertextual and intercollective networks of a sociocultural world. This is undoubtedly one reason that it had such influence over the development of anthropological and ethnographic approaches to verbal art.

Many elements of the Praguean approach were adapted to ethnographically grounded research in what came to be known during the 1960s, 1970s, and 1980s as the "ethnography of speaking." Launched primarily by Dell Hymes, John Gumperz, and their students, this paradigm combined sociolinguistics; aspects of contemporary grammatical theory; the lessons of the Americanist tradition started by Boas, Sapir, and their followers; and a heavy dosage of Prague School functionalism. The aim was to describe language and speech in their social settings, merging anthropological and linguistic approaches as fully as possible. Among the central concepts proposed were a framework for describing speech events, a differentiated approach to ways of speaking (and the genre analysis it implies), and a commitment to empirical description of how actual people speak in real social settings. Most of the idealizations basic to formalist linguistics (see Part 1) were rejected.

With its broad scope, the paradigm split off into numerous subspecialties, including the study of language contact and variation, the performance of verbal art, language in education, and the microanalysis of interaction. It was also widely criticized for a lack of theoretical unity, for its functionalist leanings, and for what turned out to be the impossibility of totally describing the "speech system" of any language. Some of these criticisms were well founded, yet they cannot negate the contribution of studies within this approach. Nor should the impossibility of exhaustive description be troubling, for totality always rests on exclusion, and that was not the aim. Whatever its programmatic limitations, the approach was and remains of enormous heuristic value, and it gave rise to important debates in a variety of areas. One of these, of direct relevance to the analysis of verbal style, was a debate among students of Native American discourse as to the proper grounds for analyzing discourse.

A critical step in the analysis of discourse is the definition of recurrent units, such as metrical measures, lines, and stanzas in a poem and thematic units and "sections" in narrative. In traditional stylistics this was part of "scansion," a term that refers specifically to the way that formal parallelism divides a poem into the smaller parts of which it is composed. Notice that in a written work, like Frost's "To Earthward," the graphic presentation of the work already imposes a scansion by its division into lines and stanzas. But in the break away from Western written texts, the issue became how to justify the "chunking" of any verbal work into relevant parts. In an oral medium, or even in a written text with no line breaks or punctuation, what would be the criteria for division? This may seem like an arcane question of little consequence to understanding, but in fact the opposite is true. The units into which a text is divided make up the intervals over which parallelism is established, and these define the positions according to which semantic equivalences are produced. Indeed, it would not be an exaggeration to say that division into units is one of the most significant phases in stylistic analysis.

Imagine if Frost's poem were presented like this:

Love at the lips was

touch as sweet as I could bear and once

that seemed too much I lived on air that crossed

me from sweet

things the flow of was it musk from hidden

grapevine springs downhill at

dusk?

Or if it were written continuously left to right, with no spaces between the words and no punctuation. In this case the parallelism is so strong and coordinated that the language almost divides itself, but it would take some analysis to arrive at Frost's scansion. And this difficulty would be all the more acute if, as is often the case in non-Western discourse, we found various principles of parallelism that failed to line up. The alliteration might suggest one way of dividing lines, the syntax another, the images based on word meanings another, and the pauses made by someone reading the poem yet another. And then imagine that there was no Robert Frost in the picture, that the text was anonymous or of obscure authorship, and that different groups gave it different readings. With these questions, we approach some of the difficulties faced by students of oral traditions as they discovered verse principles in discourse usually considered "nonpoetic."

One solution, proposed by Hymes, was to base analysis primarily (though not exclusively) on syntactic and thematic parallelism. The recurrent grammatical form of lines in certain Native American traditions appeared to define recurrent blocks of five lines, which in turn encoded recurrent kinds of thematic information. Taking a different approach, and placing a higher value on the strictly oral components of narratives as told by speakers, Dennis Tedlock proposed that a more basic principle was the breathing and pausing of a narrator—in other words, the breath groups that a speaker produced in performing a discourse: where a breath was taken and a slight pause was made and where the pacing of the narrative continued unbroken. In fact Hymes and Tedlock were analyzing discourse from different Native American cultures, and the debate was not over the empirical accuracy of their respective claims. Rather, it concerned the generalization of these results to other cultures. How might a student of, say, Yupik Eskimo (native to Alaska), Crow (a Plains group in Montana), Kalapalo (a Brazilian group of Amazonia), or Yucatec Maya proceed in analyzing discourse from these widely differing areas?

In an important article Anthony Woodbury synthesized the debate and proposed a third approach, which he illustrated with a narrative recorded during his fieldwork among Yupik speakers. His solution was to integrate syntactic and breath-pause phrasing, along with thematic units and other phonological features, into a single "rhetorical structure." Irreducible to any of its component dimensions, rhetorical structure is based on the interactions among different elements. Woodbury demonstrated with evidence from Yupik that the dimensions are analytically distinct, individually patterned, and yet interact with one another in a systematic way. This amounts to what is called in contemporary linguistics a modular approach, in which each of the component parts constitutes an independent module, and the structure of the whole derives from their interplay. It provided a way out of the impasse created by opposing alternatives, while at the same time reasserting the relevance of grammatical theory to stylistic analysis.

Concurrent with these advances in discourse analysis, ethnographers of speaking developed a fine-grained framework for describing verbal performance. In a seminal article analyzing the discourse structure of myth-telling, Hymes noted that speakers shifted between the reporting of a myth and the actual performance of its lines. This shift, which he called a "breakthrough into performance," corresponds to what Erving Goffman defined as a change in *footing* (a concept discussed more extensively in Chapter 9). That is, it seemed to mark a basic alteration in the relation between the teller and the story—from recounting the content or circumstances of mythic events to actually stepping within the mythic world and speaking from it. The language of the myth of course takes on a special, crystalline importance in such moments, much like when a storyteller breaks into quotation, with all of its attendant voice effects. Yet the change is not so much in the language itself, even though it may be signaled by various indexical shifts. Rather, it is in the relation between the speaker and his utterances.

Bauman then extended Hymes's insight into a broad framework that can be summarized in the phrase that entitled Bauman's monograph, *Verbal Art as Performance.* In the Praguean tradition verbal art was distinguished by its heightened stylistic features, as we saw with Mukarovsky's approach. Following Hymes's lead, Bauman made a major step away from formalism in asserting that what unifies verbal art is not the properties of the language but instead *how the language is actually delivered in the uttering.* By this definition even a discourse lacking stylistic elaboration can become art if it is delivered in the right way. That way is called "performance," a mode of action, not a kind of text. In performance a performer, by definition, assumes a heightened level of responsibility for the display of artistic competence. That is, his or her involvement in the utterance(s) is especially intense and subject to the evaluation of an audience. This redefinition has several consequences. The first is that artistic discourse is viewed as emergent in the events in which it is realized. No longer defined by a canonical written text, it is a kind of practice. Second, performance theory necessarily depends upon a close analysis of events of speaking, since it is in the context of the event that the artistic work lives as activity. Third, the various cues, or "keys," that mark the shift into performance take on a new importance. These include things like voice modulation, posture, gesture, and the dynamic interaction between performer and audience. Side remarks and interactions around the text now fall within the scope of analysis, since they provide the immediate discourse context of the verbal art. Fourth, because the basis of the phenomenon is the performer's involvement, the kinds of involvement typical of nonperformance must also be reconsidered. Without a sense of how speakers engage in routine talk, it would be impossible to distinguish performance as something special. And finally, there is a close relation between performance so defined and the kind of "performativity" that Austin discussed, since Austin also spoke of the consequences and responsibility incumbent on illocutionary acts (recall Austin's felicity conditions, discussed in Chapter 5). In general Bauman's theory rotated the axis of art from the object to the rendition and then reconnected it to everyday talk through a differentiated sense of how utterances are rendered. It is worth underscoring that this placed a new importance of the concept of indexicality, as the specialized footing of performance is nothing other than an indexical reframing of the utterance relative to its immediate context. Once again, it is the capacity of speech to mediate among social actors, as a function of its indexical ties, that is most basic.

What does all this imply for the notion of linguistic relativity? In a superficial sense it is clear that if poetic elements are variably present in much of everyday talk, and if what defines verbal art is a way of speaking and not a kind of language, then the mental classifications Boas, Sapir, and Whorf noted must somehow interact with verbal art—and this in a way unforeseen by Whorf and unaddressed by formalist arguments over relativity. The most sustained examination of the question to date was undertaken by Paul Friedrich (1979). Friedrich's approach is grounded in a critical reformulation of poetic language itself, breaking from the formalism of the Prague School. In place of stylistic foregrounding and the projection principle, he proposed three core attributes present in poetic language: the use of figures and tropes (including metaphor, metonymy, and others), the intensification of form through use of special marked forms of expression, and association by analogy. Beyond these three he underscored the "enormous significance of pragmatics and performance in any definition of poetic language" (1979:492), a point that links his framework to those of Hymes and Bauman. With respect to the relation between poetic language and everyday language, Friedrich's position was, if anything, more integrative than that of others in the field. Although he insisted on the importance of distinguishing among great art, things like advertising and rhetoric, and everyday speech, he was equally insistent on the ubiquity of poetic effects (albeit in varying degrees). Hence, where Boas, Whorf, and their followers seized on conceptual classification through obligatory semantic and grammatical categories, Friedrich inserted poetic dimensions and the poetic *potential* of even routine linguistic structure.

The next major shift marked by this piece involved the nonlinguistic pole of the relation: thought. As we saw, the classical statements of relativity posited a relation between language and the conceptual life of its speakers. Concepts were defined apart from affect and the imagination, under the (sometimes tacit) assumption that the real business of thinking is the grouping of ideas according to logical relations such as identity, difference, inclusion, entailment, and inference. Friedrich replaced this limited view of concepts with the more inclusive one of the imagination: "The term-idea of 'imagination' includes the emotions, sensuous image use, aesthetic apprehension and mythic forms of imagining . . . [and also] cognition, and reason—concrete, abstract and practical." With these two shifts, therefore, he reformulated the relativity hypothesis: Poetic language has a fundamental impact on the imagination of speakers. Or to use our terms, the poetic dimensions of speech help form the ways in which speakers routinely and nonroutinely imagine, thereby mediating between them and the world as they experience it. Thus instead of a two-way relation between semantic categories and the classification of experience, relativity emerges in the tensions among linguistic categories, poetic and stylistic genres, situated experience, and the imagination. Add to these the pervasive linkage of utterances to contexts via indexicals, and you no longer have a formalist relativity hypothesis. You have instead a series of intersecting factors and a variety of situated mediations.

The Ideological Dimension

One of the threads running throughout this chapter has been the idea that native speakers of any language think about their own speech practices, and their thoughts may have a significant role in defining those practices. Before entering into this topic in more detail, let's pause for a moment to contrast the perspective it implies with the one typical of traditional grammar. For Saussure, a language was the sum of *langue* and *parole,* a conventional code that serves to organize thought and make possible the processes of reference, description, and expression more generally. At no point in Saussure's approach do the speakers of a language turn their consciousness from the business of everyday talk to contemplate the language that channels it. In Chomsky's theory, as we saw, linguistic competence entails intuitions about whether an instance of language is well formed, but these intuitions are based on recognition and tacit generalization of grammatical patterns. They are not based on the conscious acts of speakers who step back from the language to reflect on it as an object. In its real functioning, language is assumed to remain invisible to native speakers, and it is only through the specialized discipline of linguistics that one can come to perceive it as it really is. Even the child learning a language is said to develop a "model" or "theory" of it, but the aim is to project the pattern of well-formedness, not to contemplate the system as such.

The difference is what separates common sense and linguistic competence from scientific reasoning and the specialized analytic skill of the linguist. The same applies to Boas's theory of the unconsciousness of the classifications effected by any language. Speakers may engage in what Boas called "secondary rationalizations," but, as the term implies, these are always after the fact. And more important, they are governed by the very system they appear to be about. In a sense this is central to the relativity hypothesis in its classical formulation. For the language is assumed to have a life of its own, beyond the reach of the conscious thoughts of its speakers. Try as they might to think about their language, their thought is always already guided by it. And the result is that the system of classifications always remains out of reach. This view of the matter guarantees that the metalinguistic musings of native speakers are distorted, peripheral. As a consequence, linguists working in the field typically take elicited judgments of grammaticality and meaning as second-order evidence for a system that lies at a deeper, unconscious level. The mediation of thought implied by the relativity hypothesis rests on the imperviousness of language, the independent variable, to thought, the dependent one.

When we recast relativity in the light of indexical forms and practices, we shifted the ground on which this classical view rests. The reason is that the ability to use indexical expressions implies the ability to judge the fit between a linguistic form and the immediate context of its production. And the way these forms shift, from utterance to utterance ("I" becomes "you," "here" becomes "there," and so forth) further implies that speakers monitor the fit continually. This does not mean that a series of conscious calculations need precede every utterance, since much of the process is rendered automatic by habit. It means instead that language has among its most basic categories forms whose semantic structure anchors speakers' awareness in the fit of form to context. Moreover, because the semantic specification of words and expressions is partial and speakers must always fill in the blanks, this awareness is continually piqued in producing and understanding speech. So long as we assume that speech follows from an abstract system that is more basic and logically prior to it, the role of awareness appears secondary and severely limited. The farther we move from that assumption, the more imposing the problem of metalinguistic consciousness becomes.

When we moved from indexicality and deixis to the ethnography of speaking, the appearance of axiomatic unity that attaches to language in the formalist view also came into question. The tendency for speech to be differentiated into distinct kinds of practice also implies the presence of metalinguistic awareness. Perhaps the most obvious sign of this tendency is the existence of sometimes very elaborate classifications of speaking according to types, as reflected in the lexicon of verbs for speaking. When a speaker labels a stretch of talk as a "promise," "insult," or "warning," this act of labeling is metalinguistic in an explicit, overt way. It involves using the language to make reference to and describe a token utterance as being a replica of a type. Here I purposely use the Peircean terms "type" and "replica" to recall the broader doctrine of interpretance in Peirce's semiotics. For if Peirce and Benveniste were right in positing interpretance as basic to any sign system, then metalinguistic interpretation is a part of all understanding. This effectively broadens the scope of the phenomenon from the finite set of labels used to designate speech types to the ubiquitous process of interpretation. In fact we can go farther and assert that interpretance is a necessary element in any relational approach to language. It is part and parcel of understanding as a constructive process. At the high end, so to speak, we find words and other verbal formulae whose central use is to describe aspects of language. But in many less explicit instances, it involves inferences and other aspects of reasoning from linguistic forms-in-context to understandings. The automatic ease with which people perform these processes in much of daily talk should not obscure the elements of the process nor the fact that when questions arise, they are able to articulate much of their reasoning. As Uriel Weinreich, Roman Jakobson, and others have observed, the ability to do this comes with linguistic competence, and all human languages can be used as their own metalanguages.

Verse and aesthetically worked discourse involve a twofold engagement of the metalinguistic dimension. In the first instance, the production and reception of such discourse relies upon speakers' ability to work with the details of expression—to align, play with, juxtapose formal elements in a concerted way. The special responsibility that a verbal artist assumes in "performance" is similarly a metalinguistic phenomenon, insofar as it amounts to recasting the relation between the expression itself and the participants in its production (the performer and the audience). But as the Pragueans and their followers showed, the internal dynamic of poetic speech rests on the intensification of form, or what Havránek called the foregrounding of form itself. Through foregrounding of form, aspects of language that are often invisible because taken for granted become the source points from which parallelisms and remarkable tropes are generated. It might even be said that without metalinguistic consciousness, there would be no poetry, that the potential of the one is interwoven with the potential of the other.

In making these remarks, I am distinguishing between two rather separate ways in which metalinguistic consciousness becomes a part of speech. The first is where specific utterances and utterance portions denote language or describe it. For instance, "'Table' is a five-letter word," "Maya is a language spoken by about 750,000 people in southern Mexico," and "'Dusk' is a time of day." This is what I called the high end of a spectrum, in which the focal function of the utterance is to individuate and comment on a linguistic object. A dictionary or grammatical description is metalinguistic in this very explicit sense. To this may be contrasted metalinguistic discourse in the more general sense of extended commentary on language, its use, its history, or contexts. In this broader sense this book is itself a metalinguistic work, although not all its individual passages comment on language as such. And it addresses itself to still broader scholarly discourse that is, in significant ways, about language. The difference between the two is gradient, more a matter of degree than of kind. Where we draw the line depends both upon how large a discourse we are considering—a sentence or a scholarly tradition—and upon how precisely we delimit language from nonlanguage. Formalists assume a clear boundary between language and the world, a boundary enshrined in the limits of grammatical description. The (presumed) presence of such a boundary makes it possible to distinguish talk about language from talk about other things. The former is metalinguistic; the latter is not.

In the present approach, by contrast, we have repeatedly questioned such a boundary, arguing instead that context saturates language, that language is in some of its features the sedimentation of practices that incorporate extralinguistic social and personal factors. To the extent that this is so, it becomes a matter of delicate judgment whether a given statement is metalinguistic. If I say, "The paper is right over there," and you respond, "That's not so," is your response metalinguistic? Yes and no. Yes, because you have ostensibly made reference to my utterance and asserted that it is false. But notice that the meaning of my utterance depends in the first instance upon its relation to the immediate situation. Without this, as we saw, the word "there" and the identity of "the paper" (i.e., *which* paper) cannot be determined. Now, you might be confused over which paper I mean, or you may think the thing is a magazine and not a paper or that the expression "right over there" is inappropriate for an object that I am actually holding in my hand. Or perhaps I pointed in the opposite direction of the paper as I spoke. In these cases you would respond to the way my words fit or do not fit with the context. Suppose you judge that I have purposely misled you, and you respond instead by simply saying, "Yeah, right," in an exasperated tone. In this case it is nowhere spelled out what you are referring to or what you mean to say about it, although most native speakers would get the point that you reject my statement, at least in its most obvious sense. Yet we would not want to assimilate this kind of response to metalanguage in the full sense. In other words, there is an enormous gray area in which we want to recognize that people are aware of and respond to verbal action, even though they may not refer directly to it or describe it.

Both metalanguage in the narrow sense and discourse about verbal practices in the broader sense involve a kind of objectification. Whether the object is a word or an entire discourse, the talk about it is, by definition, a step removed from it. This is what we mean in saying that it is talk *about* language. But as we saw with deictics and poetic language, there are elements of metalinguistic awareness in which no such remove is evident, and there is no such *aboutness* to point to as the indicator of metalanguage. These elements are part of the fabric of the utterance itself, serving to frame it, connect it to its own context, or otherwise guide its interpretation. Following a usage established by Jakobson and amplified by Michael Silverstein, we can describe these in terms of the metalinguistic function. Like the phatic, referential, and poetic functions, the metalinguistic function is variably present in most if not all discourse. The utterance "The paper is right there" illustrates this function in the choice of definite article and in the deictic expression. Insofar as these portions of the utterance connect it to its context, they are metalinguistic in the logical sense, even though they are in no obvious way "about" the utterance, nor do they stand apart from it. If metalinguistic discourse is present in much of everyday talk, the metalinguistic function is virtually unavoidable. Wherever indexicality is in play, whether in deictics or in the context dependency we discussed in Chapter 7, there is a metalinguistic connection.

It might help to think of this metalinguistic connection in terms of a simple analogy between language and the code of traffic regulations. If I say, "A stop sign indicates that the motorist is to come to a full stop," I have made an explicit meaning statement about the stop sign (cf. metalinguistic reference and description). If I then engage in a discussion about the different ways that people under varying conditions respond to traffic signals and road hazards, my discussion is broadly about those signs and their use in social life (cf. metalinguistic discourse). But if, when driving my car, I anticipate that the person in front of me will come to a stop at the corner sign, I have attended to the regulative function of the sign in practice (cf. metalinguistic function). The analogy breaks down if we push it, for various reasons, but it will serve to illustrate the different planes on which metalinguistic awareness is played out. The similarity between this and the variable realizations of poetic and referential functions further illustrates one of the basic tenets of functional linguistics, namely, that each of the functions may be present as part of the composition of virtually any routine utterance, but that in certain utterances one of them is dominant. The metalinguistic function is backgrounded in deixis, relatively more salient in poetry and metalinguistic discourse, and dominant in acts of reference to language. What the three share is that they arise out of the human capacity for self-reflexive expression and thought. No animal, machine, or idealized model can approximate human cognition unless it exercises this kind of reflexivity.

Treated in the abstract, metalanguage is forbidding. Even the word is longer than it should be. It is hard to describe in plain English and hard to grasp via common sense. We know that people think and talk about language, and most of us do it daily. But once it is tied in with the intricacies of grammar and context, its implications are obscure and far-flung, like our own blood drawn from a vein and passed through a centrifuge in a sterile environment. In the most familiar surrounds, like the kitchen, dining room, and workplace, reflexive speech goes on every day. When Natalia told Jack that the *Times* was right on the table, when Margot told Yuum to cool his heels next door, and when you read this sentence, we are all engaging in acts whose internal complexity far outstrips the simplicity of the words. It is all the more difficult to get at this because most of it is rendered invisible by its familiarity. One of the things that hides metalanguage is that reflexivity rarely shows itself as such. And for us to label it by that name is to court estrangement, like being told that something you know intimately really isn't what it appears but is something else altogether. But what is it that makes it so familiar? It is that metalinguistic statements are saturated with the same values and beliefs that infuse language as a whole, and they are part of the fabric of the discourse genres we engage in daily.

Reflexivity never takes place in a vacuum. None of the three phases of metalinguistics is native to the language lab any more than blood is native to a test tube. When we exercise this capacity, we are always evaluating an utterance, a piece of the language, or our relation to the current setting. It arises as a statement of the form "this is that" or as a mundane observation "I am here; you are there." But what delimits the this and permits its assimilation to the that, what defines the here and sustains the I, are values. We know what the words mean and what they should refer to and how they should be spoken because we belong to the world of which they are a part. Like Merleau-Ponty's phenomenal field, it is the social world, as actual potential and potential actuality, that grounds the reflexive turn. So when Margot tells Yuum to "go over there," she is acting within a world shot through with value. For one thing, her father-in-law's peace while eating is something worth defending, and it is incumbent on her to stand for it. If I had asked her why she said that, she would doubtless have had a ready answer, for value, like language, is often automatic.

Of course not everyone values the same things in the same ways or holds the same beliefs to the same degree. So although we may talk of a metalinguistic capacity as something basic and inherent in language use, it surely does not express itself in commensurate evaluations. It is another channel for difference among people, and the differences may be much more obvious than the sameness of the mechanisms through which they are expressed. For this reason, perhaps, it is better to treat the whole topic of metalanguage under the rubric of ideologies—not because social stratification causes people's values to be what they are, but because the abstraction of generalizing makes too many things sound the same. The word "metalanguage" promises more than it can deliver, and we need to recapture some of the initial variations: differences among elements of language, among kinds of discourse, among contexts of communication, and among the values in which all of the foregoing are embedded. This seems really basic if we are to recast relativity as mediation and rediscover the fascination of the issue. Neither language nor experience is a fixed entity, and neither is a simple causal reflex of the other. The two are defined in reflexive relation to one another, and difference is the condition of their interplay.

Further Readings

On Linguistic Relativity

Basso, K. H. "'Wise Words' of the Western Apache: Metaphor and Semantic Theory." In *Western Apache Language and Culture: Essays in Linguistic Anthropology.* Tucson: University of Arizona Press, 1990, pp. 53–79.

Berlin, B., and Kay, P. *Basic Color Terms: Their Universality and Evolution.* Berkeley: University of California Press, 1969.

Boas, F. "Introduction to the Handbook of American Indian Languages." In *Introduction to Handbook of American Indian Languages and Indian Linguistic Families of America North of Mexico,* edited by P. Holder. Lincoln: University of Nebraska Press, 1966 [1911]. Parts 2, 4, and 5, pp. 10–39, 55–79.

Conklin, H. C. "Color Categorization." *American Anthropologist* 75(4) (1973):931–942.

de Léon, L. 1991. "Space Games in Tzotzil: Creating a Context for Spatial Reference." Working paper, Cognitive Anthropology Research Group at the Max Planck Institute for Psycholinguistics.

Frake, C. O. "The Ethnographic Study of Cognitive Systems." In *Language and Cultural Description: Essays by C. O. Frake,* selected and introduced by A. Dil. Stanford: Stanford University Press, 1980 [1962], pp. 1–17.

Friedrich, P. "Shape in Grammar." *Language* 46 (1970):379–407.

Goodenough, W.-H. "Componential Analysis and the Study of Meaning." *Language* 32 (1956):195–216.

Greenberg, J. H., ed. *Universals of Language.* Cambridge: MIT Press, 1966.

Haviland, J. B. "Projections, Transpositions and Relativity." Working paper, Cognitive Anthropology Research Group at the Max Planck Institute for Psycholinguistics, 1991.

Hill, J., and Mannheim, B. "Language and World View." *Annual Review of Anthropology* 21 (1992):381–406.

Huddleston, R. "Componential Analysis: The Sememe and the Concept of Distinctiveness." *Canadian Journal of Linguistics* 19(1) (1974):1–17.

Hymes, D. "Two Types of Linguistic Relativity." In *Sociolinguistics,* edited by W. Bright. The Hague: Mouton, 1966, pp. 114–165.

Levinson, S. "Relativity in Spatial Description and Conception." Working paper, Cognitive Anthropology Research Group at the Max Planck Institute for Psycholinguistics, 1991.

Lounsbury, F. G. "A Semantic Analysis of the Pawnee Kinship Usage." *Language* 32(1) (1956):158–194.

———. "The Structural Analysis of Kinship Semantics." In *Cognitive Anthropology,* edited by S. A. Tyler. New York: Holt, Rinehart and Winston, 1969 [1964], pp. 193–212.

Lucy, J. "Whorf's View of the Linguistic Mediation of Thought." In *Semiotic Mediation: Sociocultural and Psychological Perspectives,* edited by E. Mertz and R. Parmentier. New York: Academic Press, 1985, pp. 73–97.

———. ed. *Reflexive Language: Reported Speech and Metapragmatics.* Cambridge: Cambridge University Press, 1991.

Sapir, E. "Language." In *Selected Writings of Edward Sapir in Language, Culture, and Personality,* edited by D. G. Mandelbaum. Berkeley: University of California Press, 1949 [1924], pp. 7–32.

Weinreich, U. "On the Semantic Structure of Language." In *Universals of Language,* edited by J. Greenberg. Cambridge: MIT Press, 1966, pp. 142–216.

Whorf, B. L. "The Relation of Habitual Thought and Behavior to Language." In *Language, Thought and Reality: Selected Writings of Benjamin Lee Whorf,* edited by J. B. Carroll. Cambridge: MIT Press, 1941, pp. 134–159.

Ethnographies of Communication

Basso, K. H. "Speaking with Names: Language and Landscape Among the Western Apache." *Cultural Anthropology* 3(2) (1988):99–130.

Bauman, R., and Sherzer, J., eds. *Explorations in the Ethnography of Speaking.* Cambridge: Cambridge University Press, 1974.

Friedrich, P. "The Linguistic Sign and Its Relative Non-arbitrariness." In *Language, Context and the Imagination: Essays.* Selected and introduced by A. Dil. Stanford: Stanford University Press, 1979 [1970]. Chap. 1, pp. 1–62.

Giglioli, P. P., ed. *Language and Social Context.* Harmondsworth, England: Penguin, 1972.

Gumperz, J. *Discourse Strategies.* Cambridge: Cambridge University Press, 1982. Chap. 2: "The Sociolinguistics of Interpersonal Communication."

Haviland, J. B. *Gossip, Reputation, and Knowledge in Zinacantan.* Chicago: University of Chicago Press, 1977.

Hymes, D. "Toward Ethnographies of Communication." In *Language and Social Context,* edited by P. P. Giglioli. Harmondsworth, England: Penguin, 1972, pp. 21–44.

———. *Foundations in Sociolinguistics: An Ethnographic Approach.* Philadelphia: University of Pennsylvania Press, 1974. Chap. 1, pp. 3–28.

Labov, W. "The Study of Language in Its Social Context." In *Language and Social Context,* edited by P. P. Giglioli. Harmondsworth, England: Penguin, 1972, pp. 283–308.

McQuown, N. A. *Language, Culture, and Education: Essays by Norman A. McQuown,* edited by A. S. Dil. Stanford: Stanford University Press, 1982.

Sapir, E. *Language: An Introduction to the Study of Speech.* New York: Harcourt Brace, 1921. Chaps. 1–2.

Sherzer, J. *Kuna Ways of Speaking: An Ethnographic Perspective.* Austin: University of Texas Press, 1983.

Silverstein, M. "Shifters, Verbal Categories and Cultural Description." In *Meaning in Anthropology,* edited by K. Basso and H. Selby. Albuquerque: School of American Research, 1976, pp. 11–55.

Discourse Style and Textuality

Bauman, R. *Verbal Art as Performance.* Prospect Heights, IL: Waveland Press, 1977.

Bauman, R., and Briggs, C. "Poetics and Performance as Critical Perspectives on Language and Social Life." *Annual Review of Anthropology* 19 (1990):59–88.

Brown, P., and Levinson, S. *Politeness: Some Universals in Language Usage.* Cambridge: Cambridge University Press, 1987. Chap. 1, pp. 1–60.

Brown, R., and Gilman, A. "Pronouns of Power and Solidarity." In *Language and Social Context,* edited by P. P. Giglioli. Harmondsworth, England: Penguin, 1972, pp. 252–282.

Cicourel, A. "Text and Discourse." *Annual Review of Anthropology* 14 (1985):159–185.

Errington, J. J. *Structure and Style in Javanese: A Semiotic View of Linguistic Etiquette.* Philadelphia: University of Pennsylvania Press, 1988.

Hanks, W. F. "Text and Textuality." *Annual Review of Anthropology* 18 (1989):95–127.

Irvine, J. "Status and Style in Language." *Annual Review of Anthropology* 14 (1986): 557–581.

Jakobson, R. "Concluding Statement: Linguistics and Poetics." In *Style in Language,* edited by T. Sebeok. Cambridge: MIT Press, 1960, pp. 350–377.

Merlan, F., and Rumsey, A. *Ku Waru: Language and Segmentary Politics in the Western Nebilyer Valley, Papua New Guinea.* Cambridge: Cambridge University Press, 1991. Chap. 1, pp. 1–19; chap. 5, pp. 88–121.

Mukarovsky, J. "Standard Language and Poetic Language." In *A Prague School Reader on Esthetics, Literary Structure, and Style,* edited and translated by P. L. Garvin. Washington, DC: Georgetown University Press, 1964, pp. 17–30.

———. "Structuralism in Esthetics and Literary Studies." In *The Prague School: Selected Writings,* edited by P. Steiner. Austin: University of Texas Press, 1982 [1941], pp. 65–82.

Sherzer, J., and Urban, G., eds. *Native South American Discourse.* The Hague: Mouton, 1986.

Tynianov, Y. *The Problem of Verse Language.* Translated by M. Sosa and B. Harvey. Ann Arbor: Ardis Press, 1981 [1924].

Urban, G. *A Discourse-Centered Approach to Culture: Native South American Myths and Rituals.* Austin: University of Texas Press, 1991. Chaps. 1–2, pp. 1–58; chaps. 4–8.

Woodbury, A. C. "Rhetorical Structure in a Central Alaskan Yupik Eskimo Traditional Narrative." In Sherzer and Urban, eds., *Native South American Discourse*, The Hague: Mouton. 1986, pp. 176–239.

The Ideological Dimension

Briggs, C. L. *Learning How to Ask: A Sociolinguistic Appraisal of the Role of the Interview in Social Science Research.* Cambridge: Cambridge University Press, 1986, pp. 79–129.

Hanks, W. F. "Metalanguage and Pragmatics of Deixis." In *Reflexive Language: Reported Speech and Metapragmatics,* edited by J. Lucy. Cambridge: Cambridge University Press, 1991, pp. 127–158.

Jakobson, R. "Metalanguage as a Linguistic Problem." In *The Framework of Language.* Ann Arbor: University of Michigan Press, 1957, pp. 81–92.

Lucy, J. "Reflexive Language and the Human Disciplines." In *Reflexive Language: Reported Speech and Metapragmatics,* edited by J. Lucy. Cambridge: Cambridge University Press, 1991, pp. 9–32.

Silverstein, M. "Language Structure and Linguistic Ideology." In *Papers from the Fifteenth Regional Meeting of the Chicago Linguistic Society,* vol. 2: *Parasession on Linguistic Units and Levels,* edited by P. Clyne, W. F. Hanks, and C. Hofbauer. Chicago: Chicago Linguistic Society, 1979, pp. 193–247.

Taylor, C. "Language and Human Nature." In *Human Agency and Language: Philosophical Papers,* vol. 1. Cambridge: Cambridge University Press, 1985, pp. 215–247.

Weinreich, U. "On the Semantic Structure of Language." In *Universals of Language,* edited by J. Greenberg. Cambridge: MIT Press, 1966, pp. 142–216.

Chapter 9

Beyond the Speaker and the Text

TO SPEAK IS TO ENTER A FIELD in which everything is moving and objects exist in relation to one another. Names, categories, and the stereotypes of common sense allow us temporarily to suspend the animation. But they are no less mutable than the things to which they seem to stick. A table is a table, a paper a paper, but beneath the labels we know that no two are really the same, and the "table" of now was "furniture" a moment ago and will be a "painting project" later. How we identify objects depends upon context, and the meanings of the words we use are so incomplete that they, too, take root in circumstances. In the previous chapter we broke down the notion that a language is a single, unitary system and replaced it with the indexical bonding of forms to utterance contexts, stylistic variation, and different ways of speaking. We underscored the point, made throughout this book, that language is permeated by human experience and that the kind of mediation basic to linguistic relativity is a reflexive one in which verbal practices routinize ways of experiencing, and these in turn make their way into the very categories of the language. This interplay is part of all speech but is nowhere more evident than in the range of metalinguistic evaluations that people make daily. For language, too, is an object experienced in relation to other objects. Its transience is made all the more final in that it can describe itself.

To speak is to take up a position in a social field in which all positions are moving and defined relative to one another. The idealized notion of a solitary speaker giving unified voice to subjective thoughts is vulnerable to the same arguments brought against language as a monolithic code. The same tendencies toward differentiation, context-dependency, and self-reflexivity that play upon language also play upon the speakers who produce it. This is not to equate speakers with language but to say that the two are intertwined. To see this more clearly, we have to separate the "speaker" from the person who happens to be speaking. The former is a social role, whereas the latter is a social agent capable of occupying many roles, some of which involve talk, some of which don't. The relativity hypothesis in its strong form is based on the primordial importance of speaking in social life.

This is one of the linchpins that holds together our understanding of human experience as based in verbal practices. But it is important to remember that between language and persons, however the two are conceived, there is the intermediary level of the various participant roles through which people come into contact with language. The very term "speaker" encodes a grand abstraction, since it applies to promisers, petitioners, liars, debaters, lovers, litigants, poets, cheaters, bullshitters, performers—and all the other more narrowly defined roles tied to speech. Like any generalization, it holds out the promise of common features that unify the differences and justify the single label. But how unitary is speaking really, and is the concept "speaker" the best we can do in describing the producers of utterances? These are the central questions of this chapter, and the short answers are "not very" and "no." The longer answers will take some explaining.

During the time that the ethnography of speaking was taking shape and theories of style and performance were being worked out, similar developments took place in the study of speech production. Goffman's work on "footing" brought into sharp relief the relation between speakers and their utterances. This resulted in the decomposition of the speaker and addressee roles into a set of more basic ones that Goffman dubbed the "production format" and the "participant framework." The result was a more precise but still abstract set of terms for analyzing the relations between parties to conversation. During this period, too, the writings of the Russian linguist Mikhail Bakhtin (who some take to be the same person as Voloshinov, writing under a pseudonym) began to appear in English translation. Bakhtin has theorized speaking in terms of what he called "dialogism." The basic insight behind this term is that when social actors speak, their words are not merely their own but reflect their engagement in a broader ideological and verbal world. Thus what might appear as straight monologue is "dialogized" by its refraction of the social horizon.

The combined result of Goffman and Bakhtin was to explode from within the appearance of a unitary speaker. Complementary to this was a very significant body of sociolinguistic research that expanded the notion of speaker to ever larger social units. These include, in rough order of inclusiveness, the speaker-addressee dyad, the multiparty interaction, the "speech community," the "community of practice," and the multiple "publics" by which an utterance or text is received. Each of these levels raises slightly different issues. It is unlikely that solutions at one level will work just right at the next. This lack of transitivity is one of the hot spots in recent theory. For instance, on the one hand, the human body plays a central role in all face-to-face interaction, which allows us to connect the work of Goffman and interactional sociolinguists with that of Merleau-Ponty. On the other hand, once we reach the level of publics, things like print mediation, broadcasting, and multiple interpretation become consequential. Language mediates among these different levels by circulating through them, but this must not obscure the existence of discontinuities. The fully saturated contextualization of examples like the exchange between Margot and Yuum raises different problems than the ones Jack faces as he reads the newspaper. Scanning the headlines, Jack engages in an interpretive community of readers, most of whom he will never meet. Though never absent, the role of corporeality is less clear and harder to argue for. We won't resolve these problems—it's too early in the game for answers—but we will work through them in such a way as to lay the groundwork for investigating them. Let's start with the speaker.

From Dialectic to Dialogue

What is the immediate context in which an actor assumes the role of "speaker"? Let's start from the motivational structure of utterances, the "why" of talk. Recalling Schutz's terms, we should distinguish the in-order-to motive from the because motive. Although meaning is never exhausted by a speaker's intentions, utterances are typically performed with certain ends in view. This is all the more evident when we are dealing with strategic interaction in which speech is a means to an end, such as informing an interlocutor, displaying knowledge, making a commitment for future action. But in general we assume that people produce speech in order to achieve some aims, even if these are obscure or hard to rationalize after the fact. We can call this a *prospective* motivation. The inverse is the *retrospective* reason for speaking. What leads up to the utterance, establishing its relevance, setting its immediate background? Perhaps it is a response to a question, a sarcastic comeback, or an interpretation of some earlier remark or experience. This orientation ties the utterance into an earlier time, be it moments or years before. Between these two orientations the utterance exists as a historical fact, far from the pure synchronic potential posited by formalism. Somewhere between the prospective and retrospective dimensions are the myriad simultaneous relations between speech and its copresent context. As we saw in Chapter 7, this context typically includes factors such as gestures coordinated with speech, bodily dispositions and movements, the spatial and temporal present, and the accessibility of objects referred to by speakers. And of course the line between the present and the past or future is a matter of degree. How we define it in a given case depends upon the kind of speech we consider. Promises, warnings, and threats portend results, whereas conclusions, inferences, and reaction reach back to what preceded them. The network of simultaneous relations between acts and contexts is the domain of pure indexicality. Indexical relations, recall, are based on coexistence and contiguity. Along with the motivational context, indexical ties define the *actuality* of the utterance.

The actuality of any utterance is a vortex of value. The motivations of a speaker are values in action, by definition, but the indexical copresent is no less subject to the defining effects of beliefs and values. This is the fallacy of any metric measure of utterance space or chronometric measure of utterance time. Right at the point where the role of value becomes definitive, objective measures intervene, with their false promise of value-free equivalence. The problem is that objectivity is itself a value, a particularly strong one in our scientific tradition, and what it provides by way of supposedly neutral measures are in fact evaluations along one dimension. As we pointed out in the previous chapter, this is one of the points on which the purely colorimetric study of color terms goes wrong. The red thread of objectivity running through all contexts is a red herring because it seeks comparability by stepping out of the dynamic of meaning production instead of into it. The comparability of temporal, spatial, or color distance lies in finding commensurate relations between the terms and their social contexts. If in one cultural context black signifies mourning and white purity, whereas in another white signifies mourning and black purity, then, in comparing the two, black is equivalent to white. The challenge is similar in defining the present of an utterance. Stopwatches give one kind of measure, but what counts as simultaneity depends upon the temporal span of the phenomenon we are looking at. In a ritual event the present may be so dilated as to include all of history, but in the last leg of a horse race, it may be down to the millisecond. Similarly, in the exchange between Margot and Yuum, the spatial extent of "here" was defined by the household as a meaningful field of interaction and the different relations between the interactants and that field. For this reason, even the three-way division among prospective, retrospective, and simultaneous dimensions of actuality is no more than a heuristic starting point. The three do not have constant values across all contexts but at best indicate a way into the problem. Once we demystify objectivity, we can ask how it is produced and defined under varying conditions.

The same applies to the production of subjectivity through speaking. When Margot told Yuum to go wait for Don Chabo and when Natalia responded to Jack by saying, "It's right on the table," both were expressing their own thoughts. Whereas Margot's directive defined the situation for Yuum and organized his response in no uncertain terms, Natalia's took the form of a simple statement of fact. Both utterances projected their speaker's perspectives on the situation, and both in different ways provided their addressees with a course of subsequent action. This capacity of speech to define situations and indicate a course of action is at the root of Austin's notion of illocutionary force. It is also part of what allows speakers to *realize themselves* through speaking. In a real sense Margot's directive said more about her as an adult Maya woman with the authority and the will to direct Yuum than it did about Don Chabo, its ostensible referent. In the same way Natalia's statement about the paper on the table located her in the scene and expressed her momentary alignment to it and to her mate. The expressive force of speaking is most obvious in emotionally charged utterances and in cases where the speaker appears to be expressing something unique to herself. But these mark the tip of an iceberg, and the construction of self through language is an ongoing process even in the most mundane circumstances.

This is not to say that the realization of the subject through talk proceeds unfettered, limited only by the free will and states of the subject. To posit this would be to ignore the fundamentally social grounding of language, the constraints on what can reasonably be said, and the numerous expectations and responsiblities summarized under the rubric of speakerhood. If Natalia had responded to Jack the way Margot did to Yuum, the result would likely have been conflict. Or if Margot spoke to her father-in-law the way she did to Yuum, there would surely have been fireworks around the house. In other words, although in the abstract sense any speaker can produce any utterance, in the social sense this is never the case. There are always constraints and consequences to speech. This marks the opposite tendency of subjective projection through speech. In the very same utterance that expresses a speaker, projecting her into the world, the world is introjected into the speaker. As Merleau-Ponty put it, it is in the world that we find ourselves, and when we look within, it is the world that we find. At its strongest, this tendency may reach overt domination, forcing a speaker to speak in a certain way. Or it may be a matter of hegemony, the invisible compulsion whereby context defines the limits of what is thinkable, including the self-image of the speaker. Insofar as language belongs to context, this is the relativity thesis at its most insidious.

We are thus going toward a view of speaking in which utterance production involves a dialectic between the expressive projection of the speaker into the world and the simultaneous construction of the speaker according to the world. In certain cases one or the other pole may be dominant, resulting in speech that is maximally creative or maximally dominated. But most of our daily discourse balances between the two extremes. That we use words charged with value implies that the weight of social context is never absent, just as the freedom to speak or remain silent implies a measure of expressivity. The same factors that constrain the meanings of linguistic forms are also the resources that enable self-realization through talk. The duality of constraint and enablement is part of the same process. In a more immediate sense, speakers rarely if ever produce talk without regard to its reception. One of the most familiar ways that social context pulls a speaker is what has come to be called recipient design. That is, parties to talk, especially effective ones, attend to the effects of their words on their addressees. As the commonsense maxim puts it, know your audience. We saw this clearly in Margot's attending to Yuum's relation to her household and in her awareness that Don Chabo was present as an overhearer to the exchange. Similarly, Natalia's response to Jack builds precisely on her knowledge that he is familiar with the spatial surround of the kitchen and dining room. This is indicated in her word choice, "It's right on the table," in which the "right" and the definite article both presuppose his familiarity with and access to the table. Furthermore, her use of "it" is coreferential with "the paper" in Jack's question. Thus among the many bridges that tie utterances into their contexts, some involve judgments about the addressee's position in the situation. It is virtually never a simple matter of a speaker's producing only her own words without regard to an interlocutor. Insofar as the indexical ground of deictic expressions requires consideration of the relations among speaker, addressee, and referent, the receiver has a role in the production of the utterance. Not only is interpretation a productive process, but *anticipated* understanding is a factor in the forming of utterances.

When people make reference to and describe themselves, the constitutive force of speech appears to be maximum. If context constrains speech, it is also produced by it. Think of an introduction in which one speaker greets another, saying,

"Hi, I'm Jack, Natalia's husband" or "Hi, my name is Andy. I work in editorial." In such cases the words uttered literally present the speaker to the addressee and define his identity for current purposes. The speech event frame is being established with the introduction of new information that can subsequently be presupposed. It is standard to maintain a distinction in linguistic description between the speech event in which talk is produced and the scene or event that is talked about. This is clearest when the two planes are separated by space or time, as in a description of events that occurred elsewhere at some other time. When reference is made to the *current* situation, through first or second person pronouns, present tense forms, or proximate deictics, the two planes are superposed: The event being talked about is (or is part of) the one in which the talk occurs. This kind of reflexivity is at the heart of performative verbs as Austin described them. In uttering "I promise," the speaker describes an event in which he makes the promise, and this event is identified with the current one. The result is that the words appear to have the "magical" effect of creating as a socially binding reality the event that they literally describe. For our purposes, what is most interesting about this phenomenon is that the speaker is simultaneously defining himself or his current situation and being defined by it. Not only does the choice of terms in which to describe oneself depend upon the situation, but the description projects the speaker as a participant in the world talked about. And this anchors the self-expression in the world of objects.

Writing about a similar range of phenomena whereby speech is simultaneously individual and collective, Bakhtin proposed the concept of "dialogism." Whereas "dialogue" is commonly understood as the interactive relation between two people engaged in talk, dialogism is the internal dynamic in the discourse of a single speaker. Although in a general sense much of the foregoing discussion concerns dialogical foundations of speech, we can make it more specific. Consider first quoted speech, in which one speaker reproduces the words of another speaker, with appropriate attribution. Margot later reports to me what Yuum had said: "So he *asked*, 'Is Don Chabo home?' " The italicized portion of her utterance is a metalinguistic verb that frames Yuum's utterance as a question. It is in the third person, past tense, making reference to him and interpreting his speech as being of the category designated by "ask." This much is Margot's interpretation, since he never used the word "ask." What follows within orthographic quotes is presented as a verbatim reproduction of his utterance. In spoken language she would likely attempt to mimic his intonation or use an intonation in which the interrogative force is made plain (e.g., with rising final contour). Although her utterance is, we can assume, part of a dialogue with me (her current addressee), it is also dialogical in the sense of including speech whose author was Yuum and speech whose author is Margot.

At a step removed from direct quotation is indirect discourse, in which the original utterance is recast in the words of the current speaker but retains its original import and at least some of its phrasing: "He asked whether Don Chabo was home." Note here that the tense is past rather than present, according to the temporal relation between Margot's current utterance and Yuum's earlier one. This is another variant of dialogism, in which different elements of Yuum's speech are retained in Margot's rendition of it. At another remove from the overt dialogism of quotation are cases in which a speaker "borrows" another person's wording or statements without attributing them. This amounts to a kind of revoicing in which the language is presented as belonging to the current speaker, whereas in fact its source is elsewhere. In publishing this can amount to plagiarism if the borrowed language is in any way proprietary and the original author claims rights over it. Of course in much of daily talk, this happens without the clear sense of a single, original author, or if there is one, the revoicing is merely a rhetorical trope. The business manager exhorts her employees, saying, "Ask not what your company can do for you, ask what you can do for your company." The ploy may be tacky or quite effective, but in either case it rests on the recognition of dialogicality. There need not be any particular author, however, and speech peppered with clichés or common formulas is no less dialogical than quotation.

At the far end of the spectrum, a speaker may subtly borrow from traditional or highly valued forms of talk in order to make a point or convince an addressee. This is particularly obvious in the rhetoric of politicians, which must be both original and capable of pushing the right buttons in the electorate. In order for an utterance to be dialogized, it is not necessary that the presence of discourse from another source be recognized as such. For certain purposes, like plagiarism, the aim is in fact to pull off the ruse unnoticed. In Bakhtin's vision *all* speech is dialogized because it draws its value from the ideological horizons of the society. To label a discourse as dialogical therefore tells us little or nothing distinctive about it. What is important is to distinguish among the different kinds and aspects of the phenomenon. Notice that its ubiquity implies that through talk speakers realize not only themselves but also their relations to others around them.

Participation Frameworks

If speakers enter into relations with their world through speaking, it is in dialogue and multiparty talk that this is at its most concrete. In the canonical cases dialogue is based on face-to-face interaction between two individuals. This is the situation on which the standard idealizations of Saussure and others are based, and it is the source of the terms "speaker" and "addressee." In their commonsense meanings these terms designate the two roles of the one producing the utterance and the one receiving it. These roles alternate in the sense that the speaker of one utterance directs talk to the addressee, who in turn becomes the speaker of the response, for which the original speaker is now the addressee. This seems to correspond well to the situation of Jack and Natalia in our opening scenario. Although we have seen that things are virtually never as simple as this makes them seem, there is already an important distinction inscribed in the terms. Namely, "speaker" and "addressee" are roles that social actors occupy for finite periods of time. This is a point we made earlier in this chapter, but here I want to highlight an interesting question that it raises. The roles themselves are usually discussed as features or, more exactly, formal objects, which are combined in the larger formal object called a speech event or conversation. This way of describing it makes them appear to be synchronic entities whose characteristics are determined solely by the facts of language, the production and auditory reception of sound. But the *occupation* of the roles is a social process, not a synchronic fact. Because of this, we should be on the lookout for indicators of how actors take up the roles, discharge and vacate them, and provide openings for others to assume them or closures to prevent them from doing so. The abstraction inherent in treating the roles apart from the question of occupancy led traditionally to a total neglect of factors based on the body. Corporeality is of course implied by the use of the vocal apparatus to make speech sounds and the auditory apparatus to perceive them. This much was already present in Saussure's talking heads model. But when it comes to occupancy, much more is implied, including posture, gaze, gestures, physical proximity, tone of voice, and timing.

Although Merleau-Ponty's approach to the corporeal schema has had no impact on sociolinguistics, to my knowledge it is right on the mark in these matters. Recall that the phenomenal field subsumes the actor's physical relation to context along with his or her awareness of that relation *and* the intuitive grasp of other potential but nonactual relations. When a speaker talks, this kind of reflexivity and awareness is constantly at play. We can see this precisely in the use of indexical items that require monitoring and encode what we might call "traffic signals" for managing interpersonal relations (see Chapter 8). Thus whatever the general arguments in favor of treating speakerhood as a process, there are also good empirical reasons for doing so.

There is a significant line of research on participant roles in sociolinguistics, including the pioneering work of R. Brown and A. Gilman (1972), Friedrich (1979: chapters 2, 3), M. Silverstein (1976), and students of the ethnography of speaking and even performance studies (see Chapter 8). But the work of Goffman (1983) stands out. Goffman came to this issue primarily out of his reflections on footing. A speaker's footing is her "alignment, set, or projected self" in relation to her words. The difference among direct, indirect, and quoted speech are footing differences in this sense, and the foregoing discussion of dialogism is germane to it as well. Goffman took these phenomena as evidence that the traditional roles had to be rethought and ultimately subdivided into a set of more finely shaded roles. His intuition was basically that a speaker producing quotation is not really a speaker in the same sense as one who produces direct discourse. Thus rather than seeing these (and all the other distinctions like them) as different ways of discharging the role of speaker, he saw them as corresponding to different roles. In place of the "speaker," he posited what he called the "production format" of the utterance. It had three parts, each one a role: (1) The "animator" is the person who makes the sounds; (2) the "author" is the one who selects the words and phrasing; (3) the "principal" is the one ultimately responsible for the opinions and statements expressed. Now these three often coincide, as they did in Jack's question to Natalia and in her response. But what about when a spokesperson delivers a text prepared by someone else, or when one person quotes another after the fact? In these cases the utterer is an animator but neither an author nor a principal. Similarly, if the press agent is charged with presenting the position of his boss to some third party, then he is animator and author but not the principal. Both in face-to-face talk and in structured interviews and public appearances, the roles are often split apart. The noncoincidence of the three is the evidence that they must be distinguished in a general analytic framework.

A similar reasoning applies to the addressee. In the exchange between Margot and Yuum, the words formed a simple dialogue, but the interaction was witnessed by myself and Don Chabo. In Goffman's terms, Margot and Yuum were "ratified participants," whereas Don Chabo and I were "overhearers." It is obvious that most daily interaction takes place in the presence of overhearers, such as bystanders and others not party to an exchange yet privy to it. In Don Chabo's case it was still more involved because he was both an overhearer and the primary referent of the exchange. This also allows us to distinguish speech addressed to an entire group from speech directed to one member of the group in the presence of the others. The overall point is that once we look closely at the relations among parties to talk, it becomes clear that the traditional dyad is an inadequate basis for description. Goffman went on to typologize kinds of talk according to the kinds of participants involved. "Dominating communication" is the main engagement between ratified participants. "Subordinate" communication is nonfocal, perhaps hidden talk among a subset of participants. It is "by-play" if the participants are ratified parties and "sideplay" if they are not. "Cross-play" is subordinate communication between a ratified and a nonratified participant. For our purposes, the details of Goffman's typology are less important than that it pushes beyond the simple dyad and opens up the possibility of a differentiated approach to multiparty talk. Indeed, this became one of the central foci of research by Goffman's students and interpreters (see C. Goodwin 1981, 1984; M. H. Goodwin 1982, 1990; Levinson 1983, 1987).

One thing that comes out clearly in Goffman's framework is the interdependence among the internal subdivisions of participant roles, the external relations among the roles, and the classification of interactions according to type. So long as the simple dyad was assumed to be the natural state of talk, the simplified versions of the roles appeared adequate. As the evidence of language variation and native typologies of speaking mounted, thanks to the work of sociolinguists and ethnographers, it became inevitable that the speaker-addressee dyad would lose its place as the measure of all talk. Thus it is not accidental that the decomposition of the roles into animator, author, principal, addressee, and overhearer was part of a broader push toward the study of different types of interaction, including multiparty talk. Once the boundaries of the dyad were breached, the inadequacy of its two parts became all too obvious. It is also clear in this framework that the relation between an individual and the language he or she speaks is mediated by social roles. This point came out in the preceding chapter, where we recast the relativity hypothesis in terms of mediation. But it is all the more compelling and concrete now. You simply cannot make inferences from utterance forms to human experience without working through the intermediate level of participation frameworks.

During the 1970s and 1980s there emerged another specialized offshoot of sociolinguistics, drawing on the work of Goffman and Harold Garfinkel. The focus was the microanalysis of routine verbal interaction, which Garfinkel initially dubbed "ethnomethodology" and subsequent scholars elaborated into "conversation analysis." Goffman and especially Garfinkel were deeply influenced by Schutz's studies of interactive relations, commonsense understanding via types, and the situational character of relevance. One of the important insights of this work, as M. H. Goodwin signaled (1990:1ff), is that human interactants continually display to each other, in the course of interaction, their own understanding of what they are doing. In other words, interaction proceeds on two levels at once: the direct engagement of the actors with the world and their evaluations regarding "what is going on here" at any point. This insight dovetails nicely with Rommetveit's proposal, following Wittgenstein, that meaning production in language is guided by the contracts speakers share regarding what kind of "game" is being played. It also builds on the phenomenological insight that actors maintain awareness of their own actions, since it is this awareness that each displays to the other party. In conversational research it led to a major focus on the empirical description of how interactants display to one another the orderliness of their talk. Thus the investigator's task of examining orderliness corresponds to the interactant's task of displaying it. The display, unlike the analytic description, is constitutive in the sense of creating the order itself. We see the same interplay in the difference between metalinguistic function, which is constitutive in situ, and discourse about language at a step removed.

If participation takes place in the social here and now of copresence, then it is subject to rapid change as an interaction progresses. What starts as a perfunctory exchange of greetings builds into a conversation in which new information is produced jointly, memories of prior interactions are brought into play, and future plans are laid. Talk by other people is reported and commented on and so becomes part of the current now. As an interaction emerges, the participation framework emerges with it. Both could be said to be up for grabs insofar as individuals or groups can propose versions that either become fact or don't but that can be contested, ignored, accepted, and so forth—all with their range of consequences and transpositions of perspective. Just as Voloshinov argued that linguistic meaning arises only in the context of utterance themes and Rommetveit argued that what can be made known by an utterance varies with the contextual frames one assumes, so conversation analysis shows that "context" is produced in dialogic and multiparty interaction. It bears the trace of this in the form of sequential organizations inherent to interaction, as well as kinds of participation inherently mediated by language. In a real sense, conversation analysis provides a new kind of irreducibility, namely, the irreducible laws of conversational interaction and their unavoidable trace on utterance form (see here Levinson 1983, Atkinson and Heritage 1984, C. Goodwin 1981).

Transposition

We started this chapter by saying that to speak is to step into an interactive field in which positions are defined relative to one another and are in constant flux. At that point the assertion may have seemed to overstate the well-known alternation between speakers and hearers typical of orderly talk. By now it is clear that both the simplicity of the roles and the supposed lockstep back and forth of speaking are false appearances. More accurately, they are idealizations devised in order to clear away the detritus of *parole* and lay bare language as a formal, synchronic system. If we push the issue a step further and attempt to join a quasi-formal perspective with the interactive one, interesting things happen. Take the case of reported speech. Neil says to Madeleine, "Meet me here tomorrow," and I subsequently report his utterance to Peter. I can say, "Neil said to Madeleine, 'Meet me here tomorrow.'" In this case I have to spell out to Peter both where and when the exchange took place. Otherwise he won't be able to interpret the deictic "here" or the adverb "tomorrow." Alternatively, I could say simply, "Neil told Madeleine yesterday to meet him there today" or "Neil told Madeleine on Saturday to meet him at the corner of Grace and Greenview on Sunday" or some such. In other words, I could resort to indirect discourse in which I have shifted the indexical elements from the initial context of Neil's utterance to the subsequent context of my own report of it. Or I could attempt to replace the indexicals with descriptive phrases that do not rely so much on the actuality of either the original exchange or the report. In all three versions of my report, I have signaled a shift in footing: I am either the animator, where Neil is the author and principal (direct quote), or the animator and author, where Neil is the principal (indirect discourse).

The problem is not that this account of the thing is wrong but that it doesn't explain much. Knowing that I am the animator but Neil is the author just isn't enough to interpret the indexicals. Neil might have penned the phrase as the opening of a poem or spoken it in jest. He would still be the author, but Peter would be clueless about the relevant references. Like metalanguage, reported speech is a form of objectification. You take an original utterance, with all its selectivity and the density of its ties to context, and you recycle part of it in another context. Whatever gets recycled has been detached and turned into an object that can be repeated. Full recovery of the original actuality is of course impossible, since both the original and the report are so selective. But we have at our disposal linguistic resources that allow us to minimize the loss and keep straight at least some of the references. The choice of metalinguistic verbs, the addition of descriptive phrases, intonation, and other means signal to an addressee what is going on. They provide the kind of displays of coherence that conversation analysts have emphasized. It is true but insufficient to say, as Goffman did, that these are keys indicating shifts in footing. They are more systematic than that, and they don't all work the same way.

The difference between direct quotation and indirect report is a matter of *transposition.* In the former the deictic term retains both its original referent and its original indexical ground. In our example, when I quote Neil's utterance, the form "here" is interpreted relative to the context of his exchange with Madeleine. The relational feature of the deictic is grounded in that utterance frame and projects a referent in relation to it. So the feature [+ proximate] attaches to Neil's utterance framework. By contrast, in the indirect report, the deictic is shifted from "here" to "there," and this change signals that the referent (the corner of Grace and Greenview) is in a relation of nonproximity. But notice that it is nonproximate *to Peter and me* as we speak. My report says nothing about Neil's whereabouts when *he* spoke. He could as well have been out of the country talking over the phone. With quoted indexical terms, we learn not only what the original speaker said but when and where he was relative to his topic. Not so with indirect report. We lose both the original words and the crucial relations among the interactants and what they were talking about. To put this in different terms, indirect discourse belongs to the participation framework of the report, whereas quotation retains its tie to the framework of the utterance that is reported. The term "transposition" applies specifically to cases like quotation, where a speaker signals that a portion of his current speech is anchored elsewhere. So when I say to Peter, "Neil told Madeleine, 'Meet me here tomorrow,'" I may be doing all the talking, but I have spoken two completely different discourses. The boundary between them comes at the onset of the quote. It instructs Peter momentarily to suspend the indexical ground of our actual present and to transpose himself into the framework of Neil and Madeleine. Other keys, such as intonation and special phrasing, can help convey this message, but none with the precision of the deictics.

These examples imply that the present of speech is a kind of palimpsest, a layering of past, present, and future frameworks all precisely articulated in the actuality of the utterance. You don't have to alternate between speaking and hearing in order to shift the roles around. All of the preceding processes would apply even if I were reminding Peter of something I had said to him in the past. The persons would be the same, but the participation frameworks of the present and the past would be different. And it is important to see that quotation is only the most obvious instance of a more widespread phenomenon. We do similar things all the time. If you think of conversation as a collaboratively produced discourse, transpositions happen each time the role of animator shifts between participants ("I" becomes "you," "this" becomes "that," and so forth). If you think of footing shifts like irony, parody, metaphor, and overstatement, relatively minor transpositions take place between the "standard" discourse and the "special talk." Although less extreme than quotation, these kinds of talk also project participation frameworks different from the ones that precede them. Transposition is basically a rarefied instance of the global capacity of speech to create new contexts on the stage of the present. We see this especially in narrative, where the skillful storyteller creates a world and moves in and out of it over the course of the telling. The challenge is to identify the varieties of transposition and footing shifts, the formal means whereby they are achieved, and the interactive processes of which they are a part.

Beyond the Face-to-face

So far we have moved from the unitary, solitary speaker to a dialectical engagement with the world, a dialogical engagement with others, and the dynamics of transposition. But even with all this, we have yet to directly discuss the role in talk of *other* social actors not physically present in the event. This is one of the often-cited criticisms of conversation analysis and indeed all phenomenologically derived theories of language: They are biased toward the experiential field of the interactants and provide little by way of analysis of the broader social backdrop. In a sense the criticism is well founded because all of the parties to talk are also parties to a larger world, the vast part of which is nowhere evident in a transcript or even a videotape of their interaction. It is fair to counter this criticism by saying that the focus of such analysis is the present, whose dynamics are more than enough to keep us busy. But this response grants the main point, that phenomenological description must be complemented by something else. The concept of dialogism and the dialectic that we sketched earlier assume a broader world but fail to analyze it in its own terms. Or better, they describe it solely from the perspective of the actual present. Even in the case of transposition, which is by definition a shift from the corporeal field into some other framework of talk, the shift takes place in, and is referred back to, the present. Notice that however elaborate a narrative transposition may be, the semantics of the indexicals always trace a path back to the actual framework in which they are embedded and ultimately interpreted. Metalinguistic frames, as in "Neil said to Madeleine yesterday, '———'" have indexicals, such as the past tense marking of the verb and the adverb "yesterday," that situate the reported speech relative to the present.

Merleau-Ponty's writings also reflect a constant concern with the situatedness of corporeal experience in the world, but it is always the world *as it appears in the phenomenal present.* Nowhere does he suspend his meditation on experience to discuss things like social structure or history apart from their emergence here and now. Ingarden comes close to this in his notion of a work as a history of concretizations, but he, too, stops short. Concretization is a process that takes place in the present, and the history made by successive instances of it always radiates from the perspective point of one or another present. There are good reasons for this, especially in the case of phenomenology. For the alternative seems to be to cut loose from actuality and adopt an objectifying "view from nowhere." This panopticon is the contrary of phenomenology, against which it defined itself, and it is the bête noire of most contemporary critical theories in the humanities. Indeed, what we have repeatedly criticized as the formalist approach to linguistic systems is a version of such a panoptical view, and that is why formalism fails when applied to the actuality of speech. But we also said from the outset that a purely relational, presentist view of language is doomed to failure. And if we have continued to hammer away at formalism, it is because it remains relevant and cannot be dismissed. The same applies to social and historical factors that transcend the scope of utterance context. To clarify the issue, let's briefly contrast Schutz's typology of social actors with Hilary Putnam's concept of the "division of linguistic labor."

As a phenomenologist, Schutz starts and ends his treatment of the life world with the experiential field of actors. In between these points, as it were, he works through the key concepts of motivation, typification, and the different "zones of relevance" (see Chapter 6). Recall that it was in the context of relevance that he proposed a typology of "sectors" in the life world. The first was the world of "consociates," those people with whom the actor has regular, face-to-face contact. At a step removed were contemporaries, those people living roughly at the same time as the actor, of whom she has knowledge but no direct familiarity. We illustrated this with the employees of the phone company and the manufacturers of objects the actor uses in everyday life. At another step removed are the actor's predecessors, all those historical personages whose existence is taken for granted and integrated into actual experience in a more vague fashion. At the farthest remove was the zone of irrelevance: all those currently, formerly, and subsequently existing agents whose existence has little or no apparent impact on the experience of the actor. Schutz's main concern was to devise a scale of relative anonymity and abstractness of typification, and in Chapter 6 we pointed out several problems with the framework. In the present context I want to stress that this way of dividing up the social world is entirely radial, with the individual actor in the center. Because of this, a contemporary can become a consociate through direct contact with the central individual. I can meet some of the employees of the phone company, who thereby enter into the warm light of consociate relations; similarly, a neighbor can move away and depart from the web of consociates, entering into the now relatively anonymous sphere of contemporaries. This movement into and out of a field of experience is what I meant in saying that the model is radial. For the entire basis for classifying people is the way they relate to the individual.

Putnam's (1975) framework is basically different and illustrates a nonradial way of integrating the broader social field into the dynamics of meaning production. Unlike Schutz, Putnam concentrates on analyzing the different semantic theories and proposing a kind of semantics that avoids some of the pitfalls of classical theories. Recall that the "intensional" meaning of a linguistic form is classically defined as a bundle of features determined according to the oppositions between the form and others related to it. This is close in spirit to Saussure's concept of paradigmatic opposition and *valeur* (see Chapter 2). The standard alternatives to intensional theories are ones based on extension. That is, the meaning of a form is the class of objects to which a term appropriately applies or of which it is "true." So for "table," instead of looking to the opposition between it and other related words, as an intensional theory would do, an extensional theory would gather together the kinds of things to which the word applies. The general extension of the word is then defined as the necessary and sufficient features common to members of the class. Now Putnam was critical of intensional approaches because they define meaning as a concept that must be known as such by a speaker. According to this, to know the meaning of a term is to be in a certain psychological state. The main justification of intensional approaches lies in the assumption that intension determines extension, that is, you can use "table" to properly describe the thing in the dining room precisely because the word has meaning x, and the thing fits the meaning.

In a move quite congenial to anthropology, Putnam argued that the intensional view was wrong because it ultimately obscured the public and social definition of meaning. This is the key move from which we go to the division of labor. For Putnam pointed out that both the semantic features usually associated with the term and the properties of objects taken to correspond to them must be valid across the linguistic community as a collectivity. In other words, meaning is not a psychological fact but a social one. This does not imply that all sectors of a linguistic community need have exactly the same meaning for a term. On the contrary, to make this assumption would be either utterly naive about social variation or a very limiting definition of what counts as a community. We know that different people understand the same words in sometimes quite different ways. And this is where the division of labor comes in: Every community of speakers uses at least some expressions whose associated features are known only by a subset of the speakers who acquire the expressions and whose use by other speakers depends upon a structured cooperation between them and the specialists (Putnam 1975:228). To put it simply, we all use at least some words whose meanings we don't really know, but we use them in rough accord with the definitions of specialists. Think of terms like "transmission," "front-end alignment," and "fuel injection" in reference to cars. Few of us would be able to provide a precise definition of any of these terms, yet we can converse adequately with a mechanic who uses them in explaining why the hatchback thumps at stop lights, shimmies at 45 miles an hour, or accelerates fast enough to get on the expressway at rush hour. I know enough about my computer to know that the hard drive crashed last month and the file directory was damaged, but I would be hard pressed to explain exactly what a crash is, technically, or how the file directory relates to the operating system. The doctor tells me I hyperextended my right shoulder swimming in waves, and I get the point, but, again, I rely on her expertise to know which muscles, tendons, and so forth are causing the pain. We might try to know as much as possible about the things in our daily lives, but Putnam's point is that we all inevitably use words according to what *we take to be* their definitions. And there is loads of evidence that we know we don't know the technical meanings. Using such words, we pause, hedge, add expressions like "sort of," "whatchamacallit," "doohickey," and "dooter" when the uncertainty gets to be too much. We defer to specialists if they are around and assume that they have the right to adjust our wording if the need arises. In other words, our ability to speak a language is at least partly based on our ability to participate in the social division of verbal skills. Notice that this makes it unnecessary, and even false, to assume that shared knowledge of a code is what makes communication possible. What makes talk possible is common membership in an interpretive community.

On the basis of these phenomena, Putnam proposed that the semantic value of any expression is made up of four factors: (1) the grammatical markers indicating the kind of expression (cf. "table" is a count noun), (2) semantic markers (cf. "table" is a solid object with a horizontal surface), (3) stereotypical features (cf. "table" is a human-made piece of furniture with a flat surface and a means of suspending or supporting it off the floor, typically used for activities like eating, writing, and so forth), and (4) its extension (i.e., the class of things to which it applies). Although each of these factors is social, the second two are strictly so. The stereotypical uses of a form rely on the kinds of practical typification that Schutz described. They have everything to do with the commonsense understandings both of objects and of the words used to denote them. The extension is actually a range of objects, and the implication of the division of linguistic labor is that this range may have discontinuities. So with the growth of specialist knowledge, the set of objects that a word designates may shift around, and some people may use it with special precision, whereas others use it more vaguely. Think of a word like "life" in relation to the abortion debate. Medical science may determine the precise onset of cell division and may have a definition of human physiology that draws the line differently than would nonspecialist advocates of one or another social policy. In the entire range of technological developments, words like "radio" or "computer" have everyday meanings that may be at variance with the extensional values of the terms when used in a high-tech laboratory. Similarly, with legal terms like "contract," "seizure," and "assault," everyday usage tends to be both broader and only partly overlapping with the technical usage.

We could multiply the examples in reference to medicine, finance, literature, visual arts, linguistics, religion, and virtually any other sphere of endeavor in which specialized knowledge refines, and may ultimately break loose from, the pathways of practical common usage. The point of Putnam's approach is that such disjunction is a feature of most if not all language use. Therefore meanings are based not on individual psychological states but on the participation of speakers in the social formation to which the language is joined. My competence to speak of the hard drive and software of my computer has more to do with my occupying a certain place in the social world, having access to computer specialists, than with my having a certain psychology.

This brings us back, then, to the issue of social organization. Putnam's discussion fails, understandably, to present a general theory of the social division of labor. He was concerned with devising an approach to semantics that tied it in to social settings. But in order to really do an analysis along the lines he proposes, we would have to look closely at social organization, the institutional structures that create specialists and legitimate their opinions, and so forth. Notice that such an account would not be based on relations to a speaking ego, as it was in Schutz's case, but on the social context directly. What makes a lawyer a specialist in words like "contract" is not her relation to any particular speaker who wants to make a written agreement for a service—not the way that being a consociate *does* depend on having a face-to-face relation. It is her having gone through a certain specialized training, passed a bar exam, and obtained a permit or license to practice in her state. With Putnam's proposal, protean though it is, we move to another level of social fact, irreducible to intersubjective experience. We could say that it *decenters* the issue of participation by proposing a form of organization based on the entire collectivity, not merely centered on the proximate participants in an utterance.

Words, like other valued objects, circulate in social groups. Many may have access to them and use them, but there are elements of their value that only a part of the group will have access to. What makes communication possible is not the perfect sharedness posited by Saussure and Chomsky but the modes of cooperation among different actors. Moreover, one corollary of this premise is that a given word has more than one possible meaning, depending upon the public to which it is directed or the participants who produce it. This is another type of mediation that impinges on linguistic practice: the intervention of social organization as a defining factor in the relation of language forms to their meanings. This intervention, or mediation, introduces a double division among participating publics.

First, we could theorize a division of the public strictly according to the distribution of discourse. Being in the loop and occupying a certain relation to an utterance constitutes one as a de facto participant. Under this view there would be as many different publics as there are trajectories for the utterance. This reintroduces the centered or radial definition of participants by making the utterance (or larger discourse) the point from which participation is defined. Overhearing, witnessing, or otherwise receiving a discourse makes one a participant in it. If we imagine this process at the level of utterances transmitted by radio, television, and print media, we can see how the reproduction and dissemination of language create a network of receivers.

As a corollary, the publics so created would be short-lived. If you missed the discourse as it passed by, then you're not a member of its public. In the limiting case every utterance would define a different public, according to who receives it at what stage of remove from its original production. And since reproduction and distribution are always selective, different parts of any discourse would have different publics, according to whether they were picked up in the process or left behind. All those context-specific aspects of an original utterance that are lost in its subsequent transmission fall away and fail to enter into the public domain. And no single public would last any longer than the circuit of production and reception by which it is defined. Under such a view the social division of linguistic labor is really an interactive division among collective agents, re-created with each new utterance (fragment) and vanishing when the utterance (fragment) ceases to be circulated.

If this were the only way that we had of defining publics, it would suffer from the very same limitations as other theories based solely on radial relations to the speaking center. But it is only half the story. For whatever the trajectory of a discourse in society, it never emerges in a vacuum. Rather, it bumps into and channels through social pathways that preexist it and persist after it has run its course. This is the other principle of division. According to this second way of conceiving publics, they are defined not by the trajectory of any single discourse but by enduring institutional forms. These other forms have their own diacritic features and histories and are driven by forces only partly dependent upon language. When Putnam talks of a division of labor and Bakhtin of ideological horizons, they have in mind social contexts defined by a plurality of factors. And dialogism, like Putnam's stereotypes and extensional classes, reflects the pervasive impact of the social on language, without elevating any act of expression to the privileged position of center. For instance, socioeconomic divisions like class, profession, educational background, and access to economic capital all have an impact on the formation of publics. Access to a discourse is not merely a given in social life but a matter of occupying a position through which the discourse circulates. The position and its occupancy outlive the act of reception. When a lawyer makes an argument before a magistrate, the relevant public goes far beyond those who happen to witness the argument. Depending upon the issue at stake and the impact of the argument, it may involve other legal experts, legislators, and subsequent litigants for whom it may set precedent. In other words, the life span of a public is both longer than the immediate reception of the discourse and structured by many factors external to it.

The duality between this second, decentered and the first, centered view of publics is not unlike the duality between subordinated and creative dimensions of art, as we discussed in the preceding chapter. In both instances the dynamic of meaning production takes place within a field of tension. On the one side the discourse expression projects a world, and on the other it meets up with a world already in full swing. Obviously, the existence of media formations, such as the press, the electronic media, and the networks of people who communicate routinely with one another, all prefigure the paths of reception for any discourse. This is why people speak "on the record," "off the record," "between you and me," "to send out a message," and so forth—because they attend to the quasi-predictable traces their utterance will leave. Once produced, utterances circulate as objects whose meaning and range of reception is beyond the control of the proximate participants.

Participant frameworks take shape, then, in the interplay between the projection of meaning by immediate participants and the more far-reaching reception of discourse by multiple publics. This raises a real question about the units of production and reception. In classical grammatical theory, as we have seen, the speaker is the producer and the addressee is the receiver. As we have progressively subdivided the speaker and multiplied the receiver roles, this picture has given way to a more global process of interaction. And the vectors of interaction are never determined solely by participation in the loop of senders and receivers. The language forms themselves bear the traces of their distribution, which both dialogizes expression and puts it in a historical context longer than the actual present. In a sense we are recapitulating here some of the classic problems of sociolinguistics, and a thoroughgoing study of these issues would have to work through the notion of the speech community.

In an early article Gumperz stated the tension between the two poles of our dual division of publics. He wrote, "The verbal system can . . . be made to refer to a wide variety of objects and concepts. At the same time, verbal interaction is a social process in which utterances are selected in accordance with socially recognized norms and expectations. It follows that linguistic phenomena are analyzable both within the contexts of language itself and within the broader context of social behavior" (Gumperz 1972:219). Unlike grammatical study, which analyzes utterances in relation to the linguistic code, a sociolinguistic study relates utterances to more general norms of behavior. The relevant universe for the latter is the speech community, which Gumperz defined as "any human aggregate characterized by regular and frequent interaction by means of a shared body of verbal signs and set off from similar aggregates by significant differences in language use" (Gumperz 1972:219). The first part of this quote focuses on what comembers of a community must share, and the latter focuses on the boundary between two or more communities. Unlike traditional grammar, sociolinguistics has always been concerned centrally with variation, and what is shared by the members of a community need not be a single language. On the contrary, it is a verbal repertoire.

A repertoire is the sum of variant codes, ways of speaking, and usage patterns employed by members of the speech community. The variants may be distinguished along two main lines, standardly called "dialectal" and "superposed" variation. Dialectal variations set apart the vernacular ways of speaking of different subgroups within the broader community. These groups may be distinguished by social and economic differences, such as class, education, and occupation, or they may actually involve different languages, such as Spanish, Greek, Polish, Black English Vernacular, and midwestern American English in a city like Chicago. What is important is that from a social standpoint the ways of speaking are distributed in the broader community according to the human groups who speak them. Superposed variation is tied to the different kinds of verbal activity in which members of a single group engage. This can be seen in the kinds of stylistic variation engaged in by a native speaker of Spanish who uses English when dealing with city officials, Spanish at the local market, specialized rhetoric when running for political office, the cadences and imagistic discourse of evangelism when speaking at church, and so forth. The idea of superposed variation is simply that we all speak in a variety of ways in social life depending upon what we are doing, who we are doing it with, and what is expected or effective for our aims. More important than the labels, these two broad axes of differentiation reflect the idea that when viewed from a social standpoint, language varies both according to who is speaking it and what they are doing as they speak. Whereas a language, like English or Spanish, may be spoken by many groups and is defined fundamentally by its linguistic coherence, a verbal repertoire is by definition tied to a single community but may subsume numerous languages.

But what is a community? This is an exceedingly difficult question to answer. One of the several ways in which recent research differs from earlier frameworks in sociolinguistics is in the basis for defining communities and in how it conceives the relations among members both within and across community boundaries. In their later work Gumperz and his collaborators have sought to analyze the kinds of miscommunication that result from talk between members of different speech groups. The idea is relatively simple in principle but very complex in practice: to speak any language is not only to instantiate its grammar but also to appropriately contextualize utterances. The very same utterance form can mean different or even opposite things depending upon how participants frame it. (This perspective on utterance meaning is wholly congruent with the approach I espouse in this book, and I have in fact been strongly influenced by Gumperz's studies of contextualization.)

Miscommunication emerges when one party to talk frames or contextualizes an utterance in a way different from the one intended by its producer. Suppose in the example of Yuum and Margot that Yuum were actually a Spanish speaker from another part of Mexico or even another country, coming in search of a shaman named Don Chabo whom he didn't know but had heard of. He finds the house and enters the yard to knock on the door and greet whoever responds. He has already made a mistake that could entirely reframe his utterance and get him in trouble. This is because by entering the yard, he has effectively entered the house, and if Don Chabo were not so broad-minded as he in fact is, he could take this as an act of disregard or violation of his privacy—all the more so if the stranger walked directly up to a resident woman and addressed her, rather than waiting respectfully at the outer gate and waiting for a man to come to him. This example involves the unwitting violation of a local standard of conduct that results in the misinterpretation of utterance. Many of the examples Gumperz and his coworkers analyzed involve miscues due to different intonation and phrasing by people who speak the same language but have different ways of contextualizing it. It is like the rudeness a native American English speaker can (mis)perceive in the flat intonation contours of Korean shopkeepers or in the miscommunications so common in other examples of interethnic talk in major cities.

Gumperz's insight is that speaking involves not only the formulation of grammatically appropriate utterances but the use of numerous "contextualization cues" that instruct the receiver how to interpret "what is going on here." Just as the conversation analysts have shown, utterance production requires that speakers display the orderliness of their actions in the doing, and these displays are prone to misconstrual. Notice that a research focus on such miscommunication goes beyond the ideas of dialectal and superposed variation by joining the two analytic units of groups and activities. An answer to the activity question, "What are we doing here?" often requires a judgment as to who is acting. And moreover, it is in the metalinguistic contextualization, and not the forms themselves, that the breakdown occurs.

To define a community as a group with a common repertoire is to link the collectivity to shared codes. True, not all members have access to the same portions of the overall repertoire, but still it is the repertoire that serves as the basic common element. An alternative definition is based on social organization independent of language. From this perspective, typical of traditional sociolinguistics, the task is to correlate language forms with the groups who use them. In virtue of the correlation, the production of a certain form indexes membership in the corresponding group. The weakness of this view is that it relegates verbal practices to the secondary position of reflecting social facts defined apart from them, and it reifies social structure as something objective and fixed.

A third, more promising alternative has emerged in the literature under the label of "communities of practice" (Lave and Wenger 1991, Eckert and McConnell-Ginet 1992, Wenger 1993). The basic idea is that the community of practice is defined as "an aggregate of people who come together around mutual engagement in an endeavor" (Eckert and McConnell-Ginet 1992:464). This way of defining community is both smaller than the traditional speech community and more dynamic than the social structure posited by correlational sociolinguistics. It also shifts the ground of definition from either language or social structure per se to the engagement of actors in some project. A family or domestic group is a community of practice in this sense, as is a sports team, a work crew, a neighborhood organization, a church congregation, the crew of a ship, members of an agricultural cooperative, and members of an academic department. Because some endeavors last longer than others, communities so defined clearly have different durations and arise under different circumstances. And because we all engage in multiple group endeavors at any time and throughout our social lives, we are members of multiple communities, simultaneously and over time.

The promise of this approach is that it provides a framework in which to define modes of participation and ways of speaking relative to the processes through which they are constituted. One such proposal was Jean Lave and Etienne Wenger's (1991) concept of "legitimate peripheral participation," which indicates the kind of participation typical of apprentices and learners of a skill. Rather than acquiring a conceptual representation of a process like woodworking, mechanics, or writing publishable academic articles, the learner comes to participate in the process as a legitimate actor, yet with less than the full responsibility for masterful execution. Workshops, practicums, clinical training, clerking for a judge, and other kinds of hands-on learning illustrate this at its clearest, but Lave and Wenger's proposal is more general than that. Adapting it to communicative practice, it implies that we are all more or less continuously learning new ways of speaking, even in our own native language, as we enter into collective endeavors of various kinds. And this learning does not involve acquiring rules or codes, but ways of acting and different kinds of participation. Furthermore, it is the overall participation framework as an emergent process that "does the learning," just as we have argued here that it is the participation framework in which an utterance acquires meaning that "does the talking."

Conclusion

What happens if we substitute the community for the participation framework as the basic unit of speech production? For one thing, the issue of motivation ceases to be defined in terms of individual intentions and projects and becomes a matter of the interlocking motivations of groups. By motivation in this context we mean both overt goals, such as the securing of political voice and legal rights, and also the aspirations and longer-range objectives of groups that may be less explicit and of which individual members may be less aware. The question of metalinguistic consciousness also shifts from psychological states of knowing, recognizing, and anticipating to a matter of historically formed orientations. The selectivity of individual awareness reemerges as the selectivity of group consciousness, formed by the interplay of sociohistorical position and the capacity for agency. Many of these ground shifts involve tensions analogous to the ones we have seen at the level of the face-to-face, but the intervening factors are a great deal more numerous and complicated. We will explore such disjunctions in detail in Chapter 12, in the context of colonial Maya practices and their trajectories. Although few would propose to entirely substitute the community, the public, or any other social aggregate for the immediate participation framework, still, it is instructive to think about the question.

For one thing, it casts into sharp relief what has become a key question in recent theory, namely, the differences between communicative phenomena at the two levels (and at the potentially many levels in between). In a real sense the traditional notion of a dyad and the more refined notion of participation frameworks fail to provide a basis for studying larger collectivities. Despite the appeal of simplicity, it doesn't make much sense to use the face-to-face as a model on which to describe complex mediated communication. Much as I would like to believe it possible, it is all but impossible that the analysis of indexical systems can explain things like the division of linguistic labor, the institutional settings of discourse reception, or the dynamics of communities of practice. It is a necessary part of a full account, just as analysis of the social field is absolutely necessary to a thorough description of indexical usage. For one thing, many of the spatial, temporal, and objectural divisions signaled by indexicals are predefined by things like architecture, activity spaces, calendars, work rhythms, and the sociocultural values of objects. The two levels of description are necessary, and neither is in itself sufficient. However we define them, social groups are not internally structured the way individuals are, and discursive fields do not typically have the centered, radial structure of a deictic field. A collective agent is neither the sum of many individual agents nor the same as a single speaker position occupied by a group. The dynamics of representation; the tensions among competing factions within the group; ways of gendering practice, power, authority, and access to resources among members of a group; and the consciousness one has of belonging in a group—these are all quite unlike the relation between an individual and his or her expression. By the same token, individual speakers and coparticipants in a face-to-face exchange are more than the reflections of group dynamics writ small.

In this chapter, we have sought to identify basic phenomena such as mediation, multiple reception, and the difference between roles and actors. And we have used such terms as a framework within which progressively to expand the unit of speech production beyond the speaker and the text. But we have reached a point in the discussion at which we must recognize that there are major disjunctions at the different levels of description. No single metalanguage for participant roles will be adequate at all levels. I have no solution to this problem, and it seems unlikely that any will be forthcoming in the near future. Rather, what we can hope to do is to cast our descriptions of face-to-face participation and larger-scale discursive formations in such a way that they intersect—or if not, that the points of divergence are made visible. We have tried to do this with the concepts of a dialectic between individual expression and the social conditions under which it arises, along with Bakhtin's dialogism, the multiparty interaction studied by conversation analysis, transposition, the formation of publics, and the different grounds for community. In the next chapters we will continue on this path, outlining an approach to communicative practice.

Further Readings

From Dialectic to Dialogue

Austin, J. L. *How to Do Things with Words,* Cambridge: Harvard University Press, 1962. Lectures 1–3, 5–11.

Bakhtin, M. M. *The Dialogic Imagination: Four Essays.* Edited by M. Holquist; translated by M. Holquist and C. Emerson. Austin: University of Texas Press, 1981.

Clark, H. "Definite Reference and Mutual Knowledge." In *Arenas of Language Use.* Chicago: University of Chicago Press, 1992. Chap. 1, pp. 9–59.

———. "Hearers and Speech Acts." In *Arenas of Language Use.* Chicago: University of Chicago Press, 1992. Chap. 7, pp. 205–247.

Hancher, M. "A Classification of Cooperative Illocutionary Acts." *Language in Society* 8 (1979):1–14.

Participation Frameworks

Atkinson, J. M., and Heritage, J., eds. *Structures of Social Action.* Cambridge: Cambridge University Press, 1984, pp. 1–17.

Goffman, E. *Forms of Talk.* Philadelphia: University of Pennsylvania Press, 1981.

Goodwin, C. *Conversational Organization: Interaction Between Speakers and Hearers.* New York: Academic Press, 1981.

———. "Notes on a Story Structure and the Organization of Participation." In *Structures of Social Action,* edited by J. M. Atkinson and J. Heritage. Cambridge: Cambridge University Press, 1984, pp. 225–246.

Goodwin, C., and Goodwin, M. H. "Assessments and the Construction of Context." In *Rethinking Context: Language as an Interactive Phenomenon,* edited by A. Duranti and C. Goodwin. Cambridge: Cambridge University Press, 1992, pp. 147–190.

Goodwin, M. H. *He-said-she-said: The Interactive Organization of Talk in an Urban Black Peer Group.* Bloomington: Indiana University Press, 1990. Chaps. 1–2, pp. 1–28.

Hanks, W. F. *Referential Practice: Language and Lived Space Among the Maya.* Chicago: University of Chicago Press, 1990. Chap. 4, pp. 135–254.

Haviland, J. B. "Con Buenos Chiles: Talk, Targets, and Teasing in Zinacantan." *Text* 6 (1986):249–282.

Levinson, S. *Pragmatics.* Cambridge: Cambridge University Press, 1983. Chap. 6, pp. 284–370.

———. "Putting Linguistics on a Proper Footing: Explorations in Goffman's Concepts of Participation." In *Goffman: An Interdisciplinary Appreciation,* edited by P. Drew and A. Woolton. Oxford: Polity Press, 1987, pp. 161–227.

McCawley, J. D. "Speech Acts and Goffman's Participant Roles." In *Proceedings of the 2nd ESCOL.* Columbus: Ohio State University, Department of Linguistics, 1986.

Schegloff, E. "On Some Gesture's Relation to Talk." In *Structures of Social Action,* edited by J. M. Atkinson and J. Heritage. Cambridge: Cambridge University Press, 1984, pp. 266–296.

Transposition

Bühler, K. *Sprachtheorie: Die Darstellungsfunktion der Sprache.* Stuttgart: Gustav Fischer Verlag, 1982.

Beyond the Face-to-face

Basso, K. H. *Western Apache Language and Culture: Essays in Linguistic Anthropology.* Tucson: University of Arizona Press, 1990.

Brenneis, D. "Language of Disputing." *Annual Review of Anthropology* 17 (1988):221–237.

Cicourel, A. "Text and Discourse." *Annual Review of Anthropology* 14 (1985):159–185.

———. "The Reproduction of Objective Knowledge: Common Sense Reasoning in Medical Decision Making." In *The Knowledge Society,* edited by G. Böhme and N. Stehr. Dordrecht: D. Reidel, 1986, pp. 87–122.

Eckert, P., and McConnell-Ginet, S. "Think Practically and Look Locally: Language and Gender as Community-based Practice." *Annual Review of Anthropology* 21 (1992):461–490.

Gal, S. "Language and Political Economy." *Annual Review of Anthropology* 18 (1989): 347–367.

Hill, J. H., and Hill, K. C. *Speaking Mexicano: Dynamics of Syncretic Language in Central Mexico.* Tucson: University of Arizona Press, 1986.

Lave, J., and Wenger, E. *Situated Learning: Legitimate Peripheral Participation.* Cambridge: Cambridge University Press, 1991.

Merlan, F., and Rumsey, A. *Ku Waru: Language and Segmentary Politics in the Western Nebilyer Valley, Papua New Guinea.* Cambridge: Cambridge University Press, 1991. Chap. 9, "Perspectives on 'Event,'" pp. 221–244.

Ochs, E. "Indexing Gender." In *Rethinking Context: Language as an Interactive Phenomenon*, edited by A. Duranti and C. Goodwin. Cambridge: Cambridge University Press, 1992, pp. 335–358.

Ochs, E., and Schieffelin, B. *Acquiring Conversational Competence.* London: Routledge & Kegan Paul, 1983.

Putnam, H. "The Meaning of 'Meaning.'" In *Philosophical Papers.* Vol. 2. Cambridge: Cambridge University Press, 1975, pp. 215–271.

Urban, G. *A Discourse-Centered Approach to Culture: Native South American Myths and Rituals.* Austin: University of Texas Press, 1991.

Wenger, E. *Communities of Practice.* Cambridge: Cambridge University Press, 1993.

Woolard, K. "Language Variation and Cultural Hegemony: Toward an Integration of Sociolinguistic and Social Theory." *American Ethnologist* 12 (1985):238–248.

PART THREE

Communicative Practices

Chapter 10

Elements of Communicative Practice

THE STUDY OF "COMMUNICATIVE PRACTICES" differs from both formalism and relationality because it combines elements of each. Although linguistic systems are governed *in part* by principles unique to language, grammar is neither self-contained nor entirely independent from the social worlds in which individual languages exist. Modes of speaking have an impact on and are influenced by linguistic structure. In order for two or more people to communicate, at whatever level of effectiveness, it is neither sufficient nor necessary that they "share" the same grammar. What they must share, to a variable degree, is the ability to orient themselves verbally, perceptually, and physically to each other and to their social world. This implies that they have commensurate but not identical categories, plus commensurate ways of locating themselves in relation to them. There are two points here: (1) Overlapping, merely comparable, or semishared categories may suffice to enable communication (contrary to the post-Saussurian assumption that understanding speech presupposes knowing the grammar). And (2) how agents situate themselves relative to one another and their context may have real consequences for their ability to communicate.

People who share categories, even to a high degree, can utterly misunderstand one another if they have different views about what is going on at the moment of their interaction. Comparable views of the present can enable engagement despite language differences. In order to communicate, people must coparticipate in an interpretive community with commensurate values regarding what counts as expression and how to view it. This kind of sharing—partial, orientational, and socially distributed—may be based on common schemes of perception that go far beyond the language.

In the same vein the relative universality of a feature of practice is less important than how it articulates with language and the social field. This typically involves ways of looking, listening, touching, physical postures, movements, and other practices of the body. One of the key differences between grammar and practice is that the latter interpenetrates language and other modes of human engagement with the world. Finally, whereas the unit of speech production in both formalist and pure relational approaches is typically taken to be the individual speaker, in a practice approach it is the socially defined relation between agents and the field that "produces" speech forms. This is not to deny the agency of individual speakers but to recognize that speech production is a social fact.

It follows that the concept of rules plays a much more limited role in a practice approach than in standard linguistic or even sociolinguistic frameworks. It is clear that there exist rules governing the grammatical structure of linguistic forms, as linguists have recognized for millennia. This does not mean that speech can be insightfully described with the metaphor of "rules of use." Rules and codes can describe the playing field and the boundaries beyond which a move will not count, but they cannot explain what goes on in strategizing and actual engagement in actions. For this, we need access to the orientations, habitual patterns, and schematic understandings of the agents themselves, as well as a more realistic view of the dynamics of the fields and frames of reception.

The Baseline of a Practice Approach

Our starting point is the three-way division of language as a semiformal system, communicative activities as semistructured processes, and actors' evaluations of these two (see Figure 10.1). These evaluations could be called *ideological* in the sense of embodying broader values, beliefs, and (sometimes) self-legitimating attitudes. They are metalinguistic, or metadiscursive, to the extent that they bear directly on language or discourse, serving to fix its meaning. However inaccurate these may appear from the perspective of form or objective aspects of activity, however much misrecognition they involve, they are nonetheless social facts as real as any others. They are part of what organizes agents' own actions and their understanding of others' actions. The three elements come together in "practice," the moment of synthesis. We must remember as we enter into this synthesis that its three dimensions, though overlapping, are analytically distinct, and they re-

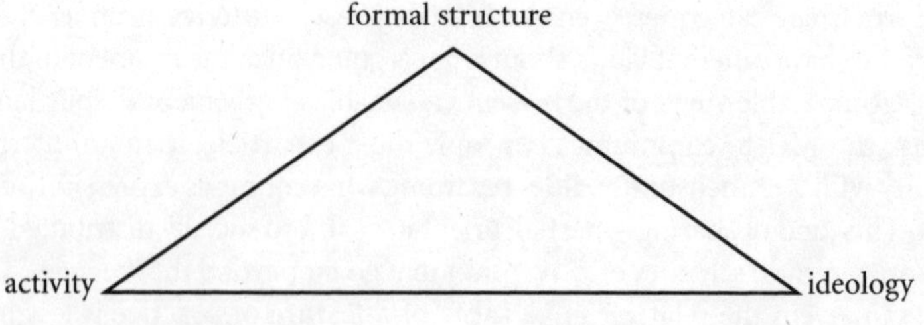

FIGURE 10.1 Three Dimensions of Communicative Practice.

quire different modes of analysis. It is tempting, depending upon one's own commitments, to try to treat activities as if they were formal systems, or language structure as if it were no more than the temporary product of activity, or ideology as merely the projection of verbal categories or the misconstrual of action. But all such attempts distort their object by denying its basic distinctness. The challenge of practice analysis is not reduction of this to a by-product of that but integration of distinct phenomena into a more holistic framework. It's a different way of generalizing, producing a different kind of generalization than those of either formal or purely relational description.

Given its basis in the historical conditions under which people live and engage in their worlds, a study of communicative practice deals as much with the actual doings of real agents as it does with the systemic potentials of symbolic forms. It is true that actors, especially effective ones, have a sense of what *could* be done under given circumstances and what is either impossible or likely to fail. This may appear at first glance to parallel the formalist concern with the generative potential of symbolic systems. But there is a key difference, for the formalist treats potential as an anonymous, combinatorial capacity inherent in the categories and rules of a system—for instance, the infinite potential of a generative grammar. Time plays no significant role in this formalist analysis, since the system is by definition a synchronic unit, and the idealized speaker-listener does little more than actualize forms prefigured by the rules. An agent in practice must on occasion estimate the *feasibility* of certain actions and must in any case have a sense, typically unreflective, of what could be pulled off with success and what will fall outside the bounds of propriety. Practical feasibility differs from formal potential in that: (1) it is a judgment call made by actors relative to a field of practice; (2) it involves a sliding scale of potential within limits, not the entire range of possible outputs of the system; (3) being tied to actuality, it is diachronic, not synchronic. In other words, it depends upon the kind of reflexivity that Merleau-Ponty put at the heart of the phenomenal field.

A judgment of practical feasibility is anything but timeless. Not only does it connect with changing circumstances, but it involves timing, knowing when to act, how long to maintain engagement, the rhythm in which to proceed, and how to deal with successive outcomes. To rush, hesitate, mistime, or stumble through an action is to fail or to invite misinterpretation, even though it may appear correct to the letter, once summarized in retrospect. Think of the response to a simple question: Yuum: "Is Don Chabo seated?" Margot: ". . . Gooverthere. . . . He's . . . drinking. Gooverthere . . . inside." As often as not, the ill-timed response is taken to indicate some hidden feelings or intentions of the speaker, perhaps nervousness or maladroitness. That is, timing is treated as significant whether one wants it to be or not. This element of practice has no analogue in formal models of language. But it is not the same as the stopwatch timing of transcripts measured in milliseconds, either. For the relevant units of duration, the significance accorded to variation and the baseline of what is expectable (and hence unnoticed) all change according to the field and the practice in question. A thoughtful pause during an oral exam is not the same as a pause of the same length after an invitation to go out with a new friend or after a witty wisecrack from a coworker. Timing, and the relations of succession and duration that make it up, is a qualitative part of practice, not the one-dimensional quantity that Saussure measured with his principle of linearity.

The Specificity of Form

The system of language does have unique properties, and we do better to recognize this than to try and pretend it isn't so. Arguments to the effect that grammar is merely a post hoc creation of academic linguists, like certain statements made by Voloshinov, Garfinkel, and some phenomenological sociologists, are simply indefensible. Not only are there many powerful universals of linguistic structure, but without some notion of grammar, it is impossible to explain the structure of even the simplest sentence. Recall the exchange with which this book began: "D'the paper come today, sweetheart?" "It's right on the table." It is pointless to attempt to explain the inversion of the subject and auxiliary verb in the question, the phonological contraction of "did" with "the," the contraction of "it" with "is" in the answer, the word order, or any similar facts without reference to English grammar. Similarly in "*kul á'an wá dón čhàabo?*" 'Is Don Chabo seated?' the morphological structure of the verb *kul á'an* is a fact of Maya grammar, and we gain nothing by denying the existence of that grammar. The boundary of the system, the degree of indeterminacy it includes, the role of context in making a general meaning specific—these are all valid issues, but they start from a recognition that the grammar does indeed have specific properties.

One of these is the kind of infinite generativity Chomsky discussed. Any human language is capable of generating an infinite set of formal objects corresponding to all permutations of phrase structures with all potentially acceptable words in all positions. The key point is that this generative potential does not describe the access that actors have to different possible utterances. On this point there are always limits, defined by factors like the social identity of the speaker, the conditions under which an utterance is made, and judgments of feasibility in the utterance situation. Generative potential is a property of a formal system, but access to the language is a matter of social capital. Even assuming that two speakers did have virtually identical knowledge of the language, the feasibility of their using that knowledge depends not upon language but upon their identity and the conditions of their interaction. And these factors can utterly alter the meaning as received.

For this reason also, the ideal of synchronic unity that applies to grammar cannot apply in the same way to activities or ideologies. Being part of activities, utterances are only partly predictable, and their occurrence depends upon timing, choices, and positionings of their producers. Some have attempted to define utterances in terms of vaguely specified types, instantiated in widely differing tokens. This appears to extend the formal conception of types from grammar to speech. If we take this path, though, we have to recognize that the notion of type is no longer the same in grammar as in utterance typology. The threshold of sameness and difference upon which the token-type relation depends has been raised to such a level as to make it almost vacuous. Even so, the type leaves unexplained most of the features of practice we are trying to get at, since these involve adjustments made on the spot, like feasibility, timing, improvisation, and features of reception not predictable by the type of the initiating utterance. At this point one wonders why the type-level regularities, whatever they are, need to be tied strictly to the unit "utterance" at all. Why *utterance* types instead of *indexical* types, *stylistic* types, or types of *social orientation*?

One way out of this morass is to let go of the notion of types, with its promise of timeless closure and unlimited replication. The aim is to generalize across verbal practices, to bring together those features that are repeatable, as distinct from those that are not. The former we will call *schematic* aspects. They imply relatively stable, prefabricated aspects of practice that actors have access to as they enter into engagement. They are schematic in the sense of being underspecified as well, having the kind of indeterminacy that Ingarden described in his notion of "blank spots" (see Chapter 6). Opposed to schematic aspects are emergent ones. By this I mean those parts of practice that emerge over the course of action, as part of action. Emergent aspects are not already given to agents prior to their engagement and so are neither prefabricated nor stable. They are in process.

In considering the status of some aspect of practice as schematic or emergent, time is critical. On the one hand, the relation to time is basic to the distinction, since schematic aspects already exist and emergent ones are in the process of becoming. On the other hand, a given feature may change from schematic to emergent during the course of practice. This happens whenever schemata are revised in use. Inversely, something that emerges as a novel form in the course of a practice can endure as a schema thereafter. Schemata are constantly being produced, through routinization, habituation, and commonsense typification (see Chapter 6). So in describing communicative practices, we need not reduce utterances to types. It is rather the ongoing tension between schematic and emergent aspects (none as complete as a type) that accounts for regularity and novelty, reproduction and production.

Similar problems arise in the case of the evaluative dimension, which I have called, loosely, ideology. Little is to be gained and much lost in the attempt to treat a collection of values bearing on language on the model of a synchronic formal system with selfsame types. For one thing, these values are heterogeneous, whereas synchronic grammars are based on the assumption of functional homogeneity in language (or at least a regular articulation of functions, as in Prague School pronouncements; see Chapters 5 and 8). The descriptive-referential value of sentences is the basis for their grammatical structure. Moreover, the reference of value orientations need not be so clear-cut and may include language and nonlanguage at the same time, making it unclear even whether a given idea is about language, and so properly *metalinguistic,* as opposed to being about something else, so not properly metalinguistic. Finally, activity and value orientations share another feature that sets them apart from grammar, namely, that they both involve the body. Just as verbal practices involve gestures, postures, perceptual experiences, and other aspects of lived space, so, too, value orientations are inscribed on body practices. Thus when we say "ideology" in this context, we denote something rather unlike classical ideologies, understood as ideas. Given the concept of habitus (see the next section), value orientations are embodied both in corporeal practices and in mental representations, being distributed over what the Cartesian perspective takes to be the different domains of mind and body.

In formal grammar there is the ideal speaker-listener who is presumed to have full competence in the language. Even if variation does occur, the idealization is a necessary part of the unity assumed to hold the system together. To conceive of an ideal ideologue, however, one who would be in command of all value orientations, is a contradiction in terms. Variation among agents is inherent; invariance is impossible. Like activities, values attaching to language and communicative practice are also diachronic. They take shape in the interplay between schematic and emergent aspects. For example, a speaker may well bring a certain value to an event of speaking, like the prestige associated with a certain register or the stigma of a regional or ethnic accent. But these values are open to change brought about by supervening experience. Whether it is a value of which the actor is aware or one beyond his or her awareness, at least some values can be confronted with experience and altered by it. They are also *diachronic* in the sense that how a given value or belief applies to a situation is a matter of judgment, and two actors can share values but disagree regarding their application to a given case. Contrast this with the relation between type and token: with the word "table" or "paper" there is little room for dispute as to the type instantiated. Tokens replicate types in a way that the application of value can never replicate value itself. What a practice signals by way of value depends upon the orientation of the observer in a way that the type-token relations do not depend upon observers. They are less open to debate.

The Process of Understanding

Mutual understanding, then, does not require that interactants share the same language system. A common language can of course help, but it is neither necessary nor sufficient. What is more basic, from a practice perspective, is that they share a sense of "what is going on here" and that they coengage in a differentiated field. This comes down to a common way of occupying their mutual present, including their sense of the setting and of their respective roles in it. Understanding an utterance is not a matter of recognition alone but entails building up its meaning, and this is a task of integration and filling in of the unsaid. If the semantic values of expressions are *partial,* as we showed in Chapters 5 and 6; if context is as much *within* literal meaning as outside of it, as we showed in Chapters 7 and 8; and if the ground of expression is the *relation* between agents and their field of engagement, as in Chapter 9, then understanding is necessarily a form of engagement. To understand an utterance is to engage with it as part of an emerging relation between oneself and one's social context, including the speaker and the surround. The process is never without precedent, but neither is it the sheer reproduction of what already exists. When Natalia understands her partner's request or Margot catches the import of Yuum's question, they must produce meanings that are missing or at best incomplete in the questions to which they respond. Understanding requires combining tacit knowledge of the interlocutor and setting with linguistic knowledge of the forms spoken, with metalinguistic knowledge of the routine frameworks in which such utterances should be heard. If competence is a matter of formal knowledge and performance the ability to execute competence, practice relies on the ability to integrate language with nonlanguage under highly variable conditions.

Objects of reference are socially typified, not sheer things as definable in an objective science. What we have called the ideological dimension bears equally on the objects of reference as on the linguistic means of reference. Whether these objects are things like newspapers and tables, other people, concepts, or indeed language itself, the horizon of values and beliefs plays a central role in defining them. To interpret speech, no less than to produce it, depends on the agent's active engagement. Following in the Saussurian tradition, we tend to associate meaning production with speech production, but in a practice framework the distribution and reception of language are equally, perhaps even more, important.

The common, if naive, assumption that printed language, like the newspaper, is more legitimate than spoken words illustrates the point. Print mediation is a mode of distribution, implying the possibility for widespread, displaced reception. When the newspaper arrives in 100,000 homes, it actualizes a network of reception. Most of the agents of reception never meet face-to-face, and they need not know just the same language in order to participate in a public. Their community is interpretive, and their unity is largely imagined. Common routines for reading, over breakfast or while commuting on public transportation, are part of the process by which meaning is produced. Moreover, there are significant differences in the ways that we read and listen to different kinds of language, both according to their position in the public and the genres of discourse they receive. It is obvious that we read the directions on an aspirin bottle at a different depth and with different goals than we read a poem or listen to an official pronouncement. Ingarden's theory of concretization makes this clear in the case of literary texts, as we saw in Chapter 6. But his basic point applies equally to the myriad kinds of everyday language with which we all engage. A differentiated approach to speech production requires a differentiated approach to reception, too.

Access to hearing and understanding is a form of capital, unevenly distributed among members of a community. Institutions like the courts, universities, churches can all be examined from the vantage point of their role in regulating how certain kinds of language are to be understood. Once we reject the idea that texts are closed objects whose meanings are contained within them, then we open up the question of who shall fix meaning. In place of a semantic representation, we get a trajectory of reception, with its concomitant multiplicity of meanings. Who says when an angry response counts as a threat or a statement of intent counts as a binding contract or an approach to some problem counts as a feasible research proposal? In the world of law enforcement, business, and research, such decisions make all the difference. Pushing the question to its extreme, we might say that the indeterminacies of meaning in speech are so great that it is only reception that produces meaning. Perhaps Saussure had it backwards: Speaking is passive and hearing is active. But we need not go so far in rejecting formalist visions as to produce their mirror opposite. The point is that meaning is made out of the interplay between production and reception, mediated by distribution. Understanding, no less than talking, is constitutive of speech.

The Plurifunctionality of Speech

In a practice approach, we start from the premise that speech is a form of engagement in the world. This has the following entailments: (1) Language and the world of human experience are everywhere interpenetrated, so that even the inner logic of a linguistic system bears the trace of the routine practices to which it is adapted. (2) To speak is to occupy the world, not only to represent it, and this occupancy entails various modes of expression, of which propositional meaning is but one. (3) Speakers and the objects they talk about are part of the same world; a division between subjects and objects is one of the *products* of linguistic practice, something people create with language, not the irremediable condition against which language must work. (4) We do many things through language, of which thinking and reasoning are a part—but not the only part. We also realize ourselves; effect changes in our worlds; connect with other people; experience beauty, rage, and tenderness; exercise authority; refuse; and pursue our interests.

The scope of verbal meaning in practice is therefore both broader and much more varied than in formalist approaches. It has to be. Even in the case of propositional meaning, a practice approach takes off from the observation, first put forth by ordinary-language philosophers (see Chapter 5), that utterances have performative dimensions. In the uttering of a descriptive statement, such as "He's having dinner" or "It's right on the table," the speaker accomplishes an act, whether it is the act of informing her interlocutor, defining a state of affairs, promising, warning, or commanding. Where practice approaches break definitively with speech act theory is in their insistence that performative effectiveness does not depend upon the preexistence of conventional speech act types. Instead, it is an emergent feature of practice, an unavoidable part of talk under conditions of differential power, authority, and legitimacy. Authorized speakers make social reality when they speak, whether or not they utter preestablished formulae like Austinian performatives. Think of statements by a representative of the court, a grammar school teacher, a religious specialist, a doctor, or anyone with the power to call the shots. The peculiarly explicit reflexivity shown by classic performatives, such as "I hereby christen this ship the SS *Magdalena,*" is only the tip of the iceberg. It depends upon a particular, language-specific dovetailing of metalinguistic with direct speech. As we have seen, this is no more than a special case of the much broader phenomena of reflexivity and objectification. Furthermore, this defining capacity of speech is not strictly limited to institutional contexts like the ones just listed. We all exercise this sort of power on a small scale repeatedly in our daily lives. In describing the world, we are often constituting it.

There is another angle to the constitutive effect of reference and description, implicit in the foregoing but more subtle. This is the role played by propositional language in inculcating certain ways of viewing the world. When day after day we say things like "Dinner's on the table; let's eat," "I'd like that on rye toast with lettuce and tomato," "One round-trip ticket to Hyde Park, please," "It's another gray day," "I'm way behind on my correspondence," "The boss just doesn't get it," we are routinizing the perspectives embedded in our descriptions. When food is on the table, we eat. We eat our sandwich a certain way, commute to a certain destination on a means of transportation for which tickets are bought. The weather is typically gray or typically sunny. Our professional responsibilities stretch us to capacity. We have a boss, and she, being a boss, doesn't appreciate our contribution. And so forth. These ways of talking habituate ways of experiencing the world of objects, something that Boas, Whorf, and Sapir understood with prescient clarity (Chapter 8). Formalism brings the truth and falsity of statements into sharp relief, but compared to the inculcation of perspectives, truth is a sideshow.

This habituation of perspectives is all the more obvious in the case of overtly evaluative statements, where the evaluation is part of a larger value structure through which the speaking agents experience themselves and the objects of description. And it gets even more subtle in the case of words like "this," "that," "around here," "over there," "I," "you," "we," "them." As we saw in Chapters 3, 7, 8, and 9, such expressions are inherently relational. In uttering any of them, speakers put themselves in a relation of inclusion, exclusion, proximity, or distance relative to the object of reference *and relative to their current interlocutor.* This dual relationality implies that the referential process is one in which subjects, objects, and social relations are simultaneously produced in the course of even the most mundane utterances. When we add to this the kind of multifunctionality explored by Prague School linguists and their intellectual descendants (Chapters 5, 8, and 9), the scope of verbal meaning expands far beyond what can be imagined in a formalist framework.

Habitus and Field

An approach to communicative practices building on the foregoing ideas necessarily implies new units of description. Just as the apparatus of synchronic types was inadequate for describing regularities of practice, so, too, the concept of "rules" is inappropriate for explaining the play between production and reproduction. Two of the concepts most centrally associated with practice theory are habitus and field. For our purposes, neither of these has the logical status of an elementary theoretical construct whose boundaries and precise definition are given in advance. Both are essentially heuristic concepts whose value is determined primarily by the kinds of description that they make possible. They correspond roughly to portions of what earlier approaches call "context," that is, the world with which linguistic forms articulate in the course of practice. In the case of habitus, we move toward context as defined by routine modes of perception, action, and evaluation, whereas the field concept moves beyond the individual agent to the broader social conditions of practice.

The concept of habitus as applied to language has a varied set of historical antecedents. In the Americanist tradition habituation has always played an important role (see Chapter 8). In his influential "Introduction to the Handbook of American Indian Languages," Boas (1966:20–21) observed that linguistic categories, by their regularity and repeatability, serve to make certain associations automatic. Against the infinite flux of actual experience, categories provide speakers with necessary tools to perceive sameness and find coherence. Whorf (1941) pushed this insight further in arguing that entire patterns of expression, or "ways of speaking," become automatic through habitual repetition. These patterns are defined not at the level of individual words or even categories, but syntactic structures, corresponding to phrases, sentences, and potentially larger units of discourse. Following the lead of Sapir (1949[1931]), Whorf went on to show that such patterns tend to take shape in reference to objective relations like containment, individuation, and enumeration of objects, which speakers then project onto other kinds of experience. Hence we speak of emotions contained in the body and the experience of duration and sequence cut up into countable units like periods, days, and lengths. Whether or not we share Whorf's judgments about the objective world, his key insight is that speakers develop whole ways of describing certain objects and then project these descriptions onto others, until, through routine repetition, they become so automatic as to go unnoticed. From a different perspective, the Prague School linguists developed the concept of automatized as opposed to foregrounded usage, where the former are expectable, partly predictable on the basis of routine reproduction (see Chapters 5 and 8). Similarly, the phenomenologists developed the concept of typification to describe the routine ways that actors group together experiences under gross, commonsense categories (see Chapter 6).

Despite important differences among them, these approaches have in common the concept that agents bring to action an immense stock of sedimented social knowledge in the form of unreflective habits and commonsense perceptions. Unlike grammar in the standard descriptions, which also organizes a great quantity of social knowledge into categories and syntagmatic structures, the notion of habituation is tied to practice. It is the repeated doing or experiencing of the habitual element that makes it habitual. The same holds for habitus, which

Bourdieu described as a "quasi postural disposition to action" (1985a:13), that is, the embodied inclination of agents to evaluate and act on the world in typical ways. Grounded in past experience and yet affecting the way that agents act, habitus is both a product of history and part of what produces history. It is sometimes said, in criticism of the concept, that habitus is merely a term for reproduction, condemning agents to repeat patterns derived from their own past experience and their position in society. This critique is incorrect, however, because a habitus is too flexible and open-ended to ensure identical reproduction; moreover, agents are not constrained to sheer repetition. Contrasting the notion with the kind of reproductive creativity implicit in grammatical models (see Chapter 4), Bourdieu (1977, 1985a) described habitus as a "generative" system of schemes. That is, it consists of what we have called the schematic aspects of practice, both in language and in the social context of practice. Unlike a grammar, but much like an ideology, habitus is highly differentiated according to the actor's place in society. Not all people who speak the same language share the same routinized dispositions to perceive objects in the same way or to engage in verbal practices the same way. The concept of habitus, then, makes three contributions to a description of verbal practice: (1) It incorporates the phenomenon of habituation, which builds regularity at the level of action without relying on conceptual rules; (2) it integrates both linguistic and nonlinguistic aspects of practice, thereby avoiding the reification of language isolated from context; and (3) being dispositional, it is perspectivally centered rather than projecting into action the view-from-nowhere common to rule-based systems. It is precisely to get out of the circle of mechanical reproduction, while still accounting for continuities, that the concept was introduced.

How, for instance, do we describe the stance or footing that Margot takes toward Yuum in their exchange? Recall from Chapter 7 that he comes to the window at dusk and asks, "Is Don Chabo seated?" She responds, "Go over there. He's drinking. Go over there [and wait] inside." Margot occupies a position in the household relative to eating, her father-in-law, and her interlocutor that predisposes her to protect her father-in-law from visitors while he eats. As a familiar of the household, Yuum has at his disposal certain sorts of speaking upon arrival. His question as posed is one of the more automatized ones, almost predictable, although his options are still multiple. The timing of his utterance, after he has crossed the threshold and is close enough to speak softly through the window, is also regular in light of his position. Yet, as I pointed out in Chapter 7, he in effect took a gamble to ignore the normal routines for greeting from the street and instead enter before speaking. There was always the chance that Don Chabo could have overridden Margot and addressed Yuum himself; thus her response was also a chance taken, however unreflectively.

These proclivities on the part of the actors to act within a certain range of alternatives lack the determinacy and universality of rules, and yet they are enduring in the sense that they last longer than the individual event under description. They are also grounded, in some crucial cases, in the corporeal awareness of the actors. As a single male, Yuum is unlikely to fix Margot, a married woman, in the eyes. He is unlikely to stretch out and display his body to her, and he would surely not touch her. Yet he does have the opportunity to traverse the threshold of her home and come within hearing of her. She in turn would not recline in front of him, fix his gaze, or allow him to see her belly. She would not reach out and shake his hand. She would not bow or curtsy to him or roll her eyes in complicity or mockery. That is, whether Margot as an individual would do any of these things, she would not do so in her capacity as the wife of her husband, the daughter-in-law of Don Chabo, or woman of the house. These aspects of her role identity as temporary occupant of the addressee position in a greeting exchange interact to produce her disposition to treat Yuum in a certain way in this event. Habitus of course goes beyond a single event, and even beyond any event (it is not as if we possess a habitus while acting but are delivered up from it while resting). But what concerns us from the viewpoint of explaining meaning production in speech is how it articulates with the scale between actual focus and horizon of potential. Without pretending to analyze it adequately here, we can see that the history of Margot's interactions with visitors, with Don Chabo, and with Yuum particularize what is a more general habitus she possesses as a social actor with a gender, a place in relation to affines and consanguines, an agent with certain rights and responsibilities.

The sociological anchor of habitus is the body in the social fields of its formation. On this point Bourdieu was particularly influenced by Marcel Mauss on body practices, and especially Merleau-Ponty on perception. Like the latter, he rejects a notion of habitus and the body based on representation, seeking rather to locate it in a more direct articulation of the body with the world (Bourdieu 1980:111). There is, as he might say, an immediate perceptual orientation between Yuum and Margot, by which they are given to one another in the immanence of the situation. More than knowing a single set of rules that they share and use as the ground for mutual understanding, the two have a "sense of the game," a practiced sense of what kind of situation they are in and what range of options are open to themselves and each other. A basic part of this knowledge has to do with the corporeal relations that they sustain as interactants and their respective spatial orientation in the household. Like language in its classical descriptions, much of body practice is unconscious in the sense of being below the threshold of one's awareness when acting. We sometimes become aware of aspects of our corporeal relation to the world when things break down, evoke physical pleasure, or require some attention. But the vast amount of the corporeal orientation in which we engage in practice is either obscure or so transparent as to be invisible (cf. Bourdieu 1980:123).

The concept of social fields is related to habitus in that it is meant to escape from the closure of formal replication while avoiding the opposite trap of imputing to actors the freedom to act without constraint. Habitus, being a set of enduring perceptual and actional schemes, is independent of fields and has the capacity to create homologies across distinct fields. Speech production takes place in a social space of objective relationships, in which people like Margot, Yuum, Don Chabo, Jack, and Natalia have social identities and ongoing relations to each other and the settings of the communicative practices. A given field can be thought of as a space of positions and position takings (Bourdieu 1983). Yuum is a visitor, Margot a resident senior woman in her household, Don Chabo the senior man. In the Maya context these positions bring with them relatively well defined expectations and some real constraints bearing on communication (Hanks 1990: chapter 3). Yet it is a matter of practical mastery how each actor occupies these positions, how far they push their respective rights and responsibilities, how close they tread to prohibited forms of practice. And of course there are not infrequent disputes over the bounds of propriety. These factors are all part of the field of domestic relations.

There are various types of field in any society, which are both similar in certain ways and distinct in others. Fields are not closed domains in which incommensurate cultural or practical logics prevail. And fields that appear disjunct at one level may in fact be part of a larger whole in which they are joined as complementary parts of a single logic. This is the case, for instance, in the fields of shamanic curing and agricultural ritual among contemporary Yucatec Maya (Hanks 1990: chapters 5, 7, 8). Still, there are significant differences between fields, and these condition the strategies that agents pursue in positioning themselves. The fields of domestic relations and agricultural practice among the Maya are clearly distinct, with different roles, divisions of labor, routine modes of temporal and spatial orientation. And yet they are profoundly related, actions undertaken in one field carrying over into the other. Practices have trajectories.

In an article treating the "literary field" in France, Bourdieu (1983) uses the field concept to emphasize the constitutive role of reception in determining the value of a literary work. Much as we have done throughout this book and Ingarden does in respect to literary works (Chapter 6), Bourdieu points to the sometimes radical shifts in meaning accorded to a work of discourse depending upon the context of its reception. Unlike Ingarden, Bourdieu goes on to posit a nearly permanent state of conflict in the literary field, in which agents struggle over access to different positions (1983:316). By foregrounding reception and the critical discourse in which works are evaluated, he shifts the problem of meaning and closure from the formal properties of the work to the dynamics of the field. This puts the production of literary works on a par with the production, through education and apprenticeship, of artists, critics, literary agents, patrons, the apparatus of publishing and advertising, and academic institutions in which readings of works are circulated through an elaborate scholarly discourse. In this way the larger field dynamics, which are inherently diachronic and stratified, are a crucial part of the reception process in which a work is defined. It is easy to imagine in the light of his discussion how one might go about sketching other fields of communicative practice, such as legal, private business, academic, domestic, ritual, medical, and even the corporeal field, in which the bodily mediated relations among agents constitute a series of positions and position takings.

Discourse Genres

In order to describe communicative practices, we need a unit of description that is greater than the single utterance but less than a language. We need a way of distinguishing kinds of practice. One way to do this would be to differentiate by the fields in which communicative practices occur, but to do this would be to imply that kinds of practice and kinds of field covary perfectly, so that a description of one would suffice to describe the other. This implication is manifestly false, since speech of various kinds occurs in virtually all fields (although some, like ritual or legal fields, may be relatively constraining). An alternative would be to rely on the types of illocutionary forces distinguished in classical speech act theory, but we have already seen the weaknesses of such an approach, which is in any case focused on single utterance types and not larger discourse practices (see Chapter 5). The unit we shall use for this level of description is the discourse genre.

From a formalist perspective, genres are types of text, or types of language, distinguished by their respective formal features and the ways they combine the features. Given what we have seen of understanding, objectification, the unit of production, the habitus, and the field of practice, a straight formalist approach to genres would be impossible. It assumes the very kind of closure of texts, encapsulation of meanings, and type-level classification of discourse that we have rejected. What we need is a way of integrating the linguistic insights of such an approach into a broader framework. An alternative basis for defining genres would be to use the native metalinguistic labels as indicators of underlying categories, such as "promise," "lie," "warn," "debate," "dispute," "request," "order" (in a restaurant), and so forth. This would make native metalinguistic ideology the basis of distinguishing genres. Although the ideological dimension plays an important role here as elsewhere in defining practice, however, there is no justification for elevating it to the sole defining factor. We know that ideologies involve misrecognition of both broader social forces and formal regularities in language as well as other distortions driven by self-justification and limitations of knowledge and access to social fields. So although both ideology and formal typology are important factors, they must be taken in tension with one another and with a more direct analysis of verbal activities as emergent processes. From the actional aspect of genres comes their diachronic and open-ended character and their linkage to the shifting perspectives of actors. The need to combine the three dimensions of formal systems, ideologies, and activities follows logically from our opening definition of practice as the synthesis of these three. The question is what such an approach would look like when applied to genres.

In broad terms genres differ in their degrees of complexity. Bakhtin's heuristic distinction between primary and secondary genres is helpful on this point. Primary genres are simple in the sense that they consist of just one kind of practice, whereas secondary genres combine two or more primary ones. For instance, novels, sermons, closing arguments, public lectures, and debates are secondary because they typically involve blends of different, simpler genres such as expository prose, poetry, persuasive rhetoric, jokes, assertions, and questions. Relatively primary genres would include practices like taking an oath, ordering food in a restaurant, requesting a copy of the newspaper, greeting a friend in the street, taking attendance at a meeting, and giving directions to a stranger. Metalanguage and reported speech are by definition secondary. I say "relatively" primary and qualify the distinction as *heuristic* because none of these would-be primary genres is necessarily simple—particularly if we build upon the notion that verbal practices are by definition multifunctional and if genres are linked to functionality, which they must be. Still, Bakhtin's division does indicate a useful scale or relative complexity.

Another general dimension along which genres differ is the criteria according to which an instance of the genre counts as complete or incomplete. Bakhtin (1986:76, Bakhtin 1985:130) called this phenomenon "finalization." Given the central importance of completeness and incompleteness in semantics and discourse analysis (see Chapters 5, 6, 7), this is a significant dimension in genre analysis as well. Finalization is not merely a matter of getting to the end of a discourse or practice; it is not tied to the presence of the final part, as it were. Instead, it is tied to the presence in the practice of whatever elements are considered to be the basic requisite of the genre. In a legal setting an oath without a Bible and a human witness lacks finalization even if the words are recited properly. The retelling of a tale that omits a crucial part in the middle lacks thematic finalization because it fails to tell what counts as the whole story. Given a theory of the levels of structure in discourse, the concept of finalization can be applied at several levels. These levels include episodes, the sections into which episodes fit, a work of discourse taken as a whole, and the reception process in which the work is invested with the fullness of meaning that comes from interpretation by a receiving public. When Ingarden argues that literary works acquire determinate meanings only through concretization in a history of receptions, he is saying that it is only in the reading and critical commentary that they are truly finalized. Similarly, when we argue that a communicative practice has meaning *potential* but acquires actual meaning only through the engagement of an interlocutor, we are locating the moment of finalization in the reception process, not the initial production.

Now some kinds of practice are relatively open to construal because they are vague or ambiguous or because their producers lack the power to fix the meaning of their own actions. The discourse of a witness under cross-examination might be a case in point. Answering questions in an order whose logic is hidden from him, the witness is led to construct a narrative that will then be intercepted as evidence, perhaps bearing on events he is ignorant of. In such a case the practice of the witness may be quite complete in terms of the individual propositions he says but without finalization in terms of the meaning that will be derived from them. By contrast, the judge who delivers a verdict engages in a practice whose official character maximizes its own finalization. The apparatus of the law, the courts, and the authority vested in the judge have the cumulative effect of making the import of the judge's words binding and closed to construal. When a criminal proceeding leads to a guilty verdict and a sentence, there is no room to construe the guilty verdict as anything other than what it is. It may be appealed, debated, and further interpreted by legal scholars, but it stands as a complete, fully concretized order at the moment of its production. As Bourdieu (1977:22) pointed out, official speech like this has the peculiarity that it makes truth while imposing the terms in which others must respond to it.

For most nonofficial genres, the temporal unfolding of practice and its changing construals in reception make it tend toward incompleteness. Whereas formalist theories start from complete tokens corresponding to complete types, the *achievement* of closure is problematic and often temporary from a practice perspective. Recalling Ingarden's theory, we might consider two kinds of incompleteness, the one due to missing parts, or blank spots, and the other due to the possibility of revision. A discourse that is incomplete in the first sense can be finalized by the work of understanding. A discourse that is incomplete in the second sense may appear finalized at any given moment but remains subject to reinterpretation and hence refinalization. Genres differ in their orientation to these two kinds of indeterminacy.

There are two other broad dimensions we can use to distinguish among genres of communicative practice. The first is the adaptation of the genre to dominant power structures in the field to which it is addressed. It is often necessary for agents to adapt their communications to the expectations and canons of acceptability of other agents in the field with which they engage. A student who studs an essay with bibliographic citations, a child who uses turns of phrase pleasing to the parent, a worker who pledges allegiance to the values of the boss, a politician who pushes buttons of his or her constituents by mentioning their concerns in a public address, a bilingual merchant who switches languages according to the preferences of customers, a motorist who respectfully addresses a policeman as "Officer"—these ways of communicating have in common that their producers adapt their practice to their addressee. They make themselves, as speakers, familiar examples of valued types of person: the assiduous student, the pleasing child, the cooperative employee, the politician "in touch with the people," and so forth. To borrow the term Bourdieu proposed, we can say that such speakers regularize their discourse by fitting it to the field of their current practice.

Closely related to regularization is officialization, the process whereby speakers signal the authentic, authoritative grounds on which they speak. To introduce oneself using a professional title, to wear the uniform of office, to speak of one's colleagues in the court or in the Senate, to refer to powerful people by first name as a display of familiarity, to describe an event using the technical language of law, medicine, military jargon, and so forth—all such moves involve building the authority of the speaker by association with dominant structures, and in this sense they enhance the quasi-official status of the person's speech. Like regularization, officialization is a way of orienting the discourse practice to dominant structures in a field. The idea is that genres as kinds of practice imply different ways of achieving such orientation.

All of the factors mentioned so far (finalization, regularization, and officialization) orient discourse genres to the reception that the practice is likely to get on the part of other agents in the field(s) to which it is addressed. They are reflexes of agents' awareness that meaning lies not in the words, but in the trajectory they take in public. A special instance of this is the use of metalinguistic framing devices, which attempt to define the practice as fitting a certain genre. These include verbs of speaking ("I promise"; "I order"; "I say to you, my fellow Americans"; "I regret to inform you"; "You are hereby notified"; "We find the defendant"), metalinguistic qualifiers ("speaking off the record," "speaking for myself," "speaking in my capacity as your attorney," "technically," "according to the law," "to the best of our knowledge"), and use of genre labels as part of the practice itself ("this announcement," "decree," "report," "document," "finding," "invitation," "petition"). Further framing devices include the use of special expressions to describe the agents engaged in the practice (patient, client, petitioner, defendant, legislator, officer), which, though not metalinguistic in the narrow sense, still refer to elements of the immediate field in which the practice is undertaken.

Overlapping with metalinguistic devices are the various indexical elements through which a discourse genre articulates with the field of its production. These include centrally the use of participant indices (so-called pronouns, demonstratives referring to persons) and the epithets for self-presentation on the part of the producer and addresser to the relevant audience or addressee. The participant frameworks described in Chapter 9 are in fact highly variable in practice, and much of the variation is organized according to genres. Think of the specific participant frameworks of legal process, involving witnesses, official interrogators, transcribers, and, depending upon the point in the process, opposing parties and a judge or other adjudicating official. Public discourse genres, particularly ones broadcast over electronic media, are adapted to complex participant frameworks involving multiple audiences (on the stage, in the auditorium or studio, in the receiving public of the broadcast), whereas genres such as medical consultation are defined as private and engaged under conditions of limited participation between patient and specialist.

The spatial orientation of genres is another instance of indexical centering. How a type of practice articulates with its setting differs from the casual ellipsis of everyday conversation to the elaborate presence of the court, the examination room, the legislative assembly, and the place of religious observance, *as all are spaces whose social values are inscribed upon the practices that take place in them.* This inscription may be evident in the words, syntax, or discourse organization of talk or in dress codes, body practices, the right to speak, the requirement of silence, and so forth. The important point is that elements of the practice genre systematically index its linkage to the spaces of engagement. The same goes for the ways that genres tie into the temporal setting of their performance, through precise marking of chronological time of onset and duration of a practice, order of events, date according to the accepted calendar. Even when the terms of this marking are not indexicals in the standard sense, their usage in a practice is indexical insofar as it defines the now, here, or we of the practice.

Genres, then, are a key part of habitus. They articulate with social fields through indexical centering, orientation to reception and dominant structures, and different kinds of finalization. Analyzed as modes of practice, they are among the best examples of habitus as a set of enduring dispositions to perceive the world and act upon it in certain ways. Genres are neither rigid formal types that can be repeated indefinitely as tokens, nor are they formless, purely momentary conjectures. Rather, they embody just the kinds of schemes for practice that constitute the habitus. And like it, they are unequally distributed among agents in any social world. For access to certain genres involves power and legitimacy and serves as a form of sociocultural capital. Through routine use, genres become natural themselves, that is, they become so familiar as to be taken for granted. Their special features are invisible to actors who experience the world through them. They are also instruments with the power to naturalize the objects and social relations they mediate. If the Americanist concept of relativity has any place in the field of contemporary theory, it must be based on genres, not categories. Through habituation and infused with the authority of their agents, genres make certain ways of thinking and experiencing so routine as to appear natural. Think of the nightly news and the way its reports naturalize violence, tragedy, and corruption, while continually reinforcing the peculiar distance and vicarious thrill of being spoken to by a reporter who is "on the scene" and yet in the home of every television viewer at the same time. Defined by the interaction among formal systems, evaluative horizons, and emergent activities, genres provide a uniquely rich area for research into communicative practice.

Further Readings

Bourdieu, P. *Outline of a Theory of Practice.* Translated by R. Nice, Cambridge: Cambridge University Press, 1977 [1972]. Chap. 3: "Generative Schemes and Practical Logic: Invention Within Limits," pp. 96–158.

———. *Le Sens pratique.* Paris: Editions de Minuit, 1980. Chap. 3, "Structure, habitus, pratiques," pp. 86–109.

———. "The Field of Cultural Production, or: the Economic World Revisited." *Poetics* 12 (1983):311–356.

———. *Questions de sociologie.* Paris: Editions de Minuit, 1984.

———. "The Genesis of the Concepts of Habitus and Field." *Sociocentrum* 2(2) (1985a):11–24.

———. "The Social Space and the Genesis of Groups." *Social Science Information* 24 (2) (1985b):195–220.

———. *Language and Symbolic Power,* edited and introduced by J. B. Thompson; translated by G. Raymond and M. Adamson. Cambridge: Harvard University Press, 1991. "General Introduction" and part 1, pp. 32–102.

Chaiklin, S., and Lave, J., eds. *Understanding Practice: Perspectives on Activity and Context.* Cambridge: Cambridge University Press, 1993.

Collins, J. "Determination and Contradiction: An Appreciation and Critique of the Work of Pierre Bourdieu on Language and Education." In *Toward a Reflexive Sociology: The Social Theory of Pierre Bourdieu,* edited by M. Postone et al. Oxford: Blackwell, 1993. Chap. 6, pp. 116–138.

Encrevé, P., "C'est Reagan qui a coulé le billet vert." *Actes de la recherche en sciences sociales* 71–72 (March 1988):109–128.

Encrevé, P., and de Fornel, M. "Le Sens en pratique." *Actes de la recherche en sciences sociales* 46 (March 1983):3–30.

Gal, S. "Language and Political Economy." *Annual Review of Anthropology* 18 (1989): 345–367.

Hanks, W. F. "Discourse Genres in a Theory of Practice." *American Ethnologist* 14(4) (1987):668–692.

———. *Referential Practice: Language and Lived Space Among the Maya.* Chicago: University of Chicago Press, 1990, pp. 3–15.

———. "Notes on Semantics in Linguistic Practice." In *Toward a Reflexive Sociology: The Social Theory of Pierre Bourdieu,* edited by M. Postone et al. Oxford: Blackwell, 1993. Chap. 7, pp. 139–155.

Irvine, J. "When Talk Isn't Cheap: Language and Political Economy." *American Ethnologist* 16 (1989):248–267.

Lave, J. *Cognition in Practice: Mind, Mathematics, and Culture in Everyday Life.* Cambridge: Cambridge University Press, 1988.

Lave, J., and Wenger, E. *Situated Learning: Legitimate Peripheral Participation.* Cambridge: Cambridge University Press, 1991.

Ochs, E. *Culture and Language Development: Language Acquisition and Language Socialization in a Samoan Village.* Cambridge: Cambridge University Press, 1988. Chap. 1: "To Know a Language," pp. 1–40; chap. 11: "Language as symbol and tool," pp. 210–227.

Ricoeur, P. "Practical Reason." In *From Text to Action,* translated by K. Blamey and J. B. Thompson. Evanston, IL: Northwestern University Press, 1991. Chap. 9, pp. 188–207.

Taylor, C. "Theories of Meaning." In *Human Agency and Language: Philosophical Papers,* vol. 1. Cambridge: Cambridge University Press, 1985, pp. 248–292.

———. "To Follow a Rule . . ." In *Toward a Reflexive Sociology: The Social Theory of Pierre Bourdieu,* edited by M. Postone et al. Oxford: Blackwell, 1993. Chap. 3, pp. 45–60.

Woolard, K. "Language Variation and Cultural Hegemony: Toward an Integration of Sociolinguistic and Social Theory." *American Ethnologist* 12 (1985):238–248.

Chapter 11

Communicative Practice in the Corporeal Field

IN THIS CHAPTER we will explore the relation between genres and culturally defined aspects of corporeality, illustrating the concepts introduced in the last chapter with examples from Yucatec Maya. The human body is at once highly local, in the sense of being a basic part of any interactive "here," whether face-to-face or mediated, and at the same time equally general insofar as values, orientations, and features of the social field are inscribed on the body and realized through it. Body practices and the domestic spaces in which they are formed are the primary locus of habitus. This does not mean that the social dynamics of practice can be reduced to a simple notion of physical presence. Rather, what might appear to be the transparent physicality of the body is in fact a complex, nuanced interplay of social and cultural forces. Corporeality is both immanent in the actual present and grounded in a world that far transcends the present. In claiming this centrality for the body, it is also important to recognize that not all communicative practices engage it in the same way or to the same degree. Indeed, it is just because corporeal dimensions play out differently in different practices that it provides a fertile area of research. In all cases what counts as "the body" depends upon the relation between human experiences and engagements and other aspects of sociocultural space. These include the lived spaces of domestic organization and residence, productive practices including agriculture and other forms of labor, daily patterns of activity, and value orientations. In general terms, language is both a means of grounding practice in the body and suspending the link to bodies.

We will consider the body under three perspectives, or "moments": as an object of evaluation through reference, description, and categorization; as itself an expressive medium, part of the form through which practices are realized; and as part of the actional field in which practice takes place. In the first moment corporeality is thematized as something talked about and explicitly under consideration. This occurs whenever people talk about the body or represent it or its parts. In the second dimension, or moment of practice, the body is not itself thematized but is part of the communicative resources through which other parts of the world are brought into focus. Think of the many expressive gestures of face, hands, and posture that are part of speech as activity and that help specify the meaning of utterances. In the third dimension corporeality is a part, sometimes tacit and sometimes quite explicit, of the field of verbal practice. When two people talk face-to-face, regardless of the topic of discussion or the gestures that they may perform, their physical occupancy of the social space is in play. This holds in non-face-to-face contexts as well, despite the presence of mediating factors that may transform or attenuate the role of bodily experience. Reading the paper, watching television, listening to the radio, talking on the phone, even communicating with spirits using divining crystals and other forms of mediation all ultimately engage the body. This third moment, in which corporeality is part of the field of production and reception, is most often ignored by intellectualist treatments of the body as an object of representation. It tends to be the least visible and the most subtle realization of corporeality in language, precisely because it is neither the focus of description nor the perceptible means of expression. And yet, as we will see, even still it is inscribed on language form and speech practice.

Maya Representations of the Body

We start, then, from the body as thematized object, something that people reflect upon and talk about.[1] Depending upon the situation, there are numerous ways of describing the body in Maya. Examples (1–4) show four nouns, each of which designates an aspect of the body. Although they are everyday words with everyday meanings, these terms are particularly common in shamanic discourse, where they figure in prayer and divination as ways of locating illness in one or another sector of the patient's body. In the division of linguistic labor in contemporary Maya settings, shamans are experts of the body. Each term has a range of meanings that establish basic connections between bodies and other things. The word *wiínklil* is used for reference to the body as size or state of corpulence. This holds for humans or any other animal. When referring specifically to humans, it can also convey "humanity, nature" in a more abstract sense.

1. ***wiínklil*** 'body'

The use of "earth" for the physical body is peculiar to shamanic prayer genres, where it occurs very commonly in reference to humans and domestic spaces.

2. ***lúˀum*** 'earth, flesh-and-bones, physical substance'

The last two terms are the standard ones in Maya for referring to "breath" and "mood," respectively,

---

[1]The linguistic forms and values sketched in this section are treated in depth in Hanks 1990.

3. *ˀìik'* 'breath, physical endurance, animacy, awareness'
4. *ˀoól* 'will, capacity for involvement and sensate experience'

Just as in Indo-European cultures, the concept of breath is directly related in Maya to the wind (meteorological) and to endurance or fatigue, as in the English "to have good wind" or "to be out of wind." It also relates to motion more generally, as we can see in related words derived from it: *yiík'-el* 'bees of a hive, ants swarming in earth'; *yiík'-al* 'force, momentum of a motion.' The same kinds of extensions occur with the "will," "mood," which can be discussed in the abstract, as part of what makes a human being, but also forms the lexical base for nearly all expressions describing momentary states of being or feeling: *kíˀimak ˀinwoól* 'I'm happy', *siís ˀinwoól* 'I'm cold', *čokβow ˀinwoól* 'I'm hot', *háˀak' ˀinwoól* 'I'm surprised', *naáy ˀinwoól* 'becalmed', and *toh ˀinwoól* 'straight (happy)'.

In examples 5–11 we see the extension of the notion of *ˀoól* over a wide range of semantic domains involving intentional or social engagements.

5. ***kušulik ˀinwoól*** 'it overwhelms me' (lit. finishes my *ˀoól*)
6. ***kubèetik ˀinwoól*** '(s)he kids me' (lit. does my *ˀoól*)
7. ***kinwok'ohˀoó(l)tik*** 'I beg' (lit. weep-*ˀoól*-it)
8. ***kinwoó(l)tik*** 'I want, wish'
9. ***yoólilil*** 'on purpose, intentionally'
10. ***yah tinwoól*** 'it pains me, I'm sorry'
11. ***máˀ tuyoól yàan iˀ*** '(s)he's not in his/her *ˀoól*' (is out of control)

Beyond these fundamental aspects of the body, there are of course many terms in Maya for body parts in the more usual sense. Examples 12–15 illustrate some of these. Each of them is also used to designate things other than body parts. The word for arm or hand is also used to denote the branches of a tree. The term for leg or foot is also the handle of long instruments like shovels or picks. The "gut" is also the circumference of any object, especially trees. The "eyes" of a plant are the fruits it bears.

12. ***ˀink'ab'*** 'my arm, hand'
13. ***ˀinwòok*** 'my leg, foot'
14. ***ˀinnak'*** 'my gut, stomach'
15. ***ˀinwič*** 'my eye(s), my face' (cf. *saásil yič* 'bright-eyed, quick')

It is usually assumed that the three dimensions of body space common to all humans are the lateral, vertical, and front/back. These would correspond to basic geometric axes of relation to the body as a center. In Maya these axes are phrased as in 16–21.

16. ***ˀimpàač*** 'my back'
17. ***ˀintáan*** 'my front'

18. ***ˀinšq̣iík*** 'my left'
19. ***ˀinšq̣nóˀoh*** 'my right'
20. ***tinwoók'ol*** 'upon, above, over me'
21. ***tinwàanal*** 'beneath, below, under me' (that is, lower than my feet if standing, buttocks if sitting, back if lying faceup, etc.)

Although I have never gathered systematic data on the question, it is my impression that of these six terms, the first two (16 and 17) are by far the most common in routine talk. Objects located in lateral or vertical relations to the body tend to be localized verbally using demonstratives or other expressions.

There is one further expression (example 22) that occurs in the same syntactic frames as these six but that has no clear analogue in English.

22. ***tinwiknal*** 'at/in my place (permanent or transitory); according to my way of thinking or acting'

On one reading, the *iknal* is like one's shadow or immediate perceptual field. It is the bodily field or zone that moves around with the person. Wherever you are at any moment, your *iknal* is there with you. On another, equally routine interpretation, the word refers to one's home, the stable domestic sphere that does not move around from moment to moment, but where one sleeps and eats with others, raises domestic animals, and stores valuable objects. In relation to the body, the boundaries of the *iknal* are fuzzy; it is a matter of relative proximity or perceptibility whether or not some object is within the sphere of your *iknal.* The domestic sphere, on the contrary, has clear boundaries, usually embodied in a stone wall, fence, or other material barrier. It is noteworthy that the term has just these two spatial interpretations, the one corporeal and the other domestic. In a third, nonspatial sense, the *iknal* is the actor's habitual way of thinking or viewing the world, much like the French *chez moi* used in reference to one's home and perspective.

In the verbs of perceiving, Maya makes a minimal, binary distinction between seeing and perceiving with some other sense. As the glosses in 23–24 show, these verbs are also used for modes of reception. To "see" another's speech is to comprehend it, to understand the overall point. To "hear" their speech is to follow its directions, to obey it or otherwise affect one's conduct in light of it.

23. ***ˀilik*** 'to see; to understand'
24. ***ˀúˀuyik*** 'to feel, hear, smell, taste; to obey'

All of the information summarized in these examples, and many others like them, is what we have called schematic as opposed to emergent. It is repeatable and anonymous in the sense that the terms apply to all humans and can be used by anyone, barring the specialized shamanic uses. Being schematic, the words are formally and semantically consistent from use to use, although not invariant, as we saw. Their meanings are also incomplete or underspecified, adding up to a sort of dotted-line outline of the body. Because of this incompleteness, when discussed out of context, the terms appear to have peculiar ranges of meaning and may even seem potentially confusing. For instance, the different senses of *iknal* could easily give rise to misunderstanding if one mistook an interlocutor's home for his or her current location. But this way of looking at the language is backwards, because the ambiguities arise only out of the abstraction of the words away from their routine contexts of use. In practice there is rarely confusion over any of these matters. The schematic aspects occur as part of emergent processes in which the blank spots are filled in by context.

I alluded to the fact that many of the body-part terms in Maya are also used in reference to things other than bodies. Vegetation is another semantic domain very closely related to corporeality, and many of the terms have ethnobotanical meanings alongside their bodily ones. Examples 25–31 illustrate this aspect in relation to the parts of a tree.

25. ***ˀuyoól*** 'the live core, sprouting point (as in palm leaves)'
26. ***ˀupàač*** 'the bark, outer surface'
27. ***ˀuyič*** 'the fruit'
28. ***ˀuk'ab'*** 'the branch(es)'
29. ***ˀuču̇un*** 'the trunk'
30. ***ˀunak'*** 'the girth (of trunk or individual branch)'
31. ***yàanal čeˀ*** 'under the tree(s)' (that is, under the overhang of its branches, not under the root system)

These examples illustrate a basic point in relation to bodies and trees: Only a small subset of the corporeal terms are deployed in relation to trees, and when they are, they have different meanings. The universe of discourse selects the value of the terms. For instance, a tree has an *ˀoól* but no *ˀìik', a pàač* 'back, bark' but no *táan* 'front'; it has *k'ab'* 'branches' but no *ˀòok 'leg'*. In other words, the paradigmatic oppositions of the terms change according to whether one is discussing trees or human bodies. The case of *pàač* is instructive in this regard, since it has three rather distinct senses according to the universe of discourse one describes with it. For [+ human], it means the upper back or area behind the body, as opposed to the front. For [+ vegetal], it means the bark or outer skin, as opposed to the inner sprouting heart. For [+ inhabited space], Maya speakers describe 'outside' as *pàač nah* (lit. 'behind house') as opposed to *ič nah* 'inside' (lit. 'eye, within house').

It is interesting to note that a tree lacks the inherent front/back orientation of the body but is given a front by a woodsman's chopping it down with an ax or machete. The action is described as *taámbesik* 'to cause (it) to have a front' and consists in the first cuts made on the tree, on the side toward which it will fall once the chopping is complete. Once these cuts have been made and the tree's front is defined by its predisposition to fall in that direction, then the side opposite the front is described as the "back." Thus the term *pàač,* which designates bark under normal conditions, shifts in reference and, in the context of felling the tree, designates the back opposite the "front." The final cuts made on the tree, which cause it to fall, are referred to as *wak'ik upàač* 'explode its back'. Although it gets a front and back, the tree never acquires the lateral orientation of the body's left and right. Such examples illustrate the way that the semantic frame of reference for terms can shift over the course of activity, thus actualizing a series of schemas as emergent phases of a larger process.

There is what appears to be a fairly widespread assumption, particularly in cognitive approaches, that the human body is a natural object, endowed with certain basic parts and axes that remain universally relevant regardless of the evaluative overlay they may receive in a given culture. With this comes the related assumption that the body is the source of metaphorical extensions, much like the cases of vegetation and domestic space sketched above. But there is a real question whether the Maya terms I have presented are in fact body-part terms or whether they designate more abstract relations of boundedness, interiority, orientation, and so forth. In order to demonstrate this, it is necessary to gather linguistic evidence that one or another domain is more basic to the semantics of the terms and to consider the alternative approaches under which the corporeal meanings are either secondary or of equal basicness. The notion of metaphorical extension is often a convenient way of hiding gratuitous assumptions about the naturalness of literal meaning. In a fuller treatment of such terms, we would also want to examine the level of specificity and generality at which parts and aspects of the body are lexically discriminated. This would lead inevitably to consideration of the distinct corporeal frames put in play by different genres of discourse, such as medical, ritual, sports, dance, and so forth. We know that different parts of the body, its movements, and relations to others are foregrounded in these kinds of talk.

Drawing together the different ways of representing the body, like the ones illustrated above, one can begin to understand the body schemas that people share as members of a single culture. These schemas have in common that they are coherent, repeatable representations of the body. All are bound up with the habitual patterns of interaction and engagement, which provide the grounds for selecting one or more as relevant to any given practice. The very knowledge and routine use of schemas like these depends crucially on aspects of social identity such as age, gender, occupation, rural versus urban residence, and so forth. My own examples show a bias toward male occupations (agricultural and shamanic) and may need revision in the light of female perspectives. At the very least there would be other schemas representing aspects of corporeal experience to which I, as a male outsider, have never had access. If we were to multiply the schemas and adjust them in order to reflect a plurality of perspectives, the result would be what might be called a "cultural repertoire" of schemas. Knowledge of this repertoire would undoubtedly contribute to an understanding of the levels of detail, values, and relations that Maya people tend to perceive among corporeal dimensions. What it would not provide, however, is a basis for understanding how knowledge of the body is adapted in the course of practices. The reason is that schemas are, by definition, generalizing, anonymous, and relatively fixed, or at least stable. The categorizations implied by schemas make up so many unoccupied rooms, designed for engagements of certain kinds but lacking the actors and the action. For the body in practice, we need to shift to another level of description.

Body as Part of the Actional Field

The most pervasive and interesting cases of corporeality are those in which the body serves not as the theme of reference and description but as the indexical ground relative to which *other* things are referred to and described. This involves partial concretizations of parts of schemas and relies on a sense of the body as background rather than foreground. For this, the minimal unit is not the schema but something closer to what Merleau-Ponty called the "*schéma corporel*" (see Chapter 6). This differs in basic ways from representational schemas. Arguing explicitly against intellectualist understanding of the body as something represented, Merleau-Ponty proposed to start from the body in motion rather than the static grid of a schema. From such a perspective, corporeality is emergent in activity, not prepackaged in cultural categories. In other words, it is constantly under revision, distributed over time.

He also rejected the idea of the body as an objective thing apart from consciousness. Rather, the *schéma corporel* is constituted in the momentary consciousness of the actor, what he called the "*prise de conscience*" in which the actor is aware of his or her own current body posture and motion. It is a reflexive process, in which perception and awareness of self interact with physical motions to produce a phenomenal "posture." Hence body as an experiential field is distributed over physical, physiological, conceptual, affective, aesthetic, and other modes of engagement in the world. Finally, Merleau-Ponty makes a move typical of phenomenologists and often troubling to others. He does not limit the *schéma corporel* to the actual bodily posture as experienced at any moment but includes within it potential postures that the actor *could* adopt but is not actually adopting. Recall from Chapter 6 that this sense of potential is unlike the formalist potential of a generative system. It is not based on closed paradigms of choice or fixed rules of combination. Instead, it is defined by prior experience, judgments of feasibility under current conditions, and a more elastic sense of what might be possible. Think of the sort of anticipations and grasp of the possible involved in crossing a busy street, jumping a puddle, or getting off a bus without falling to the ground. This notion of the body as a self-aware actuality in relation to potential is simply missing in representational schemas, however precise. It is inaccessible to both description of actual positions, however fine-grained, and to type-level definitions of potential.

I have shown elsewhere that the *schéma corporel* is the minimum necessary to describe how the body functions in indexical reference, with words like "here," "there," and the pronouns (Hanks 1990). Reflexivity is necessary in order to describe indexical grounding, that is, how utterances simultaneously make reference to and articulate with the context in which the reference is performed. The element of mobility fits well with the tendency to associate indexicals with distinctions between anticipated movement (cf. "here" and "this" when referring to the forward path) and memory of movement (cf. "there" and "that" in reference to the path already traversed). Similarly, the widely observed variability in scope of spatial terms, which makes it impossible to give a metric definition of the proximal zone encoded by words like "here," is a reflection of the horizon of potential. Such terms never encode the actual, measurable distances beyond which "here" becomes "there" or "this" becomes "that." They couldn't do so and still have the flexibility needed to articulate with indefinitely many practical situations. What they do encode is the actual potential of proximity, that the referent is within the zone that *could be* treated as proximal (for extended discussion and examples, see Hanks 1990). This relatively underspecified sense component is then combined with the actional field of utterance and thereby made precise. With Merleau-Ponty's version of the body schema, with his treatment of the phenomenal field, comes a fundamentally different way of defining actuality and potential.

The next set of examples illustrates how these concepts work in actual linguistic practices involving indexicals. Example 32 is an utterance I witnessed in which the speaker informed his interlocutor that he had thrown an object into the woods, over the visual and physical barrier of the trees. They were standing on a road by the woods at the time. The term *toloˀ* 'out there' presupposes their current visual field in combination with the natural barrier between the visually open road and enclosure of the woods. Given this barrier, any spot in the woods can be treated as outside the proximal zone of their mutual "here" (cf. Margot's use of *toloˀ* in addressing Yuum).

32. ***timpiík'č' iíntah toloˀ*** 'I heaved it out there'

Example 33 does not refer to the body of the addressee as such but to a spatial zone defined by its immediacy to the left side of the addressee's body. This presupposes the lateral orientation of the schematic body and also requires a sense of relative proximity to the body as a reference object, that is, the zone of its potential extension.

33. ***ɋaáh tašɋ'iík*** 'put it on your left'

In example 34 *téˀelaˀ* requires a pointing gesture, without which it would remain too vague to interpret precisely (and hence it would be impossible to follow the directive). The gesture frees the reference from the speaker's body as a spatial landmark, since the object could be close or far, inside or outside the space of interaction. Yet at the same time it mobilizes the body as the signaling medium of the reference. The gesture and the verbal utterance are a single constituent.

34. ***tàas téˀelaˀ*** 'bring it right here (pointing to spot nearby)'

The Maya deictic *wayeˀ* 'here' is the canonical term used for reference to places spatially immediate to the speaker. It is also commonly used in reference to the near side of an object or place, even when it is objectively far away from the speaker. Sitting in her kitchen, Elena explained to me the location of a store in town, about 15 kilometers away, where I could purchase fresh meat for the family. She described the place as

35. ***hač way taánileˀ*** ***máˀ tak'uč kiíwik***
'Right here in front of it. You don't arrive (at the) market.
hač way taánileˀ Right here in front,
téˀ kukóˀonoloˀ that's where it's sold.'

In other words, along the path leading between her current location and the landmark Oxkutzcab market, with which we were both familiar, the intermediate ground on "this side" is described as "here in front." This description in no way depends upon the inherent orientation of the landmark, which may or may not itself have a front and back. Rather, the landmark situationally defines an endpoint for the trajectory leading away from the speaker; objects along the way are represented as a fixed succession in which earlier is *taánil* 'front' and later is *pàačil* 'back' (compare other uses of "back" in the previous section). Expectably, a place beyond the market, on "the other side" of it, is referred to as *téˀ pàačiloˀ* 'there in back', never **way pàačileˀ* 'here in back'.

The core feature of "here" as characterized by *wayeˀ* is that it includes the speaker. Wherever the interactants are in relation to one another, each one is inalienably *wayeˀ*, just as each one inalienably inhabits his own corporeal schema. Sitting in a crowded bus, a girl got up and offered her seat to a woman with a child in her arms, saying,

36. ***héˀ way akutaléˀešeˀ*** 'Here, you can sit right here.'

It is significant in this utterance that the girl was offering the seat she was herself sitting in, since if this were not the case, the deictic *wayeˀ* would not be present in her utterance. The reference involves just the kind of *prise de conscience* that Merleau-Ponty described. When one enters a Maya house and is offered a chair or hammock to sit in, a strict rule of Maya etiquette, the presentative offering is *héˀ b'áˀal akutalaˀ* 'Here's something to sit on', not *héˀ way akutaleˀ* 'Here's (where) you sit, here'. The forms with *wayeˀ* are used specifically for situations in which the speaker is offering his or her own seat. They always involve a *prise de conscience* by the speaker in relation to the addressee.

I was talking with Elena by her fire when we heard the slap of Pilar patting tortillas in her kitchen across the courtyard. Elena remarked that Pilar was making tortillas, and just after she did so, we heard another slapping of cornmeal on the table.

37. pìilareˀ tu pak'ač hée b'eˀ
'Pilar's making tortillas—There! Listen! (cocking ear)'

In order to appreciate the role of corporeality in such an utterance, compare it with the description *kinwúˀ uyik upak'ač pìilar* 'I hear Pilar patting tortillas'. In the latter statement the perception is asserted. It is the main thematic object of reference. In Elena's utterance (37), by contrast, Pilar's patting tortillas is central. The auditory perception of her activity is never asserted but is necessarily presupposed.

All these examples illustrate reference to places and objects distinct from the bodies of the interlocutors and yet defined in relation to them. Being part of the actional field in this way, corporeality is a process, not a thing, an actuality whose limits are defined relative to practical potentials, not an objective condition that merely instantiates a predefined type. A speaker who makes reference to something "way over there" actualizes his or her own placement "right here," just as reference to "those other guys" embodies a reflexive self-awareness of "us." The problem for standard theories of representation is that the corporeal schema in these cases is not what is being represented. It functions rather as the ground from which *other* things are represented.

The dynamic, self-aware potentiality of the body in Merleau-Ponty's framework offers a way of describing many aspects of spatial orientation that are reduced to reified mechanics in other frameworks. This is why I say it is the minimum necessary for describing the body in practice. Still, though, it is insufficient, because it is based on the individual, the property of a single actor. In visual terms, the origin point of the perspective is a single pair of eyes. But it is impossible to describe the effects of habitus, field, and social engagement by adding up individuals, for the same reason that the social cannot be understood as a collection of individuals. We need to recast the body in social terms, to encompass the kinds of interperspectival space produced in practice. In describing each of the foregoing examples, I tried to underscore the points at which Merleau-Ponty's vision helps us to make a more precise analysis. But still, I unavoidably introduced aspects of the corporeal field that go beyond his conception, because they engage a speaker in estimating the potential mobility or extension of the addressee. Such factors require an expanded concept of the corporeal schema, one that includes agents other than the speaker. For this I will use the term "corporeal field," by which I mean the highly variable social field, or set of fields, based on bodily dimensions but occupied by more than one agent.

The Social Body

In a real sense, a social foundation for the body is already written into the concept of schemas, insofar as these are sociocultural constructs defined at the level of collective values and beliefs. To understand through schemas is already to cast the body in generalized terms. The problem is that schemas, as traditionally conceived, lose in phenomenal reality what they gain in sociocultural generality. They reduce the speaking agent to the bearer of a predefined mental structure that he is condemned to reproduce again and again. So stated, the notion of a schema presupposes a dichotomy between the social and the phenomenal, between formal categorization and emergent experiences. But such a stark division is inadequate. For the purpose of describing practice, we have had to reject or alter in a basic way the related oppositions between subjects and objects, minds and bodies, expression and representation, selfsame types and unrepeatable tokens. By reifying the boundary between form and activity, they make it impossible to describe practice in a synthetic way. The fundamental challenge of a practice approach is to get beyond them. Schemas do not have to be timeless and anonymous, as Merleau-Ponty shows, and emergent action does not have to be subjective. In relation to the body, this raises the question how situated experiences can be at once social and individual.

The simplest way of considering this question is to posit a coincidence in the perspectives of agents in interaction. Thus if one party has experience x, another party has, for all intents and purposes, the same experience. The coincidence of perspectives makes x a shared or common feature of the field. This is the *simplest* method of deriving a social fact because it works by mere addition. In an exchange like the opening one in this book, Jack and Natalia have in common their occupancy and knowledge of the domestic setting of their conversation. They are in different rooms, but both know from prior experience the respective subspaces they are occupying. The counter where Jack pours his coffee is as familiar to Natalia as the dining room table where she is sitting is familiar to him. If not in the objective actuality of their perceptual field, then in the potential horizon of perception they share a common ground. Once seated alongside one another, they share the table and the newspaper and the coffee cups as common property, to which they have roughly equal perceptual access. This is similar to the sociality of "shared knowledge" posited by formalist approaches to grammar.

Beyond this kind of sameness, there is a more subtle form of common ground, based on what Schutz called the reciprocity of perspectives (see Chapter 6). Although two interlocutors may not have the same perspective, they individually assume that their respective points of view are interchangeable and congruent for all intents and purposes (Schutz 1973:183). That is, if A could occupy B's "here," she would see the world as B does. Whatever differences do exist between their understandings are overlooked as irrelevant, until further notice. We might call reciprocity so interpreted a model based on mirroring, not addition: A reflects on B as B reflects on A, recognizing that their experiences are not shared in actuality but in potentiality. Reciprocity is one of the logical prerequisites of indexical transposition, as described in Chapter 9. It underlies the ability of conversants to move fluently between the roles of I and you when interacting: You are an addressee from my perspective, but I am an addressee from yours. It is also what makes it possible for speakers to produce and understand reported speech forms, like "She told *me*, 'I want *you* to put it right here next to *me*,' so *I* did." Recall that in such utterances, pronouns and demonstratives within the quoted speech refer to objects in the original frame of utterance, whereas nonquoted ones make reference in the current utterance frame. This is why the two italicized instances of the form "me" in the example refer to two different people, despite their identical form, whereas the italicized "you" and "I" are coreferential, despite their being formally opposed. The systematic shifting of reference that indexicals demonstrate is possible precisely because interlocutors can transpose their points of view in the manner postulated by the reciprocity principle.

Both sharedness and reciprocity can be conceived as properties of individuals, the one a simple attribute and the other a capacity to take on another's point of view. To look only at such features would be to reduce the social to the interpersonal, to invite the false assumption that corporeality is social only when people are together. Recall Merleau-Ponty's *schèma* as reflexive consciousness of actuality in motion, relative to a field of potential. We can see that the *schéma* is thoroughly social insofar as the elements of the body it synthesizes, the kinds and limits of reflexive awareness it rests on, and surely the limits of potential are all infused with value and are part of the social world. The sheer fact of reciprocity and access to transposing points of view are enabled and constrained by social position. The kind and level of sharing among agents in practice are also social products. Routine body practices, both individual and interpersonal, are inculcated and bear historically sedimented values and predispositions to act, as reflected in the definition of "habitus." These factors interact in all communicative practices, from the simplest exchange over coffee to the most elaborate ritual genres, from the face-to-face to the electronic or print mediated. What distinguishes different genres and different fields is not *whether* they engage corporeality but *how* they engage it.

The remainder of this chapter will be given over to describing a discourse genre common among contemporary speakers of Maya. Called *č'iínč' in t'àan*–literally, 'hurled speech' or, more loosely, 'speech thrown at an overhearer'—this genre will serve to illustrate how some of the elements of a practice approach to language come together in an actual case. The example is purely illustrative, and most of the basic phenomena it illustrates are also in play in other kinds of speech, although this example is especially clear.

A Maya Discourse Genre

The genre called *č'iínč'in t'àan* is a kind of engagement in which minimally three parties participate. It is canonically associated with adult women and involves two women whom I will call the attackers and a third whom I will call the target. These labels for the participant roles are intended to convey both the directionality and the aggressiveness of the genre. Like gossip, it is critical discourse between two parties regarding a third, often based on innuendo and the suggestion of impropriety. Unlike gossip, the target of this genre *must* be within earshot of the attackers and is meant to perceive the speech thrown at her. What is especially noteworthy, however, is that the target is not mentioned in the third person, as we would expect in normal gossip, but is addressed through transposition: The instigator addresses her partner as if she were the target, and the partner acts as a sort of pivot, playing the role of the target and putting words in her mouth that will be damaging to her. Imagine two people talking, call them A and B, and a third, C, within earshot but not talking with them. A addresses B with words really intended for C, and B playacts C, responding as she thinks C would respond if A's innuendos were correct. So to imply that C has a secret lover, A says to B, "Didn't I see you with your lover the other day?" and B answers, "Oh, well, yes. I'm tired of my husband." Overhearing this, C realizes that she has been impugned with the charge of adultery.

I have witnessed this genre of discourse just once, during carnival, when men were dressed up as women and circulating in the streets of Oxkutzcab, engaging in *č'iínč'in t'àan* aimed at the people of the houses they were passing. According to all the people I have discussed it with, the genre is used exclusively by adult women under normal conditions. When I suggested that men might do something similar, both men and women responded that to do so would be effeminate. The question I will examine here is how the defining features of the genre constitute a kind of practice and how, specifically, they engage the corporeal field. Being gender-marked, rapid, and often unannounced, the genre proved very difficult to record and study systematically. Accordingly, I will proceed mainly on the basis of reports from Margot, the same Maya-speaking woman who engaged in the exchange with Yuum presented in Chapter 7. The strength of Margot's reports is that they describe motivation and mention other features of context that would be tacit in actual instances of the genre. As Voloshinov pointed out, metalinguistic speech is an objective record of the evaluations of native speakers. The weakness is obviously that reports of an activity are bound to distort it by simplification, the selective focus of the one doing the reporting, and the omission of aspects of timing and delivery that the report does not accurately reproduce. My purpose is therefore to illustrate aspects of corporeal discourse and its evaluation, not to provide an adequate portrayal of this genre. To do that would require more extensive evidence of the actual forms, activities, and evaluative glosses associated with it.

The two attackers can be distinguished as instigator and pivot, as opposed to the target. As Margot put it,

38. ***ká*ˀ*atuúl persona kuč'iínč'int'àan tyó*ˀ*olal***
'Two people "throw speech at an overhearer" in order that

***uyú*ˀ*u*ˀ*k* ˀ*u , . . . ump'ée, ulaá*ˀ *untúu personá o*ˀ**
she hear it, uh, the other person.'

In saying that two people speak for an overhearer, Margot specifies that the instigator and pivot are a conversational pair, the joint producers of the hurled speech, and the target is an outsider to the exchange. Notice that the requisite participant framework involves the three parties' being sufficiently close together so that the instigator anticipates that the target will be able to hear her speech. This involves estimating the potential auditory field of the target prior to utterance. The judgment requires just the kind of reflexive awareness of potential defined by Merleau-Ponty's *prise de conscience.* Yet there is a crucial difference, because the object of awareness is not the speaker's own corporeal scheme but instead the interpersonal field of which the target is a necessary part. We can see that this delicate judgment is indeed definitional of the genre, since if the target does not hear the attack, then there is no *č'iín* 'hurling, strike'. In this case what has taken place is not speech thrown at an overhearer but standard gossip, called *ˀenredos.*

In addition to the auditory conditions on hurled speech, there is a necessary intention on the part of the instigator to hurt the target. This is not a discourse practice in which you can engage by accident or fall into by unintended indiscretion.

39. ***ˀáwra č'iínč'in t'àan eˀ, leti túun čeén tiyáˀak***
 'Now "speech thrown at an overhearer," then the speaker just says it

ˀíntensionalmèente, tyóola yúˀuk e personá oˀ
 intentionally, so that that person will hear it

pero kuyáˀak tiˀulaák' oˀ
 but she says it to her partner (interactant).'

At this point Margot recounted a case of the genre she had witnessed a few days earlier. In her telling, notice the spatial setting (a scene one sees every day in rural Yucatán): Instigator and pivot are inside their respective homesteads, leaning on the wall between them, already engaged in conversation, whereas the target is in the street en route to market. Being mobile and outside of her own domestic sphere, the target is doubly vulnerable to the attack of her enemies, whose position is reinforced by their location within the safety of their own walled domestic space.[2] As we will see, this very setting foreshadows the theme of the attack that will be hurled at the target. Whereas in examples 38–39 Margot uses the term *persona* 'person' for all three participants, now that she presents them in this spatial arrangement, she switches to *señora,* which adds the further information that all three are married. This fact is directly relevant to the theme of the attack and further anchors the exchange in the web of family values. I point out these minute details of the scene because they are the anchoring points that situate this entire scenario in the structure of values that the instigator and pivot rely on to legitimate their attack.

40. ***i. tinwúˀuyah te be, ˀeste tubèe túˀuškahakbal inkìik oˀ***
 'I heard (one case) there on the road, the road where my sister lives,

---

[2]The walls demarcating the boundaries of domestic space are ubiquitous in Yucatán and are typically about chest-high, allowing people to see over them easily. For extended discussion with figures and photos, see Hanks 1990.

ii. [. . .] káˀ atuúl señòrá oˀ [. . .] wáakbalóˀ ob bey aˀ [unintelligible] [. . .]
two ladies [. . .] were standing like this [unintelligible]

iii. uyóoˀ kòot wáak le ˀulaák' oˀ [. . .] tí eloˀ le tu hač
(arms) over the wall the other is standing. So they're really

iv. tuʠikbalóob bey oˀ tuˀéenredosóˀ ob [. . .] tí el oˀ
conversing like that. They were gossiping [. . .]. So

v. le kutíipi le señòrá oˀ [. . .] tubin hk'iíwik
when the (other) lady shows up [. . .] she's walking to (the) market.'

So instigator and pivot are face to face, already engaged in gossip, when the target comes into view. The verb *tiípil* designates the appearance of a person or object on the edge of the visual field, with the implication that the subject is approaching the perceiver. It is interesting to note that gossip in the absence of the target is what prepares the ground for hurled speech once she shows up. Judging that the target is entering the zone of auditory access, the instigator then addresses the pivot with words really meant for the target. The displacement of address is evident in the first phrase of her utterance, since the pivot, her ostensible addressee, is not going anywhere at the time. In phrase viii Margot indicates that the instigator wants her speech to be overheard. Although she does not say so, it is probable that the attack is meant not only for the target to hear but also for the benefit of all those within earshot of the scene, a sort of unbounded potential audience.

vi. pwes yáak e maá č in kin túˀun kabin
'So she says "Wow I———Where are you going?

vii. hač táah máˀalob' abestirma abáa, kih ti le yéetseñorail oˀ
You've dressed yourself well!" she says to her lady-companion.
[instigator addresses pivot]

viii. [. . .] ˀu k'aát ká ˀúˀuyáˀak yáˀak
[. . .] she wants her saying it to be heard (by the target).

ix. [. . .] ˀáam pero eske yàan máaš kimbin inwileh, kih,
[. . .] "Oh, but it's because there's someone I'm going to see," she says.

x. yàan máaš k'ab'eét inwilik, kih [laughter]
"There's someone I've got to see." [pivot responds to instigator]

In responding as she does in ix–x, the pivot acts as a surrogate for the target in the staged exchange. She receives the attack and responds in the way the attackers wish to portray the target. Notice that if the pivot were unwilling or unable to play this role, she could shut down the entire process simply by responding to the opening utterance as if it were really intended for her. She could say, "Oh, I'm glad you like my dress" or "What do you mean? I dress this way every day" or some such. The genre requires the collusion of the pivot in order to achieve completeness, which is what I mean in saying that it is by definition a joint production. In specifying that the attackers were gossiping just before this event, Margot is attending to this condition as well, since gossip is a canonical case of collusion. Finally, it is evident in this segment of Margot's description that hurled speech is a secondary genre in Bakhtin's sense because it includes quoted speech, even though the words quoted were never actually delivered by the would-be quotee.

The attack on the target is based on her clothing, that is, her choice of physical appearance. This is not the only grounds on which Maya people hurl speech, but it is interestingly corporeal and serves to underline another basic point. Physical presentation of self is saturated with value, just as the habitus is inscribed fundamentally in the practices of the body. The target is vulnerable to attack because she appears, or can be made to seem, overdressed for the routine activity of going to market. That she seems to have attended to her appearance is the grounds for inferring that she has a special person whom she wishes to impress. In the setting of this exchange, the mere fact of preparing to go to market this way invites suspicion, since the primary sphere of legitimate romantic interaction is the homestead or special events like dances and parties. The suggestion that she is overdressed puts the target in the position of having to justify herself. The pivot's response enters into this space of moral censure and states directly that the target is in an adulterous relationship. By saying "someone I really need to see," she is both understating what she conveys and relying on the idea of "seeing" as actually being with someone, which in turn implies sexual union in this context. If the innuendo and suggestion of seaminess were not enough in the words, the laughter at the end of her response assures that it is meant to imply sexual wrongdoing.

The attack is therefore invasive of the target in a quite specific sense. It recasts her physical appearance, whatever it is in fact, as reasonable grounds for suspicion about her secret behavior. It is, in other words, an attempt to dominate the target by subordinating her to accepted values of the group, values like family propriety, monogamy, and muted attractiveness in daily public settings. The same kind of attack would be unthinkable were the target a Maya man, since none of these dominant values apply, and indeed any man who would stand leaning on his wall talking with a neighbor while watching the street would himself be vulnerable to criticism. The entire relationship to lived space is different for men and therefore gendered in a strong sense. There is another kind of invasion, however, which Margot indicates clearly in the remark in example 41. She invades the private space of the target's thoughts, presuming to read her mind, as it were.

41. ***tušokik utùukul le ˀu ˀéenemìiga beyoˀ**, **yéetel***
  'She reads the thoughts of her enemy like that. And

tuburlàartik šan tumèen ubestirmail ub'áah [. . .]
  she mocks her, too, because she's gotten dressed up [. . .].

tučiína tiˀ bey oˀ [. . .] tuč'iín e tàan ti
She threw it at her like that [. . .]. She threw the speech at her.'

Once attacked, the target has various options for responding, but these also depend critically upon the corporeal field. If she is walking alone, she can only confront her attackers directly or try to ignore the attack. The former response runs the risk of a direct physical confrontation, according to Margot and other Maya people with whom I discussed this, whereas the latter can backfire if there is a larger audience who may then be left with the impression that she does have a lover at the market. This vulnerability may well reinforce the routine practice whereby Maya women tend to appear in public in groups. Assuming she is accompanied, she can then return the hurled speech in kind, using her companion as a pivot for her counterattack. This is what happened in the scene described by Margot.

42. ***héˀel oˀ ká tunúuk eˀu laák' untúul tuún oˀ***
'Right, so the other one responds then,

kómo yeétbin uˀiihá eˀ, kyáˀ al eˀ, kyáˀak eˀ,
since her daughter was going with her, she says, she says,

le ˀoó¢i pèek' oˀ, máˀ tuyilik uneh letiˀ
"The poor dog, it doesn't see its own tail,

uneh yaana kuyilik, kih
the tail of others (is what) it sees," she says.

[. . .] tuč'inah šan bey oˀ
[. . .] She threw it (back at her), too, like that.'

That the target in this case was accompanied by her daughter both provides protection and raises the stakes. For her daughter is a sort of familial moral chaperone, assuring that she does not engage in any improper rendezvous at the market and providing her with a bonafide witness of the attack. At the same time, she is compelled to fend it off effectively, lest her daughter be left in doubt. It is fascinating in this example that the target responds by referring to her tormentor as a dog. There is more here than meets the eye. As any Maya person knows from experience, Maya dogs are generally docile during the day, provided that one does not enter the space of the homestead, as marked by the wall around it. It is fairly rare, especially in town, for dogs to attack people in a public space, such as the street, in daylight. At night everything changes, and dogs become very possessive of the space in front of the homestead, including the street. Pedestrians need to pay attention and often use flashlights and stones to protect themselves from dogs who will rush them from the darkness, sometimes even biting. By treating her attacker as a dog, the target invokes this routine schema: dogs by night, gossiping women by day. But there is another element that adds delicious irony to her response. For Maya people typically address dogs in the third person. For instance, to shoo away a dog who has slinked inside the house, owners don't tell the animal directly to leave, saying, "No, get out," as we might in English. Instead, they address the animal in the third person, saying things like, "Where's that dog going!?" while looking right at it. This is another kind of transposed address, a sort of inverse of quotation, in which a phenomenal addressee (the dog) is spoken to in the third person, instead of an absent party's being presented in the first or second person, as in quote. In other words, she not only calls the instigator a dog but indexes this by addressing her in the transposed form associated with canine address. Just as the attack thematized the body, the response does too, focusing on the instigator's inability to see her own tail. The implication here is that the instigator should mind her own affairs.

In summary, then, Maya hurled speech involves many factors outlined in this and the preceding chapter. As a kind of practice, it is defined by a certain kind of participant framework and transposed address, not by the uttering of certain words. The words themselves are highly incomplete, relying on innuendo and understatement and making sense only in connection with the spatial and moral arrangement of the setting. The schematic background of corporeal valuation is in play in the relation among actors and their domestic and public spaces, the heavy gender component, the notion that physical appearance is a matter of selection and is indicative of intention, and the entire complex of perceptual access among the participants. The corporeal field is defined not by the mere arrangement of bodies in space but by the movement of the target and the stability of the attackers, the potential for auditory reception, the discrepancy between speech physically directed to one party but intended for another, the individual *prises de conscience* of the participants that they are in a setting of this kind, and their reciprocal awareness of one another. Also factored into the situation is the interperspectival element of their awareness of themselves and of each other as occupants of a joint field, and in particular the estimation of potential reception by the target of the attack. The entire field is in motion because the target is walking, and the exchange requires precise timing in order to come off. And of course the moral background of values attaching to female behavior and modes of presentation provides the ground of legitimacy without which the attacker would herself be out of line. If any of these factors is missing, then the discourse lacks finalization as an instance of hurled speech and instead becomes an instance of failed gossip (if the target is out of range), a denunciation (if the target is directly confronted without transposition), or a bizarre commentary (if the pivot mistakes the opening utterance as being directed at her rather than the target). Notice that there is nothing in the words themselves to indicate the two key transpositions that define the genre: It is the corporeal field, as the embodiment of values and the setting of practices, that provides the necessary interpretive frame for language.

Further Readings

Regarding the linguistic mediation of the body, the body in practice, and the concept of the corporeal field, see Chapter 6 above and

Bourdieu, P. *Outline of a Theory of Practice.* Translated by R. Nice. Cambridge: Cambridge University Press, 1977 [1972]. "Body as Geometer: Cosmogonic Practice," pp. 114–124.

———. *Le Sens pratique.* Paris: Editions de Minuit, 1980. Chap. 4: "La Croyance et le corps," pp. 11–134.

Eckert, P., and McConnell-Ginet, S. "Think Practically and Look Locally: Language and Gender as Community-based Practice." *Annual Review of Anthropology* 21 (1992):-461–491.

Friedrich, P. *On the Meaning of the Tarascan Suffixes of Locative Space. International Journal of American Linguistics,* memoir 23. Bloomington: Indiana University Press, 1969.

Hanks, W. F. *Referential Practice: Language and Lived Space Among the Maya.* Chicago: University of Chicago Press, 1990.

Levinson, S. "Putting Linguistics on a Proper Footing: Explorations in Goffman's Concepts of Participation." In *Goffman: An Interdisciplinary Appreciation,* edited by P. Drew and A. Woolton. Oxford: Polity Press, 1987, pp. 161–227.

Merleau-Ponty, M. "On the Phenomenology of Language." In *Signs,* translated and introduced by R. C. McCleary. Evanston, IL: Northwestern University Press, 1964, pp. 84–97.

———. *Phénoménologie de la perception.* Paris: Gallimard, 1967 [1945], pp. 114–172, 204–234.

Schutz, A. *The Phenomenology of the Social World.* Translated by G. Walsh and F. Lehnert. Evanston, IL: Northwestern University Press, 1967 [1932].

For analyses of the microrelations among speech, gaze, and gesture in conversation, see

Besnier, N. "Language and Affect." *Annual Review of Anthropology* 19 (1990):419–451.

Goodwin, C. "Notes on a Story Structure and the Organization of Participation." In *Structures of Social Action,* edited by J. M. Atkinson and J. Heritage. Cambridge: Cambridge University Press, 1984, pp. 225–246.

Heath, C. "Talk and Recipiency: Sequential Organization in Speech and Body." In *Structures of Social Action,* edited by J. M. Atkinson and J. Heritage. Cambridge: Cambridge University Press, 1984, pp. 247–265.

Schegloff, E. "On Some Gestures' Relation to Talk." In *Structures of Social Action,* edited by J. M. Atkinson and J. Heritage. Cambridge: Cambridge University Press, 1984, pp. 266–296.

For anthropological treatments of the body and spatial orientation, see

Bourdieu, P. "The Berber House." In *Rules and Meanings,* edited by M. Douglas. London: Penguin, 1980, pp. 98–110.

Comaroff, J. *Body of Power, Body of Spirit: The Culture and History of a South African People.* Chicago: University of Chicago Press, 1985.

Gell, Alfred. "How to Read a Map: Remarks on the Practical Logic of Navigation." *Man,* n.s., 20 (1985):271–286.

Mauss, M. "Techniques of the Body." *Economy and Society* 2(1) (1973):70–88.

Munn, N. D. "Visual Categories: An Approach to the Study of Representational Systems." *American Anthropologist* 68 (1966):936–950.

Turner, T. "The Social Skin." In *Not Work Alone,* edited by J. Cherfas and R. Lewin. Beverly Hills, CA: Sage Publications, 1980.

———. "Bodies and Anti-bodies: Flesh and Fetish in Contemporary Social Theory." In *Embodiment and Experience,* edited by T. Csordias. Cambridge: Cambridge University Press, 1994.

———. "Social Body and Embodied Subject: Bodiliness, Subjectivity and Sociality Among the Kayapo." *Cultural Anthropology,* May 1995.

On gossip and dispute, see

Brenneis, D. "Language and Disputing." *Annual Review of Anthropology* 18 (1989):221–237.

Goodwin, M. H. *He-said-she-said: The Interactive Organization of Talk in an Urban Black Peer Group.* Bloomington: Indiana University Press, 1990.

Haviland, J. B. *Gossip, Reputation, and Knowledge in Zinacantan.* Chicago: University of Chicago Press, 1977.

Chapter 12

Meaning in History

The Trouble with Time

When questions arise about language in history, we tend to think of the past or of how language evolves over long spans of time. This way of thinking introduces a retrospective view, whether we look "back" from the present to the origins and development of language or "forward" into the future, from which we will later look back to the present as a past from which that future unfolded. In this play of perspectives, what counts as history assumes the status of fact, something always already given and irrevocable. To "make history" is to do something that will later be factual, that will have consequences. A "historic event" is one that seems to stand out from its own past and will alter the course of subsequent events. In relation to language these questions usually point to the processes through which a contemporary form arose out of changes in sound, syntax, semantics, and usage. Viewed through the lens of their histories, contemporary languages are the products of successive changes, each representing a stage in an evolutionary development.

In a second, closely related usage, "history" designates a kind of study, the vocation of people we call historians. To "do," "write," or "study" history is commonly understood as the reconstruction or recounting of history in the first sense. This ambiguity in the noun "history" is different from what we find in nouns such as "language" (cf. linguistics), "culture" (cf. anthropology), "society" (cf. sociology), and "politics" (cf. political science). And the ambiguity is suggestive, I think, of a deeper assumption about the objectivity of history the process and the transparency of history the narrative genre. It is as if what happened can be discovered for what it was and retold as a story of chronology. The fallacy of these two assumptions should be obvious from the preceding chapters of this book. If, as we have seen, utterance production always involves the selective expression of multiple meanings that emerge out of the reception process, then there is no simple fact of the matter. Both the meaning and the objectivity of speech are produced by the publics who participate in them. Indeterminacy, multiplicity, dialogism, and transposition are inherent in the communicative process. Determinacy of meaning, unequivocal literality, authorship, and the recovery of embedded participation frameworks are all things that must be produced. They plague the historian working with language just as they plague the ethnographer or linguist, and for the same reasons.

The telling of history is filtered through the genres in which it occurs. Like writing, reported speech, and other metalinguistic operations, it is a form of objectification. It relies on the metalinguistic capacity of human discourse and takes place in a present context whose own contours inevitably shape the result. Choices among linguistic resources, including tense, aspect, indexicals, and genre labels have a decisive impact on the perspective we project on past practices. To tell the history of an utterance is therefore to work at a double remove, for the original speech must be contextualized as fully as possible, and the telling must also be contextualized. Ingarden's rule applies at both phases: The more you try to fill in the blank spots of indeterminacy, the more blank spots you introduce. At some point you step back from the infinite regress and decide that enough has been said to get the point. The key thing to keep in mind is that these judgment calls never add up to full recovery, and there is no genre of discourse that escapes from selectivity. How we think of language in history depends intimately upon how we think of it in the present.

How, then, do we come to grips with the specificity and particularity of expression, while also recognizing the systems that make expression possible? On the face of it, the question is a conceptual one, not particularly historical. And as I said at several points, this book is not in any sense a viable history of the ideas it discusses. Nor does it attempt to be. This does not mean, however, that it is ahistorical in the sense of coming from nowhere. It is situated, specific, selective, and actual, just as is any verbal production. Part of the particularity of any utterance is when it occurs, just as timing, duration, and synchronization are part of practice. If we reject the conceptual abstractness of mental representations in favor of embodied knowledge and corporeality, time enters into the picture through the rhythms of bodies in motion. In distinguishing schematic from emergent features of practice, we rely on a difference between prefabricated versus new aspects and enduring versus momentary ones. Insofar as habitus implies enduring dispositions to perceive and act in certain ways, it, too, has a hidden temporal component. The present and past to which it belongs are meaningful constructs, inflected with actors' experiences in the phenomenal present. That is, the time that concerns us here is social, cultural, and phenomenal, not the empty, anonymous spaces of chronology. The difference is a lot like the contrast between a medical chart of the human body and Merleau-Ponty's corporeal schema.

The turn to time and history is inevitable because whenever we try to define key concepts in communicative practice, such as the ones mentioned in the preceding paragraph, the definition includes temporal terms. *Practices are temporalized,* and the erasure of time is one of the most fundamental moves of formalism. This is so even when it is time itself that is the object of formalist modeling. In arguing against formal theories, we step back into the difficulties of history, in both of the above senses. The difficulties are several. In the first place the activity of doing theory and trying to describe practices is itself inscribed in time, a point Munn (1992) emphasized. Not only is this book, for instance, historically specific, but your reading of it is, too. The temporal unfolding of a single paragraph, a chapter, or the overarching direction of the book all imply emergence. Some of the terms and ideas introduced in early chapters no longer mean the same things because of the phenomenal time lag between them and this sentence. What makes this so hard is that the urge to find coherence is wrapped up in the search for fixed points, or stable perspectives, from which to describe communicative practices. It is hard enough to discuss the temporality of practices out there but doubly hard to come to grips with the temporality of this description right here.

Then, too, temporal changes tend to imply a great deal more than spatial ones. On the one hand, we have a sense that circumstances may be different from one place to another, but if the two spaces coexist in time, then they are at some level part of the same world. On the other hand, two circumstances separated by time do not so easily coexist. The later one supersedes the earlier, subsuming it and revising it in the light of supervening experience. The difference between now and then is of a greater order of magnitude than the one between here and there. And as Whorf pointed out, European languages and speech patterns provide us with numerous spatial metaphors for describing temporal relations, all of which are inherently distorting. Ultimately, it is impossible to talk about time without objectifying it because acts of reference and description always objectify, if only for a moment.

What is possible is to explore some of the temporal dimensions of practice in a way that is heuristically useful. How can we integrate time into the empirical description of communicative practices? This is the central question of this chapter. It breaks up into several smaller foci.

The first step is to recognize that the notion of a unitary time line, moving from earlier to later at a single pace in all places, is itself an artifact of the view from nowhere. Entailed in this notion is the idea that time is a substance, like flour or sand, that can be divvied up into containers like measuring cups, minutes, hours, and the little boxes for each day on a calendar. At issue here is not whether time as measured by clicks and boxes exists but rather whether it is relevant to the description of communicative practices. Like the objectivity that measures spatial distance with a yardstick and weighs material objects into pounds and kilos, time so conceived is only one of many conceptions, bound to a single value structure. For practice, we need to distinguish the various kinds of duration, synchrony, sequence, and rhythm that pertain to the kinds of actions we are studying. This is consistent with the view expressed by Munn, for whom

> "temporalization" . . . views time as [a] symbolic process continually being produced in everyday practices. People are "in" a sociocultural time of multiple dimensions (sequencing, timing, past-present-future relations, etc.) that they are forming in their "projects." In any given instance, particular temporal dimensions may be foci of attention or only tacitly known. Either way, these dimensions are lived or apprehended concretely via the various meaningful connectivities among persons, objects and space continually being made in and through the everyday world. (1992:116)

The value of temporal units varies according to context. A court proceeding may begin and end in the strike of a gavel, but this punctuality is missing entirely from other kinds of activities, like the learning of a foreign language, the writing of a book, and the sustenance of a friendship. Or better, other points of onset and termination are established according to the specifics of the activity. A threat, warning, or promise anticipates future fulfillment in a way different from a simple question or a statement of opinion. A memoir summarizes the past in ways different from the minutes of a meeting or the melancholy of nostalgia. Instead of a single line, a better image in this context is the crisscrossing of multiple spans, differing in length and density, some more curved than others. The present is neither singularly nor neatly bounded. In fact this can be seen clearly in the notion of a "frame," with its latent tie to the bounded scene within a single unit of film. Just as frame analysis leads to the recognition of embedding, transposition, and the lamination of multiple frames (see Chapter 9), so the idea of the present leads, when pushed, to recognition of diverse temporal streams intersecting as a practice emerges.

It is not only discrete acts or kinds of practice that establish different temporalities. The social fields in which practice occurs contribute as well. Maya farmers deal with temporal rhythms closely tied to the growth cycles of their crops, with different varieties of corn that mature at different rates in different kinds of soil, fruit trees that grow to maturity only after five or more years, beans that yield in a single season, and so forth. The sheer diversity of temporal factors contributing to social practices raises the question how we ever coordinate to *achieve synchrony.* From this perspective the development of things like a common calendar represents a major technological breakthrough. Similarly, the management of temporal relations becomes a critical aspect of practices, equal in importance to the other displays of coherence that conversation analysts study and the sharing of a verbal code linguists posit.

There is, then, a tension between universalizing schemes of time reckoning and the culturally meaningful perspectives on time and history according to which people act. Schutz's division between consociates, contemporaries, and predecessors is an example of the former, whereas a technology like the Georgian or Mayan calendar illustrates the latter. The problem is that universal schemes provide at least the appearance of comparability across contexts, whereas the deeper we enter into culturally specific systems, the more difficult comparison becomes. The danger is that in referring all the value constructs bearing on temporality to a single objective scheme, we run a serious risk of erasing the very qualitative distinctions we hope to explain. This does not mean that universal schemes have no value any more than that the study of deixis leads to a sheer rejection of the idea of spatial contiguity. We need to recognize that universal schemes are metalanguages that we employ for certain purposes. Like all metalanguages, they are selective, and they impose their own units and levels upon the phenomena they describe. If the aim is comparison, then it makes sense to refer different practices and cultural milieus to a common framework. But this does not justify elevating the common framework to the status of reality and relegating the variations to the status of local epiphenomena. And it requires constant attention to the factors ignored by the comparison.

Temporal elements inhere in practice on two quite separate levels. When speakers make reference to time, using temporal adverbs, day names, dates, and the like, they focalize time relations. This is an instance of categorization similar to the spatial categorizations produced in the use of distance terms; the perceptual ones produced with verbs of sensing; the affective ones marked by words like "anger," "joy," "love," and "hate"; and the corporeal ones described in the first part of Chapter 11. A study of such terms and the broader verbal resources of which they are a part can reveal much of the system of classification by which speakers objectify experience. But temporality, like corporeality, is also tacit in practices, a backgrounded aspect evident in timing, rhythm, sequence, anticipation, and memory. Like the indexical ground of reference, the tacit dimensions are an unavoidable part of the actuality of speech, even when they are not objectified. When a speaker uses expressions like "later," "tomorrow," "then," "next," "quickly," "slowly," and "right away," there is an unspoken ground of comparison tied to the present and to the normal rhythms at which an act takes place. This is one of the serious weaknesses with universal measurements of time and history: They impose the *focal* segmentations of an analytic metalanguage upon the *backgrounded* temporality of practices. This effectively flattens the two levels of figure and ground onto a single plane. But the actuality of practice is neither the sheer emergence of space, participation, and time nor the simple realization of transcendent units. It is the interplay between the two.

This all implies that the relevant units and processes involved in meaning production are both local and global, emergent and schematic. *Local units* are tied to the genre of practice under study, including things like the phases and sequencing of parts of an activity. Question-answer pairs, utterance-response sequences, narratives, ritual performances, and so forth all have relevancy structures associated with them that provide the means for distinguishing temporal units. Indeed, how they construct temporality is an important axis along which they can be compared and distinguished. These in turn interact with more *global units* corresponding to the dynamics of the fields in which they take place. Once we move to the global level of fields, discontinuity also becomes an issue. Just as the trajectory of an utterance through a field of reception is discontinuous, so, too, the multiplicity of time implies more than mere inclusion of the local within the global. Looked at as a whole, a conversational exchange or ritual event occurs within the encompassing temporal contexts of their respective settings, and these settings fragment into different temporal frameworks. This holds for any of the interactions used in this book to illustrate meaning production: the exchange between Jack and Natalia over coffee in the morning, the exchange between Margot and Yuum over supper, and the precision timing of the hurled speech in the previous chapter. The latter, for instance, was reported to have taken place during a time of the day when the two women in the street were walking to market and the other two were outside in their yards. It is unlikely that any native Maya speaker would stipulate that the genre of *č'iínč'in t'àan* occurs in the daytime, canonically during the hours when women circulate in public unaccompanied by men, and none of the people with whom I discussed it mentioned this. Yet this is true, because the requisite conditions for the genre tend in fact to arise at these times of the day. This is a good example of background temporal coordination between local timing and the more global cycle of daily activities. Still, at the level of daily cycles, we must recognize that the women going to market, the patient lying in fever in the clinic, the shaman in prayer around the corner, the merchant unloading his truck at the depot, and the journalist meeting a deadline are not all in the same time frame. Their synchrony is the product of partial coordination. You can't recognize multiple publics without also recognizing the dispersal of temporal units.

Using the terms proposed in Chapter 10, we may think of these various aspects of temporalization in relation to the three moments of practice: activity, structure, and the horizon of values embodied in habitus and cognized in ideology. The vivid present of action proceeds on the two levels of focal and backgrounded aspects, varying according to the kind and overall timing of the action. Linguistic, social, and symbolic structures provide encompassing frameworks for cultural categorizations of temporal aspects. These orient actors by providing the terms and defining the conjunctures through which they represent time and evaluate it. The horizon of values, both conceptual and embodied, binds time to myriad other aspects of human experience. They guide agents as they evaluate activities and expressive forms, both justifying their own positions and misrecognizing the factors that determine them. These three moments should not be thought of as things unrelated but as different realizations of a single communicative process. If they appear circular as we defined them in Chapter 10 and have related them to temporality here, that is because they *are* circular, to a degree. Many of the same values that emerge through activity are also embedded in linguistic categories and subject to ideological evaluation. Where the three moments differ is in their respective organizations, their relations to human experience, and their role in practice. Much of what we have said about these differences in relation to meaningful experience applies directly to the varieties of time implicated in speech.

The remainder of this chapter will explore in more detail the relation between the actuality of utterances, the quick present of talk, and the objectified versions of practice that we call history. In order to illustrate meaning in history, we will turn once again to Yucatec Maya, but this time to some of the dynamics of colonial Maya language and to the challenges posed by research on that history. Most of the really hard problems that arise in relation to temporality will go unsolved. The trouble with time is that you can't step back from it long enough to get a handle on it; and if you do manage to get some distance, it is no longer time you are talking about. This book is neither a philosophy of time nor a work of history, nor is the study of communicative practice a panacea. My aim is more modest: to demonstrate that such a study is relevant to historical research because it provides a productive perspective on some of its basic problems, and to drive home the point that there are viable alternatives to the sterile opposition between sheer synchrony and sheer diachrony.

Temporality in Communicative Practice

If time is a symbolic process, as Munn (1992) put it, then it pertains to both the products and the preconditions of practice. What we called the actuality of utterances reflects this clearly. By "actuality" I mean the social fact of an instance of speech, its meaning in terms of the agent's motivations, and its multiple ties to the indexical context in which it occurs. As Schutz pointed out, motivations have both retrospective and prospective dimensions, pointing to the past conditions leading up to the utterance and to the ends toward which it is a step. Indexical ties relate the utterance to its immediate conditions—spatial, temporal, corporeal, experiential, conceptual, and discourse-based. How we distinguish the immediate context from the broader field is a matter of judgment based on the specific features of the practice and its reception. That utterances can be repeated, reported, and otherwise transposed into novel contexts means that they have the capacity to enter into indefinitely many new contexts, articulating with similarly many presents. In so doing, the utterance forms a trajectory or span of connection between different spatiotemporal matrices. Although each step in this process is selective and no two concretizations of an utterance are really the same, still, the utterance carries with it the residua of previous presents. Like the retrospective motivations of the speaker, these residua bind the utterance to multiple pasts, but unlike motivations, these pasts need not be part of any given speaker's intentions or reasoning. Similarly, any utterance once produced becomes an object of reception and may be caught up in subsequent receptions, projecting into indefinitely many potential futures. And for the same reasons, words spoken in order that they be repeated may in fact fall by the wayside. Try as we might to control the past references and future appropriation of our speech, it is virtually impossible to do so.

This vulnerability, or fragility, of expression is both a linguistic and a social fact. In linguistic terms, it is the metalinguistic apparatus of human language that makes it possible to appropriate and attribute speech at any time to any other speaker. No phrasing, no genre, and no amount of caution in speaking can insulate an utterance from the technologies of metalanguage. Socially, it is the ubiquity of talk, the vicissitudes of human judgment, and the play among different fields of reception that open the utterance to later construals or misconstruals. As Bakhtin observed, certain forms of authoritative or dominant speech are designed to control these factors by defining their own interpretation so finally as to freeze it. But language alone can never achieve this, and the most authoritative utterance can be turned on its head by simple tropes like irony, parody, or slight shifts in wording. Similarly, social groups develop institutions such as censorship, copyright laws, ethical codes, and the entire apparatus of propriety to control speech, but the grip is tenuous at best. Viewed from the perspective of time, these facts imply that speech practices are profoundly contingent. They occur within time and are always subject to the multiple trajectories of which time is constituted.

Neither contingency nor mutability implies that meanings are cut loose from social facts, however, and this limits construal at the same time that it facilitates it. The kinds of communities posited by Putnam and correlated with language varieties in sociolinguistics are internally structured, and their interrelations are inflected with inequality. From a linguistic and purely conceptual viewpoint, all human languages are equal and all potential understandings of an utterance are equally viable. The conception of the ideal speaker-listener brings this fundamental equality to the level of the people who speak the language. In social terms, the opposite is true in all three instances. Languages are not socially equal because they are not all associated with the same kinds of prestige, nor are they equally tied to dominant values. Maya is just as complex, subtle, and generative as Spanish, but unlike Spanish it is virtually unwritten, marginal in the public and private school systems, absent from the higher courts, and often perceived as a symbol of rural or regional backwardness. Moreover, some interpretations of speech and events are dominant in groups. As a result, they may be literally unquestionable, or they may be open to debate but still backed by the weight of precedent, tacit assumptions, or more visible instruments of power. To argue for contingency is therefore not to assume that all movements of meaning are equally possible, let alone probable.

Even within the present, utterances project far beyond their immediate conditions. Dialogism binds aspects of speech to a broader discursive present. And each of the elements in that present also belongs to time, with the result that words spoken now can be caught up in other processes whose own referents and indexical bonds lead into other temporal streams. The inverse is equally true: The words of the present utterance bring aspects of their different temporalities with them. The end result of dialogism and the kinds of transposition under discussion is that the present of practice is a kind of meeting ground for centrifugal and centripetal associations, each inflected with the connections we summarize as "time." Corporeality further contributes to this dynamic by introducing body time and the motion of interacting corporeal schemas. This was particularly clear in the example of deflected speech in Chapter 11, but it is no less significant in the movements of Jack and Natalia, the coming together and separation of Margot and Yuum.

The interplay between time as represented and time as lived is basic to narrative as well. In the canonical examples, narratives recount events and actions, categorizing temporal relations through descriptive and referential expressions. These include things like tense and aspect markers, temporal connectives among sentences, framing expressions such as "once upon a time," "a little later," "and then," and so forth. These elements provide hearers with information about the world being represented. Apart from this, the narrative itself has a sequential structure, which need not correspond to the one of the story told. Flashbacks, foreshadowing, asides, and extended descriptions permit narrators to contract or expand the narrative discourse relative to the events told, and an entire novel can revolve around a single gesture. The management of time in the narrative is in principle independent of story time, and it is only in cases of iconic matching of the two that they coincide. Apart from both of these, the oral telling or reading of the narrative has its own time. The book may be read in short pieces at night before sleep; the storyteller may rush through certain sections and linger to embellish others. To put it in different terms, the participant framework of narrative is at least threefold: the performance or reception, in which the audience is critical; the narrative form itself, in which the author and discourse structure are central; and the world retold, in which narrative characters inhabit story time. In each single dimension the other two are present as background potentials. In the telling of a narrative, the three temporal planes interact to produce the work as a whole. This is the temporality of concretization.

If these dynamics come into play in the actuality of utterances, what is the "present" from the perspective of a whole language? The question is too abstract to address in anything but general terms. In the semantic schemata corresponding to words and phrases, relatively stable associations are formed between empirically distinct experiences, and this tends to naturalize language as it is experienced by speakers, making its categories at once invisible and ever-present. At the same time, under certain circumstances, the sheer torrent of differences among ways of speaking and descriptive perspectives in a community may contribute to change. Mutual adjustments between speakers, the tendencies to minimize or maximize difference, and local specializations are played out continuously in everyday discourse. Insofar as the linguistic system bears the trace of these adjustments, as we argued in previous chapters, it, too, is in constant flux. As the Prague School linguistics said, the synchrony of a system is a dynamic one, a balancing of interacting forces.

At any phase of its history, the range of potentials held ready in the schematic structure of a language are concretized in a particular configuration or range of configurations. In contemporary Maya, for instance, the expression *biš ab'èel* 'how are you? (lit. how [is] your road?)' is one of the most commonly heard greetings among people who know one another and interact on familiar terms. To my knowledge, the earliest citation of this expression is in the mid-nineteenth century, in the dictionary complied by Fray Juan Pio Perez. Earlier sources cite expressions such as *bicx a cah* 'how are you? (lit. how are you [going/doing?])' (Beltrán de Santa Rosa María 1859:165), and *bicio* 'how are you?' (Martinez Hernandez 1929: folio 51r) for what appears to be the same utterance type. What is interesting is that in the earlier forms of Maya, the same words existed as in the modern greeting, taking into account regular sound changes, yet they were not put together into the same routine expression. The semantic range of *b'èel* 'road, path, work, state of being' appears to have shifted over time, so that whereas its use was closely tied to particular acts in the colonial language, it has come to stand for the more general state of mind of a person in the modern language. In the colonial sources, in fact, it is often glossed "sin, guilt," a particular meaning clearly imported by the Catholic missionaries. That is, the overall concept of a road or path as one's "project" is concretized differently in the two stages of Maya language.

Similarly, in contemporary Maya among the many Spanish terms commonly used is the word *familia.* Whereas the standard Spanish meaning of this is "family," as in *mi familia* 'my family (esp. spouse and children)', in Maya discourse the possessed form of the word means unambiguously "wife," as in *infáamilyàa* 'my wife'. Therefore only married men use the expression, a covert gender index absent from Spanish usage of the same form. There is no evidence of this usage, so far as I can tell, in the colonial sources. Another illustration is the verb *talik* 'to touch, tap, palpitate'. In the colonial sources this verb has the general, neutral value of tactile contact with an object or the taking of it in hand (Martinez Hernandez 1929: folio 406; *Diccionario de San Francisco*:328). This general potential is realized in contemporary Maya in two ways. In the region of Valladolid, in the north of the state, it is used to describe acts of striking forcefully, whereas in the Oxkutzcab region, in the south, it is considered a vulgar term for sexual intercourse, roughly equivalent to English "screw." Similarly, the Maya term for 'mother" is *naʔ* , a word in use since the early colonial period. In Maya as spoken today, however, the more common term for mother is *màamah,* from the Spanish, whereas *naʔ* occurs *only* in the crude expression *upèel anaʔ* 'your mother's cunt'. This expression is a standard expletive, which may be variously elaborated and, when addressed to a specific addressee, is a challenge to fight. However we choose to analyze such examples, the point is that particular portions of the schematic ranges of these and similar terms are concretized in contemporary speech in ways that they were not at earlier stages of the languages. Moreover, these examples illustrate that the moral and aesthetic dimensions of language can be as significant as the referential. Change affects and may be driven by the social evaluation of any aspect of communicative practices.

Meaning in History

Temporalization, then, is a substrate of diachrony inherent in all practice. This includes both the emergence of speech in its own immediate present, from moment to moment, and the connection of this present to a broader discursive field. In contrast to this process but closely related to it is the *historicization* of speech. As understood here, this always involves objectifying practices and their verbal dimensions, through reporting, representing, and evaluating them. History, in this sense, is the product of objectification. It need not involve writing or electronic mediation, although it can. What it must involve is the metalinguistic gaze through which primary speech processes become the objects of evaluation.

In other words, history is not merely text, and text is not necessarily history. Rather, both are the products of a more general process of objectification. It is this same kind of transformation that makes a practice into a bounded event. In many cases such transformations involve looking back on something that already happened and evaluating it in a certain way. But just as the lower threshold of metalanguage is within speech itself, in the verbs of communicating and indexical keyings that frame an utterance as it occurs, so, too, the lower threshold of historicization is immanent in speech as a process. What distinguishes routine metalinguistic framing from the production of history is the degree of consciousness and the explicitness with which the objectified value is expressed.

Viewed in this light history and the processes that produce it are distinct both from language diachrony and from the study of history. The former usually consists in long-term language changes, the relations between different stages in the development of a language. What distinguishes this from history in the present sense is that the latter involves consciousness and metalinguistic objectification. These things may of course contribute to language change. But not all change is mediated by consciousness, and the kinds of systemic shift that produced the current vowel inventory of English or the current inventory of deictic terms in Maya relied on many factors apart from metalanguage. What we are calling history is tied rather to the ways in which native speakers evaluate linguistic elements. The study of history is then a second order of objectification. Gazing upon historical processes, a historian interprets and evaluates these, drawing connections and identifying chains of events that need not ever have entered the consciousness of the agents involved in them. Let's call this practice of historical interpretation "historiography," to keep it distinct from history in the first sense. We thus have three primary aspects of meaning in history: *temporalization,* which is inherent in practices as they relate to their respective fields; *historicization,* which is a product of the metalinguistic evaluation of practices; and *historiography,* the study of temporality and historicization. As we have defined them, the three correspond to different perspectives, and it should be clear that the production of history is itself a temporal process, just as the practice of historiography is both temporalized and potentially historic.

The official conquest of Yucatán by Spanish forces was in 1547, and the following years saw the development of discourse in which Spanish and Maya languages intermingled. Regional diversity was and still is a fact of life in Yucatán. Since the fall of Mayapan confederate rule in the mid-1400s, and probably long before, Yucatán was subdivided into some sixteen political geographic regions, which differed significantly in their internal structure and external relations (Farriss 1984, Roys 1957). It is likely, although as yet undemonstrated, that there were commensurate variations in the language and repertoires spoken across the peninsula. From the outset of Spanish presence in Yucatán, there were significant numbers of Maya people who allied themselves with the Europeans, whereas others resisted. With few exceptions Maya resistance was aimed not at overthrowing the new order imposed by the Spanish but at gaining access to power within the emerging social structures. As Victoria Bricker (1981), Nancy Farriss (1984), and Grant Jones (1989) show persuasively, the Yucatec Maya sought to secure for themselves a position in the colonial society. This appears to be true even when they were pursuing the strategies of flight (Farriss 1978, Jones 1989) and millenarian appeals to a purely Indian future (see Bricker 1981 and Sullivan 1989), and even while consolidating regions of resistance, such as the southern frontier, from which Spaniards were physically excluded (Jones 1989, Sullivan 1989). The principals leading these movements were usually people who had had extensive contact with the Spanish, were bilingual and bicultural to a degree, and went on to found communities in which Spanish and Maya practices were fused rather than isolated. So the diversity that preexisted the conquest continued and was further refracted by the different postures that Maya communities assumed toward the Spanish. In linguistic and cultural terms, this took the shape of varying kinds and degrees of hybridization and a highly diversified field of reception.

Colonial Yucatán was the site of a struggle over history. The Catholic church played a defining role in setting the goals of colonization and *conquista* 'conquest'. They aimed at nothing less than the remaking of Indian souls, driven in part by the millennial belief that a new world order could be created, achieving in the New World a "city of God" guided by the spiritual precepts of medieval Catholicism. The influence of the Franciscans in Yucatán was central in this regard. One of its offshoots was a discourse justifying the conquest on the grounds that the Holy Spirit had already been there prior to the arrival of the Spaniards. This was based partly on what were perceived to be traces of an already present Catholicism in Maya paganism—the use of the cruciform symbol, a practice apparently similar to baptism, and the impressive albeit debauched spirituality of the Maya people. The idea was that they had fallen under the evil influence of the devil, and the aim was to free them through tutelage in Catholic ways. Thus they defined the present in accordance with an imagined past. For our purposes, this illustrates an interesting twist on the typical retrospective character of historical objectification. Instead of defining the past according to the present, the present was objectified according to a past, a past inferred on the basis of its erstwhile traces in the present.

A great emphasis was placed upon the expression of truth and authenticity, and this gave rise to frequent metalinguistic evaluations. The relative opacity of Maya culture to the Spanish colonizers, the ardent attempts of the missionaries to refashion Maya morality, and the requirements of Spanish record keeping all served to foreground the correspondence between what people asserted to be the case and what was the case. Being both scarce and sought after, truth became a measure of value and a quality to be affirmed. This shows up in metalinguistic affirmations such as "this is true and agreed upon by all parties present," "these are our true feelings, we who are genuine nobles," and so forth. In expressions like these the deictic refers to the discourse of which it is a part, and the description is metadiscursive.

Metalinguistic evaluation was also pervasive in the translation practices of both Spanish and Maya agents. Translation is based on a series of contingent judgments about the meaning of an original statement, the appropriate rendering of that meaning in the translation, and how to handle portions of the original deemed to be "untranslatable," whether by reason of unintelligibility, subtlety of meaning, or moral-ethical reprehensiveness. In the highly charged contexts of religious conversion, legal dispute, and conflict, these judgments became focal. For instance, in rendering into Spanish evidence of idolatry among the Maya, some Franciscan friars judged the demonic incantations of Maya sorcerers to be unworthy of translation. Inversely, key words like *Dios* 'God', *cruz* 'cross', and *misa* 'mass (the sacrament)' were retained in Spanish even when used in Maya-language discourse. Such decisions are indexes of agents' consciousness of the multiple fields through which their discourse would circulate.

In attempts to read documents from the colonial period, all these factors come into play. Texts refract the fields in which they were produced and received. There are significant limitations on what can be determined with certainty, and yet by seeking to contextualize them as richly as possible, by attending to the distributions of relevant indicators, we can reveal dimensions of discourse otherwise hidden. Let's illustrate this with a brief example.

In the 1560s, shortly after the conquest of Yucatán, an acrimonious dispute erupted involving the Maya population, the Franciscans, the secular clergy, the colonists, and the nonreligious colonial administrators. Briefly put, the dispute turned on the severity of Franciscan attempts to extirpate what they considered to be the idolatrous practices of the Indians. After the initial wave of baptisms and evangelization, many Maya evidently continued to "worship idols," practicing various kinds of blood sacrifice and holding secret ritual events beyond the gaze of Franciscan surveillance. When this became clear to the Franciscans, their reaction was swift and harsh. Public trials were held, native testimony was extracted under torture, Maya idols and books were destroyed, and many members of the native nobility perished or were fined and incarcerated. The documentary record of the period, in both Maya and Spanish, gives extensive evidence of the polarizing effect of what turned out to be an unofficial inquisition.

Among the documents produced in this context were a series of letters, some bearing the signatures of Maya nobles, descrying the excesses of the friars and pleading with the Crown for help. On the face of it, these letters had the ring of truth, as they appeared to express the authentic sentiments of the Indians suffering persecution. There also emerged contradictory letters in Maya, however, praising the priests for their attempts to convert the Indians and pleading with the Crown to send *more* Franciscans. Among the best-known examples of the latter type were two series of letters, dated in February 1567, bearing the names of over thirty Maya signatories (Zimmermann 1970). If the bitter denunciations seemed true, the letters of praise seemed to fly in the face of facts and were long considered to be falsified concoctions actually authored by Franciscans attempting to defend themselves. The appearance of inauthenticity was only heightened in that the praise letters seemed to be based on a single template, all saying more or less the same thing. From a Western perspective, the similarities were too great to be coincidental, and it looked as if a single Spanish form letter had been translated into Maya, recopied a total of thirteen times, and adorned with forged Maya signatures. A month later, while the dispute was still raging, another letter in Maya was sent to the Crown, spelling out the great affection that the Maya had for the Franciscans, requesting that more be sent, and condemning the secular clergy who were beginning to outnumber Franciscans (March 9, 1567, Legajo 359 in the section "Mexico" of the Archivo General de Indias in Seville, Spain). In the light of the earlier texts, this letter, too, appeared bogus, or at least it seemed to grossly distort Maya experience. The appearance was confirmed by yet another letter, this one in Spanish, dated April 12, 1567, and signed by nobles from the province of Mani (Zimmermann 1970; cf. facsimile of map of Mani, in Figure 7.2 above). The Mani letter bitterly denounced the Franciscan excesses and alluded to other letters concocted by the Franciscans. How could the same people tortured by the frenetic friars turn around and express love for them? How could any of the praise letters be authentic expressions of their authors' feelings, if they all seemed to say the same thing in nearly the same words?

This is where a practice perspective makes a real difference. Recognizing that all speech communities are internally differentiated, we start by noting that according to local records, tribute lists, and other censuslike materials, the signatories of the praise letters came mostly from parts of the peninsula where the Franciscans had not struck with torture. The letter of denunciation came from Mani, the site at which an infamous auto-da-fé had been held, and its signatories were among the victims. In other words, the field of discourse production and reception was not unitary, and there was no single Maya perspective to which a text could be true. Second, the particular form of intertextuality defined by a series of nearly identical expressions corresponds to a discourse device well known in Maya genres: repetition. Far from indicating falsity, it suggests a ritualized attempt to produce an effect on the royal addressee. Third, although it is true that many of the signatures appear to have been written in the same scribal hand as the bodies of the texts, this was common practice. There was no tradition among the Maya, so far as we know, of affixing signatures to written texts. The important point is not whether so-and-so actually penned his name but whether he authorized its placement. On this point recall the difference between animator (cf. scribe), author, and principal. The issue is whether signatories were *principals.* Fourth, the grouping of multiple signatures on a single document is a powerful expression of political solidarity, quite apart from the content of the text. It is part of a strategy of officialization. Fifth, the texts all show particularly Maya stylistic and rhetorical features, many of which are missing from the Spanish translations because they depend on verse parallelism specific to Maya grammar. This suggests that whoever authored the letters was well versed in Maya genres or was collaborating with Maya speakers sensitive to the subtleties of high rhetoric. The discrepancy between Spanish and Maya versions is a reflex of the fragmentation of the field into disjoint interpretive communities. Finally, the March letter is much longer and more detailed than the earlier ones, and the signatures it bears are idiosyncratic. It made its way to the Archives of the Indies in Seville, suggesting that it went through the appropriate channels in the discursive field to reach the higher authorities. This trajectory further indicates that even if it were descriptively false, it is authentic, and even if it were inauthentic to the opinions of its signatories, it became truth. The letter is reproduced in facsimile as Figure 12.1 (I have added numbers in the left margin).

We turn now to the letter as the product of communicative practice in fields marked by hybridization and changing historical consciousness. The letter opens with the following salutation. The whole numbers indicate lines in the original

S. C. R. M.

Ca delos indios
y
a su mag. esta traduzida

yoklal tumul chabilon con chambel vinic canaate cayumil ti dios. yetel
tech cech noh ahau ahtepale yanix ticol cayoc lukeç lauac bal kananil tech
xan yoklal hach thonanoon tac lacal yalan auoc yalan akab hibahunon
con batabob yetel canuc teylob yan vay ti provinçia yucatan lae yoklal
vay caluumile ah otochnalonixan. coltic capat cante tuxicin cech ahaue
vchebalix achaic vmuculxan hetun cathan lae hach kanan vuilal
vay ti probinçia yucatan sant fran.co padresob toon. vchebal yalicob
vthanil dios heklay doctrina xpiana vkabae. vchebalix yalicob missa
cachaante caix vtzac vkecticonoob tac vayil thane vthanil caçicih
tahul heklai euangelio vkaba tumen españolesobe / yoklal hach kanã
vuilal vyanhal ychil cacahal. habla bacacix likul tac chi hulci obispo
tatuxchi frai fran.co toral vkabae, yulçah caix vthoxah ek padresob clerigo
vcate vkabaobe cau vacunahob ticanan cahob ychilcacahal yalabob v
thandios toon. vchebalix yalicob missa cachaante tamuk vkecticonob tume
yah tzol thanob yoklal mail yohelob vayil thane. hach manaan sant fran.co pa
dresob toon. yoklal tibij vlah benelob cau vecahob vbaob ti hach kananix
toonxan kananix vuilal vhach cultalob vay tac yaame yoklal hach vh
benob. vlob vaylae hach yohelmobix camayathanil hach tibilix vkecticonob
cuchi ah miatzobixan, hetun toon helelae maconcoon cakahçicob çança mal
habla bacacix yoklal chambel maceualon / maix cahach naatma hibic
vmucul tamuk vtukulcolob ticuchi tisant fran.co padresob heuac yoklal v
hach chichicunahob thanob cokol, tac lacal con chambel vinice cauzahob vbaob
tibail vcah suezobe vchebalix ▬ bauçic calobil yoklal hach bulanoon tu
zal pach çicin cuchi. yoklal maconcoon. cabeltic yuchiben beel cakil cabil. y.
cabelixan maitac vchibil coli tamuk caçiçinil thian tamukix capapatic.
vuich caçiçin hek laobi chambel kate cakulibin tu zicol tamuk capaticcaba
tibal ticeu yoklal manan vcux col maayox. y hic ahtepp ineob baia laobi pa
dresob. vhach homol zah cacuxolal. y. vzahonix. tu yail tukecticoon. tac çi
pilxan. hetun helelae hach cucu kahcah cacahob tiob yoklal hetun
clerigosobe machan thanobti. tihun lukul hetun sant fran.co padresobe hach
tibil vthanob toon. hach tunucix vkecticon. lay lic colticob helelac yoklal

FIGURE 12.1 *Carta de los Batabes*, March 9, 1567

ma con coon v ɔaicob yol v cambal tob ca vayil thane licix yoccic ha tuholob camchenob. laobix ɔa ha tacholob xan bala hetun cu belticob toone hach tibil yoklal yan yolob v xakinoon. v mehen dios yetel luk cahix v cah takoch yl matix v cahob tu ciciɔen tabal amehenob cech noh ahue. licix v ɔaxunticonob. tamuk v hach ɔaicon ti yolob. hach v nah. v hah cun cathan ahalach vinic yan vay lae yoklal lai ohel mail licix yilic xan/ he clerigosobe bala hun ppelili v nu cul doctrina. y. v doctrina sant franco padresob maix tan capo chiob xan yoklal ma v yamaonob mananonix ti yolob. yoklalix mataachoon calakmitob kinɔil hil cathanicob lay v il yalloe. maix yohelob cavayil thane maix cohelma v castillathanob xan. maix tan v hach ɔa v baob toon. he tu kamaan hal toonobe. lic coc cic cabaob ti tilob yetel licix ca chaic v nu cul v belob ek padresob. maix mac ma ohel mail licil v ppol malob yan tacobix v conolob bay españolesobe v amatan v conolobe yan tac vinicob conic v baal v baob. licix yoccic v baob ti juezil tamuk v ɔaic cob v cipit olalob v chi bal v ppol malob. tilavac mac cu hokol tu tanob. ti chala ti mail v chac. v beel ticob/ yoklal manaan yuchucilob ti hach yanob ti yol v yom hal v baal v baob. yoklal lay hc cu çacach tuc hicob. can çamal. hetun sant franco padresobe, ma taach v beel ticob ti bucah lae maix bal cumal ti yolob xan. hex v ɔan. v belob clerigosob lae hach kuxob toon tamuk v ɔa ɔa lic capach cabebeelte ti yotochob. lauac bal cayalicob toon yoklal yan tacob yotochob. yomix v palilobiek vinicob yan tacobix v ɔiminob. y. v thulob. hetun tu cultalob ychil cacahalobe caca lah ɔentob. y. v bal yotochob maix bal v bolil maix tan cakatab tiob yoklal cub laconob tiob. çah conix tiob xan. yoklal cah cananob. y. licix ca ɔaic yah cu chil v cuchob. tu katicob. tu benelob ti cahal cah. maix tan v bo toob. baix v cah obispo licix ca ɔaic ah cuchob ti mananix v boo hil. licix ca ɔaic v yabal v hanal[illegible]. maix tan v boton hetun ek padreob licix ca cicibotiob tu kuchul ti yabil v canan cahob. tamukix acaput botic cech noh ahau tah tepal lauac likul tu chi obispo yan vay tu provincia il yucatanme bala may tun v il baloochac a gobernador ti don luis cespedes de obiedo yoklal lay li çacach toci coon a naat v cah toon lomav chu ocanil yaobti. y. obispo yan vay ti probincia. ocanix yaobti. y. tu lacal ek padresob maix cil macob yol licil v num ciconob ti ya. caix v cham bel kal bonob ti mac cab. ti matan v benelob v chab yuchucil yic nalob a juezo timuk ca çam tic v bal caba hek lay takmob. licix v toh licon ti cotochob bale maix cohel ma v abal v chun licil v numçiconob ti ya caix v ɔacomaltob a justicia yetel ohayo españolob ... habla maix y antac v yabal v bal caba chabel ca muk y etel capatan lial canticob tu lacalob v ... vinic y anti petene habla bai ti manitac thane, hach kanan doctrina toon yok lal manac y an hetun tu cibil col ti yan sant franco padxeob y ohlal hach v yamaon tac lacal ti mana v num cah y aob. az mentibil tun cubel tic toon helelae y ohlal y antac v tioib justicia tu michob tun

FIGURE 12.1 (Continued)

y oklal hetutal v beelticob lauac memeah y a cookole y an justiçia anticoon y oklal la
y hiob lauac v abal kanã tan labebal cayumil ti dios y etel atan labebalie ced
canok ahau taytepale, hach tibilixcom he hi ca ayulec cech cayume ca acha
v yan hal tza comal y oklal tukoltzileon, caçacach y lab y ocob y aob ti y ok
y anticonob, habla hach kanamie v uilal, hetun a halach vinic y an v ailae, bin
bin hulue xane v tza ca ɔsab a ajpit olaltiob cantzac v hach anticunob, y etel okot
baix cacah tech caaturxchitob sant fran^co^ padresob toon v chebal v tal v ɔocol
v pay be doctrina v cibahob toon y oklal hach tibil v beelticob ti hach hehes ci y ut
cimicob, hach vizie v ximbalob, ena canah ca can v beelob, y oklal hach
v katob benelob teticaom tu ɔicole ena lai tah oklal lial coltic cayumintu
y oklal v hach y amaon cayamaobrean lai tach oklal coltic v y ab çalob v ay
v tzix ca avalab tu no çeibob ti provinçial cantuxchitob: tu caten l nobi
ahbenelobe y oklal çach y oçel monob ah v chbenob tayie y etel hach ɔoc
lukaamie v mayatkanob y oklalie y ohel mobie hibal kanã toon v che
bal ca tibil çab tu tan dios. y etel tibilix catacob v chayom xan ca vec
lah cob ti cahob y oklal vimo, maix mac y antoon xan hiax v ɔaicob ti
y olob v hach cambaltob v ayil thane y oklal lai v bebb ca ça mal ma
tom v malob tiy olob ç ɔil titakinob mah bu cahob ek padresob çach
ch atakim v katob çach v katob v hach y ab hal v takinob tamuk v co
coonicob v inotoon titakimil, habla çetun than lic calic tech lae maix v
tucil y oklal v hach habil y oklal lic capaktumtic y oklal hotuckal
y abil hulciob ek padresob tu pachob españolob mainã hutulob ti
y oheltob ca v ayil thane chabel hutulitiob, habla mah v cambalte oc
ci ti padreil y oklal ^tob^ maili au mariu mari e noh xibi hach paahxam liax v
pol mal bin v cah v lahobe ba ca cie y oheltob chambel than ek padresobe
y anta cob v yahob ek laitu lic cacantic v belob tech lae y oklal lic v çacach
tuchicob humachikin hibic bin y ab hebal v bahubaob dios v nah y an
toon y oklal tiy an tulacal ti lai v chu hach v nah hutul sant fran^co^
padre, mav y abal ek padresobe, mathan ba ca cobix y nahtiob
fray fran^co^ de la torre provinçial v ay helelae y oklal hach tibil v beel
y ohelie v ayil thane çach cayamaçean y oklal v çacach tzedicoon
ca chapahi tac y am ma coo coon v y atzemil ohomix colti maixtã
v helel çelexane v tam v beltic v bel v ac habi huli oydor loaysa
v xo cobon v ay lae hach y abix v inic cimictoon çach v nah ɔsab
a ajpit olal ti don luis çelelae cantzac v caxocticoon, hach ɔa cayatil
y oklal dios, ca xoc coon tu caten, y oklal y anta cob cahob hulob
y ohtob v ba ob tu tom halach v inic hiax v ɔaic v y atzil ca cocunac v pata
nob lic v muchic a ajpit olal v chebal tu v hach ɔoic cayatil, laitun
ta çoklal lial camul oktic ca ba tech caaɔsab cay atzil y oklal çetu capa
ta çoklal lial camul oktic ca ba tech ca ɔsab cay atzil
ton tac y unmlobe y etel lic ca ɔaic tech chambel pakbil ta nam hach muk
tzil lial v tal, maixetab cu chintaçal toon çach a çumuy aon mabal v bal
caba/bala çetu agoua nede [illegible] y aylae hach [illegible] v beel v y ii cah
lae tamulabo cah v bal a ca çah, ma tom v cib ximbal ti ca çal cah tu ɔicob y o
klal ma hay cu v beel, bala ɔa a ajpit olal ti y uchucil v chebal v benelob la
v ac v amac v tibilil xpianosob, caxicob v xoconob, cantzac v ceb çal
ca hati y oklal ma co cõnon con v ayil v inice hach nach tacix v yom
ca cahalob, he hi ca v hunab beelte maih çeb bin v ɔocebal tu mene, y oklal

FIGURE 12.1 (Continued)

macon coon cah vay yucatome hach pot manaan tihokal v lubil luum
vaye lai tahoklal lual cahach ok tic caba v bimah ca cah tuni a voc tu
ni akab ceh ah tepale caaab ca yatzil tihach ceb ca tac yuchucil ti
gouernador cautzac v yabhal ahbeel nalob tumen ahalach vinic yok
lal lay cakati v ceb hal hach sa v thanil ti hach tibilil cakati tihalach
vinic yoklal hach tibil yolt oon v hach yamaon ixan hach bin ix v cici anton
tetu sicole. bin ix yante dios yetel tech cech ah tepale yoklal camaat
maixan mail taach v haual yanti coon hach tibilix colti. hach caya
mai xan yoklal v yamaon he tun cathan lae coltic v saab v firmasob
cah an tulob lae bi defensorob cautzac auoheltic hach talil ticol
he ca okot batech lae, caix yetez tigouernador cautzac v natic caix v tzac
v hach anticoon cautuchite ca sib hun tech. cautzac auoheltic yail ca cah
ceh noh ahau tah tepale. hai li lae. vay ti civdad de merida. yucatan
tubolonpic v kinil yuil marco. Año de mill y quis y sesenta y siete,
dios v hach canantech. tuyabil hab tava hauhil cathan talacal
coon batabe. S. C. R. m.

v thanamilob ah nam avah tan lahulob
v ybmic acilich kabob cech ah tepale.

Don Ju.º Pech / Don Juan Can / Fran.co Chel / Fran.co Chel

Pº Ek / don pedro canche / don andres bitz / Die.º balam

Ju.º euan / Juan tun / Andres Chel / p.º de Ju.º Pok

Ju.º Zul / Ju.º Ake / luis pech / p.º Ku... / Fran.co pech

Fran.co mutul / juan chim / Fran.co can / juan magum

pedro v huchim / Juan mutul / pedro pot / Fran.co vicab

P.º diez de / Martin Gibarte / Diego rrodriguez bivian / Al.º de arevalo ynterprete

E yo ... de castro escrivano de su mag.d real pu.co y del concejo de esta cibdad de merida probinçia de yucatan y yndias del mar oçeano doy fee y testimonio verdadero que en mi presençia y de los t.s yuso escritos firmaron esta carta arriba contenida, escrita en lengua de esta probinçia las personas yndios naturales dellas cuyos nonbres de los que arriba se declaran q dixeron ser mag.s gobernadores de los pueblos q estan poblados en la probinçia de aquin thel a con tun y the can e v cama que esen estas d.has probinçias e gobernaçion de yucatan despues de la aver entendido y leido sele como en ella se conti.e y declara por persona q entiende bien la d.ha lengua y todos a una dixeron ser su bol untad escrebir la d.ha carta a su mag.d real y lo firmaron de sus nonbres los q sabian firmar y los no sabian firmaron otros por ellos y es to lo se como persona q entiendo parte de la d.ha lengua y asi lo entendi de los naturales y asi mismo lo firmaron los defensores de los d.hos naturales y el ynterprete general de esta gobernaçion a pedimento del susod.o de cuyo pedim.o di el presente en la d.ha ciudad de merida a nueve de marzo de mill e quis.os e sesenta y siete a.s siendo t.s el padre ... de la torre y los d.hos defensores e ynterprete en fee de lo qual fize mi signo

... de castro

FIGURE 12.1 (Continued)

(1–6), and the fractional numbers indicate smaller line breaks that I have introduced to facilitate discussion.

1.1 ***Yoklal tumulchabilon*** 'For we who are gathered,
1.2 ***con chambel uinic*** we common men,
1.3 ***canaate*** we understand
1.4 ***cayumil ti dios,*** our Lord in God
2.1 ***yetel tech cech*** and you who are
2.2 ***noh ahau ahtepale*** Great King and Majesty.
2.3 ***yanix ti col ca dzoc lukes*** We want you to do
2.4 ***lauac bal kananil*** something needed,
3.1 ***tech xan*** you indeed.
3.2 ***Yoklal hach thonanon taclacal*** For we are all truly humbled
3.3 ***yalan auoc*** beneath your foot,
3.4 ***yalan akab*** beneath your hand
3.5 ***hibahunon*** however many we be,
4.1 ***con batabob*** we chiefs
4.2 ***yetel canuc teylob*** and our elders
4.3 ***yan uay ti provinçia yucatan lae*** here in the Province of Yucatán.
5.1 ***yoklal uay caluumile*** For here in our land,
5.2 ***ah otochnalonixan.*** we are natives indeed.
5.3 ***coltic capat cante taxicin*** We want to recount something in your ear,
5.4 ***cech ahaue*** you king,
6.1 ***uchebalix a chaic unucul xan*** so that you might take up its response.
6.2 ***he tun cathan lae*** Here we speak:'

Several features of these opening lines of the letter indicate its locatedness in the discursive field of its time and place. Let's start with the participation framework. The authors of the text present themselves as "common men," "chiefs," and "our elders," and the direct addressee is "you who are great king and majesty" and "you king." In referring to themselves in these terms, the authors have adopted the labels most relevant to the Crown: They are common compared to the king, but they are nobles and elders relative to their local context. At this time it was Crown policy to recognize the legitimacy of noble lineages among the Maya, and these ways of presenting themselves familiarize them in terms of that policy. The epithet "great king and majesty" is a gloss on the Spanish expression *rey y majestad.* It is not the only way the Spanish could have been rendered in Maya—translations are rarely if ever unique—but it is the epithet that appears to have become routinized at this time. Although these terms were in use prior to the Spanish arrival, and *ahau* "ruler" occurs in glyphic texts, their combination in this epithet is unique to the Spanish king. Thus it is virtually a proper name, both referring to the king and indexing his uniqueness. The additional descriptions of the authors, as "gathered" (line 1.1), "truly humbled beneath your foot, beneath your hand" (lines 3.2–3.4), and "natives indeed" (line 5.2), repeat the same relations of subordination to the Crown and legitimate representatives of their communities. The expression of humility is cast in a couplet structure, which gives it the appearance of being Maya, with the foot indexing subordination and the hand indexing the executive capacity of the Crown. Actually, it is more likely to be a case of double-voicing. That is, in the Franciscan correspondence of the period, the friars often expressed loyalty to the high officials of the reign by the expression "we kiss your foot; we kiss your hand." This intertextual echo, then, positions the signatories astride the two identities as Maya and yet converted.

It is also noteworthy that indexical terms establish from the outset the "we," the "you," and the "here" (in Yucatán). One of the most provocative changes that appears to have taken place in Maya language discourse after the conquest was the introduction of such indexicals, to bind discourse to the deictic coordinates of its production and reception. In pre-Columbian hieroglyphic inscriptions, and in the more traditional Maya genres such as the prophetic histories in the Books of Chilam Balam, deictics of this sort are virtually absent. The idea is that texts were either physically bonded to their locus of production by being inscribed on monuments, or the stories they told were presented as unquestioned truth. What we find in the colonial period is the need to specify the perspective from which the truth of a discourse is asserted. This is a reflex of the radical diversification of the field under colonial rule and also likely a response to the requirements of official Spanish documents: that they be dated, located in space, and of specified authorship. That the referent of "here" includes the entire province of Yucatán and not some more restricted locus is a further signal of the address structure, since it is from the transatlantic perspective that the entire province can be totalized as a single "here." Thus it involves a covert transposition or decentering, from local to global fields. From the official vantage point, these features are requisite to the text's being legitimate. In terms of Maya discourse history, they indicate a major shift in the relation between textual forms and the actors who made them. With the emergence of a first person narrator comes a new way of evaluating text. This is further evident in the explicitly metalinguistic formula "We want to recount something in your ear, so that you might take up its response," followed by the presentative deictic "Here we speak." The reference to the king's ear implies the desired directness of contact that the letter seeks to achieve, and the "response" encodes the authors' hope that he will follow its pleadings.

Shortly after this, the letter petitions that the Crown send more Franciscans, and this, too, displays a complex metalinguistic sensibility. The friars are needed to impart the Word of God to the natives, a statement of purpose consistent with the Spanish view of the spiritual conquest. Interestingly, the letter carefully displays the authors' knowledge of the Spanish terms for the elements of evangelization: Christian Doctrine (using the Greek-derived form of *xp̄iana*), the mass, and the Gospel. This word choice indexes that the authors are indeed converted and have been well instructed by the friars, but it also signals their awareness of the duality in the discursive field. A predominantly Maya description (lines 8.1, 10.1) is immediately followed by a relative clause ("which is called") with the Spanish gloss. Notice that the "preaching" (line 9.1) is never translated into Spanish, even though the Spanish term *predicar* fits the Maya hand in glove. The rhetorical motivation for this absence of Spanish is that preaching is an activity the priests engaged in but is not itself a determinate part of the liturgy or sacred texts, and, as it says in line 9.2, the friars preached entirely in Maya. This is repeated several times in the document and was indeed one of the most salient successes of the Franciscans. Their mastery of Maya language was probably the single most important key to their effectiveness.

8.1 ***uchebal yalicob uthanil dios*** 'so they can tell us the Word of God,
8.2 ***heklay doctrina xp̄iana ukabae*** which is called the Christian Doctrine,
8.3 ***uchebalix yalicob missa ca chante*** and so they can say mass for us to watch
9.1 ***caix utzac utzecticonob*** and so they might preach to us
9.2 ***tac uayil thane*** in our language of here
10.1 ***uthanil cahçiçahul*** the word of our fellow human,
10.2 ***heklai Euangelio ukaba*** which is called the Gospel
10.3 ***tumen Espanolesobe /*** by the Spaniards /'

If the Franciscans are portrayed as the good guys, the secular clergy (clergy members unaffiliated with an order) and those who brought them are the bad guys in this text and other ones like it. Throughout the text, there is an oscillation between praise for the Franciscans and condemnation of the clergy. The clergy, who are described throughout the letter as the "black fathers," are said to preach through interpreters; avoid the company of the Maya; maintain large, wealthy households; and have children. Their ways are twisted. They abuse and frighten the Maya rather than guiding them. The assault on the secular clergy is exquisite in the latter parts of the letter. The following extracts give a taste of it.

92.1 ***hach cha takin ukatob*** 'to take money is what they wish;
92.2 ***hach ukatob*** they wish
92.3 ***uhach yabhal utakinob*** their riches to be really great'

Immediately after criticizing the clergy for their lack of poverty, the authors once again assert the deliberate truth of their words and repeat that after twenty-five years these people, who came from behind the Spanish like an evil shadow, still do not even know the local language.

93.3 ***habla hetu than lic calic tech lae***
'So here are the words in which we say to you,
94.1 ***maix u tuçil*** and it is no lie.
94.2 ***yoklal uhach hahil*** For it is the truth
94.3 ***yoklal lic capaktumtic*** that we deliberate.
94.4 ***yoklal hotuc kal*** For twenty-five
95.1 ***yabil hulciob ek padresob*** years ago black fathers arrived
95.2 ***tupachob espanolesob*** behind the Spaniards.

95.3 ***maina hu tulob ti*** And not one of them
96.1 ***yoheltob ca uayil thane*** knows our language of here.'

Throughout the attack on the secular clergy, a strong Franciscan voice is evident and almost surely indexes that the friars either colluded in the making of the document or, minimally, that their instructions provided the terms in which the secular clergy were evaluated. We know from other sources that at this time the Franciscans were in competition with secular clergy over the right to evangelize the Maya. They had been the first religious missionaries to arrive in Yucatán, and they fought to maintain their position as the sole guardians of the Maya conversion. Mastery of Maya language, prolonged living in intimate contact with Maya communities, and the vow of poverty were emblematic of their mission. That Maya authors attacked the secular clergy in the first place suggests that they were aligned with the Franciscans, but that they did so in precisely the terms of self-proclaimed Franciscan qualities goes further. It embodies the political alignment in a sustained dialogism. Although they are native nobles speaking their own language, it is the voice of their allies that they express, transposed from Spanish into Maya and submerged in the tropes of Maya rhetoric. The overall effect is to bind the Franciscans to the "here" of Yucatán and to distantiate the seculars by continuously excluding them from the participant node of "we from here." This dual voicing comes through in the self-descriptions of the authors as well, for they justify the call for more Franciscans on the grounds that without the guidance of the friars, they might fall back into the idolatrous ways of their forefathers. Here they describe themselves from the Franciscan perspective, aligning their ritual practices with the "devil."

23.4 ***yoklal hach bula noon*** 'For we were truly mired
24.1 ***tu dzalpach ciçin cuchi*** beneath the oppression of the devil in the past'

The closing of the letter once again situates it in the nonreligious political structures to which it was addressed. The signatures are mentioned, as are their *defensores* (local officials of the government charged with defending the Indians' rights) and the governor. Truth and authenticity are again affirmed, and the authors display a keen awareness of the likely trajectory of their text. The text itself is described as a "written paper," indicating its claim to legitimate status, and its authors pray that the governor will send it on to the Crown rather than keeping it in the local confines of the peninsula.

129.3 ***hetun cathan lae*** 'Here we speak.
129.4 ***coltic udzaab ufirmasob*** We want the signatures to be placed
130.1 ***cah antulob*** of our helpers
130.2 ***laobi defensorob*** the defensores
130.3 ***cau tzac auoheltic*** so that you might know
130.4 ***hach talil ti col*** that this truly comes from our heart.

131.1 ***he ca okot batech lae,*** Here we beg you
131.2 ***caix yeteh ti gouernador*** and to the governor also
131.3 ***cautzac unatic*** that he might understand it,
132.1 ***caix utzac uhach anticoon*** that he might truly help us,
132.2 ***cautuchite cadzib hun tech*** that he might send our written paper to you'

Following this, the text is dated in the Spanish calendar (March 9, 1567), the place of production is stated (Mérida), and the signatures are affixed. The smaller script at the bottom of the letter is an affirmation, by the official scribe, that the authors actually wanted to write this letter and affixed their own signatures before witnesses. Among the witnesses was Fray Francisco de la Torre (line 12), a well-known Franciscan who is mentioned with praise in the body of the letter.

Although this example is far too meager to stand for the entire discourse from which it came, it illustrates several important points that recur again and again in other documents and that are among the core features of the framework developed in this book. The depth and subtlety of the voicing are typical of contemporaneous discourse and illustrate the kinds of phenomena Bakhtin subsumed under the idea of "dialogism." They also reinforce Bakhtin's observation that voicing is value laden, and elements imported from elsewhere in the field bring with them the evaluative vantage points of their sources. The use of deictics is similarly reflective of a realignment of the values attaching to expression and the emergence of new forms of communicative practice. The self-portrayals of the authors indicate one of the most consequential forms of domination, namely, that Maya actors came to describe themselves in the terms of their oppressors. As a rhetorical strategy, this looks much like what Bourdieu called "familiarization," a way of enhancing the effectiveness of expression. But it was a dangerous game, for by routinely describing oneself in such terms, one makes the terms become habitual, and they ultimately take on the invisibility of what is "natural" or commonsensical. Submerged in this way, overt domination becomes covert hegemony.

The use of the deictics is part of the same process. Although all the forms were standard Maya, they were configured so as to accord with the requirements of Spanish discursive practice. The language choice serves at once to legitimate the claims of the authors to being true Maya nobles and to hide the hybrid sources of their text. This does *not* mean that the document is false, as the traditional view would have it, but that the social world from which it speaks was much more complicated and opaque than simple truth would allow. What we see in these apparently mundane linguistic features are the traces of a profound refashioning of Maya actors as agents of communicative practice.

Much of the preceding discussion touches on the kinds of objectification that we said produce "history." In the aspects of temporalization that situate this document and others like it in their multiple contexts, we can also see the traces of an objectifying gaze. At its lower threshold, this is inherent in the indexical centering of discourse in its participant framework, in the self-descriptions that objectify authors according to the values of their addressees, in the metalinguistic assertions of truth, and in labels of the discourse as being a "recounting in the ear of the king" and a "written paper." In physical terms, the gaze is most clearly embodied in the witnesses who must be present to assure that the text is really what it claims to be. That the main witness of this text was a Franciscan is eloquent testimony of the surveillance role of the friars. Other documents present themselves with terms including *carta* 'letter', *mapa* 'map', *deslinde de tierras* 'land survey', *ppis luum* 'land surveys', *acuerdo* 'agreement', *carta de venta* 'bill of sale', *takyah than* 'final will and testament', *testamento* 'testament', and *informe* 'report'. All such terms index the discursive categories in which the documents were framed and according to which they were meant to be understood. Just as genre labels in present-day English or Yucatec Maya imply relevancy structures, participant frameworks, and modes of reception, so, too, in the colonial materials. A proper understanding of the terms and their precise distributions in texts can reveal a great deal about the metalinguistic consciousness and rhetorical strategies of the participants.

These are of course never merely linguistic facts, even though we identify them through linguistic evidence. They are also part of a broader refiguring of local history under the dominating surveillance of the colonizers, and this duality is what makes them interesting. The remaking of history was inculcated in the Maya through teaching, preaching, and the forced practice of Spanish routines. Nearly every corner of native life was regulated, and the instruments for internalizing the regulations were set in place. Insofar as these regulations bore on language, they were metalinguistic. There is nothing magic or arcane in this observation. Far from turning world-changing events into a point of grammar, it is meant to make clear that the metalinguistic capacity of language was both a resource and a sensitive indicator of the conquest. Language provided the means of projecting domination from the level of what Maya people did every day to the level of how they understood and evaluated what they were doing.

Take the case of the southern frontier, current-day Belice, which was still unconquered in the seventeenth century. A renegade Maya "king" named Can Ek rules over a dominion centered in the Peten region of Guatemala and commands an imposing army of Maya soldiers prepared to resist the Spanish to their death. The word gets out that there are divisions in the rebel ranks and that Can Ek will not cede to Spanish rule until a preordained date, which has not yet arrived. Franciscan friars resolve to convince Can Ek that his submission to the foreigners was foretold by his own prophetic histories, once again asserting their privileged knowledge of Maya ways. For reasons that remain uncertain, Can Ek lays down arms in the last decade of the seventeenth century, on the very date that would have corresponded to a change in rule according to the Mayan calendar, as understood by the Franciscans (see Jones 1989). Did they convince him that the conquest was inevitable? Did he cede for other reasons? However we answer these provocative questions, they indicate one of the likely Spanish strategies of conversion. Seeing that Maya people had a calendrical system that they used to calibrate both the past and the future, Spanish agents used this knowledge to legitima their own designs. In other words, an indigenous mode of understanding th genre of prophecy was co-opted for the purposes of conquest.

Over the long haul, the conquest has become a supercategory in native histor cal consciousness. In present-day Yucatán many Maya adults express the prophe that the world as we know it is approaching an end, after which it will be re-cr ated. What is most striking is that the present world is defined as having com into existence at the arrival of the Spanish. The conquest marks the genesis of th world of the Christian cross. Many, including Don Chabo, believe that it will b replaced by a new creation in which the Maya are free of the oppression of th Europeans. Although such beliefs might appear quaint to us, they have been at th heart of armed revolt among the Maya on several occasions in the past, notabl during the protracted and bloody caste war of the mid-1800s. The lesson of th and the Can Ek incident is that genres of understanding, like prophetic discours are powerful resources in organizing people's beliefs both about language and th world to which it refers.

If Maya communicative practices were reconfigured in the clash with Spaniard they were not entirely replaced by the new ways. Despite the zeal and even freneti energy of the conquest, the conversion was never complete. As we have suggeste it was at best uneven, with pockets of resistance and whiplash effects across th peninsula and throughout the colonial period. To this day, Maya language is spo ken by nearly three-quarters of a million people, and much of the daily lives live out in Yucatán are saturated with the particularities of Maya culture. The Spanis language of Yucatán, the cuisine, the physical characteristics of Yucatecan peopl all bear witness to the vitality of Maya culture. Just as the Maya have been deepl hispanicized, so the predominantly Spanish sectors are marked by Maya.

In linguistic terms, this hybridization is a fundamental part of the meaning struc tures of local discourse. When a colonial document is labeled as a *carta* or *map* therefore, these terms must never be taken at face value. Rather, they index th blending of genres and the irreducible ambivalence of communicative practice The evidence of this begins with the Spanish genre labels, which occur in texts writ ten in Maya language, itself written in Spanish orthography. The signatures displa names like Pedro Puuc, Martin Pech, and Gonzalo Uitzil, in which the first name in dicates that the individual was baptized and the family name locates him in the kin ship system of Maya. Dates are invariably given in the European calendar, but the are frequently phrased in specifically Maya words. God is *Dios,* but the Virgin Mar is *kíichpam kóolebil* 'Beautiful Revered Woman'. Mass is *misa,* but the verb for at tending mass is *chaante* 'to watch (a spectacle)'. As contemporary Maya speakers pu it, everything is *sháak'áan* 'mixed together (as spices mix with food in cooking)'.

This blending is another major obstacle to literal meaning, because it mean that words, even familiar ones, are part of multiple frames of reference, each o which contains elements of the others. As we saw with the example of the 156 letter, it is not enough to scan Maya texts for the presence of "loan terms" fron Spanish, because apparently Maya terms are often used in ways that reflect thei connections to Spanish. Even when Spanish terms are set off in an otherwise Maya discourse, there is no reason to assume that they had their standard meanings. And the same applies to Yucatecan Spanish texts. With or without Maya terms, they are dialogized in a world of which Maya is an unavoidable part. This kind of blending is sometimes called "syncretism," implying that the two cultures can be separated and instances of intrusion can be located in borrowed traits. Yet this view imputes more clarity and discreteness to the process than it has, and it deflects attention from the most important fact—namely, that a new sociocultural world emerged out of the hybridization and developed its own frames of reference. The colonial actors were acutely aware of the problems hybridization posed. Their translation practices were guided by attention to possible misconstruals, and many key terms pertinent to religion, law, and government were expressly left untranslated.

Fray Pedro Beltrán de Santa Rosa María, the first native Yucatecan speaker to produce a grammar and doctrine in Maya, noted the problem in his Maya rendition of the Doctrina Christiana (1816). Earlier translations of Christian prayer contained egregious errors, he wrote, making it necessary to revise them. For instance, part of the Ave Maria, where it is said that God is above the Virgin (in heaven), was rendered in Maya as *Yumbil yan tauokol*, 'God is on top of you.' In colloquial Maya this implies sexual intercourse. The Body of Christ, referring to the host in the sacrament of Communion, had been rendered with the term *cucutil.* A fluent speaker of colloquial Maya, Beltrán noted that although this term indeed means "body," it was most commonly used to denote the penis (which he chose not to name as such but to allude to euphemistically). One could only wonder what parishioners thought they were doing in taking Communion. Beltrán also observed that the expression *Dios omnipotente* 'Almighty God' had been translated as *Ku citbil.* In purely linguistic terms, the translation was pretty good, he said, but unfortunately it coincided with the name of an indigenous "idol" that members of his community still worshiped in secret. Such examples open the possibility that Maya converts attending mass may have been worshiping their own deities or generating ribald counterreadings of the liturgy. The larger point is this: Hybridization was a fact of life in colonial Yucatán, as it is today, and it affects every phase and element of the communicative process. It is unavoidable, because of the plurality of the fields and interpretive communities. Although translations, Spanish descriptions of Maya practices, and Maya portrayals of the Spanish may all appear secondary, therefore, they are in fact *primary* sources. Just as native-speaker metalanguage distorts the speech it describes, translations and descriptions distort their objects. But both metalanguage and translations embody values directly, and these values are a prime site of hybridity.

In my own research on colonial Maya discourse, I grapple with these problems in a variety of ways. Rather than rehearse examples, of which there are too many, or state conclusions, of which there are too few secure ones, I will end by outlining some of the guiding questions in the research. These questions grew out of the search for an approach to communicative practice and have influenced the framework of this book from its inception. These have proved fruitful in the Yucatecan context, and they may provide a productive starting point for work in other areas. The following clusters of questions are focused rather narrowly on the interpretation of discourse. They are not offered as an alternative to more standard historical study. In order to be applied productively, they must be complemented by broader research, including but not limited to documentary sources in both (or all) relevant languages.

- For any textual feature, how broadly distributed is it across exemplars of its genre, across related genre types, and through time? Widely distributed features are likely candidates for the status of system conventions, whereas specialized ones may define single generic types or innovations. Feature distributions are the basis on which analytic typologies of genres can be worked out, a necessary first step toward tracing the lines of hybridization.
- Can we identify cases of innovation or improvisation through comparing standard with variant features of discourse? If so, where and when do they occur, and how do they sediment? The aim here is to discern the "edges" of a discursive formation in terms of the tension between improvised production and routinized reproduction.
- Change in communicative practices occurs in many ways, some of which can be approached through discourse analysis. At least three kinds of change are identifiable in Yucatecan discourse, each of them indicative of temporalization:

    1. The introduction of novel elements, such as the first person singular or collective author ("I," "we"), metalinguistic labels, and the use of the Spanish term *Dios,* which evidently do not appear in the earlier sources. The former are the reflexes of participation frameworks articulated to emergent, hybrid genres of practice.
    2. The shift in reference of a preexisting Maya expression when used in address to a Spanish participant. For example, the range of reference of the term *ahau* 'ruler' was limited to the king in colonial texts, in contrast to its broader usage for regional rulers in texts directed to indigenous audiences (pre-Columbian and native-addressed sources). An inverse case is provided by the expanded use of the term *yum* 'lord, father' for reference to Spanish friars and authorities in the colonial documents. By contrast, its use in indigenous sources was restricted to male kinsmen in ascending generations (e.g., denoting "father," "grandfather," "paternal uncle"). These changes can be identified only on the basis of broad-scale comparison of the distribution of the terms in many texts.
    3. The extra foregrounding and consequent semantic shifts in native terms that already existed prior to Spanish contact but took on novel associ-

ations following it. One of the clearest examples of this subtle but pervasive change is the symbol of the cross, which was in use among the Maya before Spanish contact but acquired a new salience and range of associations once linked to the omnipotent Christian deity. Such changes are difficult to analyze, since they cannot be mechanically identified but must instead be inferred from usage. They go to the heart of the expressive habits and routine assumptions of those who produced the texts.

- One of the most important foci in Maya textuality is the discourse expression of the context in which a text is produced and to which it is addressed. This holds equally for written and spoken discourse, verbal and image-based modes. In distinction to "content-based" analyses, which focus on what texts *describe*, this statement focuses on reference to authors, addressees, and other participants and on the discursive here and now in which the text arises. The question is: Are there precise commonalities in the text-to-context relations across the various genres under study? Stated more precisely, are the indexical categories configured in constant, or at least consistent, patterns? As an extension of this, how are participants and places of production referred to (including pronouns, descriptive epithets and vocatives, signatures, spatial and temporal deictics, placenames, locative descriptions, dates)?
- For any text or class of texts, what is its trajectory in the field of reception? What are the channels through which it circulates, and what can be determined regarding its interpretation by different receivers? In official documents, like the ones that end up in many archives, reception is mediated by institutional structures such as the town councils, the provincial authorities, the Council of the Indies, and the Crown. For unofficial texts, the trajectory is often obscure. One kind of evidence is the intertextual references and reports of a discourse, which indicate its sources or reception. Whereas multiple voicing can be an obstacle to determining authorship and intent, it is an invaluable resource in tracing intertextual links.

Back to the Present

Read out loud, and slowly. To say "now" is already to have lost the moment. To say "here" is to objectify part of a lived space whose extent is both greater and lesser than the referent. Greater because space and time as experienced are a mutable ground upon which the objects of reference are points projected into a universe of *n* dimensions. Less because the spatial-temporal manifold of practice is largely invisible, made discontinuous by blank spots, actual and yet uncertain. We can neither objectify it with words, nor can we avoid objectifying when we speak. There is this paradox at the center of communicative practice. It produces a synchrony, only to be superseded, overtaken by its own momentum, unable to stop the motion of meaning. It is thoroughly in time, yet its temporality is in tension with the objects it produces, objects that last despite their inconstancy. Much of the trouble with time radiates from this paradox. We rarely perceive it as such, of course, instead apprehending time through other kinds of connection in our everyday lives.

The sixteenth-century Maya nobles who gathered to sign a letter may or may not have meditated on the historical implications of their self-descriptions, but they did deliberate over their words, and they displayed a vivid consciousness of the field in which they spoke. The paradox that concerns us was never thrust forward as a topic of discussion in such texts, and there is something silly about wondering why. Other matters were more pressing, as they usually are: to get the king's ear, to show themselves worthy of being heard, to support their Franciscan friars and condemn their enemies. Their signatures show names like "don Ju^{o} pech," "p^{o} ek," "fran^{co} chel"—the hand slow and uncertain, some of the letters formed backward or scratched over and started again. This tentative hybridity, the stopping and starting, the blotting of the ink, the line breaking as the quill momentarily lost touch with the page—these are the traces of time layered and rubbed over like a palimpsest. Despite the imposing apparatus of dates, places, signatures, witnesses, seals, and the testimony of the official scribe, the now of the letter is unfixed by the hands that signed it. Those hands were in several worlds at once, not quite belonging to the moment and not quite not.

In the details of word choice and the themes addressed in the text, the same kind of instability is at play. Both simple and noble, the authors know the Spanish words of religion and political office but speak in "our language of here," "the language of our predecessors." They beg for conversion yet follow the ways of their lineages, make themselves conform to what they take to be the Spanish view of them yet do so in a language they describe as *ca ciçinil than* 'our devilish language' (line 25). Our problem is to find coherence without creating fixed points or, better, without misrecognizing the limitations of the fixity that our theories inevitably produce. For theories produce objects, only to be undermined by their own specificity. We need generalized frameworks in order to compare utterances from different worlds, and my questions come from the urge to interpret, reaching for a practical understanding of a finite corpus of texts. But they are also tentative and hybridized. And if the texts are limited, the meanings are not.

In Yucatán many of the dynamics we have seen in the colonial setting are still operative today. Returning to the field after a year away, I find new expressions and new inflections in old ones. The Maya I have studied for the past twenty years is not quite the same as it was when I lived there as a student, and my mouth is no longer as comfortable with the routines of speaking. The echoes of so many pasts have become louder, and they give pause. Many things that once appeared as Maya as maize now speak in a different voice, or at least I hear the voices differently. To study the past, especially with a commitment to language, is to put the present at risk.

It's like returning to the home of Don Chabo in Oxkutzcab and finding the entire layout of the homestead rearranged, as I did in 1993. Margot and Manuel had moved to Mérida, for the education of their children. Their house was unoccupied, a partial shell with the doors and screens removed, their yard overgrown with scrub. Yuum was nowhere to be seen; he didn't visit much any more. The kitchen had been moved way back in the yard, reoriented by 90 degrees, and covered with a tar paper roof nailed to the beams, with bottle caps used as retainers. The beams were mostly the same, having been cut at the right phase of the moon and properly dried rock hard in the sun. No longer wattle and daub, the walls were now covered with rough planks hewn from thick trees, and the structure rectangular rather than apsidal. It looked like modernization at its worst. Then I realized the style was typical of Quintana Roo, the neighboring state in which Don Chabo had traveled often to practice his shamanism as a young man, accompanied by his daughter Vidalia, an herbalist and fortune-teller. This was the golden age of his vocation, when he was dreaming new prayers almost daily, and his practice was expanding around the peninsula. He and his daughter were a team. Vidalia had moved in with him the year before to look after him in his old age, and I got the sense that this change was actually a reassertion of their bond to an itinerant past. Looking out from the kitchen, you could see four broken lines of stones, partly buried, with the remains of postholes at their corners among the weeds: the detritus of the pigsty I recalled from 1980, when I first entered the homestead. Most of the materials had been recycled and used in building the other structures around the yard. The pigs had been sold off to pay for doctor's bills. Don Chabo pointed out that most of what I thought were weeds were actually medicinal herbs that he either had planted or tended to with affection.

We entered his house and sat at the still point of the altar, which was where it had been for the past ten years. A patient arrived, a woman with a young child. I was anxious to hear him perform again, standing before the image he had inherited from his mother, the *Tres Reyes de Tizimin* (Three kings of Tizimin), a town in the north. Aside from the cruciform that he had cut from the branches of a tree at the beginning of his vocation, the Three Kings were his main *santo.* Don Chabo and the woman talked about her family life. The kid had bad diarrhea, and she was worried. He reassured her and started to pray. First the sign of the cross: *"Por la señal de la Santa Cruz, del nuestro enemigo libre nos Señor Dios Padre en el nombre del Padre, del Hijo, de los Espiritus Santo."* 'By the sign of the blessed cross, free us from our enemies, God the Father. In the name of the Father, of the Son, of the Holy Spirits.' He still combined the definite article with the possessive pronoun in "del nuestro," an archaism not used in current Spanish, and he still pluralized the Holy Spirits, a little reminder that the priest might have only one Holy Spirit, but he's got seventy-nine of them. He went on: *"Señor mio mi Jesu Cristo inyum, ilawilen, waliken, debilen tulú'umil le k'eban, kut'anabal inwok'oh ˀoól insholanpiìsh . . . "* 'Lord of mine, my Jesus Christ, my Father, look at me. I am standing, I am weak on the earth of sin. It is spoken, I beg you, I kneel. . . .' Sounds pretty Catholic in translation, but the Maya is chanted and accentuates the verse parallelism in the morphology. He is "begging" *'okoh ˀoól* in terms like the ones you see in colonial documents (cf. line 131 in the example above), but from his perspective he is lowering spirits to the altar, where they will actually visit the child and sweep his body of illness. So far, so good; the kid was settling down. This prayer is called *santiguar* 'to sanctify', a relatively minor, broad-spectrum tonic for the soul. It lasts about twelve minutes, and he frequently does ten or more in a single day. First come, first served. If you ask him about it out of context, he cannot remember most of the prayer, and I have heard him misstate his own words in response to my questions about them. Nonetheless, when performing, he reenacts the prayer with the precision of a priest saying the mass. As the prayer went on, he made reference to scores of spirits, some obviously derivative of Catholic saints, some equally obviously from Maya tradition, other ones of his own discovery.

The prayer reenacts the history of the world in its current creation, moving from the present back to the Passion of Christ and then up through the colonial period. Some of the spirits are Maya nobles from the sixteenth century, including the prophet Chilam Balam and some of the makers of the Mani map in Chapter 7. According to Don Chabo, these individuals enchanted themselves when the Spanish conquest became irreversible, existing now in the form of trees in the forest and spirits who can be moved if you have the gift. Walking the paths of his neighborhood, Don Chabo is in an unseen dialogue with the spirits in the trees, expecting to join them when his time comes. When the cataclysm comes, they will all return to walk the earth and remake it after the fall of Christianity. At one point in the prayer, when it arrives at Calvary, Don Chabo pauses briefly to rest, out of respect. Breaking the flow of his chant, he speaks in a resonant voice, "*Dios yumbil, Dios mehenbil, Dios Espiritus Santo ˀin yum*" 'God the Father, God the Son, God the Holy Spirits, My Lord'. In the phrasing of "God the Father" and "God the Son," you can hear the voice of Beltrán de Santa Rosa María and his predecessors among the Franciscans. They fixed this phrasing of the cross in the Doctrina and sermons they wrote. Beltrán knew better than to translate "God" into the near equivalent Maya word *Ku,* since this would make it too easy to confuse the Most Holy with an indigenous idol. But he couldn't stop the Don Chabos of the world from pluralizing the Holy Spirit and elevating it to the level of God. In effect, this little twist rewrites history by making the Holy Spirit a metonym for the legions of named spirits set in motion by this distinctively hybrid genre.

The visit makes a good story, and it was even better to be there. It brings us back, though, to some hard questions, since the Spanish is Maya and the Maya is Spanish. The household is newly arranged, but it reembodies interpersonal histories dense with meaning. The present, no less now than in the sixteenth century, is a field crosscut by multiple temporalities. We try to come to grips with these, using general frameworks and lots of particulars. The aim is more to see the way things fit together and fall apart than to explain them as instances of general laws. Part of this is the leveled emergence of discourse, both focal and backgrounded. Some of the shifts, from moment to moment and age to age, consist in bringing elements of the background into the foreground and vice versa. This involves objectification, playing off what people are aware of, just like the house structure involves materializing social relations in the stuff of wood, tar paper, and bottle caps. Nothing stays the same. Last year's pigsty turns up in the roof of next year's kitchen; a friar from two centuries ago speaks through the throat of a shaman, who talks with the Apostles while bringing the rain to a cornfield in the rocky hills of southern Yucatán. And as if to rub our noses in it, Don Chabo knows all along what he is doing: He is synchronizing the world, according to an ancient, autochthonous discourse. For him, his words are a testament to his Maya essence.

We started this book with a distinctly more familiar setting, two people at the table with coffee and a morning newspaper. At the beginning, we asked how we could combine the irreducibility of language the system with the relationality of its ties to context. The question has occupied us pretty much throughout the book. These two broad concepts correspond to the focal objects of different approaches to language. Sometimes the two look like conflicting ways of describing the same things, and they have led to contradictory claims about what is most central in language. Theoretical frameworks designed to explain one kind of fact often rest upon the denial or marginalization of the other. But in many instances, as we saw, they simply correspond to different aspects of language as a whole. The appearance of incompatibility is an artifact of the desire of proponents of one or another approach to lay claim to the whole of language, or at least to the most "important" or "interesting" part of it. We have argued, to the contrary, that the resulting impasse is unnecessary and has become an obstacle to understanding. You just don't have to erase speech in order to do grammar, nor the inverse. You don't have to ignore language in order to get "the big picture." The standard rhetorical tactics are familiar to all of us who work in brackish zones: to marginalize, to postpone, to claim from our chosen perspective that the other kind of fact is secondary or that it is "not part of x," where x is our favorite discipline. These tactics can be quite effective in the practical business of securing research funds, attracting students, launching publications, and defending academic departments in university settings. But they are usually without intellectual merit. At their worst, they smother creativity and act as powerful forms of censorship. Inculcated through education, they foster hegemony, misrecognition, and other debilitating by-products.

To get out of the impasse, you have to go deep into it. The first step was to get into the perspective of a formal system, a move that requires breaking with much of what common sense tells us about language. In fact, as we saw, in order to compare indefinitely many sentences, most of which never coexist as utterances, you have to suspend most of what makes it possible to navigate the simplest conversation. Only from this vantage point do the structural regularities that define types emerge. We started with language as Saussure conceived it, leaving behind the appearance of naturalness in order to foreground the arbitrary, bracketing the particular for the sake of the general, and warding off time in the name of synchrony. Jack and Natalia were no longer talking to one another as intimates in the morning. They were providing example sentences cut away from gestures, lived spaces, and interactive routines. The coffee, the news, and the tables were erased, in effect, so that the sentence forms would stand out in their paradigmatic and syntagmatic dimensions. "Motivation" no longer had to do with things like intention but was instead a measure of the grammatical complexity of form.

Having isolated *langue* this way, we turned to the relation between it and other symbolic systems.While this turn foreshadows relationality, there are different ways of doing it, and they allow for different kinds of irreducibility. Peirce's logic as semiotic turns out to be deeply relational, introducing us to the differences between types and tokens and among icons, indexes, and symbols—not as things but as *modalities* in which signs stand for objects. Although it gave little indication of what makes a given language hang together grammatically, his framework has strong conceptual affinities with Saussure's, and these Benveniste picked up on brilliantly. In Benveniste's work you see the articulation of a general semiotics with an unequivocal commitment to the distinctness and centrality of language as a special kind of system. It also underscored the idea of interpretance, which became increasingly significant as we went on. Morris's framework differed from Peirce's in being both behaviorist and formalist, an uneasy but provocative blend of approaches. Among its main contributions to our project were the distinction between denotation and designation, that is, the particular meaning of a token and the general meaning of a type; the definition of grammatical rules; and the all-important concept of metalanguage. By now we were beginning to fill in the picture of Jack and Natalia once again, putting the tables and chairs back in place, listening to their speech, asking about the coordination of gestures with utterances, wondering about the difference between what Jack meant and how Natalia interpreted his words. But having established a foothold in the irreducibility of linguistic form, we were able to maintain attention to the words they uttered even as we reanimated the scene.

At this point we paused to bring the formal perspective into sharp focus, before turning the corner toward relationality, with the complex dynamics it implies. The pause was necessary, and the timing deliberate, because contemporary grammar is much more precise, demanding, and important than can be gleaned from the early theories. We had to drive home the point that relationality can never merely *replace* irreducibility. It must *complement* it, retaining some points while forcing revision of others. This is the moment at which the two perspectives are drawn into conflict and the tension between them most closely approximates contradiction. To embody the tension, we juxtaposed Bloomfield and Chomsky with the dissenting voices of Voloshinov and Rommetveit. Bloomfield makes a coherent bridge between Morris's semiotics and Chomsky's generative grammar, sharing in the behaviorism of the former and laying the groundwork for the abstract grammar of the latter. In Bloomfield's approach to meaning, we uncovered one of the cornerstones of formalist epistemology: the concept that relative likeness among expressions, which is always a matter of degree and judgment, can be reduced analytically to a binary opposition between sameness and difference. If ck repeated his question to Natalia three mornings in a row, the newspaper ould be different, as would the time and likely the place, his intonation, and her sponse. But these differences would fall below the threshold of grammar, so ng as the morphosyntax and basic semantics of the sentence remained constant. y adjusting the threshold of difference, we can group a collection of forms under single type and establish invariance. Without this, grammar as we know it ould be impossible.

If Bloomfield adjusted the threshold of difference, Chomsky rebuilt the entire oorway through which we enter the realm of grammar. Recasting the opposition etween system and utterance into one between competence and performance, homsky equated grammar as theory with grammar as the immanent knowledge speakers. Jack and Natalia were redrawn as identical stick figures, idealized beond recognition. Yet they were possessed of unique innate abilities common to l humans, and their utterances were now sentences produced by a generative odel with infinite output. Such sweeping universalism is bound to have a price, nd we saw this with the semantic component of the grammar. The semantics was stricted to explaining things like paraphrase, equivalence, ambiguity, and anomy. It was silent on the broader issues of conveyed meaning, the force of Jack's utrance as a request for the paper and import of Natalia's response that it was ight on the table." We seemed to have reached a sort of logical extreme, which t the stage for the wholesale criticisms leveled at grammar by Voloshinov and ommetveit. Each in his way foreshadowed the contextual reasoning that lay at e heart of Part 2 of this book. The former sought to undo the Saussurian diotomies in favor of a dialectical approach to language as a social phenomenon. he latter stayed closer to the preferred examples of generative grammar, redefing the question "What does x mean?" with "What can be made known by the utring of x?" Wittgenstein's notion of language games and metalinguistic conacts was proposed as a way of explaining some of the regularities that grammar ad claimed for itself. Jack and Natalia were beginning to get some flesh back on eir bones, and we discovered it might even be possible to find coherence in their teraction through context and metalanguage.

It would have been counterproductive to part ways with formalism without rst meeting its stepchild, pragmatics, and some of its more practically minded usins from the functionalist end of the family. After all, we were searching for nthesis, and so were they. The central issue became the status of literal meaning. 's OK to criticize formalism for what it ignores, but if you really want to take its easure, you have to face up to literality. The pragmatic solution left the gramar mostly intact, positing underlying meanings of a kind pretty familiar to ammarians. To get at the rest, the speech acts, indirections, and inferences, it osited an overlay of context. The functionalists took a different approach from e outset. They rejected the equation of literal meaning with logic and pluralized e sense dimensions recognized in the semantics of language. This effectively oens the way to a concept of literality that is *already* contextual, because the nse dimensions themselves derive from the linkages between speech and context. Those linkages are called "functions." One consequence of this approach is that the invariance of designation posited by traditional grammar is replaced with literal meanings that change according to the circumstances in which they are produced. If Jack uttered the same words to Natalia in another setting, then his words would have different sense values. This amounts to saying that context is *within* the semantics, not an overlay added to it. One of the main strategies used to achieve this view has been to treat semantic representations as underspecified and literal meanings as the product of an active understanding. We illustrated this with the framework Ducrot proposed, applying it to a small set of expressions in Maya. We could just as well have discussed situation semantics, cognitive approaches, or any of several indexically based semantic frameworks. But Ducrot's proposals have the advantage of being tied in with the tradition of Saussure, Benveniste and European functionalism, and they are oriented toward empirical description of utterances.

By now we were on the path to relationality of a kind inconceivable had we not already traversed the terrain of formalism. To make the change stark, while further developing the idea of underspecification and context relativity, we turned to three phenomenologists. It is a great irony that the phenomenologists are virtually absent from contemporary linguistics, at least in the United States, since they dealt directly with discourse semantics (Ingarden), interaction and relevance (Schutz), and the body (Merleau-Ponty), all foci of current research. Of the three, Schutz is by far the most familiar because his work gave rise to the interpretive approaches from which conversation analysis developed. Ingarden's absence may have come about because his central theoretical works on discourse treat literary texts, and modern linguistics has staked its claims on so-called ordinary language. Yet his framework gave us the means to combine semantic incompleteness with understanding and experience, considerably expanding the openings created by the functional and contextual approaches we explored in Chapter 5. It became possible to conceive of Jack's question as a structure of "blank spots" and Natalia's response as the reflex of her particular concretization of it. With Schutz we fill in the additional factors of the interactive relation between the two people and the relevancy structure projected by Jack's question and his motives—both retrospective and prospective. These were the first steps toward making explicit the temporal embeddedness of understanding, a theme that formed the center of the present chapter. Merleau-Ponty, for his part, put Jack and Natalia back in their bodies, in the lived space of their interaction. Far from the mental representations of cognitive approaches, their bodies became corporeal schemas in motion, defined by their reflexive consciousness not only of their actual positions in space but the potential ones they could have adopted.

The landscape had changed, in a sense, and we were deep into relationality, from which classical formalism was almost irrecoverable. Once again the confrontation between irreducibility and relationality was starting to look like an impossible contradiction. To hone the difference to a cutting edge, we narrowed in on Voloshinov and Rommetveit. From the former, we concentrated on the pervasively social orientation of speech, the internalization of ideology, and the production of experience through expression. These three points flip the formal view of speaking on its head: Jack is no longer encoding in words a subjective intention already shaped, only to be draped in talk. His utterance shapes the intention itself, according to his orientation to Natalia, who is in turn not only his intimate companion but a social being defined by the same sociocultural horizon that defines him. Of Rommetveit's theories, we zeroed in on message structure defined as the penumbra of bridges between utterance forms and situations, with incompleteness, or what linguists call "ellipsis," posited as the natural state of language. We added to this the important observation that meaning depends on perspective and not all perspectives are shared. Maybe the exchange between Jack and Natalia mediated a difference in perspectives, so that the domestic scene was ultimately a different thing for him than it was for her. Their ability to refer to objects in it as if they were the same was actually the product of a delicate alignment achieved through the interaction itself.

Pushing the point, we spoke of "saturation by context" and entered into the world of Margot, Yuum, and Don Chabo. Instead of making a familiar setting strange, as we had with Jack and Natalia, it was time to make a strange one familiar. I purposely selected this example because it was the same exchange we had used to study Ducrot's approach to meaning, but this time we let in a lot more ethnography. Ethnography comes with the turf, and without it the example could not be explained nor the opacity of the words laid bare. This, then, set the stage for revisiting indexicality, for indexicals are the single most important resource that speakers dispose of in bridging utterance forms to interpretive frames. The big point was that irreducibility and relationality, which are perspectives no less than are the mundane ones of Jack and Natalia, can best be synthesized through empirical description. They originate in the world, and it is there, not in the abstraction of theory, that they must be rejoined.

We had come this far without even considering the influence of habit on the routine thought patterns of speakers, without asking what a generalized framework for context would look like, and without taking the obvious step of relating verbal styles and repertoires to meaning. All of these things were at play in our examples, and they had to be dealt with in order to compare them. They marked the next intervals on our way. The idea that linguistic categories and routine speech patterns influence how people think is one of the founding concepts in the Americanist tradition, dating back to Boas's early writings, and still on the table today. So salient is the concept of relativity that it might seem ironic in a book of this sort that we waited until Chapter 8 to bring it up. But this book is not an essay on the history of ideas, and this particular idea is subtle enough to require preparation. Also, the aim was to redefine relativity in terms of incompleteness and indexicality, to recast it as a problem in the mediation of meaning. The splitting up of any language into styles and repertoires implies a plurality of categorizations, ruling out any simple attempt to correlate a language with a way of thought. When you add to this the reflexive turn of metalinguistic ideologies, a new kind of relativity is set in motion. Instead of language, speech, and thought, you have a good half dozen elements, including immediate contexts, more extended ones, the emergent semantic relations produced in verse, the penumbra of values infusing both language varieties and the things they are used to talk about. It takes some care to discuss relativity without sliding back into the hidden premises of formalism, but that was the challenge.

When we cut the idea of speech production loose from the solitary speaker, we turned another corner. The words of Jack, Natalia, Margot, and Yuum were not really their own—not in any simple way. They were the product of a dialectic between their respective motives, including their orientations to their partners in talk and the value constructs in which their actions took on meaning. The participant structures of talk turned out to be more subtle than we had suspected, perhaps, and speech more vulnerable to transposition, appropriation, and multiple reception. You had to think in terms of communities and divisions of labor in order to follow the social trajectories of utterances, and that meant that neither speakers nor straight-up dyads would do the trick. Looking at it all, traced out like the path through a labyrinth full of dead ends and discontinuities, you wonder how talk is possible in the first place. Or to borrow a turn of phrase from Goffman, it makes you wonder how we ever limit the process enough to control meaning. Good questions, to my lights.

This is where we moved into the home stretch, sort of. We had enough behind us to rethink some of the major points and put them into a new synthesis. With luck we could avoid some of the snares and dead ends encountered along the way, without forgetting the positive lessons of the road. I've called the synthesis "communicative practice." The first word is meant to be more general than language but still centered on how people jointly make meaning. The second word indexes its focus on process, where this is shaped by language and other symbolic systems, the particulars of activity, and the socially specific values that always inform experience. We want to pull back from sheer dichotomies like subject/object, type/token, form/use, synchrony/diachrony, and production/reception. We don't want to delete these ideas outright, just put them in their proper place as moments in a greater process—in order to make space for productive reception, dynamic synchrony, the structuring of form by use, the making of types through utterance tokens, the objectivity of subjects, and the subjectivity of objects. Habitus, field, and genre all help, so long as you remember that the schemas of habitus are incomplete, the boundaries between fields shift around and have to be made by human agents, and genres are modes of action, not types of language. A lot of this converges on the body, but not the stick figures of before or the physiological system of a doctor or even the reflexive subject of Merleau-Ponty. Habitus is in the body as much as it is in the mind, but this body is defined through corporeal fields. This means it is *interperspectival,* or, as we put it, the zero-point of corporeal perspective is occupied by more than one set of eyes. Looking for good examples, we returned to Yucatán, showing the different senses of the body through Maya communicative practices. Any native speaker knows the basic body-part terms, but only those engaged in a corporeal field with three or more members get to play with the hurled speech of *č'iín č'in t'àan.*

And so I have narrativized a process of reading and writing whose emergence was part of a multistranded temporality, only some of which I can be aware of. I pulled out some themes, and left others to lie where they were, guideposts that work only if you come on them from the right angle. It has been an exercise in metalinguistic objectification, making history out of practice after the fact. But it is not really *after* the fact, not any more. Objectification inheres in practice as it unfolds, and it becomes a kind of practice itself, when you pull it into the foreground and set about doing it in earnest. Each step forward has within it a return. The past is recast in the consequences of the present, which would have been different without the past. And so forth. That's the thing about the present. To make it meaningful, you've got to fill in the blanks, but then you've got a different present. Plus a new set of blanks to contend with.

Further Readings

Barrera Vasquez, A., et al. *Diccionario Maya Cordemex.* Mérida, Mexico: Ediciones Cordemex, 1980.

Beltrán de Santa Rosa María, P. *Declaración de la Doctrina Christiana en el idioma Yucateco.* Mérida, Mexico, 1816 [1740].

Bricker, V. R. *The Indian Christ, the Indian King, the Historical Substrate of Maya Myth and Ritual.* Austin: University of Texas Press, 1981.

Cogolludo, Fray Diego López de. *Historia de Yucatán.* Graz, Austria: Akademische Druck, 1971 [1656].

Comaroff, Jean, and Comaroff, John. *Of Revelation and Revolution: Christianity, Colonialism, and Consciousness in South Africa.* Chicago: University of Chicago Press, 1991.

Fabian, J. *Language and Colonial Power.* Cambridge: Cambridge University Press, 1986, pp. 1–91.

Farriss, N. "Nucleation vs. Dispersal: The Dynamics of Population Movement in Colonial Yucatán." *Hispanic American Historical Review* 58 (1978):187–216.

———. *Maya Society Under Colonial Rule: The Collective Enterprise of Survival.* Princeton: Princeton University Press, 1984.

Gonzalez Cicero, S. M. *Perspectiva religiosa en yucatán, 1517–1571.* Mexico, D.F.: El Colegio de México, 1978.

Hanks, W. F. "Rhetoric of Royal Address." Paper presented at the American Anthropological Association annual meeting, Washington, DC, 1985.

———. "Authenticity and Ambivalence in the Text: A Colonial Maya Case." *American Ethnologist* 13(4) (1986):721–744.

———. "Discourse Genres in a Theory of Practice." *American Ethnologist* 14(4) (1987):688–692.

Jones, G. D. *Maya Resistance to Spanish Rule: Time and History on a Colonial Frontier.* Albuquerque: University of New Mexico Press, 1989.

Kulick, D. *Language Shift and Cultural Reproduction: Socialization, Self, and Syncretism in a Papua New Guinean Village.* Cambridge: Cambridge University Press, 1992. Introduction, pp. 1–26.

Martinez Hernandez, J. *Diccionario de Motul, Maya-Español Atribuido a Fray Antonio de Ciudad Real.* Mérida, Mexico: Talleres de la Compania Tipografica Yucateca, 1929.

McQuown, N. A. "Classical Yucatec (Maya)." In *Handbook of Middle American Indians,* vol. 5: *Linguistics.* Austin: University of Texas Press, 1967, pp. 201–247.

Morley, S., and Brainerd, G. W. *The Ancient Maya.* Revised fourth edition by R. Sharer. Stanford: Stanford University Press, 1983.

Munn, N. D. "Visual Categories: An Approach to the Study of Representational Systems." *American Anthropologist* 68 (1966):936–950.

———. *The Fame of Gawa: A Symbolic Study of Value Transformation in a Massim (Papua New Guinea) Society.* Cambridge: Cambridge University Press, 1986.

Perez, J. P. *Diccionario de la lengua maya.* Mérida, Mexico: Imprenta Literaria de Juan Molina Solís, 1866–1877.

Quezada, S. "Encomienda, cabildo y gubernatura indígena en Yucatán, 1541–1583." *Historia Mexicana* 34 (4) (April–June 1985):662–684.

Restall, M. B. "The World of the Cah: Postconquest Yucatec Maya Society." Ph.D. dissertation, University of California, Los Angeles, 1992.

Ricoeur, P. *From Text to Action.* Translated by K. Blamey and J. B. Thompson. Evanston, IL: Northwestern University Press, 1991. Introduction, pp. 1–24; chap. 2, "The Task of Hermeneutics," pp. 53–74; chap. 5, "What Is a Text?" pp. 105–124.

Roys, Ralph L. *The Political Geography of the Yucatán Maya.* Washington, DC: Carnegie Institution, 1957.

Stocking, G., ed. *Colonial Situations: Essays on the Contextualization of Ethnographic Knowledge.* Madison: University of Wisconsin Press, 1991.

Tozzer, A. M., trans. and ed. *Relación de las cosas de Yucatán, by Fray Diego de Landa.* Cambridge: Peabody Museum of American Archeology and Ethnology, Harvard University, 1941.

Zimmermann, G. *Briefe der indianischen Nobilität aus Neuspanien an Karl V um die Mitte des 16 Jahrhunderts.* Munich: Kommissionsverlag Klaus Renner, 1970.

Bibliography

Atkinson, J. M., and Heritage, J., eds. *Structures of Social Action.* Cambridge: Cambridge University Press, 1984.

Austin, J. L. *How to Do Things with Words.* Cambridge: Harvard University Press, 1962.

Baker, G. P., and Hacker, P. M. S. *Wittgenstein: Understanding and Meaning.* Oxford: Blackwell, 1980.

Bakhtin, M. M. *The Dialogic Imagination: Four Essays.* Edited by M. Holquist; translated by M. Holquist and C. Emerson. Austin: University of Texas Press, 1981.

———. *The Formal Method in Literary Scholarship: A Critical Introduction to Sociological Poetics.* Translated by A. J. Wehrle. Cambridge: Harvard University Press, 1985 [1928].

———. *Speech Genres and Other Essays.* Edited by M. Holquist and C. Emerson; translated by V. McGee. Austin: University of Texas Press, 1986.

Barrera Vasquez, A., et al. *Diccionario Maya Cordemex.* Mérida, Mexico: Ediciones Cordemex, 1980.

Barwise, J. "On the Circumstantial Relation Between Meaning and Content." In *Meaning and Mental Representations,* edited by U. Eco et al. Bloomington: Indiana University Press, 1988.

Barwise, J., and Perry, J. *Situations and Attitudes.* Cambridge: MIT Press, 1983.

Basso, E. "Contextualization in Kalapalo Narratives." In *Rethinking Context: Language as an Interactive Phenomenon,* edited by A. Duranti and C. Goodwin. Cambridge: Cambridge University Press, 1992.

Basso, K. H. "Speaking with Names: Language and Landscape Among the Western Apache." *Cultural Anthropology* 3(2) (1988):99–130.

———. *Western Apache Language and Culture: Essays in Linguistic Anthropology.* Tucson: University of Arizona Press, 1990.

Bauman, R. *Verbal Art as Performance.* Prospect Heights, IL: Waveland Press, 1977.

Bauman, R., and Briggs, C. "Poetics and Performance as Critical Perspectives on Language and Social Life." *Annual Review of Anthropology* 19 (1990):59–88.

Bauman, R., and Sherzer, J., eds. *Explorations in the Ethnography of Speaking.* Cambridge: Cambridge University Press, 1974.

Beltrán de Santa Rosa María, P. *Declaración de la Doctrina Christiana en el idioma Yucateco.* Mérida, Mexico, 1816 [1740].

———. *Arte de el idioma Maya reducido a succintas reglas y semi-lexicon Yucateco.* Mérida, Mexico: J. D. Espinosa, 1859.

Benveniste, E. *Problèmes de linguistique générale,* 2 vols. I. Paris: Gallimard, 1966 and 1974.

———. "The Semiology of Language." In *Semiotics: An Introductory Anthology,* edited by R. Innis. Bloomington: Indiana University Press, 1985.

Berlin, B., and Kay, P. *Basic Color Terms: Their Universality and Evolution.* Berkeley: University of California Press, 1969.

Besnier, N. "Language and Affect." *Annual Review of Anthropology* 19 (1990):419–451.

Bloomfield, L. "On Recent Work in General Linguistics." *Modern Philology* 25 (1927):211–230.

———. "Meaning." *Monatshefte für deutschen Unterricht* 35 (1943):101–116.

———. "Secondary and Tertiary Responses to Language." *Language* 20 (1944):45–55.

———. *A Leonard Bloomfield Anthology.* Edited by C. Hockett. Bloomington: Indiana University Press, 1970.

———. *Language.* Chicago: University of Chicago Press, 1984 [1933].

Boas, F. "Introduction to the Handbook of American Indian Languages." In *Introduction to the Handbook of American Indian Languages and Indian Linguistic Families of America North of Mexico,* edited by P. Holder. Lincoln: University of Nebraska Press, 1966 [1911].

Bourdieu, P. *Outline of a Theory of Practice.* Translated by R. Nice. Cambridge: Cambridge University Press, 1977 [1972].

———. "The Berber House." In *Rules and Meanings,* edited by M. Douglas. London: Penguin, 1980.

———. *Le Sens pratique.* Paris: Editions dc Minuit, 1980.

———. "The Field of Cultural Production, or: the Economic World Revisited." *Poetics* 12 (1983):311–356.

———. *Questions de sociologie.* Paris: Editions de Minuit, 1984.

———. "The Genesis of the Concepts of Habitus and Field." *Sociocentrum* 2(2) (1985a):11–24.

———. "The Social Space and the Genesis of Groups." *Social Science Information* 24(2) (1985b):195–220.

———. *Language and Symbolic Power.* Edited and introduced by J. B. Thompson; translated by G. Raymond and M. Adamson. Cambridge: Harvard University Press, 1991.

Brenneis, D. "Language and Disputing." *Annual Review of Anthropology* 18 (1989):221–237.

Bricker, V. R. *The Indian Christ, the Indian King, the Historical Substrate of Maya Myth and Ritual.* Austin: University of Texas Press, 1981.

Briggs, C. L. *Learning How to Ask: A Sociolinguistic Appraisal of the Role of the Interview in Social Science Research.* Cambridge: Cambridge University Press, 1986.

Brown, P., and Levinson, S. *Politeness: Some Universals in Language Usage.* Cambridge: Cambridge University Press, 1987.

Brown, R., and Gilman, A. "Pronouns of Power and Solidarity." In *Language and Social Context,* edited by P. P. Giglioli. Harmondsworth, England: Penguin, 1972.

Bühler, K. "The Deictic Field of Language and Deictic Words." In *Speech, Place, and Action: Studies in Deixis and Related Topics,* edited by R. J. Jarvella and W. Klein. New York: Wiley, 1982.

———. *Sprachtheorie: Die Darstellungsfunktion der Sprache.* Stuttgart: Gustav Fischer Verlag, 1982.

Burks, A. W. "Icon, Index and Symbol." *Philosophy and Phenomenological Research* 9 (1949):673–689.

Cassirer, E. "Le Langage et la construction du monde des objets." In *Essais sur le langage,* edited by J.-C. Pariente. Paris: Editions de Minuit, 1969.

Chaiklin, S., and Lave, J., eds. *Understanding Practice: Perspectives on Activity and Context.* Cambridge: Cambridge University Press, 1993.

Chomsky, N. *Syntactic Structures.* The Hague: Mouton, 1957.

———. Review of *Verbal Behavior,* by B. F. Skinner *Language* 35 (1959):26–58.

———. *Aspects of the Theory of Syntax.* Cambridge: MIT Press, 1965.

———. "Methodological Preliminaries." In *The Philosophy of Linguistics,* edited by J. Katz. Oxford: Oxford University Press, 1985.

Chomsky, N., and Halle, M. *The Sound Pattern of English.* New York: Harper and Row, 1968.

Cicourel, A. "Text and Discourse." *Annual Review of Anthropology* 14 (1985):159–185.

———. "The Reproduction of Objective Knowledge: Common Sense Reasoning in Medical Decision Making." In *The Knowledge Society,* edited by G. Böhme and N. Stehr. Dordrecht: D. Reidel, 1986.

———. "The Interpenetration of Communicative Contexts: Examples from Medical Encounters." In *Rethinking Context: Language as an Interactive Phenomenon,* edited by A. Duranti and C. Goodwin. Cambridge: Cambridge University Press, 1992.

Clark, H. *Arenas of Language Use.* Chicago: University of Chicago Press, 1992.

Cogolludo, Fray Diego López de. *Historia de Yucatan.* Graz, Austria: Akademische Druck, 1971 [1656].

Coleman, L., and Kay, P. "Prototype Semantics: The English Verb *Lie.*" *Language* 57(1) (1981):26–44.

Collins, J. "Determination and Contradiction: An Appreciation and Critique of the Work of Pierre Bourdieu on Language and Education." In *Toward a Reflexive Sociology: The Social Theory of Pierre Bourdieu,* edited by M. Postone et al. Oxford: Blackwell, 1993.

Comaroff, J. *Body of Power, Body of Spirit: The Culture and History of a South African People.* Chicago: University of Chicago Press, 1985.

Comaroff, Jean, and Comaroff, John. *Of Revelation and Revolution: Christianity, Colonialism, and Consciousness in South Africa.* Chicago: University of Chicago Press, 1991.

Conklin, H. C. "Hanunóo Color Categories." *Southwestern Journal of Anthropology* 11(4) (1955):339–344.

———. Review article: *Color Categorization. American Anthropologist* 75(4) (1973): 931–942.

de Léon, L. 1991. "Space Games in Tzotzil: Creating a Context for Spatial Reference." Working paper, Cognitive Anthropology Research Group at the Max Planck Institute for Psycholinguistics.

Devitt, M., and Sterelny, K. *Language and Reality: An Introduction to the Philosophy of Language.* Cambridge: MIT Press, 1987.

DuBois, J. "Meaning Without Intention: Lessons from Divination." In *Responsibility and Evidence in Oral Discourse,* edited by J. H. Hill and J. T. Irvine. Cambridge: Cambridge University Press, 1993.

Ducrot, O. *Le Dire et le dit.* Paris: Editions de Minuit, 1984.

Duranti, A., and Goodwin, C., eds. *Rethinking Context: Language as an Interactive Phenomenon.* Cambridge: Cambridge University Press, 1992.

Eckert, P., and McConnell-Ginet, S. "Think Practically and Look Locally: Language and Gender as Community-based Practice." *Annual Review of Anthropology* 21 (1992): 461–490.

Eco, U., et al., eds. *Meaning and Mental Representations.* Bloomington: Indiana University Press, 1988.

Encrevé, P. "C'est Reagan qui a coulé le billet vert." *Actes de la recherche en sciences sociales* 71–72 (March 1988):109–128.

Encrevé, P., and de Fornel, M. "Le Sens pratique, construction de la référence et structure sociale de l'interaction dans le couple question/résponse." *Actes de la recherche en sciences sociales* 43 (March 1983):3–30.

Errington, J. J. *Structure and Style in Javanese: A Semiotic View of Linguistic Etiquette.* Philadelphia: University of Pennsylvania Press, 1988.

Fabian, J. *Language and Colonial Power.* Cambridge: Cambridge University Press, 1986.

Falk, Eugene H. *The Poetics of Roman Ingarden.* Chapel Hill: University of North Carolina Press, 1981.

Farriss, N. "Nucleation vs. Dispersal: The Dynamics of Population Movement in Colonial Yucatan." *Hispanic American Historical Review* 58 (1978):187–216.

———. *Maya Society Under Colonial Rule: The Collective Enterprise of Survival.* Princeton: Princeton University Press, 1984.

Fauconnier, G. "Quantification, Roles and Domains." In *Meaning and Mental Representations,* edited by U. Eco et al. Bloomington: Indiana University Press, 1988.

Fillmore, C. "Types of Lexical Information." In *Semantics: An Interdisciplinary Reader in Philosophy, Linguistics, and Psychology,* edited by D. Steinberg and L. Jakobovits. Cambridge: Cambridge University Press, 1971.

———. "Frames and the Semantics of Understanding." *Quaderni di semantica* 6(2) (1985):222–254.

Frake, C. O. *Language and Cultural Description: Essays by C. O. Frake.* Selected and introduced by A. Dil. Stanford: Stanford University Press, 1980.

Friedrich, P., *On the Meaning of the Tarascan Suffixes of Locative Space. International Journal of American Linguistics,* memoir 23. Bloomington: Indiana University Press, 1969.

———. "Shape in Grammar." *Language* 46 (1970):379–407.

———. *Language, Context and the Imagination: Essays.* Selected and introduced by A. Dil. Stanford: Stanford University Press, 1979.

Gal, S. "Language and Political Economy." *Annual Review of Anthropology* 18 (1989): 347–367.

Garver, N. "Varieties of Use and Mention." *Philosophy and Phenomenological Research* 26 (1965):230–238.

Gell, Alfred. "How to Read a Map: Remarks on the Practical Logic of Navigation." *Man,* n.s., 20 (1985):271–286.

Giglioli, P. P., ed. *Language and Social Context.* Harmondsworth, England: Penguin, 1972.

Goffman, E. "The Neglected Situation." In *Language and Social Context,* edited by P. P. Giglioli. Harmondsworth, England: Penguin, 1972.

———. *Forms of Talk.* Philadelphia: University of Pennsylvania Press, 1981.

Gonzalez Cicero, S. M. *Perspectiva religiosa en yucatán, 1517–1571.* Mexico, D.F.: El Colegio de México, 1978.

Goodenough, W.-H. "Componential Analysis and the Study of Meaning." *Language* 32 (1956):195–216.

Goodman, N. *Ways of Worldmaking.* Cambridge, MA: Hackett, 1978.

Goodwin, C. *Conversational Organization: Interaction Between Speakers and Hearers.* New York: Academic Press, 1981.

———. "Notes on a Story Structure and the Organization of Participation." In *Structures of Social Action,* edited by J. M. Atkinson and J. Heritage. Cambridge: Cambridge University Press, 1984.

Goodwin, C., and Goodwin, M. H. "Assessments and the Construction of Context." In *Rethinking Context: Language as an Interactive Phenomenon,* edited by A. Duranti and C. Goodwin. Cambridge: Cambridge University Press, 1992.

Goodwin, M. H. "Processes of Dispute Management Among Urban Black Children." *American Ethnologist* 9 (1982):76–96.

———. *He-said-she-said: The Interactive Organization of Talk in an Urban Black Peer Group.* Bloomington: Indiana University Press, 1990.

Greenberg, J. H., ed. *Universals of Language.* Cambridge: MIT Press, 1966.

Grice, H. P. "Meaning." In *Semantics: An Interdisciplinary Reader in Philosophy, Linguistics, and Psychology,* edited by D. Steinberg and L. Jakobovits. Cambridge: Cambridge University Press, 1971.

Gumperz, J. "The Speech Community." In *Language and Social Context,* edited by P. P. Giglioli. Harmondsworth, England: Penguin, 1972 [1968].

———. *Discourse Strategies.* Cambridge: Cambridge University Press, 1982.

———. "Contextualization and Understanding." In *Rethinking Context: Language as an Interactive Phenomenon,* edited by A. Duranti and C. Goodwin. Cambridge: Cambridge University Press, 1992.

Hancher, M. "A Classification of Cooperative Illocutionary Acts." *Language in Society* 8 (1979):1–14.

Hanks, W. F. "Rhetoric of Royal Address." Paper presented at the American Anthropological Association annual meeting, Washington, DC, 1985.

———. "Authenticity and Ambivalence in the Text: A Colonial Maya Case." *American Ethnologist* 13(4) (1986):721–744.

———. "Discourse Genres in a Theory of Practice." *American Ethnologist* 14(4) (1987):688–692.

———. "Text and Textuality." *Annual Review of Anthropology* 18 (1989):95–127.

———. *Referential Practice: Language and Lived Space Among the Maya.* Chicago: University of Chicago Press, 1990.

———. "The Indexical Ground of Deictic Reference." In *Rethinking Context: Language as an Interactive Phenomenon,* edited by A. Duranti and C. Goodwin. Cambridge: Cambridge University Press, 1992.

———. "Metalanguage and Pragmatics of Deixis." In *Reflexive Language: Reported Speech and Metapragmatics,* edited by J. Lucy. Cambridge: Cambridge University Press, 1993.

———. "Notes on Semantics in Linguistic Practice." In *Towards a Reflexive Sociology: The Social Theory of Pierre Bourdieu,* edited by M. Postone et al. Oxford: Blackwell, 1993.

Harman, G. "Three Levels of Meaning." In *Semantics: An Interdisciplinary Reader in Philosophy, Linguistics, and Psychology,* edited by D. Steinberg and L. Jakobovits. Cambridge: Cambridge University Press, 1971.

———. "Against Universal Semantic Representation." In *Proceedings of the Texas Conference on Performatives, Presuppositions and Implicatures,* edited by A. Rogers et al. Washington, DC: Center for Applied Linguistics, 1977.

Harris, Z. "Distributional Structure." *Word* 10(2-3) (1954):775–793.

Haviland, J. B. *Gossip, Reputation, and Knowledge in Zinacantan.* Chicago: University of Chicago Press, 1977.

———. "Con Buenos Chiles: Talk, Targets, and Teasing in Zinacantan." *Text* 6 (1986): 249–282.

———. "Projections, Transpositions and Relativity." Working paper, Cognitive Anthropology Research Group at the Max Planck Institute for Psycholinguistics, 1991.

Havránek, B. "The Functional Differentiation of the Standard Language." In *A Prague School Reader on Esthetics, Literary Structure, and Style,* edited and translated by P. L. Garvin. Washington, DC: Georgetown University Press, 1964.

Heath, C. "Talk and Recipiency: Sequential Organization in Speech and Body." In *Structures of Social Action,* edited by J. M. Atkinson and J. Heritage. Cambridge: Cambridge University Press, 1984.

Hill, J. H., and Hill, K. C. *Speaking Mexicano: Dynamics of Syncretic Language in Central Mexico.* Tucson: University of Arizona Press, 1986.

Hill, J. H., and Mannheim, B. "Language and World View." *Annual Review of Anthropology* 21 (1992):381–406.

Huddleston, R. "Componential Analysis: The Sememe and the Concept of Distinctiveness." *Canadian Journal of Linguistics* 19(1) (1974):1–17.

Husserl, E. "Origin of Geometry." In *Phenomenology and Sociology: Selected Readings,* edited by T. Luckmann. New York: Penguin, 1978.

Hymes, D. "Two Types of Linguistic Relativity." In *Sociolinguistics,* edited by W. Bright. The Hague: Mouton, 1966.

———. "Linguistics: The Field." *International Encyclopedia of Social Sciences* 9 (1968): 351–371.

———. 1972. Review of *Noam Chomsky,* by J. Lyons. *Language* 48 (1972):416–427.

———. "Toward Ethnographies of Communication." In *Language and Social Context,* edited by P. P. Giglioli. Harmondsworth, England: Penguin, 1972.

———. *Foundations in Sociolinguistics: An Ethnographic Approach.* Philadelphia: University of Pennsylvania Press, 1974.

———. "In Vain I Tried to Tell You." In *Essays in Native American Ethnopoetics.* Philadelphia: University of Pennsylvania Press, 1981.

Hymes, D., and Fought, J. *American Structuralism.* The Hague: Mouton, 1981.

Ingarden, R. *The Cognition of the Literary Work of Art.* Translated by R. A. Crowley and K. R. Olson. Evanston, IL: Northwestern University Press, 1973.

———. *The Literary Work of Art: An Investigation on the Borderlines of Ontology, Logic and Theory of Literature.* Translated by G. G. Grabowicz. Evanston, IL: Northwestern University Press, 1973.

Irvine, J. "Status and Style in Language." *Annual Review of Anthropology* 14 (1986): 557–581.

———. "When Talk Isn't Cheap: Language and Political Economy." *American Ethnologist* 16 (1989):248–267.

Jakobson, R. *The Framework of Language.* Ann Arbor: University of Michigan Press, 1957.

———. "Concluding Statement: Linguistics and Poetics." In *Style in Language,* edited by T. Sebeok. Cambridge: MIT Press, 1960.

———. "Signe zéro." In *Readings in Linguistics,* vol. 2, edited by E. Hamp, F. W. Householder, and R. Austerlitz. Chicago: University of Chicago Press, 1966 [1939].

———. *Selected Writings of Roman Jakobson,* vol. 2. The Hague: Mouton, 1971.

———. *Six Lectures on Sound and Meaning.* Translated by J. Mepham. Cambridge: MIT Press, 1978.

Jones, G. D. *Maya Resistance to Spanish Rule: Time and History on a Colonial Frontier.* Albuquerque: University of New Mexico Press, 1989.

Katz, J. "Semantic Theory." In *Semantics: An Interdisciplinary Reader in Philosophy, Linguistics, and Psychology,* edited by D. Steinberg and L. Jakobovits. Cambridge: Cambridge University Press, 1971.

Kellner, H. "On the Cognitive Significance of the System of Language in Communication." In *Phenomenology and Sociology: Selected Readings,* edited by T. Luckmann. New York: Penguin, 1978.

Kulick, D. *Language Shift and Cultural Reproduction: Socialization, Self, and Syncretism in a Papua New Guinean Village.* Cambridge: Cambridge University Press, 1992.

Labov, W. "The Study of Language in Its Social Context." In *Language and Social Context,* edited by P. P. Giglioli. Harmondsworth, England: Penguin, 1972.

Lakoff, G. "Cognitive Semantics." In *Meaning and Mental Representations,* edited by U. Eco et al. Bloomington: Indiana University Press, 1988.

Langacker, R. W. *Foundations of Cognitive Grammar,* vol. 1: *Theoretical Prerequisites.* Stanford: Stanford University Press, 1987.

———. *Foundations of Cognitive Grammar,* vol. 2: *Descriptive Application.* Stanford: Stanford University Press, 1991.

Lave, J. *Cognition in Practice: Mind, Mathematics, and Culture in Everyday Life.* Cambridge: Cambridge University Press, 1988.

Lave, J., and Wenger, E. *Situated Learning: Legitimate Peripheral Participation.* Cambridge: Cambridge University Press, 1991.

Lee, B. *Talking Heads: Languages, Meta-Languages and the Semiotics of Subjectivity.* Chapel Hill: Duke University Press. In Press.

Lees, R. Review of *Syntactic Structures,* by N. Chomsky. *Language* 33 (1957):375–407.

Levinson, S. *Pragmatics.* Cambridge: Cambridge University Press, 1983.

———. "Putting Linguistics on a Proper Footing: Explorations in Goffman's Concepts of Participation." In *Goffman: An Interdisciplinary Appreciation,* edited by P. Drew and A. Woolton. Oxford: Polity Press, 1987.

———. "Relativity in Spatial Description and Conception." Working paper, Cognitive Anthropology Research Group at the Max Planck Institute for Psycholinguistics, 1991.

Lindstrom, L. "Context Contests: Debatable Truth Statements on Tanna (Vanuatu)." In *Rethinking Context: Language as an Interactive Phenomenon,* edited by A. Duranti and C. Goodwin. Cambridge: Cambridge University Press, 1992.

Lounsbury, F. G. "A Semantic Analysis of the Pawnee Kinship Usage." *Language* 32(1) (1956):158–194.

———. "The Structural Analysis of Kinship Semantics." In *Cognitive Anthropology,* edited by S. A. Tyler. New York: Holt, Rinehart and Winston, 1969 [1964].

Lucy, J. "Whorf's View of the Linguistic Mediation of Thought." In *Semiotic Mediation: Sociocultural and Psychological Perspectives,* edited by E. Mertz and R. Parmentier. New York: Academic Press, 1985.

———, ed. *Reflexive Language: Reported Speech and Metapragmatics.* Cambridge: Cambridge University Press, 1991.

Lyons, J. *Semantics,* vol. 1. Cambridge: Cambridge University Press, 1977.

Maclay, H. "Overview." In *Semantics: An Interdisciplinary Reader in Philosophy, Linguistics, and Psychology,* edited by D. Steinberg and L. Jakobovits. Cambridge: Cambridge University Press, 1971.

Martinez Hernandez, J. *Diccionario de Motul, Maya-Español Atribuido a Fray Antonio de Ciudad Real.* Mérida, Mexico: Talleres de la Compania Tipográfica Yucateca, 1929.

Mauss, M. "Techniques of the Body." *Economy and Society* 2(1) (1973):70–88.

McCawley, J. D. "Speech Acts and Goffman's Participant Roles." In *Proceedings of the 2nd ESCOL.* Columbus: Ohio State University, Department of Linguistics, 1986.

McQuown, N. A. "Classical Yucatec (Maya)." In *Handbook of Middle American Indians,* vol. 5: *Linguistics.* Austin: University of Texas Press, 1967.

———. *Language, Culture, and Education: Essays by Norman A. McQuown,* edited by A. S. Dil. Stanford: Stanford University Press, 1982.

———. *Catedra extraordinaria "Alfonso Caso y Andrade": el microanalisis de entrevistas.* Mexico, D.F.: Instituto de Investigaciones Antropológicas, Universidad Nacional Autónoma de México, 1983.

Mead, G. H. *The Philosophy of the Present.* Chicago: University of Chicago Press, 1980.

Merlan, F., and Rumsey, A. *Ku Waru: Language and Segmentary Politics in the Western Nebilyer Valley, Papua New Guinea.* Cambridge: Cambridge University Press, 1991.

Merleau-Ponty, M. *Signs.* Translated and introduced by R. C. McCleary. Evanston, IL: Northwestern University Press, 1964.

———. *Phénoménologie de la perception.* Paris: Gallimard, 1967 [1945].

Morgan, J. "Sentence Fragments and the Notion 'Sentence.'" In *Issues in Linguistics: Papers in Honor of Henry and Renée Kahane,* edited by B. B. Kachru et al. Urbana: University of Illinois Press, 1973.

Morley, S., and Brainerd, G. W. *The Ancient Maya.* Revised fourth edition by R. Sharer. Stanford: Stanford University Press, 1983.

Morris, C. *Foundations of the Theory of Signs.* Chicago: University of Chicago Press, 1971 [1938].

Mukarovsky, J. "Standard Language and Poetic Language." In *A Prague School Reader on Esthetics, Literary Structure, and Style,* edited and translated by P. L. Garvin. Washington, DC: Georgetown University Press, 1964.

———. "Structuralism in Esthetics and Literary Studies." In *The Prague School: Selected Writings,* edited by P. Steiner. Austin: University of Texas Press, 1982 [1941].

Munn, N. D. "Visual Categories: An Approach to the Study of Representational Systems." *American Anthropologist* 68 (1966):936–950.

———. *The Fame of Gawa: A Symbolic Study of Value Transformation in a Massim (Papua New Guinea) Society.* Cambridge: Cambridge University Press, 1986.

———. "The Cultural Anthropology of Time: A Critical Essay." *Annual Review of Anthropology* 21 (1992):93–123.

Newmeyer, F. *Grammatical Theory: Its Limits and Its Possibilities.* Chicago: University of Chicago Press, 1983.

Ochs, E. *Culture and Language Development: Language Acquisition and Language Socialization in a Samoan Village.* Cambridge: Cambridge University Press, 1988.

———. "Indexing Gender." In *Rethinking Context: Language as an Interactive Phenomenon,* edited by A. Duranti and C. Goodwin. Cambridge: Cambridge University Press, 1992.

Ochs, E., and Schieffelin, B. *Acquiring Conversational Competence.* London: Routledge & Kegan Paul, 1983.

Peirce, C. S. *Philosophical Writings of Peirce.* Edited by J. Buchler. New York: Dover Publications, 1955.

Perez, J. P. *Diccionario de la lengua maya.* Mérida, Mexico: Imprenta Literaria de Juan Molina Solís, 1866–1877.

Polanyi, M. *On Personal Knowledge: Towards a Post-Critical Philosophy.* Chicago: University of Chicago Press, 1974.

Putnam, H. "Some Issues in the Theory of Grammar." In *On Noam Chomsky: Critical Essays,* edited by G. Harman. New York: Doubleday, 1974.

———. "Is Semantics Possible?" In *Mind, Language and Reality: Philosophical Papers,* vol. 1. Cambridge: Cambridge University Press, 1975.

Quezada, S. "Encomienda, cabildo y gubernatura indígena en Yucatán, 1541–1583." *Historia Mexicana* 34(4), (April-June 1985):662–684.

Quine, W. "Methodological Reflections on Current Linguistic Theory." In *On Noam Chomsky: Critical Essays,* edited by G. Harman. New York: Doubleday, 1974.

Redfield, R., and Villa Rojas, A. *Chan Kom: A Maya Village.* Chicago: University of Chicago Press, 1962 [1934].

Restall, M. B. "The World of the Cah: Postconquest Yucatec Maya Society." Ph.D. dissertation, University of California, Los Angeles, 1992.

Ricoeur, P. *From Text to Action.* Translated by K. Blamey and J. B. Thompson. Evanston, IL: Northwestern University Press, 1991.

Rommetveit, R. *On Message Structure: A Framework for the Study of Language and Communication.* New York: Wiley, 1974.

Ross, J. R. "Constraints on Variables in Syntax." Ph.D. dissertation, MIT, 1967.

Roys, Ralph L. *The Political Geography of the Yucatan Maya.* Washington, DC: Carnegie Institution, 1957.

Sadock, J. *Toward a Linguistic Theory of Speech Acts.* New York: Academic Press, 1974.

Sag, I. A., and Hankamer, J. "Deep and Surface Anaphora." *Linguistic Inquiry* 7(3) (1976):391–426.

Sapir, E. *Language: An Introduction to the Study of Speech.* New York: Harcourt Brace, 1921.

———. *Selected Writings of Edward Sapir in Language, Culture, and Personality.* Edited by D. G. Mandelbaum. Berkeley: University of California Press, 1949.

Saussure, F. de. *Course in General Linguistics.* Translated by W. Baskin. New York: McGraw-Hill, 1966.

———. *Cours de linguistique générale.* Edited by Tullio de Mauro. Paris: Payothèque, 1974.

Schegloff, E. "On Some Gestures' Relation to Talk." In *Structures of Social Action,* edited by J. M. Atkinson and J. Heritage. Cambridge: Cambridge University Press, 1984.

Schutz, A. *The Phenomenology of the Social World.* Translated by G. Walsh and F. Lehnert. Evanston, IL: Northwestern University Press, 1967 [1932].

———. *On Phenomenology and Social Relations.* Edited by H. R. Wagner. Chicago: University of Chicago Press, 1970.

———. *Collected Papers,* vol. 1: *The Problem of Social Reality.* Edited by M. Natanson. The Hague: Mouton, 1973.

Searle, J. "What Is a Speech Act?" In *Language and Social Context,* edited by P. P. Giglioli. Harmondsworth, England: Penguin, 1972.

———. *Speech Acts: An Essay in the Philosophy of Language.* Cambridge: Cambridge University Press, 1976.

Sherzer, J. *Kuna Ways of Speaking: An Ethnographic Perspective.* Austin: University of Texas Press, 1983.

Sherzer, J., and Urban, G., eds. *Native South American Discourse.* The Hague: Mouton, 1986.

Silverman, D., and Torode, B. "Husserl's Two Phenomenologies." In *The Material Word: Some Theories of Language and Its Limits.* London: Routledge & Kegan Paul, 1980.

Silverstein, M. "Shifters, Verbal Categories and Cultural Description." In *Meaning in Anthropology,* edited by K. Basso and H. Selby. Albuquerque: School of American Research, 1976.

———. "Language Structure and Linguistic Ideology." In *Papers from the Fifteenth Regional Meeting of the Chicago Linguistic Society,* vol. 2: *Parasession on Linguistic Units and Levels,* edited by P. Clyne, W. F. Hanks, and C. Hofbauer. Chicago: Chicago Linguistic Society, 1979.

Spiegelberg, H. *The Phenomenological Movement: A Historical Introduction.* The Hague: Nijhoff, 1960.

Stocking, G., ed. *A Franz Boas Reader: The Shaping of American Anthropology, 1883–1911.* Chicago: University of Chicago Press, 1982.

———. *Colonial Situations: Essays on the Contextualization of Ethnographic Knowledge.* Madison: University of Wisconsin Press, 1991.

Sullivan, P. *Unfinished Conversations: Mayas and Foreigners Between Two Wars.* New York: Knopf, 1989.

Taylor, C. In *Human Agency and Language: Philosophical Papers,* vol. 1. Cambridge: Cambridge University Press, 1985.

———. "To Follow a Rule . . ." In *Towards a Reflexive Sociology: The Social Theory of Pierre Bourdieu,* edited by M. Postone et al. Oxford: Blackwell, 1993.

Tozzer, A. M., trans. and ed. *Relación de las cosas de Yucatan, by Fray Diego de Landa.* Cambridge: Peabody Museum of American Archeology and Ethnology, Harvard University, 1941.

Trubetzkoy, N. *Principles of Phonology.* Translated by C. A. M. Baltaxe. Berkeley: University of California Press, 1969.

Turner, T. "The Social Skin." In *Not Work Alone,* edited by J. Cherfas and R. Lewin. Beverly Hills, CA: Sage Publications, 1980.

———. "Bodies and Anti-bodies: Flesh and Fetish in Contemporary Social Theory." In *Embodiment and Experience,* edited by T. Csordias. Cambridge: Cambridge University Press, 1994.

———. "Social Body and Embodied Subject: Bodiliness, Subjectivity and Sociality Among the Kayapo." *Cultural Anthropology,* May 1995.

Tynianov, Y. *The Problem of Verse Language.* Translated by M. Sosa and B. Harvey. Ann Arbor: Ardis Press, 1981 [1924].

Urban, G. *A Discourse-Centered Approach to Culture: Native South American Myths and Rituals.* Austin: University of Texas Press, 1991.

Voloshinov, V. N. *Marxism and the Philosophy of Language.* Translated by L. Matejka and I. R. Titunik. Cambridge: Harvard University Press, 1986 [1929].

Weinreich, U. "On the Semantic Structure of Language." In *Universals of Language,* edited by J. Greenberg. Cambridge: MIT Press, 1966.

———. "Semantics and Semiotics." *International Encyclopedia of Social Science* 14 (1968):164–169.

———. "Explorations in Semantic Theory." In *Semantics: An Interdisciplinary Reader in Philosophy, Linguistics, and Psychology,* edited by D. Steinberg and L. Jakobovits. Cambridge: Cambridge University Press, 1971.

Wenger, E. *Communities of Practice.* Cambridge: Cambridge University Press, 1993.

Whorf, B. L. "The Relation of Habitual Thought and Behavior to Language." In *Language, Thought and Reality: Selected Writings of Benjamin Lee Whorf,* edited by J. B. Carroll. Cambridge: MIT Press, 1941.

Wittgenstein, L. *Philosophical Investigations.* Oxford: Blackwell, 1953.

Woolard, K. "Language Variation and Cultural Hegemony: Toward an Integration of Sociolinguistic and Social Theory." *American Ethnologist* 12 (1985):238–248.

Ziff, P. "On Grice's Account of Meaning." In *Semantics: An Interdisciplinary Reader in Philosophy, Linguistics, and Psychology,* edited by D. Steinberg and L. Jakobovits. Cambridge: Cambridge University Press, 1971.

Zimmermann, G. *Briefe der indianischen Nobilität aus Neuspanien an Karl V um die Mitte des 16 Jahrhunderts.* Munich: Kommissionsverlag Klaus Renner, 1970.

About the Book and Author

Written in an informal style with engaging examples, this introduction to the study of language in context presents a provocative new approach to communicative practice. Emphasizing the dual status of language as linguistic system and as social fact, William Hanks offers fresh insights into the dynamics of context, the indeterminacy of cultural forms, and the relation between human experience and the making of meaning.

Drawing on a broad range of theory and empirical research, Hanks explores the varieties of reflexivity in language, relating them to linguistic structure, textuality, and genres of practice. He shows how the human body both anchors the communicative process and provides a reference point for displaced and mediated speech. Tracing the movement of meaning through social fields and communities, Hanks casts new light on the ways that utterances are fragmented and objectified in social life. Speech emerges as a contingent process in which the production and reception of meaning are tied into multiple dimensions of time and context and history rests on the objectification of practice.

Hanks's penetrating readings of classic works in linguistics, philosophy, and social theory are complemented by suggestions for further reading. Within the framework of communicative practice, he integrates elements of formal grammar and semiotics, phenomenology, cultural anthropology, and contemporary sociology. Neither a history nor a summary of the field, *Language and Communicative Practices* is a critical synthesis of the dialectics of meaning that inform all language and speech.

William F. Hanks is professor of anthropology and linguistics at the University of Chicago. He has been a visiting professor at the University of Paris, L'École des Hautes Études en Sciences Sociales, and Casa de America in Madrid.

Index